WTO – World Economic Order, World Trade Law

MAX PLANCK COMMENTARIES ON WORLD TRADE LAW

Editors

Rüdiger Wolfrum
Peter-Tobias Stoll

1. Peter-Tobias Stoll and Frank Schorkopf, *WTO – World Economic Order, World Trade Law.* *(2006)* *ISBN 90-04-14496-X*

MAX PLANCK COMMENTARIES ON WORLD TRADE LAW

WTO

—

World Economic Order, World Trade Law

BY

PETER-TOBIAS STOLL
FRANK SCHORKOPF

with the assistance of Arthur Steinmann

Max Planck Institute for
Comparative Public Law and International Law

MARTINUS NIJHOFF PUBLISHERS
LEIDEN/BOSTON

This is the English version of *WTO – Welthandelsordnung und Welthandelsrecht*.

A C.I.P. record for this book is available from the Library of Congress.

Printed on acid-free paper.

ISSN 1574-907X
ISBN 90-04-14496-X

Koninklijke Brill NV incorporates the imprints Brill Academic Publishers, Martinus Nijhoff Publishers and VSP.

http://www.brill.nl

Printed and bound in the Netherlands.

CONTENTS

LIST OF ABBREVIATIONS

ACP	African, Caribbean and Pacific Group (Lomé/Cotonou Conventions)
AD	Anti-dumping measures
ADA	Anti-Dumping Agreement
AGOA	African Growth and Opportunity Act
AJIL	American Journal of International Law
AMS	Aggregate measurement of support (in Agreement on Agriculture)
AoA	Agreement on Agriculture
ASCM	Agreement on Subsidies and Countervailing Measures
ATC	Agreement on Textiles and Clothing
BGBl.	Bundesgesetzblatt (German Federal Law Gazette)
BISD	Basic Instruments and Selected Documents (published by GATT)
BT-Drs.	Bundestagsdrucksache
BVerfG	Bundesverfassungsgericht (Federal Constitutional Court)
CAP	Common Agricultural Policy (EU)
CBD	Convention on Biological Diversity
CBERA	Caribbean Basin Economic Recovery Act
CITES	Convention on International Trade in Endangered Species of Wild Fauna and Flora
CMLR	Common Market Law Review
CN	Combined Nomenclature
CPC	Central Product Classification
CTD	Committee on Trade and Development
CTE	Committee on Trade and Environment
CVD	Countervailing duty (subsidies)
DCs	developing countries
DOC	Department of Commerce
DRAMS	Anti-Dumping Duty On Dynamic Random Access Memory Semiconductors
DSB	Dispute Settlement Body
DSU	Understanding on Rules and Procedures Governing the Settlement of Disputes (Dispute Settlement Understanding)
EBA	Everything but Arms Inititative
EBOR	European Business Organization Law Review
EC	European Communities
ECJ	European Court of Justice
ECR	European Court Reports
ECT	Treaty of the European Community

ECOSOC	Economic and Social Council
EEC	European Economic Community
EFTA	European Free Trade Association
EIPR	European Intellectual Property Review
EJIL	European Journal of International Law
ELRR	Economic and Labour Relations Review
EPÜ	Europäisches Patentübereinkommen
EU	European Union (officially European Communities in WTO)
EuGRZ	Europäische Grundrechte Zeitschrift
EuR	Europarecht
Eurostat	Statistical Office of the European Communities
EuZW	Europäische Zeitschrift für Wirtschaftsrecht
EUT	Treaty of the European Union
EWS	Europäisches Wirtschafts- und Steuerrecht
FAC	Food Aid Convention
FAO	Food and Agriculture Organization (of the United Nations)
FSC	Foreign Sales Corporations
FTAA	Free Trade Agreements of the Americas
GATS	General Agreement on Trade in Services
GATT	General Agreement on Tariffs and Trade
GDP	Gross Domestic Product
GH	Grabitz/Hilf, Recht der Europäischen Union (Kommentor)
GMO	Genetically Modified Organism
GNP	Gross National Product
GPA	Agreement on Government Procurement
GRUR Int.	Gewerblicher Rechtsschutz und Urheberrecht Internationaler Teil
GSP	Generalized System of Preferences
GURT	Gene-use Restriction Technology
GYIL	German Yearbook International Law
HS	Harmonized Commodity Description and Coding System
HVILJ	Harvard International Law Journal
HWP	Harmonized Work Programme
IATA	International Air-Transport Association
ICC	International Chamber of Commerce
ICITO	Interim Commission for the International Trade Organization
ICRIER	Indian Council for Research on International Economic Relations New Delhi Working Papers
ICSID	International Centre for Settlement of Investment Disputes
IE	Independent Entity
IEC	International Electrotechnical Commission
ILM	International Legal Materials
ILO	International Labour Organization
IMF	International Monetary Fund

IOE	Office International des Epizooties
IPIC	Treaty on Intellectual Property in respect of Integrated Circuits
IPPC	International Plant Protection Convention
IPE	Intellectual Property Right
ISO	International Organization for Standardization
ITA	Information Technologies Agreement
ITC	International Trade Centre
ITO	International Trade Organization
JIEL	Journal of International Economic Law
JILP	Journal of International Law and Politics
JMWP	Jean Monnet Working Paper
JOB	Joint Concept Paper
JWT	Journal of World Trade
JZ	Juristenzeitung
LDCs	Least Developed Countries
LIBERTAD	Cuban Liberty and Democratic Solidarity
lit.	Litera
LIC	Agreement on Import Licensing Procedures
MAI	Multilateral Agreement on Investment
MEA	Multilateral environmental agreement
MFA	Multifibre Arrangement Regarding International Trade in Textiles
MFN	Most-favoured-nation
MIGA	Multilateral Investment Guarantee Agency
MRAs	Mutual Recognition Agreements
NAFTA	North American Free Trade Agreement
NAMA	Market Access for Non-agricultural Products
NGO	Non-governmental Organization
NJW	Neue Jursitische Wochenschrift
NME	Non-market economy
NT	National Treatment
NTB	Non-tariffs barriers
OCTG	Oil Country Tubular Goods
OECD	Organization for Economic Co-operation and Development
OMA	Orderly Market Agreement
OMC	Organisation Mondiale de Commerce (World Trade Organization)
PGE	Permanent Group of Experts (Agreement on Subsidies and Countervailing Measures)
PPM	Process and Production Methods
PSE	Producer subsidy equivalent (agriculture)
PSI	Pre-shipment inspection
RIW	Recht der Internationalen Wirtschaft
SCM	Subsidies and Countervailing Measures
S&D, SDT	Special and differential treatment (for developing countries)
SEO	Subsidies Enforcement Office

SG	Agreement on Safeguards
SGA	Selling, General and Administrative
SPS	Sanitary and phytosanitary measures
SSG	Special Safeguard (in Agreement on Agriculture)
TARIC	Tarif Intégré de la Communauté Integrated Tariff of the European Community
TBT	Technical barriers to trade
TMB	Textiles Monitoring Body
TNC	Trade Negotiations Committee
TPRB	Trade Policy Review Body
TPRM	Trade Policy Review Mechanism
TRIMs	Trade-related investment measures
TRIMS	Agreement on Trade Related Investment Measures
TRIPS	Trade-related aspects of intellectual property rights
TSB	Textiles Surveillance Body
UK	United Kingdom
UN	United Nations
UNCTAD	UN Conference on Trade and Development
UNDP	UN Development Programme
UNYB	United Nations Yearbook
UNTS	United Nations Treaty Series
URAA	Uruguay Round Agreement Act
U.S.C.A.	United States Code Annoated
USITC	US International Trade Commission
USTR	United States Trade Representative
VDLT	Vienna Convention on the Law of Treaties
VER	Voluntary export restraint
WCO	World Customs Organization
WCT	World Copyright Treaty
WGTCP	Working Group on the Interaction between Trade and Competition Policy
WIPO	World Intellectual Property Organization
WPPT	WIPO Performances and Phonograms Treaty
WTO	World Trade Organization
ZaöRV	Zeitschrift für ausländisches öffentliches Recht und Völkerrecht
ZEuS	Zeitschrift für Europarechtliche Studien

TABLE OF CASES

Appellate Body

Panel (WTO and GAT)

Panel (Art. 22.6 DSU)

European Court of Justice (ECJ)

Court of First Instance

Bundesverfassungsgericht (German Federal Constitutional Court)

PREFACE

Since the establishment of the World Trade Organization (WTO) and the entry into force of its legal order a decade ago, the world trade law has moved from the fringes of international law into the limelight of public and academic interest. Beside the legal significance the WTO became the forum political debates that centre around the topics such as globalization, justice in the world trade order and sustainable development.

[. . .]

The book's conception and text is based on the original German version, that has been published under the title "WTO – Welthandelsordnung und Welthandelsrecht" in September 2002. For the English translation we have extensively revised and updated the chapters, footnotes and the selection of literature.

We would like to thank *Arthur Steinmann* has translated most of the chapters and coordinated the work in Göttingen, *Graham Williams* has prepared working translations for a few chapters [. . .]

P.-T.S. F.S.

INTRODUCTION

I. *World Economy and World Trade Law*

1 The founding of the World Trade Organization, and the entry into force of its rules on January 1, 1995 marked a **turning point in the development of international economic relations**. Following a long period of lesser significance and effectiveness of the international trade system, the WTO today can be considered the most relevant regulatory body in global economic relations. However, its impressive institutional framework and complex body of law, should not lull one into forgetting that its coverage is still limited. International financial matters are dealt with by the World Bank and the International Monetary Fund. Furthermore, important other issues, as, for example, investment, have scarcely been addressed by the WTO so far, but primarily remain the subject of numerous bilateral treaties.[1] Moreover, the international system of technical and economic cooperation is significant. In addition, a multitude of other organizations are active in the area of international economic relations. These include the United Nations, the United Nations Conference on Trade and Development (UNCTAD), regional economic organizations, as well as the OECD and the International Chamber of Commerce (ICC). Together, these various institutions and regulations form the world economic legal and institutional order.

2 The concept of **order**, as commonly used in this area, is also similarly used in national economic policy and law. It characterises a set of principles, laws and institutions which governs social or economic activities. In this sense, the WTO can be seen as an important pillar of the **world trade order**, which mainly builds on the principles of the liberalization of trade and non-discrimination. In addition, it is also worth noting that this world trade order is only one part of an extensive world economic system which contains the above-mentioned elements.

---

[1] It should be noted, however, that a more comprehensive regime on investments is on the agenda of the ongoing Doha round, paras 799 *et seq.*

II. *World Trade in Numbers*

3 **International trade**, i.e. the exchange of goods and services, as well as investments, has grown steadily since the end of the Second World War. However, trade activities differ considerably between regions. While Asia has seen an increase in its share of world trade, the figures show a decrease as far as Africa is concerned. In 2003, world exports amounted to some 7,294 billion US-Dollars, representing a fifth of the worldwide gross national product. These developments have many causes. However, it can hardly be doubted that the opening up of national markets by lowering tariffs and reducing trade barriers made an important contribution to it.

Development of world trade (export) by regions and selected national economies 1948–2003 – *Billion US$ and Percentage*[2]

	1948	1953	1963	1973	1983	1993	2003
	Billion US Dollar						
World	58.0	84.0	157.0	579.0	1838.0	3671.0	7249.0
	Percentage						
North America	27.3	24.2	19.3	16.9	15.4	16.6	13.7
Western Europe	31.5	34.9	41.4	45.4	38.9	45.0	43.1
Africa	7.3	6.5	5.7	4.8	4.5	2.5	2.4
Asia	13.6	13.1	12.4	14.9	19.1	26.1	26.1
Japan	0.4	1.5	3.5	6.4	8.0	9.9	6.5
China	0.9	1.2	1.3	1.0	1.2	2.5	6.0
Tiger States	3.0	2.7	2.4	3.4	5.3	9.2	9.7
GATT/WTO Members	60.4	68.7	72.8	81.8	76.5	89.5	94.3

4 In 2003, the **European Union** was the largest exporter (19,4%), followed by the USA (12,7%), Japan (8,3%), China (7,7%) and Canada (4,8%). As far as imports are concerned, the EU ranks second (18,7%) after the US (21,8%).[3]

5 Trade in commercial services is growing and today amounts to approximately one fifth of world trade. In 2000 commercial **services**[4] worth some 1,450 million US Dollars were exported. However, those figures are likely even to underestimate the role of the service sector due to inconsistent methods of calculation and difficulties with the collection of data. For instance, services of foreign suppliers provided by way of commercial pres-

[2] Source: WTO Annual Report, International Trade Statistics 2004, 30.

[3] Source: WTO, Leading exporters and importers in world merchandise trade (excluding intra-EU (15) trade), 2003, http://www.wto.org/english/res_e/statis_e/its2004_e/section1_e/i06.xls.

[4] The heading of commercial services includes areas such as transport services, travel services and other industry related services. For further definitions, see also para. 540.

ence are not included. In 2000, the EU's share of exported commercial services was 41.2%, followed by those of the USA (18.67%), Japan (4.69%) and Canada (2.49%). Within this period, 40% of the EU's trade in commercial services was with the USA, while only 13% was with European Free Trade Association States, 6% with African States, and 18% with Asia.[5]

III. *Literature, Information and Research Tools*

Marci Hoffman, International Economic Law and the Internet: Content, Quality and Research Methods, JIEL 4 (2001) 4, 231–244; *Juan M. Mesa*, Legal and Documentary Research at WTO: The New Documents On-Line Database, JIEL 4 (2001) 4, 245–259; *Marci Hoffman & Jill Mc. Watson* (eds), ASIL Guide to Electronic Resources of International Law, ASIL Bulletin No. 14, 2nd ed., Washington 2002.

1. *Documents of the WTO*

6 **Official documents** of the WTO[6] are available on the Internet for free in the three authentic languages, English, Spanish and French[7] – as long as they are not classified or kept confidential for a particular length of time.[8] The documents can be searched with the help of the document symbol, which is assigned on the basis of the WTO document nomenclature. This nomenclature reflects the relevant body and the type and content of the document. Each document symbol consists of a combination of letters, digits and additional specifications.[9] The following general indications are used, and appear as the first letter of a document symbol:

G	trade in goods
IP	intellectual property
JOBS	unsigned documents
S	trade in commercial services
WT	WTO committees
OFFICE	Administration
SCHD	schedules of concessions and commitments
PLURI	plurilateral agreements

[5] Source: Eurostat and IWF, see also Eurostat, Statistics summary Nr. 117/20014: EU-Figures for the Ministerial Conference at Doha, <http://europa.eu.int/comm/eurostat/>.

[6] <http://www.wto.org>.

[7] <http://docsonline.wto.org/>.

[8] For details, see the General Council's accepted principles and the procedure of release, WT/L/160/Rev. 1, 8.7.1996.

[9] E.g.: G/SPS/W/63/Rev.1 – (collection/series/type/digit/status).

The letters after the stroke specify the subject matter more closely. For instance, documents concerning anti-dumping matters are denoted by the letters G/ADP[. . .], whereas WT/DS[. . .] relates to dispute settlement. The type of the document is further specified by another letter as follows:

M	minutes
N	notification
Q	question/reply
R	report
W	working paper

Further indications concern the document's status:

Add.	addendum
Corr.	corrigendum
Rev.	revision
Suppl.	Supplement

7 The WTO Secretariat produces a number of **publications**, which can in most cases be downloaded. These include the annual reports, international trade statistics; studies and parts of reports relevant to trade policy reviews (see para. 27). The reports and awards of the Panel and Appellate Body under the DSU are accessible by way of the WTO database (<http://www.wto.org/english/tratop_e/dispu_e/dispu_e.htm>) and are also published on paper.[10]

8 The ***Analytical Index* – Guide to GATT Law and Practice** (6th ed., Geneva) is a particularly useful reference tool for legal practitioners. It is published by the Secretariat and includes relevant decisions concerning the particular provisions of the GATT. A collection of important decisions, reports, protocols and other documents of the GATT 1947 generated between 1952 and 1995 has been published by the GATT Secretariat under the title: Basic Instruments and Selected Documents (BISD). It is based on an initial four-volume edition. Since 1953, "Supplements"[11] have been published annually. The BISD has also been published in a microfiche edition.

9 The WTO has published its first edition of a **WTO *Analytical Index*, covering the period from** 1 January 1995 to 30 June 2001, which is also accessible via the Internet.[12] The **Appellate Body Repertory of Reports and Awards**[13] covers the case law of the Appellate Body between 1995–

[10] WTO Dispute Settlement Reports 1996–2003, Cambridge University Press.
[11] Example of citation: BISD 39S/62 = Basic Instruments and Selected Documents, 39th Supplement, Page 62.
[12] <http://www.wto.org/english/res_e/booksp_e/analytic_index_e/ analytic_index_e.htm>.
[13] <http://www.wto.org/english/tratop_e/dispu_e/repertory_e/repertory_e.htm>.

2004 by reference to cases, subject matter and relevant provisions. The **WTO Focus Newsletter covers** current activities of the WTO and recent developments. It is freely available and can be ordered by way of electronic subscription.[14]

2. *Literature*

a. *Textbooks, Monographs, and Collections (Selection)*

Bhagwati, Jagdish & Panagariya, Arvind & Srinivasan, Thirukodikaval	Lectures in International Trade, 2nd ed., Cambridge 1998
Bhala, Raj & Kennedy, Kevin	World Trade Law: The GATT-WTO System, Regional Arrangements, and U.S. Law, Charlottesville 1998, with Supplement 1999
Carreau, Dominique & Juillard, Patrick	Droit international économique, Paris 2003
Corden, W. Max	Trade Policy and Economic Welfare, 2nd ed., Oxford 1997
Cottier, Thomas	GATT-Uruguay Round, Bern 1995
Dam, Kenneth W.	The GATT, Law and International Economic Organization, Chicago 1970
Flory, Thiébaut	L'organisation mondiale du commerce, Brussels 1997
Hilf, Meinhard & Oeter, Stefan (eds.)	WTO-Recht, Baden-Baden 2005
Hoekman, Bernard M. & Kostecki, Michel M.	The Political Economy of the World Trading System, 2nd ed., Oxford 2001
Hudec, Robert E.	The GATT Legal System and World Trade Diplomacy, 2nd ed., Salem 1990

[14] <http://www.wto.org/english/res_e/focus_e/focus_e.htm>. For further sources, see the link, "Resources", on <http://www.wto.org/english/res_e/res_e.htm>.

Jackson, John H.	The World Trading System, 2nd ed., Cambridge/London 1997
Jackson, John H.	The World Trade Organization – Constitution and Jurisprudence, London 1998
Jackson, John H. & Sykes, Alan O. (eds.)	Implementing the Uruguay Round, Oxford 1997
Krugman, Paul R. & Obstfeld, Maurice	International Economics, Theory and Politics, 5th ed., Reading 2000
Lowenfeld, Andreas F.	International Economic Law, Oxford 2001
Matsushita, Mitsuo & Schoenbaum, Thomas & Mavroidis Petros C.	The World Trade Organization, Oxford 2003
Meerhaeghe, Marcel A. van	International Economic Institutions, 7th ed., Dordrecht 1998
Ortino, Federico & Petersmann, Ernst-Ulrich (eds)	The WTO Dispute Settlement System 1995–2003, The Hague et al. 2004
Palmeter David & Mavroidis, Petros C.	Dispute Settlement in the World Trade Organization, Practice and Procedure, 2nd ed., Cambridge 2004
Picone, Paolo & Ligusto, Aldro	Diritto dell'organizzazione mondiale del commercio, Padova 2002
Seidl-Hohenveldern, Ignaz	International Economic Law, 3rd ed., The Hague 1999
Stern, Brigitte & Ruiz Fabri, Hélène	The Case-Law of the WTO, Leiden/Boston, Vol. 1 2004, Vol. 2 2005
Trebilcock, Michael J. & Howse, Robert	The Regulation of International Trade, 3rd ed., London, 2004
Senti, Richard & Conlan, Patricia	WTO: Regulation of World Trade after the Uruguay Round, Zurich 1998
Siebert, Horst	World Economy, 2nd ed., London/New York 2002

Sykes, Alan O. & Davey, William J. & Jackson, John H.	Cases and Legal Problems of International Economic Relations, 3rd ed., St. Paul 2002
Viner, Jacob	A Problem in International Trade, Chicago 1923
Weiler, Joseph H. H. (ed.)	The EU, the WTO, and the NAFTA, Oxford/New York 2000

b. *Manuals*

- WTO Secretariat, Guide to GATT Law and Practice (Analytical Index), 6th ed., 2 Vol. Geneva 1995.
- WTO Secretariat, Guide to Dispute Settlement, 2002.
- WTO Secretariat, WTO analytical index, Geneva 2003.
- WTO Secretariat, A Handbook on the WTO Dispute Settlement System, 2004.
- Dennin, Joseph F., (ed.), Law & Practice of the World Trade Organization, (Loose leaf) New York 2001.
- Pescatore, Pierre & Davey, William & Lowenfeld, Andreas (eds): Handbook of WTO/GATT Dispute Settlement, 11th ed. (March 2002), (Loose leaf) New York 1992.
- Prieß, Hans-Joachim & Berrisch, Georg (eds), WTO-Handbook, Munich 2003.
- Wolfrum, Rüdiger & Stoll, Peter-Tobias (eds), Max-Planck-Commentaries on WTO Law, 2005.

c. *Collections of Legal Texts*

World Trade Organization	The Legal Texts – Results of the Uruguay Round of Multilateral Trade Negotiations, 2nd ed., Cambridge 1999
World Trade Organization	The WTO Dispute Settlement Procedures, 2nd ed., Cambridge/Geneva 2001
Tietje, Christian	Welthandelsorganisation, 2nd ed., Munich 2003
Zamora, Stephen & Brand, Ronald A. (eds)	Basic Documents of International Economic Law, Chicago 1990
Henkin, Louis & Smit, Hans & Pugh, Richard C. & Schachter, Oscar	International Law: Cases and Materials 4th ed., St. Paul 2001

Kunig, Philip & Lau, N. & Meng, Werner	International Economic law – Basic Documents, 2nd ed., Berlin 1993
Cheng, Chia-Jui (ed.)	Basic Documents on International Trade Law, 3rd ed., 1999
Hilf, Meinhard & Schorkopf, Frank (eds)	WTO-LawRecht, Text Collection English/German, 2nd ed., Hamburg 2003

d. *Journals*

10 In the journals field, very few are aimed specifically at WTO law. These include

- Journal of International Economic Law (JIEL)
- Journal of World Trade (JWT)
- World Trade Review

A number of other titles regularly include reports and articles on this area of law

- American Journal of International Law (AJIL)
- Aussenwirtschaft
- Brooklyn Journal of International Law
- Common Market Law Review
- Europäische Zeitschrift für Wirtschaftsrecht (EuZW)
- European Journal of International Law (EJIL)
- European Journal of Political Economy
- Fordham International Law Journal
- Harvard International Law Journal (HVILJ)
- International and Comparative Law Quarterly
- Legal Issues of Economic Integration
- Leiden Journal of International Law
- Michigan Journal of International Law
- Minnesota Journal of Global Trade
- Recht der Internationalen Wirtschaft (RIW)
- Review of International Economics
- The World Economy
- World Competition
- World Trade and Arbitration Materials
- Zeitschrift für ausländisches öffentliches Recht und Völkerrecht (ZaöRV)

e. *Information services*

11 There are also **information services** on offer, to allow tracking of the latest developments in international trade law, and especially WTO law. These are offered both in printed form and on the **Internet**. "Bridges Weekly Digest" is a weekly information letter of a non-governmental organisation, the International Centre for Trade and Sustainable Develop-

ment (<http:// www.ictsd.org>), which is freely available. Another valuable information source is the World Trade Law website (http://www.worldtradelaw.net), which has a commercial section, but also contains free material.

f. *Internet sites for WTO Law*[15]

European Commission, Directorate General Trade	*http://europa.eu.int/comm/trade/index_en.htm*
Int. Centre for Trade and Sustainable Development	*http://www.ictsd.org*
International Law Association – Int. Trade Law Com.	*http://www.ila-hq.org*
International Chamber of Commerce (ICC)	*http://www.iccwbo.org*
International Monetary Fund (IMF)	*http://www.imf.org*
North American Free Trade Agreement (NAFTA)	*http://www.nafta-sec-alena.org/*
Organization for Economic Cooperation and Development (OECD)	*http://www.oecd.org*
Trade and Development Centre	*http://www.itd.org/*
UN Commission on International Trade Law	*http://www.uncitral.org*
UN Conference on Trade and Development (UNCTAD)	*http://www.unctad.org*
United States Trade Representative (USTR)	*http://www.ustr.gov*
World Bank	*http://www.worldbank.org*
World Custom Organization (WCO)	*http://www.wcoomd.org*
World Trade Organization	*http://www.wto.org*

[15] See JIEL 5 (2002) 1, 251–264 and JIEL 7 (2004) 1, 199–201, for more detailed lists of links regarding the WTO and international trade law.

g. *Research Tools on the Internet*

Michigan State University – global EDGE (Statistics)	*http://globaledge.msu.edu/ibrd/*
Institute of International Economic Law, Georgetown University	*http://www.ll.georgetown.edu/intl/iiel/home.htm*
New York University School of Law, WTO and GATT and Research	*http://www.law.nyu.edu/library/wtoguide.html*
Max-Planck-Institute of comparative public and international law – UN Library	*http://www.virtual-institute.de/de/UNDepot/Inhalt.cfm*
Transnational Law Database – Lex Mercatoria	*http://www.tldb.de*

CHAPTER ONE

HISTORY AND ORGANIZATIONAL STRUCTURE

John H. Jackson, Restructuring the GATT System, 1990; *Thomas Cottier*, The GATT-Uruguay Round, 1995; *Gerald A. Bunting*, GATT and the evolution of the global trade system, St. John's journal of legal commentary 11 (1996) 2, 505–521; *Richard Senti*, WTO the new world trade order: a survey, 1997; *John H. Jackson*, Global Economics and International Economic Law, JIEL 1 (1998) 1, 1–23; *Daniel C. Esty*, Non-governmental organizations at the World Trade Organization, JIEL 1 (1998) 1, 123–147; *Jagdish Bhagwati & Matthias Hirsch* (Eds), The Uruguay round and beyond: essays in honour of Arthur Dunkel, 1998; *John Croome: WTO-Secretariat*, Guide to the Uruguay Round agreements, 1999; *Wolfgang Benedek*, Developing the constitutional order of the WTO – the role of NGOs, in: *idem* (Ed.), Development and developing international and European law, 1999, 228–250; *WTO-Secretariat*, From GATT to WTO, 2000; *Frederick M. Abbott*, Distributed governance at the WTO-WIPO, JIEL 3 (2000) 1, 63–81; *Dukgeun Ahn*, Linkages between international financial and trade institutions, JWT 34 (2000) 4, 1–35; *Sandeep Chauhan*, GATT to WTO: Gandhian alternative to new international economic order, 2001; *Mitsuo Matsushita*, The World Trade Organisation, 2003; *Roderick Abbott*, The role of the World Trade Organization, Bitburger Gespräche 41 (2003), 135–142; *Mohammend S. B. Korotana*, Cases, materials and commentary on the WTO law, 2004; *Julio A. Lacarte*, Transparency, public debate and participation by NGOs in the WTO, JIEL 7 (2004) 3, 683–686; *Georg Matthias Berrisch*, Cancun – was nun?, RIW 50 (2004) 1, 69–75; *Guido Glania*, Various approaches for institutional reforms within the WTO, Aussenwirtschaft 59 (2004) 1, 7–28; *Petros C. Mavroidis* (Ed.), The WTO and international trade law, 2005; *Nicholas Perdikis* (Ed.), The WTO and the regulation of international trade, 2005; as well as the corresponding chapters of the monographs enlisted in the introduction.

I. *The Evolution of the World Trade Order*

12 The experience of the Great Depression of the 1930s played an important role in the **formation of the international economic order after the Second World War**. The United Nations Organization (UNO), founded in 1945, pays tribute to this experience through the establishment of a special principal organ, the Economic and Social Council (ECOSOC). In addition, Art. 55 of the Charter of the United Nations commits the Member States to far-reaching cooperation on economic and social issues. It thus accommodates the notion that peace cannot be understood to mean merely the absence of violence, but can

also include economic and social aspects that are essential for the effective preservation of peace.[1]

13 Still during World War II, at the Bretton Woods Conference in 1944, a new order for the coordination of international financial relations had been set up in the form of the World Bank and the International Monetary Fund (IMF). In the field of world trade, the ECOSOC was intended to create a similar system that would – under its surveillance as a United Nations specialized agency – regulate cooperation between States with regard to world trade. The United Nations Conference on Trade and Employment that had been convened for this purpose in 1947 adopted the **Havana Charter** (named after the conference location) establishing the International Trade Organization (**ITO**).[2] In addition to the formation of such an organization, the ITO Charter contained comprehensive and far-reaching international trade regulations. For example, it made provisions for commitments regarding economic development, the labour market, trade in natural resources, and even included a special chapter on the regulation of competition. These regulations, which in different respects went far beyond a mere free trade concept, encountered firm rejection by the US Senate (paras 681 *et seq.*) when it was called upon to ratify the Charter. In consequence, the originally US-led initiative eventually failed through lack of US support.[3]

14 As a preparatory effort, the States participating at the conference, with the support of an interim commission,[4] had negotiated separately about the reciprocal reduction of tariffs. In the course of these negotiations the States agreed several general rules that were meant later to become part of the Havana Charter. There was considerable interest in bringing these agreements into force quickly as a means of overcoming the economic crisis in the U.S., and achieving the war economies' transition into a free market. So, the **Protocol** of October 30, 1947[5] provided for the preliminary application of the rules from January 1, 1948. Since, according to the Protocol, conflicting national law was to remain unaltered (so-called "grandfather clause"), and since there was therefore no need for

[1] *Wolfrum*, in: *Simma* (ed.) The Charter of the United Nations, 2nd ed., Art. 55, para. 2; regarding the positive notion of peace see *Frowein*, in: *Simma* (ed.), The Charter of the United Nations, 2nd ed., Art. 1, para. 5.

[2] United Nations Conference on Trade and Employment, UNYB 1947–48, 522 *et seq.* 972 *et seq.* The notion of employment shows the influence of John Maynard Keynes and his economic policy ideas at the Bretton Woods Conference, which he attended personally.

[3] The rejection was possible especially because the business community's pressure for consent had been considerably reduced due to the preliminary application of the GATT and the tariff reductions connected thereto.

[4] Interim Commission for the International Trade Organization (ICITO).

[5] Protocol of Provisional Application of the General Agreement of Tariffs and Trade, UNTS, 55, 308.

ratification by Congress, the US government was able to conclude the agreement by itself in exercise of its temporary negotiation authority with respect to tariff reductions. The **General Agreement on Tariffs and Trade (GATT)**,[6] having become effective on this basis, was administered by the Interim Commission whose term of office was prolonged especially for this purpose. Later on the commission was appointed the Secretariat of the GATT.[7] Following the unsuccessful attempt to establish the ITO, the GATT, which had originally been set up as a merely interim arrangement, became a permanent institution. During the course of several decades, due to the needs of the CONTRACTING PARTIES for coordination, cooperation and dispute settlement in the context of the agreement, the GATT evolved more and more into a *de facto* organization.

15 During six more rounds of negotiations – the so-called **GATT Rounds** – the parties progressively agreed upon more and more far ranging tariff concessions, which formed the core of separate agreements with open membership. It was supplemented by additional regulations on subsidies and countervailing duties, technical barriers to trade, import licence procedures, public procurement and anti-dumping.[8]

16 The eighth GATT Round started with a Ministerial Conference in Punta del Este, Uruguay, in 1986, in the middle of a crisis for the GATT: its regulations were no longer in tune with the realities of world trade, especially the increasing role of trade in services; furthermore, the GATT's authority was challenged by the emergence of dissenting silent or explicit agreements between individual Member States, by its inefficient consensus-based dispute settlement mechanism, and by unilateral trade sanctions. In the course of the eight-year-long negotiations in the **Uruguay Round** which ended in 1994, basically a new, consolidated and essentially enlarged system for the world trade order was finally set up on the basis of the (old) GATT.

17 In contrast to the GATT Rounds until then, a "single undertaking approach" prevailed in the Uruguay Round, according to which the traditional structuring of the legal order into separate agreements was maintained, while the regulations and negotiation results contained therein could, however, be accepted or rejected by the States only in their entirety as a package.[9] The final act of the Uruguay Round, negotiations on which began in Marrakesh in December 1993 and which was signed on

[6] Dated 30 October 1947, in the version valid since 1 March 1969, UNTS 55, 94.

[7] Resolution Establishing an Interim Commission for the ITO, UNYB 1947–48, 978 *et seq.*

[8] The following GATT rounds should be mentioned: 1949 Annecy, 1950–51 Torquay, 1956 Geneva, 1960–62 Dillon, 1964–67 "Kennedy-Round", 1973–79 "Tokyo-Round".

[9] A so-called "GATT à la carte" and the disruption of the unity of the WTO legal order connected with it was to be avoided considering the negative experiences of the Tokyo Round.

April 15, 1994, therefore contains no less than 46 agreements and 25 resolutions.[10] Of fundamental importance in this context is the **Agreement Establishing the World Trade Organization (WTO Agreement)**,[11] to which the other agreements are attached in groups. It entered into force on January 1, 1995, following 76 ratifications. According to Art. I WTO Agreement,[12] the World Trade Organization (WTO) came into being on the same day.

18 The fourth Ministerial Conference at Doha/Quatar adopted a mandate to start a new round of trade negotiations that become known as the "Doha Round".[13] An extensive work programme, including tariff negotiations, implementation issues, as well as the reform of WTO law on anti-dumping, subsidies, regional trade agreements and dispute settlement, was started. However, the deadline of January 1, 2005 has expired without the finalization of the agenda.

II. *The WTO as World Trade Order and World Trade Organization*

19 Like the GATT, the WTO is understood as the embodiment of a regime with corresponding institutional foundations and legal regulations (para. 2).

20 Listing the **objectives** of the world trade order, section one of the Preamble to the WTO Agreement mentions: raising the standard of living, ensuring full employment and a large and steadily growing volume of income and effective demand, expanding the production of and trade in goods and services, while allowing for the optimal use of the world's resources in accordance with the objective of sustainable development. Further goals named are the protection and preservation of the environment and the enhancement of the means for doing so. The second section of the Preamble refers to the interests of developing countries and the need for economic development.[14] Compared to these higher-ranking economic and political goals, and taking into account the respon-

---

[10] Final Act Embodying the Results of the Uruguay Round of Multilateral Trade Negotiations, LT/UR/A/1, 15 April 1994.

[11] Agreement Establishing the World Trade Organization, LT/UR/A/2, 15 April 1994; entered into force on 1 January 1995.

[12] The numbering of the provisions in the different WTO Agreements is not uniform. For the most part, Roman numerals are used for the numbering of the articles. However, in several agreements Arabic numbering is also applied. With regard to paragraphs a colon or full stop is used.

[13] Ministerial Declaration adopted on 14 November 2001, WT/MIN(01)/DEC/1, 20 November 2001.

[14] The question whether and to what extent the WTO serves free trade or dictates the freedom of trade is discussed below in the section on the principles of the WTO, see paras 61 *et seq.*

sibility of other international organizations and State sovereignty, section three of the Preamble confines the role of the WTO to the substantial reduction of tariffs and other barriers to trade and to the elimination of discriminatory treatment in international trade relations by means of reciprocal and mutually advantageous arrangements.

III. *The WTO as an Organization*

21 According to Art. II:1 WTO Agreement, the WTO constitutes the common institutional framework for the conduct of trade relations among its Members in the areas set out in the individual agreements and associated legal instruments. The WTO's **area of responsibility** thus having been defined, Art. III WTO Agreement specifies its **tasks and functions**. The general and commonly found task description – the administration of the corresponding legal statutes including their implementation – is broadened by paragraph one, which expressly mentions the WTO's task of furthering the objectives of the agreements. Explicitly mentioned is the function of administering dispute settlement and the periodical, political review of the trade policies of the Members.

22 At the same time, the WTO shall explicitly serve its Members as a **forum for negotiations**. This function is not limited to matters relating to existing agreements (Art. III:2:1 WTO Agreement), but includes the possibility that the WTO may serve as a forum for "further negotiations" concerning multilateral trade issues, and as a framework for the implementation of the results of such negotiations. Finally, alongside the general authorization to cooperate with other international organizations,[15] Art. III:5 WTO Agreement explicitly provides for cooperation with the International Monetary Fund and the World Bank with a view to achieving greater coherence in global economic policy-making.[16]

23 The responsibilities of the WTO, which considerably surpass those of the GATT, are clearly geared towards a **dynamic further development** of the world trade order. Corresponding multi-faceted assignments for review and organization are, on the other hand, included in the individual agreements. Overall, this dynamic is described as a so-called "built-in agenda" and results in a staged, continuous negotiation process that

[15] See Art. V:1 WTO Agreement.

[16] See the WTO Agreements with the International Monetary Fund (IMF) and the International Bank for Reconstruction and Development, the International Development Association (World Bank), WT/L/195 of 18 November 1996; for the IMF-WTO relationship see *Siegel*, AJIL 96 (2000) 2, 561 *et seq.*

is, for the most part, assigned to the competent bodies. At the same time, as additional instruments for the further development of the world trade order, negotiating rounds are carried out, which can henceforth be based on Art. III:2:1 WTO Agreement, even in cases concerning new subjects (paras 716, 725 *et seq.*). Currently, such negotiations take place in the "Doha round".[17] However, as the current experience underlines, the institutional momentum towards a dynamic development generates a considerable pressure for success that may be considered overly ambitious.

IV. *Bodies and Organizational Structure*

24 The WTO has an extensively sub-divided structure, including the following three **main bodies** referred to in the WTO Agreement: the Ministerial Conference, serving as the representative body (Art. IV:1), the General Council as the executive body (Art. IV:2), and the Secretariat in charge of administrative affairs (Art. VI).

25 The **Ministerial Conference** is the principal organ of the WTO. It is open to all Members and meets at least once every two years.[18] It has full authority to take decisions on all matters under any of the Multilateral Trade Agreements, if requested by a Member to do so (Art. IV:1 WTO Agreement). In addition, the Ministerial Conference has particular powers that are partly subject to special procedures and majority requirements. It is also responsible for appointing the Director General of the WTO, and for adopting the staff regulations (Art. VI:2 and 3 WTO Agreement). It further has the authority to set up committees, amongst which are committee on Trade and Development as well as the Committees on Budget, Finance and Administration (Art. IV:7 WTO Agreement). It has important powers with regard to authentically interpreting (Art. IX:2 WTO Agreement) and amending (Art. X:1 WTO Agreement) the Multilateral Trade Agreements, and it is authorized to waive an obligation imposed on a Member, provided there are exceptional circumstances (Art. IX:3 WTO Agreement, see para. 170 *et seq.*). Furthermore it can turn a multilateral agreement into a plurilateral agreement, as

---

[17] See paras 799 *et seq.*

[18] A recent report submitted to the Director-General of the WTO written by eight eminent WTO-scholars on "The Future of the WTO – Addressing institutional challenges in the new millennium", referred to as the "Sutherland Report" after the chairman of the Consultative Board, Mr. *Peter Sutherland*, advises, *inter alia*, that in future the Ministerial Conference should meet annually and that the Director-General should report to the ministers in writing on a six-month basis (Sutherland Report, 2004, Principle Conclusions, para. 28). Whether this recommendation will be implemented remains to be seen.

well as, *vice versa*, declare plurilateral agreements to be multilateral agreements (Art. X:9 WTO Agreement).[19] Finally, it is the responsibility of the Ministerial Conference to decide on the negotiation and regulation of new subjects (Art. III:2 WTO Agreement), as well as the acceptance of new Members (Art. XII:2 WTO Agreement).

26 The **General Council** (Art. IV:2 WTO Agreement) is a permanent executive body that, in the interval between meetings of the Ministerial Conference, carries out the functions of the latter, and, in addition, has special responsibilities of its own. It meets as appropriate (Art. IV:2 s. 1, Art. IV:3 and Art. IV s. 1 WTO Agreement) and consists of representatives of all Members.[20] As regards its special function, the General Council can thus not be distinguished from the Ministerial Conference by the group of the Members represented on it, but rather with regard to their rank: while the Ministerial Conference is designed for high-ranking political participation, the General Council, meeting at the site of the Secretariat in Geneva, is carried out by the representatives of the Members accredited to it. The Council has the right to establish its own rules of procedure and, furthermore, to approve the respective rules of procedure of the different committees in accordance with Art. IV:5 WTO Agreement.

27 The General Council, in particular, carries out important functions regarding the **settlement of disputes** and the **review of the trade policy** of the Members. These functions are, however, not directly allocated to the Council but are, from a formalistic point of view, rendered institutionally independent: the Understanding on Rules and Procedures Governing the Settlement of Disputes (DSU)[21] and the Trade Policy Review Mechanism (TPRM)[22] provide for **institutional independence** also with regard to the organizational structure, and, as such, provide for a committee for dispute settlement (Dispute Settlement Body, DSB) and a body for the review of trade policies (Trade Policy Review Body, TPRB). In the present structure of the WTO, this institutional independence has not, however, been achieved through separate bodies. According to Art. IV:3 and 4 WTO Agreement, the work of the two bodies is rather allocated to the General Council, which can however establish its own rules of procedure and appoint its own chairman for these special functions.

---

[19] With respect to the differentiation between plurilateral and multilateral agreements, see para. 51.

[20] It is therefore not designed for a limited number of representatively selected and rotating members as is the case with the Security Council and the ECOSOC of the United Nations.

[21] Understanding on Rules and Procedures Governing the Settlement of Disputes (DSU); see also the Rules of Conduct for the Understanding on Rules and Procedures Governing the Settlement of Disputes, WT/DSB/RC/1, 11 December 1996.

[22] Annex 3 to the WTO Agreement.

28 In contrast to the Ministerial Conference, the General Council has the explicit authority to create its own **subsidiary organs**. According to Art. IV:5 WTO Agreement three special Councils: The Council for Trade in Goods, the Council for Trade in Services and the Council for Trade-Related Aspects of Intellectual Property Rights are allocated to the General Council, and carry out their activities under the general guidance of the latter. Participation in these councils is open to all Members. The Councils meet as necessary. They establish their respective rules of procedure subject to the approval of the General Council and can, as necessary, appoint subordinate committees which again themselves have the right to set up their own rules of procedure subject to the approval of the respective Councils.

29 The **special bodies of the General Council** have the general function of overseeing the operation and functioning of the respective agreements, i.e., the multilateral trade agreements relating to the trade in goods according to Annex 1 A of the WTO Agreement, the General Agreement on Trade in Services (GATS),[23] and the Agreement on Trade Related Aspects of Intellectual Property Rights (TRIPS).[24] Additional special functions arise out of these agreements themselves and can, furthermore, be allocated to special bodies.

30 The **Secretariat of the WTO** (Art. VI WTO Agreement) works under the guidance of a Director-General who is appointed by the Ministerial Conference.[25] Since the decision-making power rests exclusively in the hands of the Members, the main task of the Secretariat is the logistic, technical and professional support of the councils and committees, the developing countries, the dissemination of information to the media and the (world) public as well as the organization of the Ministerial Conferences. In addition to that, the Secretariat gives advice to States interested in acceding to the WTO and it offers its legal expertise in the context of dispute settlement. In 2005, the Secretariat has 615 regular staff. Its costs, which amount to about CHF 169 million in 2005, are borne by the Members. A Member's respective share is calculated by reference to its share of world trade in goods, services and intellectual property.[26] In

[23] General Agreement on Trade in Services (GATS), English version: OJ EC No. L 336/190 of 23 December 1994.

[24] Agreement on Trade Related Aspects of Intellectual Property Rights (TRIPS), English version: OJ EC No. L 336/213 of 23 December 1994.

[25] Still named "Executive Secretary" under the GATT 1947 (see Art. XXVI:4), later, without changing the text of the treaty, renamed "Director-General", see decision of 23 March 1965. This term was now also adopted in Art. VI:1 WTO Agreement. See also the Procedures for the Appointment of the Directors General, WT/GC/W/482/Rev.1 6 December 2002.

[26] The minimum quota of a Member with respect to the funding of the annual budget is

addition, the WTO has extra-budgetary resources at its disposal that are donated by industrial countries on a voluntary basis. This money is used to finance technical aid for developing and transformation countries, i.e., in particular the education and further training of personnel.[27]

31 The powers, duties, conditions of service and term of office of the **Director-General** are determined by the Ministerial Conference.[28] The Director-General has comprehensive authority with respect to the staff of the Secretariat, while the Ministerial Conference is competent to make general regulations in this regard.[29] The Director-General and the personnel of the Secretariat enjoy the status of international officials pursuant to the general rules.[30] Art. VI:4 WTO Agreement extensively regulates their integrity and independence: instructions from any body external to the WTO may neither be sought nor accepted. The Members are requested to refrain from exercising influence. In addition, the Director-General and the staff of the Secretariat are to refrain from activities that may reflect on their position as international officials.[31]

0.015% equals CHF 25.110, – in 2005; in 2005 the United States contributed CHF 26.45 M., Germany 14.85 M., Japan 10.25 M. and United Kingdom 9.55 M.

[27] The trade-related technical assistance to developing countries provided by the WTO has to be distinguished from the support rendered by the Advisory Centre on WTO Law, which is a private organizations outside the WTO legal framework, see <http://www.acwl.ch>). The centre is to provide legal training, support and advice on WTO law and dispute settlement procedures to developing countries, in particular to the least developed among them, and to countries with economies in transition. For the Integrated Framework for Trade-Related Technical Assistance to least-developed countries (IF) see the Integrated Framework Steering Committee, Joint Communiqué by the Six Agencies of the Integrated Framework – IMF, ITC, UNCTAD, UNDP, World Bank and WTO of 15 July 2003, WT/IFSC/5, <http://www.integratedframework.org/index.html>.

[28] Following the resignation of *Renato Ruggiero* (1995–1999) from the office of Director-General in April 1999, a months-long struggle for the succession took place between the US and some of the EU Member States on the one hand, and the Asian countries under the leadership of Thailand on the other hand. The compromise that was finally reached provided for the partitioning of the mandate of the Director-General into two periods: the former Prime Minister of New Zealand, *Mike Moore* took office on 1 September 1999, to be replaced three years later by the Vice Prime Minister and Trade Minister of Thailand, *Supachai Panitchpakdi*, see the decision of the General Council of 22 July 1999 WT/L/308 and the communication of Thailand WT/L/438 dated 20 December 2001; on 1 September 2005 *Pascal Lamy* will become Director-General of the WTO. For the procedure of appointment of directors-general compare WT/L/509, 20 January 2003.

[29] In the decision of 7 October 1998, Conditions of Service Applicable to the Staff of the WTO Secretariat (WT/GC/W/102/Rev.1), the General Council adopted comprehensive staff regulations, which provide for the establishment of a pension fund. With regard to the administrative decisions of the Director-General, there is the possibility of legal protection through reference to the Administrative Tribunal of the International Labour Organization.

[30] See *Brownlie*, Principles of Public International Law, 5th ed., 1998, 682 *et seq.*

[31] See staff regulation No. 1.4 and the codex for the staff of the Secretariat, Council Decision of 7 October 1998, WT/GC/W/103.

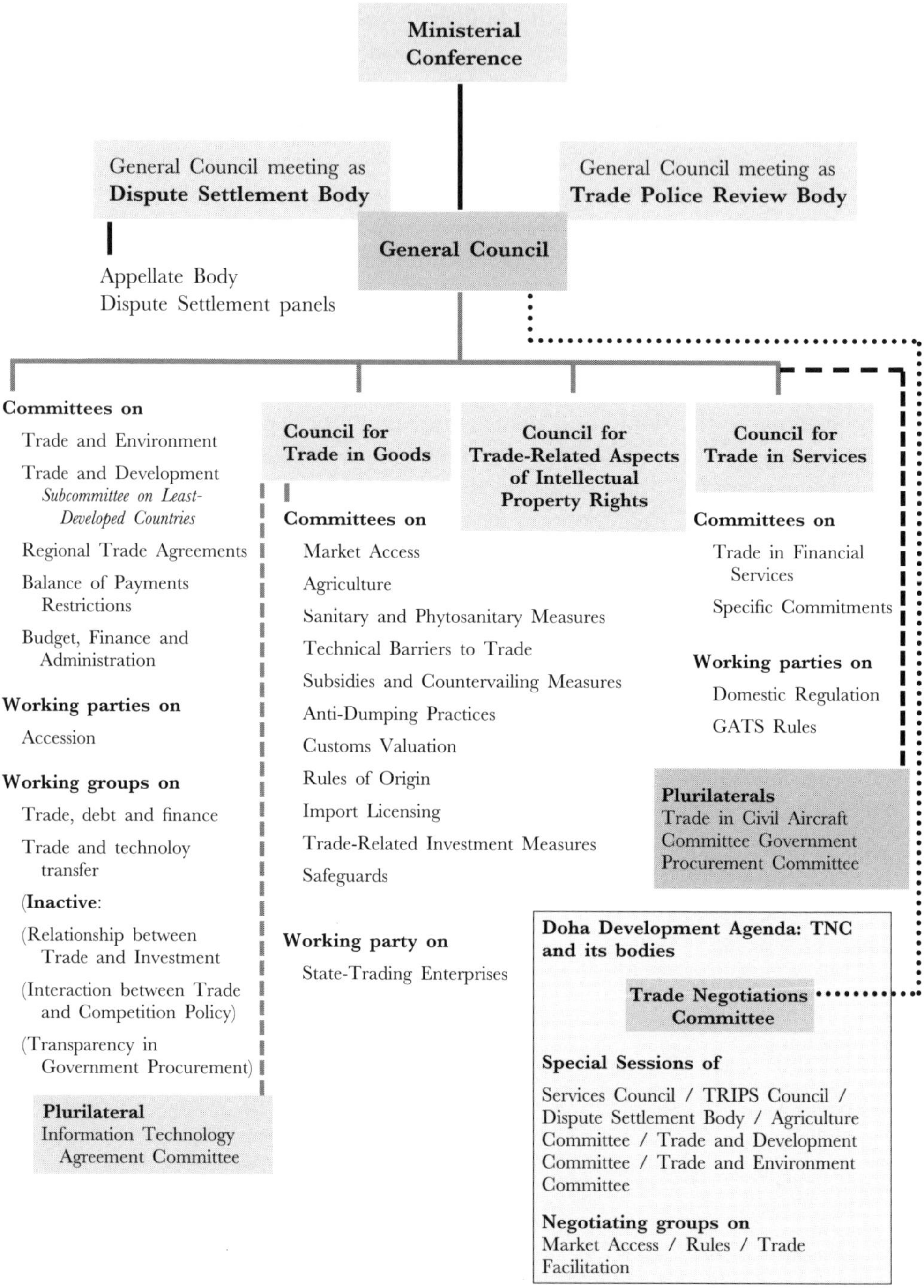

Organizational Structure of the WTO (based on a chart of the WTO Secretariat, see <http://www.wto.org/english/thewto_e/whatis_e/tif_e/org2_e.htm>)

32 The institutional structure laid out in the WTO Agreement is complemented by **additional bodies and institutions** that are provided for under the different Agreements, or that have in the meanwhile been set up by the General Council or the Ministerial Conference. These include the institutions stipulated in the Plurilateral Trade Agreements;[32] they operate within the institutional framework of the WTO and shall keep the General Council informed of their activities on a regular basis (Art. IV:8 WTO Agreement).

V. *Membership and Accession*

33 Ten years after its establishment, the WTO can be called a **nearly universal organization.**[33] In addition to the original members of the GATT, which became original Members of the WTO in accordance with Art. XI WTO Agreement, many States or independent customs territories joined the newly created organization for the first time, in view of the successful conclusion of the Uruguay Round. China and Taiwan were admitted at the end of 2001,[34] while other important requests for admission, such as, amongst others, from Russia and Saudi-Arabia, are currently being negotiated.[35]

34 The legal basis for the **accession** of new Members is Art. XII WTO Agreement.[36] Art. XII:1 stipulates that the accession of new Members depends on terms subject to negotiation. In contrast to the practice of other international organizations, the WTO seeks from an applicant, in addition to the recognition of the rights and duties contained in the basic agreements, special concessions in the form of the agreements referred to in Art. XII:1 WTO Agreement. As a rule, these refer to the reduction of tariffs and other trade barriers and – generally – to measures for trade liberalization. These procedures thus take into account the peculiarity of the WTO system – a system, after all, that, in addition to the regulations contained in the single agreements, is based on continuously negotiated,

---

[32] Agreement on Trade in Civil Aircraft, Agreement on Government Procurement, English version: OJ EC No. L 336/273 resp. 290 resp. 305 of 23 December 1994.

[33] As of 1 September 2005, the WTO counted 148 Member States.

[34] See Protocols of Accession at: <http://www.wto.org/english/thewto_e/acc_e/completeacc_e.htm>.

[35] For the current status of accession procedures see the Technical Note on the Accession Process – Note by the Secretariat – State of Play and Information on Current Accessions – Revision, WT/ACC/11/Rev.5, 21 April 2005.

[36] The WTO Secretariat has drafted a detailled accession procedure, see Note on the Accession to the World Trade Organization, Procedures for Negotiations under Article XII, WT/ACC/1 (1995) and Technical Note on the Accession Process, WT/ACC/10/Rev.2 (2004).

tariff concessions, and that therefore also requires of newly joining Members that they, too, make concessions upon accession. The procedure for new admissions is that a special committee is set up for each request for admission (Working Party on Accession) in the context of which the applicant negotiates with the WTO Members about such concessions and reaches a draft agreement accordingly. The decision on accession then rests with the Ministerial Conference (Art. XII:2 WTO Agreement) and requires a two-thirds majority of the Members' votes.[37] However, in 1995 the General Council specified this provision insofar, as on matters *inter alia* related to accessions under Art. XII, the General Council will seek a decision by **consensus** pursuant to the general rule in Art. IX:1 WTO Agreement and the respective GATT practice (see para. 40).[38]

35 Where accession candidates are particularly important as in the case of, e.g., the People's Republic of China, successive **bilateral negotiation rounds** with significant trading partners, such as the United States and the EU, have taken place additionally, the results of which are then extended to all other WTO Members by way of the most-favoured nation principle (para. 119).

36 **The membership of the European Union (EU)** is now explicitly provided for in Art. XI:1 WTO Agreement, where the term "European Communities" is used.[39] Moreover, the 25 EU Member States are also individually Members of the WTO (footnote 39). The case of the European Union is also accommodated by a special provision (Art. IX:1 2 WTO Agreement). This regulates the case where the European Union as such exercises its voting power and stipulates that in that case it can exercise the same number of votes as it has Member States.

37 Like other international organizations, the WTO grants special privileges to the group of **developing countries** and, distinguishes between the

---

[37] For an extensive elaboration on the accession process see the report of the WTO Secretariat, WT/ACC/7/Rev.2, 1 November 2000.

[38] See Decision-making Procedures under Articles IX and XII of the WTO Agreement, Statement by the Chairman as agreed by the General Council on 15 November 1995, WT/L/93.

[39] The European (Economic) Community was not a formal Member of the GATT. However, it was accepted that the communities had *de facto* membership over and above that of its individual Member States. A formal recognition of the European Economic Community as a customs union did not occur. Since no agreement could be reached on the GATT compatibility of the Treaties of Rome, the CONTRACTING PARTIES in 1958 decided to postpone a final clarification of the matter (see BISD 7/71). *De facto* this meant recognition of the practice carried out up to that time. While Art. XI WTO Agreement refers to the European Communities, formally only the European Community (EC) has signed and ratified the agreement. From a legal point of view only the European Community (EC) is a WTO Member, and therefore subject of rights and obligations. While commonly the term "Europan Union" is used, this usage of terminology is legally incorrect. We refer to the "European Union" in order to avoid confusion.

group of Developing Countries (DC) and a specially defined sub-group, the Least-Developed Countries (LDC).[40] Regarding a definition of the latter group, Art. XI:2 WTO Agreement refers to recognition by the United Nations.[41] In the absence of an explicit definition of the group of developing countries in the WTO Agreements, the categorization is made on the basis of a declaration by the respective State, which can, however, be contested by other Members. This has occurred in certain fields in the past, for example in the area of intellectual property. For States which accede to the WTO as new Members, their status is defined during the accession negotiations.

38 The WTO has specifically addressed the problems of developing, and especially least-developed countries in the complex accession process. In this respect, the General Council has decided that the Secretariat shall assist in the process of accession of LDCs and that the transitional periods as contained in the WTO agreements shall apply to acceding LDCs, taking into account their individual development, financial and trade needs.[42] The first LDCs to finalize their accession were Nepal and Cambodia,[43] while the accession process of Vanuatu is curretly halted at that country's request.

39 The WTO allows for an observer status of governments and international intergovernmental organizations. The purpose of government **observer status** in the General Council and its subsidiary bodies is to foster the acquaintance with the WTO and its activities, and to prepare and initiate negotiations for accession to the WTO Agreement of the observer. International intergovernmental organizations can request observer status in the WTO if they have "competence and a direct interest in trade policy matters", or who have responsibilities related to those of the WTO (see Art. V:1 WTO Agreement).

[40] The different special regulations for developing countries are dealt with later in the context of the topic-related sections and chapters, as well as in the context of the part on the ongoing Doha-Round.

[41] Currently, the list of the United Nations classifies as least-developed countries 49 States, 30 of which are Members of the WTO. Amongst these are, *inter alia*, Angola, Bangladesh, Niger, Senegal, and Uganda, see UN-Doc: A/CONF.191/11, 8 June 2001. A definition for developing countries is only used in one instance in the WTO Agreements, namely in Annex VII of the Agreement on Subsidies and Countervailing Measures, referring to developing countries as mentioned in Art. 27.2 (a) of that agreement.

[42] Decision of the General Council on Accession of Least-Developed Countries, WT/L/508, 20 January 2003. See in this respect also the Work Programme for the Least Developed Countries (LDCs) adopted by the Sub-Committee on Least-Developed Countries, WT/COMTD/LC/11, 13 February 2002, implementing paras 9 and 42 of the Doha Declaration. See on Doha paras 799 *et seq.*

[43] Accession of the Kingdom of Nepal and Accession of the Kingdom of Cambodia, Decisions of 11 September 2003, WT/MIN(03)/18 and WT(MIN(03)/19.

VI. *Procedures and Decision-Making*

40 According to Art. IX:1 WTO Agreement, the WTO shall continue the practice of decision-making by **consensus**. In this so-called consensus procedure, which is also practised in other international organizations, a proposed decision is considered to be adopted when no Member explicitly objects.[44] Art. IX:1 WTO Agreement, however, provides for decision-making by simple majority if consensus cannot be arrived at. In this context the European Union possesses as many votes as it has Member States (para. 36). This basic rule – majority, if not consensus – is subject to exceptions that provide for a stricter form of decision-making in the case of particular subjects. For example, in some cases only decision making by consensus is permissible. These exceptions serve either the absolute protection of minorities[45] or the operability of the WTO procedures, e.g. in the dispute settlement procedure (para. 219), in which the course of proceedings can only be *hindered* by the consensus of the Members. In addition, the legal order of the WTO provides for different kinds of qualified majorities. A three-fourths majority is, e.g., applicable for authentic treaty interpretations (Art. IX:2 WTO Agreement) and for exceptional waivers of treaty obligations (Art. IX:3 WTO Agreement).

41 A **two-thirds majority** is necessary for decisions on the annual budget (Art. VII:3 WTO Agreement), the accession of new members (Art. XII:2 WTO Agreement), and for amendments of treaty provisions (Art. X:1 and 3, 4, 5 WTO Agreement). Amendments that alter the rights and obligations of the Members become effective for only those Members that have given their consent to them.[46]

VII. *The WTO in the Context of the International System and the Global Economic Order*

42 In relation to the United Nations and its system of specialized international organizations, the WTO, like the GATT 1947, is given the status of a **de facto specialized agency**.[47] Whether the WTO has actually

[44] See footnote 1 to Art. IX.

[45] See, e.g., Art. 12.1 of the Agreement on Sanitary and Phytosanitary Measures (SPS), provision 33 of the Rules of Procedure for Meetings of the Committee on Sanitary and Phytosanitary Measures, G/SPS/48/Rev.1, 28 April 1997.

[46] In case the Members decide by three-fourths majority that the amendment is of such a nature, namely (significantly) altering the rights and obligations of the Members, that Members who have not agreed to the amendment may be free to withdraw from the WTO. Continued membership in this case is subject to a separate decision by the Ministerial Conference.

[47] The relationship with the United Nations results from the fact that the GATT, as part of the bigger context of the unrealized International Trade Organization (ITO), goes back to

assumed this status is doubted by some. The General Council has several times characterized the status of the WTO in the following way: "Recalling that the WTO is a *sui generis* organization established outside the United Nations system."[48]

43 In addition to the above-mentioned (paras 1, 13) special relation to the World Bank as well as the International Monetary Fund according to Art. III:5 WTO Agreement, Art. V:1 WTO Agreement authorizes the General Council to make appropriate arrangements for effective **cooperation with other intergovernmental organizations**. Moreover, the special bodies of the Council and other institutions within the WTO are authorized in many individual provisions to cooperate with other international organizations. Some formal agreements on cooperation and relations have been negotiated with the international organizations concerned, or less formal agreements have been reached (paras 44 *et seq.*, paras 326, 452, 610). In addition to more or less formalized and institutionalized forms of cooperation, a number of **other international organizations** have **observer status** in the bodies of the WTO (para. 39).[49]

44 The different cooperative relationships also take into account the fact that the Uruguay Round considerably extended the regulatory area of the World Trade Organization, so that it now consciously includes areas in which other international organizations have been active hitherto. This extension is especially eye-catching in the field of intellectual property, for which the World Intellectual Property Organization (**WIPO**) was and is responsible. This extension of the operating range of the World Trade Organization is also a sign of the reversal of a political trend, in which the World Trade Regime – now in the form of the WTO – has acquired subject matters which were previously dealt with by other international organizations or bodies.

45 The establishment of the WTO brought with it a drastic decline in importance of, in particular, the United Nations Conference on Trade and Development (**UNCTAD**). The latter dominated the world trade diplomacy in the world economic policies, in particular in the years between 1970 and 1980, and was intended to restructure interstate cooperation in global economic relations in the sense of a "new world economic order" in favour of the developing countries.

---

an initiative of the United Nations. Due to the provisional legal basis for the validity of the GATT 1947 as an international treaty and the equally provisional basis on which the GATT Secretariat was constituted and operated, this status as a specialized agency was only *de facto*.

[48] WT/GC/W/102/Rev.1, 7 October 1998.

[49] United Nations, International Monetary Fund, World Bank, Food and Agricultural Organization (FAO), UNCTAD, WIPO, and OECD.

46 By agreement between the relevant bodies, the continuing operation of the **International Trade Centre** (ITC), which had originally been set up as a common initiative of the UNCTAD and the GATT to support developing countries in their external trade activities, was ensured.[50]

47 Earlier, the Organization for Economic Co-operation and Development (**OECD**), was considered to represent industrialized countries and to perform the role of a counterweight to UNCTAD. In the meantime, the role of the OECD has changed as a result of the accession of some relevant developing countries. Its significance has decreased overall as, on the one hand, it cannot to the samè extent as the WTO claim to be universal, and, on the other hand, it no longer represents a closed spectrum of interests. As the failed negotiations for a Multilateral Agreement on Investments (MAI) demonstrate, the OECD finds it difficult to assert a constructive role for world economic relations alongside the WTO.[51]

48 Art. V:2 WTO Agreement equally provides for **cooperation with non-governmental organizations (NGOs),** in addition to cooperation with intergovernmental organizations. On a high normative level the provision thus stays abreast of the increasing significance of non-governmental organizations in international relations, and, in particular, in world economic relations. With regard to the interface of the World Trade Organization with the topics of the environment, economic development, social standards and human rights (paras 764 *et seq.*, 776 *et seq.*), the non-governmental organizations play an especially important role. As a consequence of the provision and with a view to the greater participation of the public, or the so-called "international civil society", the WTO since its coming into being has significantly changed its public relations policy, and has, for example, made a large number of its documents available to the public.[52] Concerning the non-governmental organizations in detail, a decision provides for their far-reaching participation that, however, compared with that of other international organizations such as the environmental organizations, does not allow for equally extensive forms of participation.[53]

49 Regarding the importance of coordination with other intergovernmental organizations, of transparency and a dialogue with civil society the recent

[50] On the activities of the ITC see the annual report for 2004, ITC/AG/XXXVIII/202 of 23 February 2005 at: <http://www.intracen.org>.

[51] In the past, the OECD has been successful in the control of multinational enterprises, and the fields of competition law as well as investment, and it has adopted several non-binding, but practically important, regulations in this area.

[52] General Council Decision on Procedures for the Circulation and Derestriction of WTO Documents – Revision of 18 July 1996, WT/L/160/Rev.1.

[53] Guideline for Arrangements on Relations with Non-Governmental Organizations – Decision adopted by the General Council on 18 July 1996, WT/L/162.

so-called "*Sutherland Report*" has made some recommendations. It recognizes the importance of close cooperation with other intergovernmental institutions in view of the potential contributions of such institutions to the WTO. In respect to the treatment of NGOs, it calls for a further development of the 1996 guidelines and more resources for such relationships with civil society.[54]

VIII. *The WTO and its Legal Order*

50 As holds true for the GATT, the special significance of the WTO consists in its **establishment of a legal order for world economic relations**. The reinforced and considerably extended substantive provisions contribute to this in the same way as the elimination of unilateral measures and the now considerably more effective and streamlined dispute settlement.

51 The WTO legal order is based on the sum of altogether 46 agreements which formally constitute **Annexes** to the WTO Agreement. The essential trade provisions are located in Annex 1, the "Understanding on Rules and Procedures Governing the Settlement of Disputes" is contained in Annex 2, and the "Trade Policy Review Mechanism" is included in Annex 3. In addition, Annex 4 lists the so-called plurilateral trade agreements. In contrast to the so-called multilateral trade agreements, the membership in these **plurilateral agreements** is optional. Also, they have a special role with regard to their institutions and decision-making.[55]

52 **Annex 1**, containing the multilateral trade agreements, is divided into a large first **Part A** that concerns all agreements on the trade in goods, and therewith the original subject matter of the GATT 1947. **Part B** contains the new General Agreement on Trade in Services (**GATS**) and **Part C** comprises the Agreements on Trade-Related Aspects of Intellectual Property (**TRIPS**).

53 The regulations on trade in goods contained in **Annex 1 Part A** are based on old regulations of the GATT 1947, and incorporate the latter agreement and its entire *acquis* according to a number of special provisions, essentially regulated in the General Agreement on Tariffs and Trade

[54] The Future of the WTO – Addressing Institutional Challenges in the New Millennium, Report by the Consultative Board to the Director-General *Supachai Panitchpakdi*, WTO, 2004, Chapter V and VI and Principal Conclusions and Recommendations, paras 6–14.

[55] See, inter alia, Art. II:3 and IV:8 WTO Agreement. At the time of the entry into force of the WTO the following were included: Annex 4 (a) Agreement on Trade in Civil Aircraft, Annex 4 (b) Agreement on Government Procurement, Annex 4 (c) International Dairy Agreement, and Annex 4 (d) International Bovine Meat Agreement. The latter two expired at the end of 1997.

1994. In addition, there is a series of special agreements which can be partly traced back to corresponding regulations of the GATT 1947, and, in particular, to the Tokyo Round.

54 In contrast to what the arrangement of the various agreements into the different attachments and sub-sections of the WTO Agreement might suggest, there is **no general, constitutive hierarchy** between the agreements. Corresponding to the structure of international public law, the agreements of the WTO are of equal rank in relation to each other. The relationship between them is in general determined by the general principles of international treaty law, and therefore, since the rule *lex posterior derogat legi priori* is inapplicable by reason of the simultaneous conclusion of the agreements, primarily the speciality of provisions (*lex specialis*) is the governing principle.

55 However, before the rule *lex specialis derogat legi generali* can be applied, multiple **explicit regulations on the relationship between the individual agreements** have to be considered which, with regard to their content, again boil down to the principle of speciality. In principle, it results from the special WTO regulations and the general rules of international public law that the various special provisions of the WTO legal order have preference over the general rules, and in particular, the provisions of the GATT 1994.[56]

56 As the practice of dispute settlement shows, in the face of the amplitude of regulations and with regard to their internal relationship, a delimitation is often extremely **difficult**. For example, the relationship between the regulations on trade in goods (GATT) and the GATS has been controversial more than once.[57] In addition, the delimitation is especially critical in the area of the SPS and the TBT in their relationship to the general provision of Art. XX GATT 1994.[58]

57 In addition to the individual agreements, **interpretations** play a significant role in the WTO legal order. They can be adopted by a three-fourths majority of the Ministerial Conference and the General Council, by virtue of their mandate for **authoritative interpretation** according to

---

[56] See the general interpretation rule with respect to Annex 1 A WTO Agreement.

[57] *Canada – Periodicals*, WT/DS31/AB/R, 30 June 1997, 17 *et seq.*; *European Communities – Bananas*, WT/DS27/AB/R, 9 September 1997, para. 217 *et seq.*

[58] Both the SPS and the TBT recognize the right of Members to issue technical regulations; both describe this right by means of regulations which regard the development and the application of such technical provisions, while containing a number of similar provisions. Finally, the TBT defines its range of application in Art. 1.5 in part by reference to the SPS. While the latter explains in more detail the general exceptional provision of Art. XX *lit.* b GATT 1994, the former defines the exact obligation of the Members according to Art. III GATT 1994. In both cases it is problematic whether and to what extent the general provisions remain applicable alongside the special agreements. See also paras 410 *et seq.*

Art. IX:2 WTO Agreement. Such interpretations are binding on the WTO, the bodies and its Members, and need to be taken into account in the case of dispute settlement. The WTO has adopted a number of interpretations regarding the old GATT 1947, and it has also in recent times made new interpretations. The margin of interpretation that the WTO body is entitled to is, in relation to the alteration of the treaty, difficult to determine.

58 Aside from the agreements and interpretations, there are numerous **decisions** of the Ministerial Conference, the General Council and the other bodies of the WTO, as well as decisions of the Ministerial Conference at the end of WTO trade rounds. Such decisions concern internal organizational questions of the WTO, such as the organization's institutional structure, the configuration of the bodies, its financial matters, and the topics to be addressed by the individual bodies. They can also address the Members in, however, non-binding form. General decisions have no legally binding effect in relation to the Members due to the absence of corresponding explicit authorization. They can, however, be considered for the interpretation of WTO law.

59 The "**internal law**" of the WTO, i.e., the rules of procedure of the individual bodies, the rules on the annual budget, the regulations of service, and other regulations, also belongs to this category. The surveillance and implementation of the substantive international trade law contained in the agreements and possible interpretations is ensured by the dispute settlement mechanism and the Trade Policy Review Mechanism. The former concern the quasi-judicial control of possible rule violations at the request of a Member, and the latter serves in a general sense as an *a priori* and politically, not legally, oriented control of the general trade policy of the respective Members. In addition, surveillance of and compliance with, as well as the implementation of, the agreements is assured by multiple notification obligations and by individual procedures of control contained in the individual agreements.

CHAPTER TWO

CONCEPTS AND LEGAL STRUCTURE

A. Yusuf Abdulqawe, "Differential and more Favourable Treatment": The GATT Enabling Clause, JWT 14 (1980) 488–507; *Jan Tumlir*, International Economic Order and Democratic Constitutionalism, ORDO 34 (1983), 71–83; *idem*, Economic policy as a constitutional problem, London, 1984; *Jan Tumlir*, Protectionism, Trade Policy in a Democratic Society, 1985; *Ernst-Ulrich Petersmann*, Grey Area Trade Policy and the Rule of Law, JWT 22 (1988) 2, 23–44; *idem*, Constitutional Functions and Constitutional Problems of International Economic Law, 1991; *Frieder Roessler*, The Constitutional Function of the Multilateral Trade Order, in: *Meinhard Hilf & Ernst-Ulrich Petersmann* (Eds), National Constitutions and International Economic Law, Deventer 1993, 53–62; *Ernst-Ulrich Petersmann*, Rights and Duties of States and Rights and Duties of Their Citizens – Towards the "Constitutionalization" of the Bretton-Woods-System Fifty Years after its Foundation, Recht zwischen Umbruch und Bewahrung, Festschrift für Rudolf Bernhardt, 1995, 1087–1128; *Warren F. Schwartz*, Toward a positive theory of the most favored nation obligation and its exceptions in the WTO/GATT system, International review of law and economics 16 (1996) 1, 27–51; *Yi Wang*, Most-favoured-nation treatment under the General Agreement on Trade in Services, JWT 30 (1996) 1, 91–124; *Peter-Tobias Stoll*, Freihandel und Verfassung, ZaöRV 57 (1997) 1, 83–146; *Warren F. Schwartz & Alan O. Sykes*, The economics of the most favored nation clause, in: *Jagdeep S. Bhandari* (Ed.), Economic dimensions in international law, 1997, 43–79; *Y. S. Lee & Jai S. Mah*, Reflections on the agreement on safeguards in the WTO, World competition 21 (1998) 6, 25–31; *Alan O. Sykes*, Comparative advantage and the normative economics of international trade policy, JIEL 1 (1998) 1, 49–82; *John H. Jackson*, The World Trading System, 2nd ed. 1997; *WTO-Secretariat*, The Fundamental WTO Principles of National Treatment, Most-Favoured-Nation Treatment and Transparency, WT/WGTCP/W/114, 14 April 1999; *Edward S. Tsai*, "Like" is a four-letter word – GATT Article III's "like product" conundrum, Berkeley journal of international law 17 (1999) 1, 26–60; *Bernard Jansen & Maurits Lugard*, Some considerations on trade barriers erected for non-economic reasons and WTO obligations, JIEL 2 (1999) 3, 530–536; *Robert E. Hudec*, "Like Product": The Difference in Meaning in GATT Articles I and III, in Regulatory Barriers and the Principle of Non-Discrimination in World Trade Law, in: *Thomas Cottier & Petros C. Mavroidis* (Eds), Regulatory barriers and the principle of non-discrimination in World trade law, 2000, 101–123; *Petros C. Mavroidis*, "Like Products": Some Thoughts at the Positive and Normative Level, in Regulatory Barriers and the Principle of Non-Discrimination in World Trade Law in: *Thomas Cottier & Petros C. Mavroidis* (Eds), Regulatory barriers and the principle of non-discrimination in World trade law, 2000, 125–135; *Meinhard Hilf*, Power, Rules and Principles – Which Orientation for WTO/GATT Law?, JIEL 4 (2001) 1, 111–130; *Lothar Ehring, De Facto* Discrimination in WTO Law: National and Most-Favoured-Nation Treatment – or Equal Treatment?, JMWP 12 (2001); *Axel Desmedt*, Proportionality in WTO Law, JIEL 4 (2001) 3, 441–480; *Lorand Bartels*, Article XX of GATT and the Problem of Extraterritorial Jurisdiction, JWT 36 (2002) 2, 353–403; *WTO-Secretariat*, GATT/WTO Dispute Settlement Practice Relating to GATT Article XX, Paragraphs (b), (d) and (g), WT/CTE/W/203, 8 March 2002; *Christoph T. Feddersen*, Der ordre public in der WTO. Auslegung und Bedeutung des Art. XX *lit.* a) GATT im Rahmen der WTO-Streitbeilegung, 2002; *Robert E. Hudec*, Free trade, souverignty and democracy, World Trade Review, 1 (2002) 2, 211–222; *Chris Milner & Robert Read*, Introduction: The GATT Uruguay Round, trade liberalization and the WTO, Trade liberalization, competition and the WTO 2002, 1–19; *Mitsuo Matsushita*, Basic principles of the WTO and the role of competition policy, Journal of world investment: law, economics, politics 3 (2002) 4, 567–584; *Meinhard Hilf & Sebastian Puth*, The principle of proportionality on its way into WTO/GATT law, European integration and international co-ordination, 2002, 199–218; *Ole Kristian Fauchald*, Flexibility and predictability under the World Trade Organization's non discrimination clause, JWT 37 (2003) 3, 443–482; *Paul Beynon*, Community mutual recognition agreements, technical barriers to trade and the WTO's most favoured nation principle, European Law review 28 (2003) 2, 231–249; *Michael Hart & Bill Dymond*, Special and differential treatment and the Doha "Development" Round, JWT 37 (2003) 2, 395–415; *Chad P. Brown & Rachel Rachel McCulloch*, Nondiscrimination and the WTO Agreement on Safeguards, World Trade Review 2 (2003) 3, 327–348; *Jennifer L. Stamberger*, The legality of conditional preferences to developing countries under the GATT Enabling Clause, Chicago journal of international law 4 (2003) 2, 607–618; *Stefano Inama*, Trade preferences and the World Trade Organization negotiations on market access, JWT 37 (2003) 5, 959–976; *Marc Baccetta*, Adjusting to trade liberalization, 2003; *Peter Lindsay*, The ambiguity of GATT Article XXI, Duke law journal 52 (2003) 6, 1277–1313; *WTO-Secretariat*, Technical Barriers to trade, 2004; *Jon R. Johnson*, The WTO decision – MFN, national treatment, trims and export subsidies, Auto pact: investment, labour and the WTO, 2004, 73–109; *Henrik Horn & Petros C. Mavroidis*, Still hazy after all these years: The interpretation of national treatment in the GATT/WTO case-law on tax discrimination, EJIL 15 (2004) 1, 39–69; *Robert Read*, Like products, health & environmental exceptions, Estey Centre journal of international law and trade policy 5 (2004) 2, 123–146; *Peter M. Gerhart & Michael S. Baron*, Understanding national treatment, Indiana international & comparative law review 14 (2004) 3, 505–552; *Gabrielle Marceau & Joel P. Trachtman*, GATT, TBT and SPS: a map of WTO law of domestic regulation of goods, The WTO Dispute Settlement System 1995–2003, 2004, 275–340; *Spencer Henson* (Ed.), The WTO and technical barriers to trade, 2005.

60 Understanding the current world trade order with its complex institutional structure and its vast body of law requires an orientation which refers to the general principles and takes into account the underlying economic concepts.

I. *Foundations and Objectives*

1. *"Free Trade" – a Description in Need of Clarification*

61 The system of the world trade order, as once constituted in the GATT and nowadays in the WTO, is often, and at first sight not surprisingly, associated with the idea of **free trade**. This common attribution however, requires some **clarification**.

62 The system of the world trade order is based on the **economic theory** of free trade as originally developed by *David Ricardo* (1774–1823), which has been underpinned by further economic research and historical evidence. It basically implies that all participating States profit from open trade, even if their economies differ in terms of competitiveness and development, and even if states unilaterally open their market. However, as is true for any theoretical approach, it is based on certain presumptions, which require careful consideration. As far as the theory of free trade is concerned, it has to be borne in mind that it refers to the prosperity of a society as a whole. It does not address questions about the distribution of this prosperity and the priorities of economic development.

63 However, it would be misleading to assume that the world trading system fully reflects the **policy conclusions** that may be considered to follow from free trade theory. While the system of the world trade order as constituted in the WTO may well be understood as aiming at producing prosperity gains through trade liberalization, its policy objectives are far more complex and less strictly connected to concepts which are associated with the term "free trade".

2. *Higher-ranking Economic Policy Goals and Interrelations in the Context of the International System*

64 As far as the objectives of the WTO are concerned, it can be asserted that according to the relevant provisions of the WTO Agreement **free trade is neither the only nor the overriding purpose**. Incidentally, this term does not appear at all in the preamble to the WTO Agreement. Rather, when looking at the fundamental objectives set out in it, which claims legal force in contrast to a common misconception,[1] other economic policy objectives are mentioned.

65 The Preamble in its first consideration lists several **overriding and paramount objectives**: raising standards of living, ensuring full em-

[1] According to Art. 31 para. 2 of the Vienna Convention on the Law of Treaties of 23 June 1969, UNTS 331, 1155, the provisions in the preamble to an international treaty have legal validity for its interpretation.

ployment and a large and steadily growing volume of real income and effective demand, and expanding the production of and trade in goods and services. Moreover, it addresses the "optimal use of the world's resources in accordance with the objective of sustainable development", and the aim "both to protect and preserve the environment and to enhance the means for doing so".

66 These basic objectives exhibit similarities to the language in other instruments such as, for instance, the Treaty of the European Community (Art. 2 ECT) and the founding instruments **of the World Bank, the International Monetary Fund**, and finally **Art. 55 of the Charter of the United Nations**. They recall that the world trade system was once meant to form a sub-structure of the United Nations Economic and Social Council (ECOSOC) in the larger context of the ITO (paras 13 *et seq.*). Hitherto, the GATT and the WTO have, from a formal viewpoint, not yet assumed this position. They nevertheless blend into the developed architecture of the world economic system. Connected by similar objectives, which conceptually, with their emphasis on full employment, still reflect strong *Keynesian* influences, the WTO on thc one hand, and the World Bank and International Monetary Fund on the other, are given a particular, subject-area-specific role. The WTO's cooperation with other organizations, mentioned in several instances, is meant to achieve the coordination of subject-area-specific operation, and to ensure a continued focus on the overarching objectives as mentioned.[2] This architecture and objective historically had the purpose of preventing individual organisations from dominating and skewing the objectives. The fact that this is nevertheless cause for complaint today can be traced back less to a systematic deficiency of the WTO but rather to the fact that the United Nations Economic and Social Council, which was supposed to assume supervisory political control and leadership, has not been able to fulfil this function hitherto.

67 In the second recital clause of the Preamble, the WTO Agreement addresses the need for **economic development** and the interest in ensuring that developing countries, and in particular the least developed countries (LCDs), secure their respective share in the growth of international trade.

68 Only in the third recital clause does the Preamble envisage "reciprocal and mutually advantageous arrangements directed to the substantial **reduction of tariffs and other barriers to trade** and to the elimination of discriminatory treatment in international trade relations."[3] The

---

[2] Concerning its realization the WTO Agreement and Art. XXXVIII:2 *lit.* c GATT 1994 also refer to other international organizations.

[3] Emphasis added.

liberalization of trade therefore does not appear to be an end in itself, but rather a sub-objective or instrument in the pursuit of other, higher-ranking economic policy objectives.

3. *Not Free Trade – but Liberalization and Non-discrimination*

69 When looking at the preamble in its entirety and bearing in mind that the term "free trade" is not expressly mentioned, it becomes apparent that the policy concepts associated with the term play an altogether limited role in the context of the WTO.

70 At the same time, it has to be emphasised that the preamble expressly refers to the **elimination of discrimination** in international trade relations. The issue of non-discrimination is not in any way merely a subordinate side-aspect of trade liberalization. Instead, it has its own significance, as is already demonstrated by the fact that the obligations to non-discrimination applies regardless of whether or not obligations to liberalise exist in the relevant sector (see paras 118 *et seq.*). The element of non-discrimination shows that the trade order does not merely pursue the reduction of trade barriers but includes more principled concepts, which, in the case of non-discrimination are those of competitive equality and equity.

4. *Trade Liberalization, not Market Integration*

71 One also has to be **careful** when attempting to draw further conclusions from the free trade orientation of the world trade order with regard to **national economic systems**.

72 The idea of free trade is often and consistently **associated with** a system of national, liberal economic constitution, one of a **market economy**. In fact, some interrelations between free trade and a free-market system on the national level appear to be obvious. There is a close connection between a rather free, market economic system of an national economy and the liberal arrangement of its external economic relations.

73 Last but not least, it is for this reason that the GATT was interpreted by scholars with great beneficial insight from the perspective of the **economic critique of the welfare state**.[4]

[4] See generally: *Tumlir*, Protectionism, Trade Policy in a Democratic Society, 1985; *idem*, Economic policy as a constitutional problem, 1984; *idem*, International Economic Order and Democratic Constitutionalism, ORDO 34 (1983), 71–83; *Roessler*, The Constitutional Function of the Multilateral Trade Order, in: *Hilf & Petersmann* (Eds), National Constitutions and International Economic Law, Deventer 1993, 53–62; *Petersmann*, Constitutional Functions and Constitutional Problems of International Economic Law, 1991.

74 This theoretical context, however, is not directly reflected **in the world trade order** and its legal system. The GATT/WTO system does not include precepts or obligations with regard to the design of the Members' internal economic systems. The Members are states with different economic systems including those with a declared socialist orientation.[5] Thus, the sovereignty of States remains untouched.

75 While the world trade system does not interfere with the basic concepts of the economic system of its Members, it is very much concerned with the **instruments of economic policy**. The WTO envisages a number of obligations for and limitations on the sovereign operation of its Members. Here, however, special, indirect relationships arise between the world trade order and national economic systems. They rely largely on the fact that the WTO's rules and requirements for the use of trade-effective, economic policy instruments as well as the interest of the states in negotiating reciprocal market access rights have **repercussions on** the structure and the procedures of **national economic policies.**

76 For example, the interest of national branches of trade in access to foreign markets can be realized only if the Member concerned makes concessions in return with regard to the opening up of its own markets. Measures providing for the protection of one's own structurally weak sectors or giving effect to their support are thereby called into question. Driven by own national export interests, **pressure** is thus exerted **upon the national economic policy, counteracting** the otherwise often powerful **particularistic interests in the protection** of certain, structurally weak sectors. It must be noted that the world trade order does not in any way prohibit the support of certain sectors or groups, or the promotion of structural change (paras 489 *et seq.*). It does however, by means of the prohibition of quantitative restrictions and subsidies, exclude several **particular inefficient and wealth-reducing instruments**. These appear very attractive from a political point of view, since, when they are applied, it remains nearly impossible to discern which advantages are made available to the economic sectors to be protected, and what costs these measures bring with them for society as a whole.[6]

77 These and similar measures and functions have, justly, been understood as a "second line entrenchment **of the national economic constitution**".[7] All in all, the result is that the world economic order does not set any

[5] See, e.g., *Hoekman & Kostecki*, The Political Economy of the World Trading System, 179 *et seq.*
[6] In this regard, see the statistical data on subsidies in Chapter 5 para. 489.
[7] See *Tumlir*, International Economic Order and Democratic Constitutionalism, ORDO 34 (1983), 71–83 at 80.

requirements with regard to the design of the economic systems of Members but it nevertheless certainly influences national economic policy.[8]

5. *No Free Trade Constitution in the Sense of Individual Liberties – No Right to Market Integration*

78 Finally, it must be pointed out that the world trade order, despite its free trade orientation, does not represent an international "*Free Trade* Constitution". Unlike the law of the EU, the GATT contains **no individual guarantee of the freedom to trade**, apart from the insignificant guarantee of the freedom of transit in accordance with Art. V GATT 1994.[9] For the purpose of clarification, it must be mentioned that the system of the world trade order, while lacking individual entitlements concerning the freedom to trade,[10] contains precise rules of non-discrimination in the sense of most favoured nation treatment and national treatment.

79 Such **individual rights to non-discrimination** have other, but nevertheless very significant, guarantee functions with regard to the safeguarding of unimpeded trade. Their effect is, from a legal point of view, however reduced, owing to the fact that, according to the present state of the law, these provisions are not directly applicable, so that they cannot be directly invoked by individuals at the national level (paras 687 *et seq.*).

80 Unlike the EU, the WTO thus does not contain individual rights and liberties which can be invoked by the individual and which apply in preference to national law, and which may importantly promote and secure trade liberalization. It is thus distinctly less far-reaching than other trade liberalization regimes, which aim at **economic integration** and include the concept of a common market or even future political integration.

81 Without the driving force of directly applicable individual trade rights which take priority over national law, **the liberalization of trade rests entirely with the Members**, which, by the way, very well take on interests and complaints of individuals, and thus indirectly bring the rights and interests of individuals into play.[11]

[8] See in this regard also the excellent overview of the arguments used in the recent *Sutherland Report*, The Future of the WTO – Addressing Institutional Challenges in the New Millennium, Report by the Consultative Board to the Director-General *Supachai Panitchpakdi*, WTO, 2004, "Globalization and the WTO – the case for liberalizing trade", paras 1 to 57.

[9] Such trade or foreign trade freedom is not always guaranteed on the national level either. The US Constitution, for example, does not contain any such guarantee.

[10] In this respect the Accession Protocol of the People's Republic of China must be seen as a peculiarity in the WTO system, as it does contain in its para. 5 an explicit "Right to Trade", applicable to all enterprises in China. In effect, this right to trade makes effective the national treatment obligation inherent in Art. III GATT to all intra-Chinese trade. In addition, the freedom to import and export goods is expressly mentioned, WT/L/432, 23 November 2001.

[11] Some States and the EU have created special procedures for this purpose, see paras 708 *et seq.* below.

82 According to the world trade order, individual Members in principle incur **no obligation to open up their markets unilaterally**. This is a significant difference as compared to European economic integration, which includes the obligation on all member states to eliminate, over the course of a transitional period, tariff barriers amongst each other in favour of a common market with a common external tariff.[12] In contrast to the concept of market integration, the world trade order thus contains, neither in the form of an individual liberty nor as an international legal obligation of Members, a basic rule to admit trade and to reduce corresponding individual state restrictions.

83 Rather, the world trade order counts on the mutual interest of the Members in access to foreign markets and on the **mechanism for negotiating and regulating this reciprocal market access in detail**. For this purpose, the world trade order makes available a forum of negotiations and procedures as well as a substantive legal framework. It moreover nowadays contains an obligation on the Members readily to agree to such negotiations and to cooperate with other Members (see Art. XXVIIIbis GATT 1994 and Art. XIX GATS).

6. *Development as a Fundamental Objective*

84 The Preambular text of the WTO Agreement makes it very clear that trade should not only be conducted "with a view of raising standards of living" as a general, overarching objective of the Agreement, but also in its second consideration explicitly recognizes the "need for positive efforts designed to ensure that developing countries, and especially the least developed among them, secure a share in the growth in international trade commensurate with the needs of their economic development." Enhancing the **economic development** of developing countries (DCs) is thus made one of the aims of the WTO itself.

85 With this aim the WTO follows in the **footsteps of the GATT** order. While in the ITO negotiations the majority of states involved in the multilateral negotiations had been developing countries, the provisional application of the GATT 1947 had been pushed by mainly developed states.[13] Due to the birth defect of the GATT through the failure of ratification of the ITO Charter, the rules and regulations directed at the enhancement of developing country economies did not come into force. Thus, the GATT 1947 was originally left with only a single provision on the special needs of economies in development or in reconstruction, **Art. XVIII**, allowing for special balance of payments exceptions. Following

[12] See Art. 3 (1) *lit.* a and Art. 25 ECT.
[13] Only 10 of the original 23 signatories to the GATT were developing countries.

negotiations in the GATT framework and the speedy recovery of the European economies after the end of the Second World War, Art. XVIII was renamed to become an instrument only applicable to Members "the economy of which can only support low standards of living and is in the early stages of development".[14]

86 As early as the 1957 Ministerial Session the needs of developing countries were at the center of attention of the GATT order. Following this session, a prominent economist, *Gottfried Haberler* was entrusted with the task to examine trends in commodity prices and the effects on developing county economies. The 1958 **Haberler-Report** must be seen as setting the tone for the future GATT, and now WTO, rationale towards its rules for developing countries. The Haberler-Report came to the conclusion that "there are special considerations affecting the position of under-developed primary producing countries which justify a greater use of trade controls by them than by the highly industrialized countries [. . .]. Finally, insofar as import restrictions can turn the international terms of trade in favour of the restricting country, it can be argued that poorer countries should have a **somewhat greater freedom in their use** than richer countries."[15]

87 Following the "Programme for Expansion of International Trade", which already mentioned the possibility and desirability of preferential tariff regimes for developing coutries, the so-called "Kennedy Round" of 1964 brought further developments for developing coutry treatment in the GATT. Institutionally, a **Committee and Trade and Development** (CTD), as well as the **International Trade Center** (ITC)[16] were established, while the rules originally included in the ITO Charter on development and reconstruction were now introduced into the GATT 1947 framework with its new Part IV.

88 As a reaction to the first **United Nations Conference on Trade and Development (UNCTAD)**, during which a "uninanimous agreement in favour of the early establishment of a mutually acceptable sytem of generalized, non-reciprocal and non-dicriminatory preferences which would be beneficial to the developing countries" was reached, the rationale of the Haberler report was included in the GATT rules. To the one, following the introduction of a unilateral Australian preferential tariff system for developing countries, a waiver for all developed Members of the GATT for such **Generalized System of Preferences (GSP)** was

[14] Originally Art. XVIII was also designed to allow special national measures for reconstruction purposes.

[15] GATT (1958), Trends in Agricultural Trade: Report by a Panel of Experts (The Haberler Report), Geneva.

[16] As a joint agency with UNCTAD.

agreed upon for a duration of 10 years.[17] Many developed Members established preferential tariff regimes for developing and least-developed countries which are still in force today.[18]

89 Finally, in the wake of the experiences with the GSP Regimes, the Tokyo Round saw a further establishment and consolidation of the special treatment of developing countries. While the 1971 waiver on GSP systems was limited to a duration of 10 years, a new and unlimited waiver was sought by developing countries. Also, the central elements of the Haberler-Report were finally to be formally included in the GATT legal order. The agreement reached on these issues was and remains the central document dealing with the treatment of developing countries. Cumbersomely named the "Decision on Differential and More-Favourable Treatment, Reciprocity and Fuller Participation of Developing Countries", this decision came to be known as the **"Enabling Clause"**.[19] The decision enables developed countries to provide **"special and differential treatment"** to developing countries, and thus functions as an exception to the principle of most favoured nation treatment.[20]

II. *Prevalence of the Law and Rule of Law*

90 A fundamental principle of the WTO is the organization of world trade relations by legal means. This becomes clear when we see that the Members are **bound under international law** by the Agreements and the concessions made.

1. *"Peculiarities" of WTO Law and its Operation*

91 Even today, after the entry into force of the WTO Agreement and all its annexes and after the establishment of the organization, there is reason to recall the binding effects of its norms under international law. With the entry into force of the Agreement, the special construction of the **provisional applicability of the GATT 1947 was no longer necessary**. While the latter had not significantly diminished the effect of the GATT, it had given rise to doubts about its continuity and had, by virtue of explicit regulation, not prevented but rather allowed the

---

17 Decision of 25 June 1971, L/3545.

18 See e.g. the EU GSP-regime, based on Council Regulation (EC) No 2501/2001, OJ L/346/1, 31 December 2001; as amended by Council Regulation No 2211/2003 of 15 December 2003, OJ L 332/1, 19 December 2003.

19 Decision of 28 November 1979, L/4903.

20 See in this respect the decision of the Appellate Body in *European Communities* – Tariff Treatment of Developing Countries, WT/DS246/AB/R, 7 April 2004, para. 99.

application of older, conflicting law of individual Members ("grandfather clauses"). The establishment of the WTO as a fully-fledged international organization **ended the institutional restrictions**, which even the GATT Secretariat as a preliminary entity had been subject to.

92 Nevertheless, **obstinate and long nourished doubts about the effectivity of the world trade order** persist. The GATT has long been regarded as a *sui generis* regulatory system that was barely capable of categorization within the system of international law. Its provisional application in a tentative manner may have contributed to this difficulty, as may have its peculiar system of rulemaking and enforcement, which included some elements of a diplomatic-political character.

93 In this regard, the DSU, with its reference in Art. 3.2 to the customary rules of interpretation of public international law, now contains the important and helpful notice that the **legal order of the WTO forms a part of public international law**.[21]

94 More so than questions of formal classification under public international law, it is arguably the operating mode and also the self-perception and self-presentation of the GATT that have contributed to this prevalent, but nevertheless often blurred, qualification. In fact, the CONTRACTING PARTIES and the GATT Secretariat had for a long time nourished a political culture that was primarily aimed at preserving the diplomatic balance, in which consultation played an important role for the settlement of disputes, and in which the impression was given that the existing rules could be altered by the will of the parties concerned. To a large extent, such appraisals only describe, in a generalized manner, a conduct which is expressly governed by the WTO legal order and is mirrored by respective procedures and instruments as provided for by the WTO agreements. This holds true for consultations as an instrument of dispute settlement as well as for the different forms of negotiation and alteration of treaty rules and concessions. Thus, the **validity** of the WTO legal order **in international law** is thereby **not put into question**.

95 Moreover, in later phases of the GATT a tendency evolved to circumvent its provisions in a legally questionable way by bilateral agreement, provoking a general **erosion** and reduction of efficiency. The WTO explicitly counteracts this tendency by a number of special provisions.[22] However, it is only the efficiency and not the effect of the law that is questioned by the practice of evasion.

---

[21] In detail on this matter *Pauwelyn*, The Role of Public International Law in the WTO: How Far Can We Go?, AJIL 95 (2001) 3, 535 *et seq.*

[22] Those are the so-called "Voluntary Export Restraints" (VERs) and the "Orderly Market Agreements" (OMAs). See Art. 11:1 *lit.* b Agreement of Safeguards, paras 165 *et seq.*

96 These questions are of practical importance in particular with regard to the **case law of the ECJ on the direct applicability** of provisions of WTO law.[23] The Court does not question that the WTO agreements form part of Community law. However, it does not deem its provisions to be suitable for direct application, as it considers the WTO rules and obligations to be subject to reciprocity and negotiation between the members of the world trade order. It would be only slightly exaggeragted to state that this interpretation by the Court seems to be intended to grant the EU a certain degree of leeway temporarily, in order to uphold EU policies and regulations which are inconsistent with the WTO, in the hope that a favourable solution will be reached through negotiations. This point of view sounds strangely shiftless for a court that has more than once, and sensationally, helped the individual citizen to claim his rights against the Member States and the European institutions, and that has fostered the European Market and the European basic freedoms. However, it should be noted, that so far, none of the Members provides for direct effect of WTO rules within its legal order.[24]

2. *Effectiveness and Enforcement of WTO Law*

97 The legality of WTO rules is secured by the system of **dispute settlement**. The dispute settlement mechanism not only serves to solve disputes and secure the particular benefits which Members may expect as a result of the conclusion of individual Agreements and the concessions of other Members. It is, as emphasized by the Understanding on Rules and Procedures Governing the Settlement of Disputes (DSU), governed by the law of the WTO and is committed to its enforcement in the joint interests of all Members. At the same time, Art. 3.8 DSU, for example, facilitates access to a dispute settlement procedure. In the case of an infringement of provisions of the WTO legal order, it presumes the nullification or impairment of benefits, which are a condition for the initiation of dispute settlement proceedings in accordance with Art. XXIII GATT 1994 (para. 207).

98 The legal order binds and disciplines the foreign trade policy of individual Members. Within the scope of its rules, it inhibits forceful pursuit of their own interests. The protection of individual Members from the power of others plays an important role in world economic relations, in which trade volume, political influence and financial resources are very unequally distributed and are subject to legal restrictions only in a

[23] See most recently ECJ, Judgment of 1 March 2005, C-377/02, not yet reported – *Léon van Parys*; ECJ, C-93/02 P, European Court Reports 2003, 10497 – *Biret International*; paras 681 *et seq.* below.

[24] *Stoll*, Freihandel und Verfassung, ZaöRV 57 (1997) 1, 83–146 at 92.

limited way. The streamlining and the juridical alignment of the dispute settlement mechanism and the prohibition of unilateral measures within the WTO have precisely been understood as a further decisive step away from a power-oriented and towards a **rule-oriented approach.**[25]

3. *The Rule of Law*

99 The significance of the binding force of WTO rules, however, is neither limited to its formality and legally binding effect nor by the exclusive applicability to the interstate level. It also includes an element of the rule of law and extends to the level of the Member States. As a matter of fact, it finally is also of concern to individual market participants.[26]

100 A starting point for a rule of law is already visible in the way relations between Members are organized and in their relation to the organization jointly funded by them. Like other developed regimes of international law, the WTO does not content itself with formally binding its Members to the substantive law. It rather contains **far-reaching, procedural and substantive rules for the creation, amendment, implementation and interpretation of WTO rules**. The Members are, in relation to each other as well as to the WTO, subject to extensive obligations to publish, notify and report on the content and enforcement of their trade policies. They are supported by the TPRM as an *a priori* instrument of control. Substantively, the exertion of rights is in many cases bound by a criterion of proportionality.

101 The legal order of the WTO however also contains a number of provisions which are aimed at guaranteeing the rule of law in the arrangement of the Members' legal order with regard to law-making, administration and judicial control, and which provide for corresponding obligations of the Members.[27] Their purpose is to **ensure, according to the rule of law, that the Members enact and implement their trade policies**, and thereby to provide legal security for individual trade transactions and their participants.

[25] On this matter see *Hilf*, Power, Rules and Principles – Which Orientation for WTO/GATT Law, JIEL 4 (2001) 1, 111, 114 *et seq.*

[26] *United States – Section 301–310 of the Trade Act of 1974*, WT/DS152/R, 22 December 1999, paras 7.71 *et seq.*

[27] See fundamentally Art. X GATT 1994: Publication and Administration of Trade Regulations: Art. X:1, Publication of the respective regulations, Art. X:2, no enforcement prior to official publication, Art. X:3 *lit.* a, impartial and just administration, Art. X:3 *lit.* b, maintenance or institution of judicial, arbitral and administrative procedures for review. See also the Agreement on Implementation of Article VI GATT 1994: Art. 6 – Participation in the procedure and procedural rights, Art. 12 – Publication, Art. 13 – judicial review, and the extensive provisions in Part III of TRIPS regarding national procedures for the enforcement of intellectual property, see *Petersmann*, Constitutional Functions and Constitutional Problems of International Economic Law, 1991, 222 *et seq.*

102 In addition, in individual areas the WTO contains extensive **obligations with regard to the national legal systems** of its Members. For example, the Anti-dumping Agreement includes precise requirements concerning the procedure and the substantive criteria of national anti-dumping procedures. The GATS contains diverse rules on the design of national law. To a much greater extent this is the case with the TRIPS, in which the Members have agreed to the precise organization of national legal systems with respect to the enforcement of intellectual property rights, including detailed requirements such as temporary relief and possible sanctions of penal law.

III. *Reciprocity as a Fundamental Structural Characteristic*

103 As described above, the **liberalization** of world trade as the objective of the world trade order is pursued through **individually negotiated, accurately defined individual steps on the basis of reciprocity**. This principle of reciprocity is an important principle of the structure of the world trade order. It shapes the proceding liberalization in the form of negotiations, in which States make concessions on the basis of reciprocity and which, in the form of extensive lists, are part of the legal system of the world trade order. It also commands the effectiveness and enforcement of these legally binding concessions.

1. *Economic and Political Meaning and Function*

104 From an economic point of view, the **principle of reciprocity is paradoxical**. As set out above, unilateral liberalization of trade creates welfare gains when the economy as a whole is considered (see para. 62). From this theoretical perspective, it would appear to be in the interest of states to abandon trade barriers unilaterally. From this theoretical point of view it must appear paradoxical that the Members rarely undertake further liberalization unilaterally.

105 **Delaying** liberalizing steps which – **from a theoretical perspective – are in one's own interest can be understood as a tactical move**. From this perspective, delaying one's own liberalizing steps has the purpose of maintaining a basis for negotiation, in order thereby to persuade other States themselves to offer further liberalization.

106 The meaning and function of the reciprocal element of the WTO become much clearer economically and politically, when one takes into account that governments, under real world conditions, do not strictly follow the rational recommendations inherent in free trade theory and

do not exclusively aim at maximizing overall national economic welfare. They often take into consideration that the opening of markets may have different consequences when one looks at the individual economic branches and the different groups in society. It can hardly be ignored that, while **liberalization** of trade is useful for an economy in its entirety, there are however **very clearly winners and losers** when considering individual economic subjects, enterprises and sectors. The competitive pressure caused by liberalization of trade is of use to the economy in question and to all participants in that economy which need the product concerned for consumption or further production. On the other hand, the increased competition puts the corresponding national sectors under pressure and perhaps forces them into a structural change often including considerable social consequences.[28]

107 A rational national economic policy may be capable of fostering structural change by making use of the gains of liberalization, and to mitigate the social consequences by carrying out a policy of distribution. This concept, however, is based on a very simple picture of the structure of national governments and their decision-making processes. In this view, they appear as independent entities that can for the most part comply freely with economic insights and **rational choice**. When considering the findings of political economics, however, a very much more differentiated picture of the decision-making structures of political institutions and a considerably more advanced interpretation of the world trade system and its fundamental principle of reciprocity becomes apparent. Political institutions and governments can then not be considered as independent actors which merely follow an abstract rationality of welfare maximization by opening up trade. Such political institutions, and the groups and individuals that they build on, are rather deeply rooted in society and dependent on its consent not just when it comes to elections. The decision-making process is thus influenced by the respective interests of the institutional groups and individuals, but the interests of the relevant economic sectors and social groups also play an important role. The expression and the ability to assert such interests follow their own rules. Amongst these is the rule that the very general and elusive, diffuse general interest of society in a welfare increase through trade liberalization is comparatively less assertive than the precisely describable interests of particular and well established groups of society, as decribed by the theory of **collective action**.[29] One can even

[28] The industrial nations of Western Europe have experienced such processes of structural change, for example, in the economic sectors of clothing and textiles, steel production and shipbuilding.

[29] See *Olson*, The Logic of Collective Action, 1977.

further ask, what is the "interest of society" and how can it be conceptualized in a democratic state with its constituational framework for the formation and enforcement of society's will under the majority rule?

108 If one takes these realities into account, the result is that the **concept of trade policy** of the individual states is **to some extent determined** by minority interests of the society in question, and departs to a varying degree from the focus on overall social welfare. Within the EU, this exertion of influence is even more complex as, in addition to the existing interest groups – in particular, consumers and enterprises – the Member States themselves need to be considered. As has already been indicated, the world economic order's principle of reciprocity under these conditions makes it easier for governments to resist the exertion of the influence of interest groups that favour continued trade protection. This is because they can refer to the fact that other competitive and export-oriented sectors of the economy are dependent upon open foreign markets, and thus, owing to the principle of reciprocity, concessions will have to be made with respect to the opening of one's own market. The principle of reciprocity which, by reason of these effects has considerably fostered the success of the world trade order, is the basis for the structures of the legal system of the world trade order in many respects.

2. *Reciprocity as an Element of Negotiation, Obligation and Enforcement*

109 As far as the original and further liberalization of trade is concerned, corresponding to the principle of reciprocity the negotiation procedures are organized into special **negotiation rounds**. Their course and procedures are arranged in such a way as to foster the readiness of the Members to make further concessions in return for corresponding offers from other Members. In a fundamental way, this is regulated in Art. XXVIIIbis GATT 1994, which deals with tariff negotiations.[30]

110 The concessions reached are, according to Art. II GATT 1994, legally binding. With regards to the **existence and operation of concessions once made, the principle of reciprocity continues to have effect**. If a Member wants to modify or withdraw its concessions because it is no longer able or willing to keep them, reciprocal concessions of other Members have to be negotiated anew, see Art. XXVIII GATT 1994.

111 The **principle of reciprocity** also affects **enforcement**. According to Art. XXIII:1 GATT 1994, dispute settlement proceedings may be initiated only if a Member claims the impairment or nullification of

[30] On this matter see also paras 305 *et seq.*

benefits accruing to it directly or indirectly under the GATT. These benefits include essentially access to foreign markets achieved through corresponding concessions. It must be emphasized with regard to the significance of the principle of reciprocity that, according to the legal grounds for the initiation of disputes as provided for in Art. XXIII:1 GATT 1994, this is not an option only if the impairment of benefits is due to a legal infringement (*lit.* a). A Member can equally initiate dispute settlement proceedings if the alleged impairment of benefits is attributable to a measure by another Member regardless of whether or not it is contrary to existing WTO provisions (*lit.* b, see paras 207 *et seq.*). The alternative case in Art. XXIII:1 *lit.* b GATT 1994 shows that dispute settlement proceedings not only deal with infringements according to *lit.* a, but also serves to safeguard legitimate expectations if these are threatened not by a violation of law but in other ways through a measure of other Members.

112 Finally, the **principle of reciprocity** is considered with regard to the "sanctions" which may be imposed in the course of dispute settlement proceedings by a Member whose benefits have been impaired. Art. 22.4 DSU stipulates that the **suspension of concessions** and other obligations authorized as a "sanction" must be equivalent to the level of the nullification or impairment (paras 280 *et seq.*).

3. *Most-Favoured-Nation Treatment as a Modification of the Element of Reciprocity*

113 In the context of the world trade order a considerable modification is, however, of significance for the understanding of reciprocity. For a multi-tude of reasons, amongst which are unity and manageability, the world trade order subjects the reciprocally negotiated concessions to **most-favoured-nation treatment**. A concession by an individual Member is therefore to be granted to all other Members regardless of what concessions they have made or are ready to make (Art. I:1 GATT 1994).

114 It cannot be ignored that this most-favoured-nation principle can **limit the effectiveness** of the principle of reciprocity with regards to the achievement of new trade liberalizations, as Members may be hesitant to offer liberalizing steps in view of the potential for free-riding by other Members. This has been considered a major reason for the recent tendency of Members to conclude Regional Trade Agreements (RTAs) (see Art. XXIV GATT 1994, Art. V GATS, see also para. 805).[31] In

[31] With statistical data and further references *Crawford & Fiorentino*, The changing Landscape of Regional Trade Agreements, WTO Discussion Paper No. 8, 2005; *Hilpold*, Regional integration

some special sectors of the trade in services, exceptions to this principle have been explicitly permitted. Art. II:2 GATS allows for a deviation from the most-favoured-nation principle (para. 120).

4. *Reciprocity as Special Characteristic of the WTO?*

115 The principle of reciprocity has also played an important role with regard to the **characterization of the world trade system** as a whole. Not infrequently the opinion is voiced that the legal system in its entirety is notably influenced by reciprocity. This assessment has played a special role in the established case law of the European Court of Justice regarding the question of direct applicability of the WTO provisions (paras 687 *et seq.*).

116 However, a closer look reveals, that a distinction has to be made in view of different elements of the WTO legal order. A special and increased reciprocal relationship clearly exists first of all with respect to concessions between Members.

117 Essential other elements of the WTO legal order can to a much lesser **extent be explained as the result of an individual giving and taking as part of negotiations**. This holds true in view of the provisions on non-discrimination and those that incorporate legally binding effect and the rule of law of the world trade order.

IV. *Non-discrimination: Most-Favoured-Nation Treatment and National Treatment*

118 The elimination of discrimination in international relations is one of the essential objectives of the WTO, ranking equally with the reduction of tariffs and other barriers to trade. The fundamental **principle of non-discrimination** contains two elements: the principle of most-favoured-nation treatment, and the principle of national treatment. Both can be found in all three major pillars of the WTO legal order: most-favoured-nation treatment in Art. I:1 GATT 1994, Art. II GATS, and Art. 4 TRIPS, and national treatment in Art. III GATT 1994, Art. XVII GATS, and Art. 3 TRIPS.

according to Article XXIV GATT, Max Planck Yearbook of United Nations law 7 (2003), 219. See also Chapter II, The Erosion of Non-Discrimination, paras 58–107 of the so-called *Sutherland* Report, "The Future of the WTO", 2004. According to para. 74, the prevalence of preferential trade agreement has led to the fact that the EU applies MFN tariff rates to a total of only nine countries, albeit including the US, Canada, Korea, China, Hong Kong and Japan.

1. *Most-Favoured-Nation Treatment (MFN)*

119 **Art. I:1 GATT 1994, the fundamental provision** on most-favoured-nation treatment, provides that "any advantage, favour, privilege or immunity granted by any contracting party to any product originating in or destined for any other country shall be accorded immediately and unconditionally to the like product originating in or destined for the territories of all other contracting parties." The provision refers to "duties and charges of any kind imposed on or in connection with importation or exportation or imposed on the international transfer of payments for imports or exports", and to "the method of levying such duties and charges", and to "all rules and formalities in connection with importation and exportation." In addition, the most-favoured-nation principle is mentioned in plenty of other provisions of the GATT 1994 and related agreements.[32]

120 The corresponding provision on most-favoured-nation treatment in Art. II:1 **GATS** is shorter and accords "immediately and unconditionally to services and service suppliers of any other Member treatment no less favourable than that it accords to like services and service suppliers of any other country". This principle refers to "any measure covered by this Agreement." Many GATS provisions also include the idea of most-favoured-nation treatment, as does Art. 4 TRIPS.[33]

a. *Meaning and Function of Most-Favoured-Nation Treatment*

121 The principle of most-favoured-nation treatment has **historic roots going back beyond** the GATT 1947. It is applicable not only in the legal system of the WTO but also in many other areas of international economic law, such as in investment protection treaties. It can be regarded as an expression and a formulation of the principle of sovereign equality of states. Its significance within the world trade order rests first of all in the automatic extension of the concessions made to one Member to all other WTO Members. At the same time, most-favoured-nation treatment assures the simplification and clarity of the structure of obligations, without which the world trade order would lose its manageability and would be barely workable.

---

[32] See Art. III:7 GATT 1994 – Quantitative regulations relating to the mixture, processing, or use of products; Art. IV *lit.* b – Screen time for films; Art. V:2 – Flag of vessels, place of origin, departure, entry, exit or destination; Art. V:5 – Transit; Art. V:6 – Transit and direct consignment; Art. IX:1 – Marking requirements; Art. XIII:1 – Quantitative prohibitions and restrictions; Art. XVII:1 *lit.* a – Application for State trading enterprises; Art. XVIII:20 – Economic development; Art. XX – General exceptions. See *Senti*, WTO, paras 383 *et seq.*

[33] Art. VII:3 – Recognition of professional qualifications; Art. VIII – Application for monopolies and exclusive service providers; Art. X – Negotiations on the question of safeguard measures; Art. XII – Balance-of-payments exceptions; Art. XIV – General exceptions; Art. XV – Subsidies; Art. XVI – Market access; Art. XXI – Negotiation on modification of concessions. See *Senti*, WTO, paras 385 *et seq.*

122 On the other hand, the most-favoured-nation principle has a constitutive role for relations among States at the level of the world trade order: As mentioned, the GATT does itself not oblige its Members to open themselves up to free trade. However, it offers procedures and mechanisms with the help of which Members can enter into such obligations on the basis of reciprocal concessions.[34] The most-favoured-nation principle plays a fundamental role in this context. It **ensures**, first of all, the **value of a reciprocal concession** by preventing the other party from subsequently offering separate, even further reaching concessions to another Member which would devalue the consideration given for the concession in question.[35]

123 Moreover, it ensures the **manageability** of the world trade system, which would otherwise break down into an infinite number of different bilateral trade arrangements (see para. 114).[36]

124 Furthermore, it leads to a **multiplication of liberalizing effects** which, as soon as they are conceded by a state, benefit all other states.[37] At the same time, this ensures that all states participate in the current state of development of the world trade system.

125 Finally, the most-favoured-nation principle helps to reduce the impact of **differences in power between the Members**.[38] By way of most-favoured-nation treatment, it is possible for smaller Members and newcomers to benefit from concessions as well.[39]

126 The background to this are further and more far-reaching economic policy aims and functions. The principle of most-favoured-nation treatment prohibits differentiation between exporters or goods from different States, and therefore leaves the **decision on import, acquisition, and consumption to the market**.

---

[34] On the relationship between reciprocity and most-favoured-nation treatment see *Hudec*, Tiger in the House: A Critical Appraisal of the Case against Discriminatory Trade Measures, in: *Petersmann & Hilf* (Eds) National Constitutions and International Economic Law, 1993, 165–212; *Hoekman & Kostecki*, The Political Economy and the World Trading System, 31 *et seq.*

[35] *Tumlir*, GATT Rules, 8 *et seq.*

[36] According to *Petersmann*, Rights and Duties of States and Their Citizens; Festschrift *Bernhardt*, 1106 nearly 7,000 treaties would have to be concluded in order bilaterally to regulate the results of the Uruguay Round.

[37] *Langer*, Grundlagen einer internationalen Wirtschaftsverfassung, 1995, 109 *et seq.*

[38] *Petersmann*, Constitutional Functions, 229; *Langer*, (footnote 37 above), 112 *et seq.*

[39] It cannot be ignored that a "free-rider" problem is connected with most-favoured-nation treatment, causing a certain tension with regard to the states' interest in reciprocity. The EU, in particular, during the Uruguay Round therefore called for the relativization of the principle, especially with respect to the rule on safeguards in accordance with Art. XIX GATT 1994. Part of the problem is resolved by the requirement to make concessions in the course of obtaining original membership of the WTO or as a prerequisite for accession. Furthermore, most-favoured-nation treatment, due to its functions explained above, belongs to the very foundations of the world trade order.

127 The most-favoured-nation principle, finally, also expresses a **distinct element of competitive equality**.

b. *Like Products or Services*

128 When applying the principle of most-favoured-nation treatment in accordance with Art. I:1 GATT 1994 ("like products"), or Art. II:1 GATS ("like services and service suppliers"), as is the case with respect to the principle of national treatment (paras 139 *et seq.*), the "likeness" of the respective products or services is relevant.[40] Proposals for more extensive regulation of this question were made during the negotiation of the GATT, but were eventually not pursued.[41] In 1970, the GATT working group on border tax adjustment developed the following **criteria**: 1. the product's property, nature and quality, 2. the product's end-uses, 3. consumers' tastes and habits, and 4. tariff classification.[42]

129 Further development of the assessment of likeness has largely been **left to dispute settlement**. The first case concerned the panel decision of 1952 in "Belgian Family Allowances".[43] In the following, the concept of likeness was dealt with in GATT,[44] as well as WTO dispute settlement organs, which have extensively elaborated on this issue, while stressing the case-by-case approach on the matter.[45]

130 However, they primarily concerned **Art. III:4 GATT 1994**. The Appellate Body saw a uniform approach in the different references to "like products". However, it also pointed out that the term had to be interpreted **in the light of the context of the regulation**. Using an accordion as a metaphor, it indicated that the span of "likeness" of products would have to be drawn closer or wider depending on the context of the regulation.[46] For an assessment of likeness in different contexts one will therefore be able to refer to the statements in the dispute

[40] The question of "likeness" arises, also with regard to Art. II:2, III:2, III:4, VI:1, IX:1, IX:2 *lit.* c, XIII:1, XVI:4, and XIX:1 GATT 1994 as well as with respect to the Agreement on Subsidies and Countervailing Measures and the Antidumping Agreement, see extensive analysis of the Appellate Body in *European Communities – Measures Affecting Asbestos and Asbestos-Containing Products*, WT/DS135/AB/R of 12 March 2001, para. 88.

[41] See with regard to those proposals *Jackson*, World Trade and the Law of GATT, 1969, 260 *et seq.*

[42] Report of Working Party on Border Tax Adjustments of 2 December 1970, BISD 18S/97, para. 18; confirmed e.g. in *European Communities – Asbestos*, (footnote. 40 above), paras 101 *et seq.*, See also para. 144 below.

[43] GATT, BISD, 1S/59 (1953).

[44] *Canada – Measure Affecting the Sale of Gold Coins*, L/5863 of 17 September 1985; *Japan – Custom Duties, Taxes and Labeling Practices on Imported Wines and Alcoholic Beverages* of 13 October 1987, BISD 34S/83.

[45] See e.g., *United States – Gasoline*, WT/DS2//R of 29 January 1996, paras 6.5 *et seq.*; *European Communities – Bananas*, WT/DS27/R of 22 May 1997, paras 7.62 *et seq.*, and *India – Measures Affecting the Automotive Sector*, WT/DS146/R, WT/DS175/R of 21 December 2001, paras 1,173 *et seq.*

[46] *European Communities – Asbestos*, (footnote 40 above), para. 88.

settlement proceedings with respect to Art. III:4 GATT 1994, but, in a second step, one will have to consider the spirit and purpose of the relevant provision – here Art. I:1 GATT 1994 – as a means of correction.

c. *Exceptions to the Principle of Most-Favoured-Nation*

131 Next to the **general exceptions** of the WTO legal system, which of course apply also to Art. I:1 (paras 151 *et seq.*), some specific exceptions to this central pillar of the WTO order must be mentioned, which apply under certain, restricted conditions.

132 First of all, Art. I itself, in its paragraph 4 allows for the continuation of **historic preferences** which, however, are today of almost no significance.[47]

133 Very important, on the contrary, are those exceptional elements that are to provide for the **preferential treatment of developing countries** (paras 84 *et seq.*). In this context, the so-called **"enabling clause"** must be mentioned in particular, which allows for the preferential treatment of developing countries. It was adopted in 1979 as a decision of the CONTRACTING PARTIES of the GATT, and was meant to protect the general system of preferences which had been introduced by the United Nations Conference on Trade and Development.[48] In a recent case the Appellate Body has clarified the legal nature of the Enabling Clause an an exception to the general principle of most-favoured nation.[49] In doing so, the Appellate Body has nevertheless, and importantly, accepted the Enabling Clause as being an "integral part of the GATT 1994".[50]

134 Apart from the "enabling clause", special arrangements in favour of (developing) countries can be secured by means of **exceptional authorizations** – the so-called **waivers**. According to Art. IX:3 and 4 WTO Agreement, such waivers are also permissible for other purposes, provided the substantive and procedural conditions contained in these provisions are met. The preference system of the European Union vis-à-vis the so-called African-Caribbean-Pacific (ACP) countries as established

[47] *Senti*, WTO, para. 389 *et seq.*

[48] GATT CONTRACTING PARTIES, Decision on Differential and more Favourable Treatment, Reciprocity and Fuller Participation of Developing Countries, L/4903 28 November 1979, GATT, BISD 26S/203 (1980), para. 1 reads: "Notwithstanding the provisions of Article I of the General Agreement, contracting parties may accord differential and more favourable treatment to developing countries, without according such treatment to other contracting parties." see generally on this matter *Yusuf*, "Differential and more Favourable Treatment": The GATT Enabling Clause, JWT 14 (1980), 488 and *Keck & Low*, Special & Differential Treatment in the WTO: Why, When and How?, WTO Staff Working Paper ERSD-2004-03, 2004.

[49] *European Communities – Tariff Preferences*, WT/DW246/AB/R, 7 April 2004, para. 99.

[50] *Ibid.*, para. 90 and footnote 192, in which the Appellate Body refers to the wording of para. 1 (b)(iv) of Annex 1A incorporating the GATT 1994 into the WTO Agreement.

under the **Cotonou Agreement** – the former Lomé Agreement –, for example, is based on such a waiver.[51]

135 Another form of deviation from the most-favoured-nation principle is provided for in Art. XXIV GATT 1994 and Art. V GATS with regard to **customs unions and customs communities**, or economic integration (see the wording in Art. V GATS). Provided that the substantive and procedural conditions stipulated in the two regulations have been fulfilled, the Member States may, for the purpose of establishing a customs community or customs union, reduce trade barriers amongst themselves, without in return having to grant most-favoured-nation treatment to other states. This regulation also applies to the EU and its customs union.

136 Both the **GATS and the TRIPS** provide for deviations from the most-favoured-nation principle in a very specific way. According to **Art. II:2 GATS**, Members can opt for exemptions from most-favoured-nation treatment in certain cases. Such exemptions are to be listed in a specific annex to the GATS agreement and further details are regulated in the **"Annex on Art. II Exemptions"**. Para. 3 of the annex provides for a review of all exemptions granted for a period of more than 5 years. Furthermore, such exemptions shall in principle be valid for no more than 10 years (para. 6), and, in any case, they shall be subject to negotiation in subsequent trade liberalizing rounds. Finally, under para. 2 of the Annex any new applications for such exemptions shall be dealt with in accordance with Art. IX:3 WTO Agreement and thus be treated in the same way as waivers. These regulations highlight a tendency to handle such exemptions restrictively and to reduce them over time.

137 The reason for creating these exemptions is the fact that the **most-favoured-nation principle can also inhibit progress in trade liberalization** in certain circumstances. This is the case when individual Members fear that their concessions will be of great profit to other Members without the latter being ready to make balanced concessions in return.

138 Another exemption is contained in **Art. 4 TRIPS**, which spells out the most-favoured nation principle but at the same time clarifies that any advantage, favour, privilege, or immunity deriving from other agreements is exempted (*lit.* a–d). Thus, the TRIPS most-favoured-nation

[51] This is necessary in particular because the preference system under the Cotonou Agreement does not refer to all developing countries, but only to those belonging to the ACP Group. Similarly, the US African Growth and Opportunity Act (AGOA) and the Caribbean Basin Economic Recovery Act (CBERA) only apply to a certain region and therefore necessitate a waiver from WTO rules.

standard does not require Members to pass on to nationals of all WTO Members a legal advantage resulting from their being party to some other international agreement.

2. *National Treatment (NT)*

139 The principle of national treatment also has a function for the world economic order far beyond the prohibition of discrimination in individual cases.

a. *Meaning and Function*

140 National treatment basically calls for a de-nationalization of internal markets by way of prohibiting discrimination against goods and services on the basis of their foreign origin. It therewith inhibits the use of internal tax and regulatory measures to cause trade restrictions. The latter are accordingly only permissible at the border crossing. National treatment thus protects the rule of tariffication (para. 330 *et seq.*), i.e., the conversion of all forms of trade restrictions into tariffs.

141 The Appellate Body fundamentally clarified the purpose of Art. III GATT 1994 in ***Japan* – Alcoholic Beverages** as follows:

> The broad and fundamental purpose of Article III is to avoid protectionism in the application of internal tax and regulatory measures. More specifically, the purpose of Article III is to ensure that internal measures not be applied to imported and domestic products so as to afford protection to domestic production. Toward this end, Article III obliges Members of the WTO to provide *equality of competitive conditions for imported products in relation to domestic products.* [. . .]. Article III protects expectations not of any particular trade volume but rather of the equal competitive relationship between imported and domestic products.[52]

142 The concept which is set out in Art. III:1 GATT 1994 according to the view of the Appellate Body may be summarized as that the requirement of national treatment shall prevent the Members from applying internal tax and regulatory measures which affect the **competitive relationship** between domestic and imported products in such way as to protect domestic production.[53]

b. *Like Products and Services*

143 The principle of national treatment refers to **like products** and **like services**. The interpretation of the indefinite term of likeness is there-

[52] *Japan – Alcoholic Beverages*, WT/DS8/AB/R, WT/DS10/AB/R und WT/DS11/AB/R, 4 October 1996, paras 109 *et seq.* Emphasis used by the Appellate Body, as cited in its decision in *European Communities – Asbestos*, WT/DS 135/AB/R (footnote 40 above), para. 97. Quotations ommitted.

[53] *European Communities – Asbestos*, WT/DS 135/AB/R (footnote 40 above), para. 98.

fore of great importance. The problem is however that the GATT – and on the same basis now the GATS[54] – uses the term *like product* in different contexts.[55]

144 An often used starting point for determining likeness in the sense of Art. III:4 GATT 1994 are the **four criteria** named in the report of the GATT working group on **border tax adjustments** (para. 128). The Panel and the Appellate Body, however, emphasize in their decisions that there is no precise definition and that the term *like product* must be interpreted on a case-by-case basis.[56]

145 This fundamental understanding forms the basis of both Art. III:2 and Art. III:4 GATT 1994. In contrast to Art III:4 GATT 1994, which refers to the internal sale, offering for sale, purchase, transportation, distribution or use of products, further differentiation must be undertaken in the context of Art. III:2 GATT concerning internal taxes and other internal charges. The provision contains two obligations: while the requirement of equal treatment in Art. III:2 s. 1 refers to *like products*, Art. III:2 s. 2 applies to "*directly competitive or substitutable product[s].*" The differentiation results from the relevant note in Annex I to the GATT 1994. According to the Appellate Body, this is the reason the term 'like product' has a **narrower meaning** in the context of **Art. III:2 s. 1 GATT 1994** than the same wording in Art. III:4 GATT 1994.[57]

c. *No Less Favourable Treatment*

146 The principle of national treatment prohibits the granting of **less favourable** treatment to foreign products or services than is accorded to like national products and services.[58]

147 It does **not mandatorily require formally equal treatment** of national and foreign products and services, and it is not limited to that either. Legally different regulations are a strong indication of a breach of the principle of national treatment. However, this principle does not necessitate formally equal, but rather no less favourable, treatment. According to the criterion of no less favourable treatment compliance with the principle of national treatment can in individual cases thus also be achieved when a regulation is formally different. Also, the

---

[54] See Art. II:1 GATS: "like services and service suppliers of any other country".

[55] See Art. I:1, II:2, III:2, III:4, VI:1, IX:1; XI:2 *lit.* c, XIII:1, XVI:4 und XIX:1 GATT 1994. The concept of *like product* is the basis for the Agreement on Subsidies and Countervailing Measures, the Antidumping Agreement, and the Agreement on Safeguards.

[56] *Japan – Alcoholic Beverages*, WT/DS8/AB/R (footnote 52 above), para. 114.

[57] *European Communities – Asbestos*, WT/DS 135/AB/R (footnote 40 above), paras 93 *et seq.*

[58] See *Italian Discrimination against Imported Agricultural Machinery*, paras 11–13, BISD 7S/60, 64. The significance of this second element was recently clarified by the Appellate Body in an *obiter dictum* in *European Communities – Asbestos*, WT/DS 135/AB/R, (footnote 40 above), para. 100.

national treatment principle does not bar a Member from affording more advantageous treatment to goods or services of foreign origin.

148 On the other hand, **formally equal treatment does not *a priori* exclude infringement** of the national treatment principle. This requirement also includes *de facto* discriminating measures which do not go back to the origin of a product or service, but which however in their practical consequences primarily affect foreign products or services. The vital criterion for the valuation of this question is the **aim and the effect** of a measure (aims and effect test).[59]

d. *Exceptions to the Principle of National Treatment*

149 An important exemption from the principle of national treatment is contained in Art. III:8 *lit.* a GATT 1994. According to this provision, the principle does not apply to legal norms "governing the **procurement by governmental agencies** of products purchased for governmental purposes and not with a view to commercial resale or with a view to use in the production of goods for commercial sale".[60] According to Art. XIII:1 GATS, this exception is also valid for corresponding services.

150 Incidentally, the security exceptions in accordance with Art. XXI GATT 1994 and Art. XIVbis GATS apply as well as the justification stipulated in Art. XX GATT 1994 (paras 174 *et seq.*).

V. *The System of Exceptions*

151 The system of the world trade order provides for a number of exceptions allowing Members to deviate from their obligations with regard to certain objectives and interests. They refer to different grounds of justification and are, to a different extent, conditioned upon **substantive and procedural requirements**.

152 An important group of exceptions concerns **economic policy situations** – the protection of the balance of payments (para. 157) or a possible endangerment of or damage to national sectors of industry (para. 162). A second group concerns exceptions in favour of other **national interests in regulation, protection or enforcement**. Amongst these are in particular the protection of public order and morals, and the different policies for the protection of health, environment and national resources (para. 174). Finally, there are exceptions for the protection of national security (para. 197).

---

[59] In this regard see also *Ehring*, De facto discrimination in world trade law, JWT 36 (2002) 5, 921.

[60] As regards the Agreement on Government Procurement, see paras 526 *et seq.*

153 The significance of the exceptions rests increasingly in their ability to establish **interfaces with other** national and international **policy issues**. There are clear interrelations with the world monetary system and its activity, with agreements on resources, and with national and international health and environmental policies (paras 739 *et seq.*).

154 To some extent, interests in regulation have come to be of such importance and potential for conflict that **more comprehensive regulations have been established on the basis of the exception rules**. This is true, for instance, for the SPS agreement, which clarifies the exception contained in Art. XX *lit.* b GATT 1994 (Art. 2.2 SPS) and Art. 8 for the TRIPs Agreement, which emerged on the basis of conflicting view about the scope of Art. XX *lit.* d GATT 1994.

155 The manifold exceptions reveal a **system of rule and exception** that has first been designed to allow Members to exercise their sovereign right to pursue certain policy objectives nationally. At the same time, however, the system became increasingly subjected to further regulations of procedures and substantive criteria in the context of the WTO. The exceptions cause a deviation from the general rules, amongst which are included the rules on reciprocity. The exceptions are linked in part to some mechanism for compensating other Members in view of this potential distortion of reciprocity.

1. *The "Economic Policy" Exceptions: Balance of Payment Measures, Protection Clauses, and Waivers*

156 The "economic policy" exceptions are characterized by their direct pursuit of national economic interests.[61]

a. *Balance of Payment Measures*

157 These include, first of all, authorization for the introduction of **trade restrictions to safeguard the balance of payments** (Art. XII GATT 1994), which permits Members exceptionally to deviate from Art. XI GATT 1994, and to restrict the quantity or value of merchandise permitted to be imported. The extensive regulation contains substantive conditions (Art. XII:2), requirements (Art. XII:3) and procedural prerequisites (Art. XII:4). In case of a "persistent and widespread" application of the exemption, complementary measures of monetary cooperation with the involvement of "appropriate intergovernmental organizations" shall be considered (Art. XII:5). Art. XVIII B GATT 1994 contains a

[61] *Senti*, WTO, 200 *et seq.*; *Bogdandy*, The International Trade Law, in: *Grabitz & Ipso* (Eds), U.S. Trade Barriers, 73 (89), see *Benedek*, Die Rechtsordnung des GATT aus völkerrechtlicher Sicht, 1990, 160.

similar provision with regard to developing countries, extending the scope to the protection of infant industries.

158 Along with the GATT 1994, the **Understanding on the Balance-of-Payments Provisions of the General Agreement on Tariffs and Trade 1994** entered into force, which clarifies the two exceptions in accordance with Art. XII and XVIII B GATT 1994. The agreement addresses the questions of the configuration and enforcement of such measures, and provides for notification, documentation, and consultation procedures.

159 The abovementioned agreement stipulates the **precedence of** the less trade-disruptive, **price-based measures**, such as, amongst others, "import surcharges" and "import deposit requirements" (para. 2). Only where these measures are not adequate are quantitative restrictions on imports permissible following a declaration. Both types of measures are furthermore to be limited to the extent necessary (para. 4).

160 In order to minimize any protectonist effects,[62] the restrictions shall be **administered in a transparent manner**. *Inter alia*, adequate justification is to be given with respect to the selection of the products subject to restriction.

161 Moreover, the agreement regulates the **dismantling** of such restrictions. The Members first of all have the duty to publish timetables as soon as possible. In addition, there is a special **procedure for consultation** which shall be carried out by the **Committee on Balance of Payment Restrictions**. It is based on two different legal grounds: Art. XII:4 GATT 1994 on the one hand, and Art. XVIII:12 GATT 1994 on the other, depending on whether the general exception of Art. XII or the special rule for developing countries in Art. XVIII B GATT 1994 is relevant. However, they differ only with regard to time limits (Art. XII:4 *lit.* b or Art. XVIII:12 *lit.* b). The procedure is to be carried out upon the establishment or intensification of such restrictions, but also at recurrent intervals with regard to the reduction of restrictions. In detail, the procedure follows a decision of the GATT Council dated 28 April 1970.[63]

b. *Safeguard Clauses and the "Agreement on Safeguards"*

162 The exception in Art. XIX GATT 1994 aims at the **protection of national sectors of industry** from excessive import competition. It concerns cases in which, "as a result of unforeseen developments and

[62] Para. 4 s. 2: "In order to minimize any incidental protective effects [. . .]."

[63] Procedures for Consultations on Balance-of-Payment Restrictions, 28 April 1970, BISD 18S/48–53, LT/UR/A-1A/1/GATT/U/3, 15 April 1994.

of the effect of the obligations incurred by a contracting party under this Agreement, including tariff concessions, any product is being imported into the territory of that contracting party in such increased quantities and under such conditions as to cause or threaten serious injury to domestic producers in that territory of like or directly competitive products [. . .]". The Member shall then be free, "in respect of such product, and to the extent and for such time as may be necessary to prevent or remedy such injury, to suspend the obligation in whole or in part or to withdraw or modify the concession".

163 Art. XIX GATT 1994 allows for "emergency actions" which may be "invoked only in situations when, as a result of obligations incurred under the GATT 1994, an importing Member finds itself confronted with developments it had not **'foreseen'** or **'expected'** when it incurred that obligation."[64] Art. XIX:2 GATT 1994 provides that notice is to be given to the other Members before the measure is implemented, in order to allow them to review it. According to paragraph 3, an agreement amongst the Members is not necessary for the application of the measure. If no agreement is reached, the **other Members** may, however, under certain conditions set out in paragraph 3, "suspend [. . .] the application [. . .] of such substantially equivalent **concessions or other obligations**."

164 Under the GATT, the use of Art. XIX GATT 1947 had gotten "out of hand".[65] Furthermore, the provision had not been able to prevent states, in order to circumvent the notification and consultation duties required by Art. XIX and the most-favoured-nation principle, from controlling important sectors of world trade outside the GATT regime by way of so-called **grey area measures**, namely voluntary export restraints (VERs), and orderly market agreements (OMAs).[66] Their compatibility with the GATT had been disputed, but had never been ultimately clarified.[67]

---

[64] *Korea – Definitive Safeguard Measure on Imports of Certain Dairy Products*, WT/DS98/AB/R, 14 December 1999, para. 86. This question was also at the heart of the highly public case on US safeguards on steel products, in which safeguards introduced by the Bush administration were found to be in violation of provisions of the Safeguards Agreement, *US – Definitive Safeguard Measures on Imports of Certain Steel Products*, WT/DS248/AB/R, 10 November 2003.

[65] *Bronckers*, Selective Safeguard Measures in Multilateral Trade Relations, Issues of Protectionism in GATT, European Community and United States Law, 1985; *Kleen*, The Safeguards Issue in the Uruguay Round – A Comprehensive Approach, JWT 23 (1989) 5, 73 *et seq.*; *Hamilton & Whalley*, Safeguards, in: *Schott* (Ed.), Completing the Uruguay Round, 79 *et seq.*

[66] On the nature and design of VER, see the background note of the GATT Secretariat "Grey-Area" Measures, MTN.GNG/NG9/W/6, 16 September 1987.

[67] On the arguable compatibility of the US-Canada Soft Lumber Agreement of 1996 with the GATT 1994, see *Lee*, Revival of Grey-Area Measures?, JWT 36 (2002) 1, 155 *et seq.*

165 During the Uruguay Round, reform of the provision was attempted, leading to the conclusion of the **"Agreement on Safeguards"** (SG). The agreement undertakes a radical step. According to Art. 10 SG, the Members shall **terminate** all safeguards taken pursuant to Art. XIX GATT 1947 within a certain period.

166 Art. 11 SG provides for the "prohibition and elimination of certain measures". The Members shall thus not take any emergency action as set out in Art. XIX GATT 1994, unless such action is in accordance with the agreement. Furthermore, Art. 11.1 *lit.* b SG **explicitly excludes grey area measures**, such as voluntary restraints, "orderly marketing arrangements" and any other similar measures.[68] Again, there is a procedure for the abolition of such measures.

167 On the basis of the thus re-established regulatory authority of the GATT, conditions for the application and use of such safeguards were regulated. Art. 2.2 SG now clearly stipulates that such safeguard measures must be designed and applied in such a way as not to refer merely to a single source, that is, to a single exporting country. Thereby, the so-called **selectivity of safeguard measures** has been addressed, which had played an essential role in the negotiations.[69] It concerns the question whether and under what conditions states may restrict imports from certain states in breach of the most-favoured-nation principle. In special cases it is possible, though, to allocate quotas among different exporting countries, Art. 5.1 *lit.* a SG.

168 Special rules apply to **China** in this respect – in light of the heavy increase of Chinese textile imports into the EU, the EU has threatened to impose safeguard measures against these imports.[70] According to the rules as contained in Art. XIX GATT and the Safeguards Agreement, such country-specific safeguard measures would not be permissible. However, China has accepted a "transitional product-specific safeguard mechanism" to apply for a timeperiod of 12 years in its Accession Protocol.[71]

[68] Art. 11 *lit.* b says: "Furthermore, a Member shall not seek, take or maintain any voluntary export restraints, orderly marketing arrangements or any other similar measures on the export or the import side. These include actions taken by a single Member as well as actions under agreements, arrangements and understandings entered into by two or more Members. Any such measure in effect on the date of entry into force of the WTO Agreement shall be brought into conformity with this Agreement or phased out in accordance with paragraph 2."

[69] *Hamilton & Whalley*, (footnote 65 above), 84 *et seq.*

[70] See the Press Release of 24 April 2005 of DG Trade of the EU Commission.

[71] WT/L/432, 23 November 2001, para. 16. The EU has integrated this specific safeguard provision into the relevant Council Regulation 3030/93, OJ L 275 in form of Article 10a for textiles. See in this respect also the Notice on the Application of Article 10a of Council Regulation 3030/93 Concerning a Textiles Specific Safeguards Clause, OJ C 101/02, 27 April 2005.

169 Art. 12 SG governs notification and consultation obligations, Art. 13 SG provides for supervision by a "Committee on Safeguards" under the authority of the Council of Trade in Goods. According to Art. 11.2 SG, the states may, however, each retain one grey-area measure.[72]

c. *General Exceptions – "Waivers"*

170 Another form of exception is the authorization according to Art. XXV:5 GATT 1994 – the so-called "waivers". The provision, "in exceptional circumstances", provides for the ability to free a Member from certain obligations by way of a decision approved by a two-thirds majority of the CONTRACTING PARTIES. This decision-making requirement constitutes the specific feature of the waiver. It gives an especially strong political character to this exception which explains why Art. XXV:5 GATT 1994 contains almost no substantive requirements.

171 The Understanding in Respect of Waivers of Obligations under the GATT 1994 aims to restrict "waivers" in the sense of Art. XXV:5 GATT 1994.[73] It provides that all existing waivers shall **terminate after a certain period of time**, at the latest two years after the entry into force of the WTO (para. 2). New, strict procedures are laid down for the extension of an existing waiver or the authorization of a new waiver (para. 1). According to these, such request must include a description of the measures which the Member proposes to take, explain the specific policy objectives, and, furthermore, state the reasons which prevent the Member from achieving its policy objectives by measures consistent with its obligations under the GATT.

172 In addition, **Art. IX:3 WTO Agreement** governs the decision of the Ministerial Conference on the authorization of a waiver. Waivers are granted in exceptional circumstances upon the request of the Ministerial Conference, and in this case, and in contrast to the general principle of the unanimous vote, a three-thirds majority is expressed to be sufficient for their authorization. Art. IX:3 and 4 WTO Agreement lay down further deadlines and procedural requirements. Moreover, it must be emphasized that waivers are tied to certain conditions, and must name the date on which they terminate (Art. IX:4). Where the period exceeds one year, the Ministerial Conference shall review the waiver no later than one year after it is granted, and thereafter annually until the waiver terminates.

---

[72] The Annex to the SG so far only lists one such measure: the agreement on voluntary restrictions for cars between the EU and Japan, which was, however, terminated by 31 December 1999.

[73] See, e.g., the US waiver for agricultural products, para. 350.

173 List of waivers according to Art. IX WTO Agreement

Member	Sector	Start	End
El Salvador	Impl. Of Art. VII GATT	8 July 2002	7 March 2005
LDCs	Art. 70.9 TRIPS	8 July 2002	1 January 2016
Canada	CARIBCAN	14 October 1996	31 December 2006
Developing Countries	LDC Preferences	15 June 1999	30 June 2009
Switzerland	Preferences Albania and Bosnia-Hercegovina	18 July 2001	31 March 2004
United States	Frotmer Trust Territory of the Pacific Islands	14 October 1996	31 December 2006
Cuba	Art. XV:6 GATT	20 December 2001	31 December 2006
Colombia	Art. 5.2 TRIMS	20 December 2001	31 December 2006
Europan Communities	Preferences Western Balcans	8 December 2000	31 December 2006
European Communities	Transitional Regime Bananas	8 December 2000	31 December 2006
European Communities	ACP Partnership (Cotonou Agreement)	14 November 2001	31 December 2007
United States	Caribbean Basin Economic Recovery Act	15 November 1995	31 December 2005
11 Members	Kimberly Process Certifiaction Scheme for Rough Diamonds	15 May 2003	31 December 2006
EU/ACP-Countries	Cotonou-Agreement	14 November 2001	31 December 2007
Developing Countries	Preferential Treatment for the Least Developed Countries (LDCs)	15 June 1999	30 June 2009

2. *The "General" Exceptions: Public Morals and Protective Policies*

a. *Basics*

174 Of special significance among the exemption provisions is **Art. XX GATT 1994**. The provision lists a total of ten special exception cases in which Members will not be prevented from adopting and enforcing certain measures. Amongst these exceptions are, *inter alia*, the protection of public morals (*lit.* a), the protection of human, animal or plant health and the protection of exhaustible natural resources (*lit.* b and g, paras 184, 190), matters of law enforcement (*lit.* d), the protection of cultural treasures (*lit.* f), measures against prison labour (*lit.* e), and the protection of scarce domestic products and commodities (*lit.* h–j). These specific elements are preceded by general conditions contained in the first sentence of Art. XX, often called the *chapeau*. With regard to the admissibility of a measure under Art. XX GATT 1994 it is expedient first to determine whether the measure conflicts with an obligation or a regulation of the WTO. Should this be the case, it must be established (2) whether an exception applies factually, and (3) whether its special requirements are met (paras 183 *et seq.*). Finally (4), it must be ascertained whether the general requirements as stipulated in the *chapeau* – no unjustified or arbitrary discrimination (para. 194) and no disguised restriction on trade (para. 196) – are satisfied.

175 Art. XX GATT 1994 was designed to **protect the sovereignty** of the Members. The provision is intended to clarify that Members are

not prevented by their WTO obligations from undertaking measures to achieve the goals and purposes provided for in the exceptions. As long as the requirements of the individual exceptions are met and the general conditions contained in the *chapeau* are adhered to, Members may "adopt and enforce" measures conflicting with their obligations under the WTO. In application of the general rules, the burden of proof of the existence of the conditions of Art. XX GATT 1994, if contested, rests with the Party wishing to invoke it. This holds true for the individual exceptions and their requirements as well for adherence to the general conditions of the *chapeau*.

176 It is to be emphasized that **conflict** with the rules of the world trade order is **not necessarily the consequence** when pursuing the aims and motives set out in Art. XX GATT 1994. On many occasions, national measures will come under consideration that will not affect trade and its regulation by the WTO. Moreover, it must be borne in mind that the law of the WTO leaves a certain room for manoeuvre. While, to name an example, import restrictions are prohibited in accordance with Art. XI GATT 1994 (paras 333 *et seq.*), regulations within the national market are however subject only to the rule of national treatment in accordance with Art. III:4 GATT 1994 (paras 140 *et seq.*). If like products cannot be manufactured within a country, a limiting criterion for comparison is missing.[74] The exception of Art. XX GATT 1994 thus only applies when a national measure and its application conflict with with other WTO rules.

177 The authority arising from Art. XX GATT 1994 is far-reaching. Corresponding to the regulation's structure, the Members have considerable latitude. In addition, the exception is **not subject to a full proportionality test in the stricter sense**, according to which interest in the achievement of the objectives set out in the exception has to be restrictively balanced against the extent to which there is a departure from the rules of the world trade order.

178 However, the exceptional permission described above is not limitless. The provision establishes limits for Members by means of the **selection of the relevant objectives** and policy areas for which exceptions are created, and by means of their definition. The exceptions, in addition, contain further **limitations**.

179 In particular, it must be noted that, according to the binding English version of the GATT 1994, the exceptions in *lit.* a – protection of

[74] The Appellate Body has explicitly opposed the view that the interpretation of Art. III:4 GATT 1994 should be guided by the principles of Art. XX GATT 1994. In this context, it stated that both provisions must be interpreted on their own, independently of the other's existence, *European Communities – Asbestos*, WT/DS135/AB/R, 12 March 2001, para. 115.

public morals, *lit.* b – protection of human, animal, and plant health, and *lit.* d – matters of law enforcement, are dependent upon the condition that the "measures [are] **necessary**" for obtaining the objectives described. Such "necessity" is assumed when there is no less trade-infringing measure available for achieving the goal described. It must be pointed out, however, that the SPS and the TBT, which, amongst others, have the purpose of putting Art. XX *lit.* b GATT 1994 to practice, contain more far-reaching criteria which come close to a more comprehensive proportionality test.

180 Art. XX *lit.* c (import and export of gold and silver), *lit.* e (products of prison labour), and *lit.* g (conservation of exhaustible natural resources) require a certain **relationship** ("[. . .] relating to [. . .]") between the objective described in the exception clause and the measure.

181 It is still largely unclear whether measures in accordance with Art. XX GATT 1994 require that a Member interested in taking them must be able to assert a **link between** its **regulatory regime and** the relevant **purpose or object of protection**. The wording of the provision refers to this relationship only in *lit.* f, where the protection of "national treasures of [cultural] value" is expressly referred to. With regards to *lit.* g and the protection of sea turtles, the Appellate Body, without definitely clarifying the question, decided it was sufficient that such turtles also crossed maritime areas subject to sovereign rights of the US (paras 753 *et seq.*). With regard to *lit.* a, b, and d, one will have to assume that some relationship with the national regulatory and protective interests of the Member concerned will be required.

182 A special role with regard to the relevant relationship is assumed by *lit.* e, which permits measures concerning products of prison labour, and thereby refers to a circumstance within another Member. One might view this as confirmation of the Members' authority to make prison labour abroad a connecting factor for national measures at home. Art. XX *lit.* h GATT 1994 concerns the execution of an international agreement, and thereby alludes to the implementation of an international regulatory interest. All in all, it becomes apparent that, with respect to the necessary requirement, a case-specific assessment of the respectively relevant exceptions has to be undertaken.

b. *The Individual Exceptions*

183 First amongst the exceptions is the protection of **public morals, Art. XX *lit.* a** GATT 1994. In practice, this exception has however played scarcely any role. It must be assumed that the Members themselves are allowed to define the contents of "public morals" and the possible measures for their protection within wide limits.

184 Of far greater relevance is the protection of **human, animal or plant life or heath** in accordance with **Art. XX *lit.* b** GATT 1994. This provision determines in a general manner the relationship between the world trade order and health, consumer, and environmental policies, and has frequently played an important role in disputes. With regard to sanitary and phytosanitary measures, the provision is further elaborated on by the SPS Agreement (paras 415 *et seq.*).

185 With regard in particular to necessity (para. 179) one may well assume that Members will have a limited margin for determining risk and designing corresponding measures. The determination of the **level of protection** is a different matter, as it is a political decision. It is subject to the sovereign determination of the Members, and includes the ability to opt for a complete exclusion of a risk.[75] With regard to the protection of the environment, Art. XX *lit.* b GATT 1994 is today often superseded by the overriding exception clause of Art. XX *lit.* g GATT 1994 (para. 190).

186 **Art. XX *lit.* c** GATT 1994 provides for an exception with regard to the **import and export of gold and silver**, which today should no longer play a considerable role.

187 Members may, in accordance with **Art. XX *lit.* d** GATT 1994, also claim an exception with regard to measures necessary for the **application of certain legal provisions**. A non-exhaustive list includes rules relating to customs enforcement, the enforcement of monopolies operated under the GATT 1994, and regulations on the protection of patents, trade marks and copyrights, as well as the prevention of deceptive practices. The provision has had significance in particular with regard to two disputes under the GATT, concerning the rejection of what were possibly patent infringing imported goods.[76] These two disputes were the starting point for negotiations about the later TRIPS, which now contains in its Art. 51 *et seq.* special provisions for measures at the border, and reinforces the right of Members to adopt measures against restrictions on competition in the context of patent licensing contracts.

188 Of some relevance is the right of Members to take measures **"relating to the products of prison labour", Art. XX *lit.* e** GATT 1994, and thus in particular to restrict their import. The exception is significant, first, in view of the structure of Art. XX GATT 1994, because it refers to conditions and circumstances obtaining in a foreign jurisdiction. The provision may also be understood to refer to an international

[75] See in this respect the concept of "zero risk" contained in *European Community – Hormones*, WT/DS26/AB/R, WT/DS48/AB/R, paras 178 *et seq.*

[76] *United States – Imports of Certain Automotive Spring Assemblies* of 26 May 1983, L/5333–30S/107.

principle of law. Therefore, the provision is often referred to as a model for the integration of social norms and standards in the WTO system (paras 764 *et seq.*). The opinion is also sometimes voiced that Art. XX *lit.* e GATT 1994 may be applied in the sense of a wider interpretation with regard to other forms of forced labour.[77]

189 In accordance with **Art. XX *lit.* f** GATT 1994, Members may also take measures to protect "**national treasures** of artistic, historic or archaeological value". The exception thereby refers to the relationship of the world trade order with cultural policies. This relationship is also expressed in further provisions, such as the special provisions on films,[78] and is sometimes discussed under the term 'cultural exception'.

190 The **conservation and use of natural resources** is addressed in Art. XX GATT 1994 by three different exceptions – ***lit.* g, h, and i**. The measures for the **"conservation of exhaustible natural resources"** referred to in Art. XX *lit.* g GATT 1994 are qualified by the condition that "such measures are made effective in conjunction with restrictions on domestic production or consumption". This provision, originally created with regard to mineral resources, increasingly plays a role in the area of environmental protection, as nowadays it is recognized that living resources and environmental goods are also included (see paras 755 *et seq.*).[79] In addition, *lit.* h concerns international agreements on natural resources. *Lit.* i allows export restrictions to ensure national demand.

191 Finally, Art. XX *lit.* j GATT 1994 deals with measures for the **acquisition or distribution of products** in general or local short supply. It has not been much applied and is not likely to play a larger role in the future.

c. *The General Requirements of Justification – Chapeau*

192 In addition to the fulfilment of one of the exceptions just mentioned, Art. XX GATT 1994 requires that the **conditions of the *chapeau* be met**. These conditions have been understood as an expression of the principle of good faith, and as a barrier to abuse. They thus limit the right of Members to invoke the exception rule.

193 These requirements have a rather different starting point from the individual exceptions. While the latter refer to the adoption or implemen-

[77] This was the central question in a domestic US case against a state law of Massachusetts, which limited the ability of state organs to procure goods and services from firms in business relations with Myanmar (Burma). See on the government procurement issues in this respect paras 526 *et seq.* and for an overview *Fitzgerald*, Massachusetts, Burma, and the World Trade Organization, Cornell International Law Journal 34 (2001) 1, 1 *et seq.*

[78] See Art. IV GATT.

[79] See for example *United – States–Shrimp*, WT/DS58/AB/R, 12 October 1998, paras 128.

tation of measures, the *chapeau* lays down requirements for the application of measures. The Panel and the Appellate Body have frequently indicated that primarily the **practical application of a measure**, and only then its subject matter and content, shall be subject to the assessment, while the measure must be considered in the general context of the regulation.

194 Accordingly, Art. XX GATT 1994 first of all demands that the application of a measure may not lead to **arbitrary or unjustifiable discrimination** between countries in which the same conditions prevail. The requirement shows certain parallels to the general principle of non-discrimination (paras 118 *et seq.*). In looking at conditions in different countries, it refers not only to exporting, but also to importing countries and concerns conditions in different exporting countries.[80] It comprises, first of all, the unequal treatment of Members when equal conditions prevail. Moreover, it also concerns cases of formally equal treatment when unequal conditions apply. The latter – and thus the failure to have regard to essential circumstances in the individual Members concerned – has been characterized as the absence of necessary flexibility.

195 Furthermore, it is also inferred from the requirement of Art. XX – *chapeau* – that Members wanting to take and apply a measure may under certain circumstances incur the obligation to negotiate in good faith with the exporting countries concerned about remedies and about achieving protection objectives through the conclusion of an international agreement (para. 759).[81]

196 Finally, Art. XX GATT 1994 requires in its *chapeau* that the application of a measure may not lead to a **disguised restriction on international trade**. The content of this criterion came to be disclosed only in the course of dispute settlement. First, it includes a publicity aspect, already inherent in the term "disguised". The existence of arbitrary and unjustified discrimination has been identified as a further element. Finally, the protectionist objective as expressed in design, architecture and revealing structure of the measure has been pointed to.

3. *Security Exceptions*

197 Art. XXI GATT 1994, Art. XIVbis GATS and Art. 73 TRIPS contain very similar exceptions with regard to the protection of security. Accordingly, the WTO rules must not be understood as obliging any Member to **furnish any information** "the disclosure of which it

[80] See the Appellate Body in *United States–Gasoline*, WT/DS2/AB/R, 29 April 1996, p. 22.
[81] *United States – Shrimp*, WT/D58/AB/R, 12 October 1998.

considers contrary to its essential security interests" (Art. XXI *lit.* a GATT 1994), or to prevent it from taking certain more closely defined measures "which it considers **necessary for the protection of its security interests**". Further, no provision of WTO law may be understood as preventing "any contracting party from taking any action in pursuance of its obligations under the United Nations Charter for the maintenance of international peace and security". This means a reference to the system of **collective security** established under the Charter of the United Nations.

CHAPTER THREE

DISPUTE SETTLEMENT

Pierre Pescatore & William J. Davey & Andreas F. Lowenfeld (Eds), Handbook of WTO, GATT Dispute Settlement, (Loose-leaf) 1992; *Robert E. Hudec*, Enforcing international trade law: the evolution of the modern GATT legal system, 1993; *Ernst-Ulrich Petersmann*, The Dispute Settlement System of the World Trade Organization and the Evolution of the GATT Dispute Settlement System since 1948, CMLR 31 (1994) 5, 1157–1244; *Peter-Tobias Stoll*, Die WTO: Neue Welthandelsorganisation, neue Welthandelsordnung, ZaöRV 54 (1994) 2, 241–343; *Christian Schede*, The strengthening of the multilateral system: Article 23 of the WTO dispute settlement understanding; dismantling unilateral retalitation under Section 301 of the 1974 Trade Act?, World competition 20 (1996) 1, 109–138; *Ernst-Ulrich Petersmann* (Ed.), The GATT/WTO dispute settlement system: international law, international organizations and dispute settlement, 1997; *John H. Jackson*, The Dispute Settlement Understanding: misunderstandings on the nature of legal obligation, AJIL 91 (1997), 60–64; *Ernst-Ulrich Petersmann* (Ed.), International trade law and the GATT/WTO dispute settlement system, 1997; *Carl-August Fleischhauer & John H. Jackson*, New institutional forms of dispute settlement: The World Trade Organization (WTO) Appellate Body, the International Tribunal for the Law of the Sea and the United Nations Compensation Commission, in: *Wybo Heere* (Ed.), Contemporaty international law issues: new forms, new applications, 1998, 383–396; *James Cameron* (Ed.), Dispute resolution in the World Trade Organisation, 1998; *Thomas Cottier*, Dispute settlement in the World Trade Organization: characteristics and structural implications for the European Union, CMLR 35 (1998) 2, 325–378; *David Palmeter*, The WTO Appellate Body needs remand authority, JWT 32 (1998) 1, 41–44; *John H. Jackson*, Dispute settlement and the WTO: emerging problems, JIEL 1 (1998) 3, 329–351; *Gabrielle Marceau*, A call for coherence in international law: Praises for the prohibition against "clinical isolation" in WTO dispute settlement, JWT 33 (1999) 5, 87–152; *Peter-Tobias Stoll & Arthur Steinmann*, WTO: The Implementation Stage, Max PlanckYearbook of United Nations Law 3 (1999), 407–437; *Joel P. Trachtman*, The domain of WTO dispute resolution, Harvard international law journal 40 (1999) 2, 333–377; *Robert E. Hudec*, The new WTO dispute settlement procedure: an overview of the first three years, Minnesota journal of global trade 8 (1999) 1, 1–53; *Marco C. Bronckers* & *John H. Jackson*, Outside counsel in WTO dispute process, JIEL 2 (1999) 1, 155–158; *Friedl Weiss*, Improving WTO dispute settlement procedures: issues and lessons from the practice of other international courts and tribunals, 2000; *Joseph H. Weiler*, The Rule of Lawyers and Diplomats: Reflections on the Internal and External Legitimacy of WTO Dispute Settlement, JMWP 9, 2000; *Georg C. Umbricht*, An 'Amicus Curiae Brief' on Amicus Curiae Briefs at the WTO, JIEL 4 (2001) 4, 773–794; *Erich Vranes*, Principles and emerging problems of WTO cross retaliation, EuZW 12 (2001) 1, 10–15; *Edwin Vermulst*, WTO dispute settlement with respect to trade contingency measures, JWT 35 (2001) 2, 209–228; *James Cameron*, Principles of international law in the WTO dispute settlement body, The international and comparative law quarterly 50 (2001) 2, 248–298; *Matthew S. Dunne*, Redefining power orientation, Law and policy in international business 34 (2002) 1, 277–342; *Peter Gallagher*, Guide to dispute settlement, 2002; *Christopher T. Timura*, Cross-examining expertise in the WTO dispute settlement process, Michigan journal of international law 23 (2002) 3, 709–732; *Petros C. Mavroidis*, Amicus curiae briefs before the WTO, European integration and international co-ordination 2002, 317–329; *Joost Pauwelyn*, The use of experts in WTO dispute settlement, The international and comparative law quarterly, 51 (2002) 2, 325–364; *Kym Anderson*, Peculiarities of retaliation in WTO dispute settlement, World trade review 1 (2002) 2, 123–134; *Hunter R. Clark*, The WTO banana dispute settlement and its implications for trade relations between the United States and the European Union, Cornell international law journal 35 (2002) 2, 291–306; *Ernst-Ulrich Petersmann*, WTO negotiators meet academics, JIEL 6 (2003) 1, 237–250; *Zhu Lanye*, The effects of the WTO Dispute Settlement Panel and Appellate Body reports, Temple international and comparative law journal 17 (2003) 1, 221–236; *Claus-Dieter Ehlersmann*, WTO dispute settlement and competition law, Fordham international law journal 26 (2003) 6, 1505–1561; *Joel P. Trachtmann*, Costs and benefits of private participation in WTO dispute settlement, Harvard international law journal 44 (2003) 1, 221–250; *Barbara R. Monroe*, WTO dispute settlement procedure bibliography, JIEL 6 (2003) 3, 745–759; *Axel Bree*, Harmonization of the dispute settlement mechanisms of the multilateral environmental agreements and the world trade agreements, 2003; *Richard O. Cunningham*, Dispute settlement through the lens of "free flow of trade", JIEL 6 (2003) 1, 155–170; *John Greenwald*, WTO dispute settlement, JIEL 6 (2003) 1, 113–124; *Matthias Oesch*, Standards of review in WTO dispute resolution, 2003; *Karen J. Alter*, Resolving or exacerbating disputes?, International affairs 79 (2003) 4, 783–800; *Donald MacRae*, Claus-Dieter Ehlermann's presentation on "the role and record of dispute settlement panels and the Appellate Body of the WTO", JIEL 6 (2003) 3, 709–717; *D. Palmeter & P. C. Mavroidis*, Dispute Settlement in The World Trade Organization, 2nd ed., 2004; *John H. Jackson*, International law status of WTO dispute settlement reports, AJIL 98 (2004) 1, 109–123; *Gregory Shaffer*, Recognizing public goods in WTO dispute settlement: Who participates? Who decides?, JIEL 7 (2004) 2, 459–482; *Brigitte Stern & Hélène Ruiz Fabri* (Eds), La jurisprudence de l'OMC / The Case-Law of the WTO 1996–1997, 2004 and 1998–1999, 2005; *Frederico Ortino* (Ed.), The WTO Dispute Settlement System 1995–2003, 2004; *Donald MacRae*, What is the future of WTO dispute settlement?, JIEL 7 (2004) 1, 3–21; *Hans Mahncke*, US steel tariffs and the WTO dispute resolution mechanism, Leiden journal of international law 17 (2004) 3, 615–624; *Kara Leitner*, WTO dispute settlement 1995–2003, JIEL 7 (2004) 1, 169–181; *WTO-Secretariat*, A handbook on the WTO dispute settlement system, 2004; *Petros C. Mavroidis* (Ed.), The WTO and international trade law/dispute settlement, 2005; *Nicholas Perdikis* (Ed.), The WTO and the regulation of international trade, 2005.

198 A particularly remarkable aspect of the WTO, in comparison with other international regimes, is that it has a strong **legally based element of dispute settlement and enforcement**. Besides the abstract review of the trade policies of Member States by the Trade Policy Review Mechanism (Paras 27, 51), the WTO Agreement includes in Annex 2 rules for the peaceful settlement of specific disputes – the Dispute

Settlement Understanding (DSU).[1] The DSU provides for specific institutions which act within a two-tiered quasi-legal procedure, with a further phase dealing with implementation matters, and finally, with possible countermeasures in cases of failure to implement the ruling.

199 Chapter VII of the **Havana Charter** already sets out a very specific system of dispute settlement for the ill-fated International Trade Organisation. It included elements of voluntary arbitral jurisdiction, a special function of the Executive Board comprising arbitral awards, recommendations and "appropriate and compensatory" measures, as well as reference to the Conference of the ITO as the main organ (Art. 95). Additionally, the possibility of an "advisory opinion" of the International Court of Justice was explicitly provided for (Art. 96). Finally, Art. 92 excluded all unilateral measures.

200 After the failure of the Havana Charter, the **GATT 1947** was used in isolation and on a provisional basis. It **contained only two special components** for dispute settlement: Art. XXII, which included a requirement for consultations, and Art. XXIII, which provided for permissable claims, action by the CONTRACTING PARTIES and the possibility of sanctions. Accordingly, dispute settlement under the GATT 1947 was reserved for the CONTRACTING PARTIES as the only organ. In investigating the conflict with respect to factual and legal issues, the CONTRACTING PARTIES used specific working groups, in which all contracting countries could take part.

201 Since this was soon seen as inefficient, **Panels**[2] were established,[3] and this procedure was later **institutionalized.**[4] Membership of these Panels was later restricted to three persons.[5] A major problem of this in itself useful mechanism was that the final decision on the conflict was left to the CONTRACTING PARTIES, which had to decide by positive consensus, including the conflicting parties. This gave the losing party

[1] Understanding on Rules and Procedures Governing the Settlement of Disputes.

[2] The expression "panel" is the short form of "panel of experts"; as in the anglo-american legal system the members of a jury are called a panel, with the choice of this expression the intention might have been to stress the panels' impartiality. In contrast to the practice under GATT 1947, there were no representatives of the disputing parties or of the leading economic countries present in the first panel under the DSU.

[3] The first incidence of this new procedure was the "*Treatment by Germany of Import of Sardines*" case, Panel report adopted on 31 October 1952, G/26, BISD 1S/53.

[4] Decision of 5 April 1966, BISD 14 S/18.

[5] Decision of 12 April 1989, Improvements to the GATT Dispute Settlement Rules and Procedures, L/6849, BISD 36S/61.The practice of using three persons as panelists was reverted to before these binding improvements, see in this respect para. 6 (iii) of the Agreed Description of the Customary Practices of the GATT in the Field of Dispute Settlement, annexed to the Understanding on Dispute Settlement, BISD 26S/210, 28 November 1979.

the opportunity not only to reject the Panel report as a whole, but also numerous possibilities delay the ruling. The dispute settlement procedure was therefore susceptible to the enforcement of particular interests by means of political power.[6]

202 The damage done to the confidence in this procedure led to **unilateral measures**, taken at first by the United States, then by other GATT Members and later by the EU. This **erosion** of the legal order of world trade relations was a central topic at the Uruguay Round, and led to a noticeable strengthening and improvement of the dispute settlement mechanism.

I. *Legal Basis*

203 Dispute Settlement in the WTO is based on the interaction of various legal rules. According to the Appellate Body, all such rules form an **integrated system of dispute settlement** within the DSU.[7]

204 **Institutional questions** are dealt with by the WTO Agreement.[8] Alongside these institutional questions, the **DSU** is of central significance, covering general procedural questions of Panel and Appellate Body proceedings. The DSU refers to disputes brought under the agreements of the WTO framework, including those relating to the WTO Agreement or the DSU itself, but excluding the TPRM.[9]

205 However, the causes for action are ruled upon by the particular agreements, see Art. 1.1 and Appendix 1 DSU. Furthermore, a number of agreements within the WTO framework contain **specific provisions** for dispute settlement, which are repeated in Appendix 2 of the DSU and prevail over the general rules and procedures in case of conflict.[10]

---

[6] Members made only careful use of those possibilities the GATT offered. A survey shows that Members blocked the establishment of a panel or the adoption of a report in only a few cases. More often, they used the opportunity to delay the decision and in the meantime searched for a solution through negotiation, see *Hudec*, The new WTO dispute settlement procedure, Minnesota Journal of Global Trade 8 (1999) 1, 1 *et seq.* It can therefore be concluded that the dispute settlement system under the GATT had important and remarkable achievements.

[7] *Guatemala – Anti-Dumping Investigation Regarding Portland Cement from Mexico*, Appellate Body Report, WT/DS60/AB/R, 2 November 1998, para. 66: "We see the special or additional rules and procedures of a particular covered Agreement as fitting together with the generally applicable rules and procedures of the DSU to form a comprehensive, integrated dispute settlement system for the WTO Agreement".

[8] Art. III:3 and IV:3 WTO Agreement.

[9] DSU Art. 1.1 and Appendix 1 and TPRM A (e). The reason for this is that the TPRM sets out its own closed mechanism to ensure accordance with the WTO framework, which does not refer to individual conflicts.

[10] Art. 1.2 s. 2 DSU.

206 Part of that integrated system are **decisions and rules** of the GATT[11] and under the **WTO**, as well as procedural rules for the appellate review.[12]

207 Among the provisions, which define the basis of disputes by defining admissible claims, **Art. XXII and XXIII GATT 1994** are particularly relevant, as they represent the rules of dispute settlement under GATT and are frequently referred to by other agreements. Art. XXIII GATT 1994 describes the circumstances in which a Member may begin dispute settlement proceedings. It refers mainly to the special relationship of reciprocity of rights and obligations within the GATT (see paras 103 *et seq.*).

208 A fundamental prerequisite for the admissibility of claims is the **nullification or impairment** of benefits which Members are entitled to, either directly or indirectly under the legal order of the WTO, or an impediment to the attainment of any objective of the General Agreement. According to Art. XXIII GATT 1994, the nullification or impairment of benefits can be claimed in three different ways: first, a Member may assert such a nullification or impediment, in the classical sense as an instrument for enforcement, if another Member refuses to carry out its obligations under the Agreement, Art. XXIII:1 *lit.* a GATT 1994.

209 Secondly, Art. XXIII GATT 1994 also envisages a so-called **non-violation complaint**. With this, a Member may assert the nullification or impairment of benefits if they are not based upon an infringement of legal obligations, but on factual circumstances independent thereof, no matter whether or not they are lawful.[13]

210 Thirdly, the assertion of nullification or impairment of benefits is possible in **"any other situation"**, Art. XXIII *lit.* c GATT 1994. This allows members to claim nullification or impairment of benefits which are based neither on violation of rules, nor on a measure taken by a member, but which are the result of other circumstances.

---

[11] See Art. 3.1 DSU, which clarifies that the principles of dispute settlement as applied under Art. XXII and XXIII GATT are to be adhered to.

[12] Working Procedures for the Appellate Review, WT/AB/WP/5, 1 January 2005. See also the explanation in WT/AB/WP/W/9, 7 October 2004 concerning the changes to the last version.

[13] See *Cottier & Nadkavukaren Schefer*, Non-Violation Complaints in GATT/WTO Dispute Settlement: Past, Present and Future, in: *Petersmann* (Ed.) International Trade Law and the GATT/WTO Dispute Settlement System, 1997, 148 *et seq.*

II. *Aims and Objectives of WTO Dispute Settlement*

211 WTO Dispute Settlement pursues various aims: *primarily*, the **settlement of disputes** between individual Members in a legally prescribed and court-like – juridical – procedure, in which the DSU explicitly favours an amicable solution and therefore points to political opportunities for settlement of trade conflicts.[14] The emphasis on political elements of dispute settlement, which played a significant role in the history of dispute settlement in the WTO, is even more underscored by the reference to conciliation and mediation in Art. 5 DSU,[15] and the fact that prior consultations are a mandatory requirement for dispute settlement.[16]

212 Dispute settlement under the WTO, *secondly*, serves to **protect the reciprocal rights and obligations** of the Members and, therefore, to maintain the functioning of the legal framework and the WTO itself.[17] In this sense, dispute settlement serves the general interests of the Members in implementing the legal framework of the WTO.[18] This function is carried out in particular by Art. 3.8 DSU, which substantiates the nullification or impairment of benefits as a requirement for the use of dispute settlement through a rule of presumption: nullification or impairment of benefits is presumed if provisions of the WTO framwork are infringed. In this case, it is for the members concerned to disprove the accusation.

213 A further – the *third* – objective of dispute settlement in the WTO is the **clarification of the existing provisions** in conjunction with the rules of customary international law on the interpretation of treaties.[19] This classical and important function of dispute settlement is limited in the context of the DSU with the aim of **limiting judicial activism**. This can already be seen in the fact that the term "clarification" is used, rather than "interpretation".

---

[14] Art. 3.7 s. 3 DSU.

[15] If a cases where a developing country is involved see Art. 3.12 DSU and the Decision of 5 April 1966 on Procedures under Article XXIII, BISD 14S/18; least-developed-countries can claim special and differential treatment under Art. 24.2 DSU.

[16] Art. 4 DSU.

[17] Art. 3.3 DSU; to the objectives of consultations see *Mexico – High Fructose Corn Syrup* (21.5), WT/DS132/AB/R/W, 22 October 2001, para. 54.

[18] On this level of enforcement of the rules in the general interest, the system of dispute settlement stands alongside the already mentioned element of the TPRM, see paras 27, 95.

[19] The formulation in Art. 3.2 is due to the fact that not all Members of the WTO are members of the Vienna Convention on the Laws of Treaties of 23 May 1969, (see para. 261); these rules may however apply as customary international law rules beyond the group of members of that convention; compare *India – Patent Protection for Pharmaceutical and Agricultural Chemical Products*, WS/DS50/AB/R, 19 December 1997, paras 45 *et seq.*, *European Communities – Poultry*, WT/DS69/AB/R, 13 January 1998, para. 7.

214 Furthermore, Art. 3.2 s.3 DSU emphasises that decisions in the framework of dispute settlement can **neither add to nor diminish the rights and obligations of the Members**. Additionally, Art. 3.9 DSU refers to the exclusive competence of the Ministerial Conference and General Council to decide on authoritative interpretations of the WTO Agreements.[20] The Appellate Body has in numerous cases emphasized that this exclusive competence has to be strictly observed.[21] In other cases, however, both the Panel and the Appellate Body have obviously extensively used their scope for interpretation. However, it is worth noting that the dispute settlement mechanism of the WTO is much more restricted in respect of judicial activism than other such mechanisms in international law.

III. *The Institutions of Dispute Settlement*

215 The strength of the dispute settlement system of the WTO lies in the fact that the entire procedure is strictly regulated. This regulation is accompanied by **institutionalization**, which is provided for in the WTO Agreement. There are many bodies to be consulted in this tightly organized system for the settlement of disputes: the Dispute Settlement Body (DSB), which gives conclusive legally binding rulings, the Panel, the Appellate Body, the Secretariat, the Arbitrator, and the expert institutions. The rules of procedure for dispute settlement, including rules on independence, conflict of interests and impartiality, apply to all these institutions.[22]

1. *Dispute Settlement Body*

216 As has already been described above (paras 200 *et seq.*), the fundamental step in the development of the dispute settlement system was the appointment of expert committees – the so-called panels – which gradually and eventually undertook the tasks of dispute settlement on the basis of specific corresponding rules. Originally, the CONTRACTING PARTIES, as the main organ of the GATT 1947, were entitled to undertake this task and it was understood to be a largely political course of action. The Dispute Settlement Body insofar represents on the one hand a **continuum for the competence of a political main organ**

[20] See Art. IX:2 WTO Agreement.

[21] See, e.g. *Japan – Alcoholic Beverages*, WT/DS8/17, WT/DS10/17, WT/DS11/15, 30 July 1997, p. 13; *United States – Wool Shirts and Blouses*, WT/DS33/AB/R, 25 April 1997, p. 19 *et seq.*

[22] Rules of Conduct for the Understanding on Rules and Procedures Governing the Settlement of Disputes, WT/DSB/RC/1, 11 December 1996, see also WT/AB/WP/W/2, 22 January 1997.

and therefore an element of diplomatic dispute settlement, and embodies on the other hand an – albeit imperfect – institutional independence.

217 The DSB has been created as an independent organ, but its activities are administered by the General Council, which, in this special function, has specific working procedures and may elect a special chairperson (para. 26). From a functional point of view, the political-diplomatic elements assert themselves with the existence of the DSB. As regards the competence of the DSB, it has, first of all, all rights with respect to the **organization of the dispute settlement system and its institutions**. The typical autonomy in questions of organization and working procedure, that attributes to a classical system of jurisdiction, is not yet in place in the WTO.

218 Moreover, the DSB is responsible for **certain guiding decisions** at the different stages of the **dispute settlement procedure**. These include rulings regarding the establishment, composition and mandate of the Panel, as well as the adoption of its reports or the reports of the Appellate Body. Furthermore, this also includes, on the level of implementation of a Panel or an Appellate Body report, decisions on measures for implementation or possible trade sanctions.

219 These wide-ranging rights of the DSB, not only in respect of the organization of the dispute settlement mechanism, but also in the different stages of the procedures, are mitigated by the fact that the DSB decides by **negative** (or: reverse) **consensus**. The DSB can only change the course of the different stages and their results in the very unlikely case that there is consensus by all Members, including the disputing parties, to do so. With this, the DSU has abolished an important shortcoming of the GATT 1947 (para. 201). In the GATT dispute settlement mechanism, consensus by all contracting parties including the disputing parties was required for the adoption of a Panel report. This form of procedure frequently led to the blocking of or at least delays in the adoption and implementation of Panel reports. Save for the exceptional situation of negative consensus, the **action of the DSB** in the specific procedures can therefore be best characterized as **notarial**.

220 With respect to **surveillance of the implementation** of Panel or Appellate Body rulings, the DSB has further compentences.[23] The DSB has continual rights to information and notification in cases in which Members are obliged by decisions of dispute settlement institutions to change their trade policies.

[23] See Art. 21.6.

2. *Panel*

221 Panels are appointed on an **ad hoc** basis by the DSB for each specific case at the request of one party. The DSB must appoint a Panel at the second meeting if the dispute cannot be settled by consultations in accordance with Art. 4 DSU. At the first meeting of the DSB following the application the positive consensus principle of Art. 6.1 DSU is to be applied, so that the Member concerned may still impede the establishment of a Panel. As the conflicts about the EU market regulations for bananas and the subsidies for civil aircraft show, some Members make use of this right in order to gain time or to express their disapproval.[24]

222 Contrary to dispute settlement under GATT 1947, decision-making in the DSB is turned round: while consensus of the CONTRACTING PARTIES was formerly necessary for the establishment of a Panel, the DSB is now obliged to establish a Panel at the second meeting if it does not by consensus decide not to do so (negative consensus, Art. 6.1 DSU). This is often called the **"right to a Panel"**.

223 According to Art. 8.5 s.1 DSU, the Panel must be composed of **three** highly qualified **persons**, who should be members of the public service.[25] Panel members are independent and may not be citizens of any of the countries involved in the conflict (Art. 8.3 DSU). These persons may also serve on more than one Panel at the same time (Art. 9.3 DSU).

224 The Secretariat plays an important role in the **composition** of individual Panels in accordance with Art. 8.6 DSU: it maintains a list of qualified persons.[26] According to Art. 8.6, the Secretariat proposes members for the Panel which the parties may refuse only for compelling reasons. Despite the Secretariat's important role, the composition of the Panel mainly depends on the agreement of the parties, as Art. 8.7 DSU states indirectly. If the parties have still not agreed on its members 20 days after the Panel's formal establishment, the Director-General, at the request of one of the parties, appoints the members of the Panel.

---

[24] See most recently WT/DS317, *United States – Measures affecting trade in large civil aircraft*, Request for Panel, WT/DS317/2, 3 June 2005; WT/DS316 – *European Communities and certain Member States* – Measures affecting trade in large civil aircraft, Request for Panel, WT/DS317/2, 3 June 2005.

[25] This arises out of the history of the GATT dispute settlement, where only state representatives could serve on the panel. Later, persons who did not belong to the public service, especially those in the academic area, could also be appointed. The names of those persons shall be held on a special list of experts, see Art. 8.1 and 8.4 DSU.

[26] Indicative List of Governmental and Non-governmental Panelists, WT/DSB/33, 6 March 2003. Last addendum WT/DSB/33/Add.2, 12 January 2005. According to Art. 8.4 S.2 DSU this list also contains the earlier GATT "Roster of Non-Governmental Panelists", 30 November 1984, BISD 31S/9.

225 Like the composition of the Panel, its **mandate** is also granted only for a specific case. This shows clearly the historical origin of dispute settlement as a political-diplomatic procedure which should originally merely prepare the political decision. The relevant political organ reserved to itself the decision on who and to what extent should work on and resolve a specific dispute. Differing from a court with its rules of procedure, each individual Panel gets its own specific mandate. Art. 7.1 DSU provides for a standard clause developed from GATT practice, which applies automatically if nothing is agreed to the contrary by the contracting parties within 20 days of the establishment of a Panel.[27] In practice, parties have to some extent made use of the ability to change the mandate of the Panel, and have thus attempted to limit the ambit of the matter in dispute.

3. *Appellate Body*

226 One of the main improvements of the dispute settlement system under the WTO is the introduction of a **second decision-making level**, which can, on request, review the decision of a Panel. Next to Art. 17 DSU the "Working Procedures for Appellate Review" cover the appeal procedure.[28]

227 Unlike the Panel process, the appeal process is assigned to a **standing organ**, the Appellate Body. It is composed of seven persons. The **members** of the Appellate Body are appointed by the DSB for four years, with the possibilitiy of one re-election (Art. 17.2). They should be known and reputable experts with special knowledge in the areas of law and international trade, and they must be independent of the governments of the states involved. The membership of the Appellate Body should also be representative of the membership of the WTO. Members must always be available at short notice, and must also be up to date with the activities of the WTO, especially in the area of dispute settlement. The Members of the Appellate Body serve in rotation, i.e., three persons are chosen out of the membership for each individual case.[29] They are not allowed to take part in discussions on disputes which could lead to a direct or indirect conflict of interests

---

[27] The clause in Art. 7.1 DSU is: "To examine, in the light of the relevant provisions in (name of the covered agreement(s) cited by the parties to the dispute), the matter referred to the DSB by (name of party) in document [...] and to make such findings as will assist the DSB in making the recommendations or in giving the rulings provided for in that/those agreement(s)." This clause expresses clearly the historic, political-diplomatic idea of dispute settlement through the decision of a political organ, here the DSB, although the DSB has in an overall view no function with regard to the contents of the decision.

[28] WT/AB/WP/5, 1 January 2005, see footnote 12 above.

[29] Art. 17.1 s.3 DSU.

(Art. 17.3 DSU).[30] The Appellate Body has decided on its own Working Procedures after consultation with the chairperson of the DSB and the Director-General, and has transmitted these to the Members.

4. *The Secretariat*

228 The Secretariat also plays an important role in dispute settlement.[31] It has a decisive influence on the **selection of Panel members** (Art. 8.4 and Art. 8.6 DSU), serves as registrar for the applications and submissions of the parties (Art. 12.6 DSU), and supports the Panel and its members. This last function is of particular significance for the representation of developing countries in dispute settlement procedures (Art. 27.2 DSU). The role of the secretariat is also criticized, since it can exert considerable influence on the outcome of a dispute through the drafting of résumés of Panel reports.[32]

5. *Other Institutions*

229 Besides these regularly involved organs and institutions, the DSU provides for the use of **expert review groups**[33] within the Panel procedure and the appointment of arbitrators in certain cases.[34]

IV. *The Dispute Settlement Procedure*

230 The dispute settlement procedure is divided into **three parts**: consultation, Panel or Appellate procedure, and enforcement. This is all tied in to a very tight time frame, which should, in the sense of effective law enforcement, prevent any undue delays. The aim of the DSU is that an enforcable decision should in principle be reached within a period of 12 months.[35]

---

[30] An inside view of the Appellate Body is given by *Ehlermann*, Six Years on the Bench of the "World Trade Court", JWT 36 (2002), 605.

[31] See Art. 27 DSU.

[32] See *Weiler*, The Rule of Lawyers and the Ethos of Diplomats: Reflections on the Internal and External Legitimacy of WTO Dispute Settlement, JMWP 9/2000, 13 *et seq.*

[33] See Art. 13.2 and Appendix 4 DSU.

[34] See Art. 21.3 *lit.* c, 22.6 and 7 as well as Art. 25 DSU. For the last mentioned proceeding, see the ruling in *United States – Copyright*, WT/DS160/ARB25/1, 9 November 2001, which dealt with the level of compensation to be paid. In this proceeding, the EU was awarded an annual compensation of € 1,219,900. This was the only instance in which the special arbitral procedure of Art. 25 has been used to date.

[35] See Art. 20, which foresees a maximum procedure from establishmet of the Panel up to the decision of the Appellate Body of 12 months. A maximum period of two months of consultations havc to bc added.

1. *Consultation*

231 The dispute settlement procedure begins with so-called consultations, in which the members concerned attempt to reconcile their differences. Consultations can be understood as an element of **diplomatic and political dispute settlement** and are the **mandatory stage** before the juridical dispute settlement. The aim, as demonstrated by Art. 4.3 s.1 DSU, is to achieve a solution which is mutually acceptable to all the parties. Consultations and procedures to be applied thereby are in the hands of the parties. The consultations are confidential and do not affect the rights of the parties in the further proceedings (Art. 4.6 DSU).

232 As Art. 4.1 DSU states, the consultation procedure is used just by the **Members** and rests entirely in their hands. Consultations are offered by written request from one Member to the other (Art. 4.3 and Art. 4.4 S. 2 DSU).[36] The dispute settlement institutions are only informed of these consultations by notification in accordance with Art. 4.4 DSU.

233 Art. 4 DSU includes a series of provisions which should ensure that the disputing parties make efforts in good faith to settle the conflict. This includes a **time limit** of ten days in which to respond to the original request for consultation (Art. 4.3 DSU) and a time limit for the start of consultations of 30 days after the request is submitted. In total, 60 days from the submission of the request are set aside for consultations: if no agreement is reached within this period, the applicant party may request the establishment of a Panel. The same applies if the other party does not respond to the request or the opening of consultations, or if both parties agree that a settlement by consultations would not be successful.[37]

234 Apart from these rules, which serve the purpose of ensuring transparency and clarity in the conflict, the DSU contains **no further substantial provisions**, but leaves it to the parties to decide on how to use the consultation stage. With regard to the substance of the consultations as a precondition for the request for a Panel, the DSU limits itself to the formal requirements of the procedure or the failure to observe the strict time limits. Whether and to what extent the parties made an effort during the consultation stage constructively to settle the conflict is irrelevant to the admissibility of a request for the establishment of a Panel.[38]

---

[36] Under the GATT 1947, the consultation procedure was governed by Art. XXII GATT.

[37] In *Mexico-High Fructose Corn Syrup*, no consultations were held at all. However, as Mexico had only claimed a breach of the procedural provisions of the DSU during the compliance panel stage, the Appellate Body found that it was estopped from bringing such a claim that late in the proceedings, WT/DS132/AB/RW, 22 October 2001, para. 50 and 75.

[38] Corresponding arguments are often rejected by the Panel, see *European Communities* –

235 The DSU in Art. 5 also names **further instruments** for such **diplomatic means of political dispute resolution**: good offices, conciliation and mediation. Unlike consultations these methods are characterised by the fact that an uninvolved third party supports the conflicting parties in finding a solution to the conflict. Art. 5.6 DSU provides that the Director General can offer good offices, conciliation and mediation. However, this does not exclude the employment of officials, international organizations, States or individuals. Fundamentally, the utilisation of such methods presupposes a degree of agreement between the conflicting parties. Good offices, conciliation and mediation can be used in conjunction with consultations and can even be continued during the panel procedure.[39] Very little is known about the utilisation of such offices, since one of the fundamental prerequisites for success is confidentiality.[40]

2. *The Formal Dispute Settlement Procedure: Panel and Appellate Body*

236 If the parties are unsuccessful in resolving the dispute by consultations or with the help of a third party, then the formal dispute settlement procedure of the WTO starts with the request for **establishment of a panel**. Such a request must be made in writing and must include information about the consultations carried out and the legal basis for the complaint, so that the point of conflict becomes clear (Art. 4.4 s.2 DSU). If the complaining party wishes a mandate different from that formulated in Art. 7.1 DSU (para. 225), it must propose its formulation. The further details for the procedures before the Panel are contained in Art. 12 and Appendix 3 DSU.

237 These include special requirements for the **time-frame** of the Panel procedure. A strict sequence for the procedural steps is provided for, with corresponding time limits, so that normally, according to Art. 12.8 s.1 DSU, the procedure lasts for six months. In contrast to the strict time frame and the underlying interest in an effective enforcement of the laws lies the interest in the high quality of the results of the Panels, as stipulated in Art. 12.2 DSU. Therefore, it is possible to modify the time frame, having regard to the different interests and concerns involved.

Bananas, WT/DS27/R, 22 May 1997, para. 7.19 *et seq.*; *Korea – Alcohol*, WT/DS75/R and WT/DS84/R, 17 September 1998, para. 10.18 *et seq.; Turkey – Textiles*, WT/DS34/R 31 May 1999, para. 9.22 *et seq.*

[39] Art. 5.4 and 5.5 DSU.

[40] However, see Communication from the Director-General of 13 July 2001, Article 5 of the Dispute Settlement Understanding, WT/DSB/25 and General Council, Request for Mediation by the *Philippines, Thailand and the European Communities*, WT/GC/71, WT/GC/66 and WT/GC/66/Add.1.

In cases of urgency it is possible to shorten the time frame, especially if perishable goods are concerned.[41] Equally, the overall time-frame can be extended up to nine months if the Panel is not able to present its final report within six months (Art. 12.9 s.2 DSU). Such extension may arise if the facts of the case are complicated or give rise to complex legal questions. This is especially so if the Panel requires the assistance of Specific Expert Groups in accordance with Art. 13.2 and Appendix 4 DSU. Normally, the Panel itself decides on its time frame – according to Art. 13.2 it has the duty to set the time frame following its establishment.

238 Outside the ambit of these time limits, **proceedings can also be suspended** for up to 12 months if the complaining party submits a request with the aim of settling the dispute in another way (Art. 12.12 s.1 DSU). If the proceedings are not resumed after this period, the Panel's mandate lapses.[42]

239 Within its time frame, the **Panel procedure is divided into different sections**, which are laid down in the DSU and Appendix 3: after negotiations and discussions between the Panel and the disputing parties about questions of procedure, which are not expressly mentioned in the provisions, the actual Panel procedure begins with the **first substantive meeting**. Part of this meeting is reserved for the statements of and discussion with third parties involved in the proceedings.[43]

240 After the written submissions and the responses have been made, there is a **second substantive meeting**. After these two meetings, the Panel concludes the part of its interim report which contains the descriptive sections of its draft report, summarizing the facts and legal subject matter of the action, and forwards it to the parties for a response.

241 With the submission of the interim report the **interim review stage** begins (Art. 15 DSU). It regularly takes one week and the parties have the opportunity to seek a review of parts of the interim report. After that, a review meeting can take place.

242 Subsequently, the Panel drafts the **final report** and forwards it to the parties to give them a final chance to find a solution amongst themselves. After a further time limit, the final report is sent to the other Members and officially to the DSB, so that it is again involved in the dispute.

---

[41] Art. 12.8 s.2 DSU.
[42] Art. 12.12 s.3 DSU.
[43] For involvment of third parties in the proceeding, see paras 252 *et seq.*

243 The DSU regulates in detail in which form the Panels may **seek information on the facts of the case**. According to Art. 13.1 DSU they have the right to gather information and technical advice from every person or institution they consider to be adequate. The standard of adequacy is determined by the Panel. Before this occurs, the public authorities of the Members involved have to be informed. The Panel may also adress questions to Members. If confidential information is given, it should not be made public without the formal authorisation of the person, institution or authority providing it.[44]

244 Art. 13.2 DSU allows the Panel to seek information and expert opinion from **every appropriate source**.[45] With regard to questions concerning technical or academic questions, the Panel may ask for written expert opinions of an **Expert Review Group** (para. 229), whose establishment and work are regulated by Appendix 4 DSU.[46] Such Expert Review Groups are subordinated to the Panel, which specifies their function and proceedings, although the general rules are provided for in Appendix 4.

245 According to this, persons with a relevant profession or knowledge of the subject shall be appointed, whereas nationals of the conflicting parties may be appointed only if the information is not available from any other source. Just like the Panel, these expert groups may also gather information and advice from every appropriate source. Members shall answer without delay.[47] All information has to be offered to the parties, although confidential information is given indirectly by way of summary. As with the intermediate procedure in the Panel proceedings, the Expert Groups draft a provisional report and give the parties the opportunity to draft a response before a final report is made, which is sent to the conflicting parties and the Panel. Art. 13.2 and number 6 of Appendix 4 DSU state explicitly that the final report has a solely advisory function and is therefore not binding.

246 Practice shows that the Panels more and more often **appoint individuals as experts** rather than establishing an Expert Review Group in accordance with Art. 13.2 DSU. The reasons for this development are the procedural requirements which the expert groups have to fulfill: such group has to submit a collective report which requires a consensus

---

[44] This provision is supplemented by the confidentiality rule in panel proceedings in Art. 14 DSU. For the practice of the Appellate Body in dealing with business secrets, see *Canada – Aircraft*, WT/DS70/AB/R of 2 August 1999, para. 141 *et seq.*

[45] For the discussion of the question of admissibility of "*amicus curiae* briefs", see paras 259, 297.

[46] See also the rules on expert groups in Art. 11.2 SPS and Art 14.2 TBT.

[47] In *Turkey – Textiles*, WT/DS34/R, 31 May 1999 the Panel consulted the EU, which was not formally involved in the conflict, with a request for information.

position among the experts. The Appellate Body has affirmed that this action is compatible with the DSU.[48]

247 After the distribution of the Panel report in the DSB, a party to the dispute can **appeal** the report. There is no specific period mentioned in the DSU that restricts the parties' right to appeal. As Art. 16.4 DSU provides that the DSB shall be adopted within 60 days after its circulation, these 60 days mark the maximum time for the notification of an appeal.[49] The appeal can only be made on issues of law covered in the panel report and legal interpretations developed by the panel (Art. 17.6 DSU).

248 The **procedural details** are covered in Art. 17 DSU and in the Working Procedures which has been drafted by the Appellate Body.[50] Ten days after the appeal, the applicant must make a written submission which substantiates the grounds for appeal. In particular, it must specify the challenges and the legal arguments on which the appeal is based. This submission must also include a precise statement of the provisions of the relevant agreements and other legal sources relied on and the nature of the decision or ruling sought (para. 21 of the Working Procedures).

249 The procedure before the Appellate Body is limited to a strict **time frame**, which it sets itself. Normally, the proceedings should not take longer than 60 days, counting from the date on which a party to the dispute formally notifies its decision to appeal.[51] The Working Procedures contain further specific rules covering multiple appeals and the persons involved. Para. 29 covers in particular the non-appearance of a party. It provides that if a submission is not filed within the required time period or if a party does not appear, the Appellate Body may, after the hearing, give an appropriate decision, which may also include the dismissal of the appeal.

250 The Appellate Body can **decide** as follows: it can uphold, amend or dismiss the findings and conclusions of the Panel.[52] The final report of the Appellate Body must be approved by the DSB within 30 days of its circulation, if the DSB does not dismiss it by consensus.[53]

---

[48] *European Communities – Hormones*, WT/DS26/R, WT/DS48/R, 18 August 1997, paras 8.7–8.8, as confirmed by the Appellate Body, WT/DS26/AB/R, WT/DS48/AB/R, 16 January 1998, paras 146 *et. seq.*, See also more recently *European Communities – Asbestos*, WT/DS135/R, 28 September 2000, paras 5.19, 8.10.

[49] Art. 16.1 DSU allows for a mimimum of 20 days before a circulate report can be considered for adoption.

[50] See footnote 28 above.

[51] Art. 17.5 DSU.

[52] However, the Appellate Body cannot remand a case back to the original panel for further factual clarification. See in this respect para. 295.

[53] Art. 17.14 DSU.

3. *Conflicting Parties and Others Involved in the Procedure*

251 The dispute settlement procedure of the WTO is provided **solely to its Members**. In principle, the DSU is designed for the clarification of legal questions between conflicting parties. However, it also contains provisions for the involvement of third parties.

252 The **participation of "third" parties** in the consultation procedure is governed by Art. 4.11 DSU. According to this, a Member may take part in the consultation procedure if it claims a substantial trade interest,[54] if it has informed the parties, and if the responding party agrees to the claim that there is a relevant trade interest. The request shall be accepted by the respondent, if he agrees that the claim of substantial interest is well-founded. If this decision is negative, the third party may – alternatively – request entirely independent consultations.

253 Art. 10.2 s.1 DSU grants the position of a **"third party"** in a panel procedure to any Member who has a substantial interest in the issue and has notified this interest to the DSB. The third party will be heard by the panel and can make written submissions. These submissions shall also be given to the disputing parties and shall be reflected in the panel report (Art. 10.2 s. 2 DSU). According to Art. 10.3 DSU, third parties are entitled to be present at the first meeting and a part of this first hearing will be dedicated to them (para. 239). According to Art. 10.4 DSU a third party can itself begin dispute settlement proceedings if it is of the opinion that its benefits are nullified or impaired (para. 208). Such a dispute shall be referred to the original panel wherever possible. It has to be emphasised that there is no obligation to disclose any further submissions of the parties to third parties beyond the first substantive meeting (Art. 10.3 DSU).[55]

254 On the level of the **appeal procedure**, **third parties** may, according to Art. 17.4 DSU, make written submissions to, and be given an opportunity to be heard by, the Appellate Body, if they have notified the DSB of a substantial interest in terms of Art. 10.2 DSU.[56] Nevertheless, a third party is not entitled to appeal a Panel report itself.

255 In the panel procedure, there are two possibilities for the involvement of multiple parties. According to Art. 9.1 DSU, a Member may join

---

[54] Whether this requirement is an equivalent to "legal interest" see *European Communities – Bananas III*, WT/DS27/AB/R, para. 132.

[55] This has lead to problems in the compliance panel procedure, in which, due to the strict time-frames, only one meeting is held with the parties. The Appellate Body has clarified that third parties are thus entitled to all relevant documents for this "first" (and only) meeting, including the rebuttal submissions, *United States – Tax Treatment for "Foreign Sales Corporations" (FSC)*, WT/DS108/AB/RW, 14 January 2002, para. 251.

[56] See paras 24 and 27(3) of the Working Procedures for Appellate Review (see note 28 above).

in the complaint, and a single panel should be established to examine such complaints whenever feasible,[57] while taking into account the rights of all Members concerned. According to Art. 9.2 DSU, it must be ensured that the individual applicants enjoy the same rights they would have had if separate panels had examined the complaints. In particular, the panel shall submit separate reports on the dispute concerned if one of the parties so requests. If the establishment of a single panel is not possible, Art. 9.3 states that, to the greatest extent possible, the same persons shall serve as panelists on each of the separate panels and the timetables for the panel process in such disputes shall be harmonized. All individual complainants have their own right of appeal (Art. 17.4 DSU).

4. *The Participation of Lawyers, Legal Advisors, and Non-governmental Organisations*

256 Dispute settlement in the WTO largely lies in the **hands of the Members** and is generally carried out by governments or their delegates and representatives. The meetings of the Panel and the Appellate Body are not public because of their overriding aim of finding a positive solution to the dispute (Art. 3.7 DSU). Confidentiality could be conducive to reaching an amicable solution to the conflict.[58]

257 With regard to the requirement for legal advice or legal expertise, many governments rely on scholars, **lawyers** and other advisors. These can officially take part in the proceedings and speak, as long as they are **official members of a delegation** and have been notified as such.[59] On the other hand, the Panel and Appellate Body have so far strictly refused to accept these lawyers or legal advisers as sole representatives or counsel.

258 A similar problem arises with **non-governmental organizations**, which can provide special expertise or may have a particular interest in the dispute. The parties may well submit relevant statements to the procedure, if they introduce them as part of their own submissions. It would also be possible for representatives of non-governmental organisations officially to take part in the proceedings if they are appointed

[57] According to the decision of the Panel in *India – Patents*, WT/DS79/R, 24 August 1998, paras 7.11 *et seq.* members are not obliged to coordinate their complaints. The rules in Art. 9 DSU are only recommendations and cannot alter the rules and obligations of Members as contained in the DSU.

[58] Art. 2 of Appendix 3 DSU, with regard to the panel and Art. 17:10 S.1 DSU, with regard to the Appellate Body.

[59] *European Communities – Regime for the Importation, Sale and Distribution of Bananas*, WT/DS27/AB/R, 9 September 1997, I.A.10.

as members of the delegation and are notified as such. For instance, the Advisory Center on WTO Law, which has been established in 2001, offers support for developing countries in dispute settlement procedures (para. 30).

259 A further question is whether non-governmental organisations can take part in the proceeding independently of the conflicting parties. The Appellate Body basically affirms the authority of the Appellate Body and Panels to consider **statements from non-governmental organisations** in terms of an *amicus curiae brief*[60] at their discretion. In this regard, the Appellate Body refers to Art. 13 and 17 DSU and has adopted an Additional Procedure to its Working Procedures.[61] However, the **hearing** of representatives of such organisations has so far been **refused**. Further rights, for example on the basis of public participation, do not exist.

V. *Applicable Rules, Interpretation and Legal Effect*

260 The applicable laws and regulations comprising the standard of review in dispute settlement are the Agreements and acts of the WTO (Art. 3.2 DSU). Furthermore, panels have more than once consulted **other international treaties**, if they have been relevant for particular disputes. Under this provision these rules have been taken into account even where the mandate of the Panel has not provided for them explicitly.[62]

261 According to Art. 3.2 s.2 DSU, the standard for interpretation are the **"customary rules for interpretation of public international law."** In practice, the Panel refers, for reasons of simplicity, to the Vienna Convention on the Law of Treaties,[63] in which most of the rules for

[60] *Amicus curiae briefs* are an institution of especially American procedural law. With such statements, third parties not directly involved in the trial attempt to convince the court of the correctness of a certain result. For this see *Umbricht*, An "Amicus Curia Brief" on Amicus Curia Briefs at the WTO, JIEL 4 (2001) 4, 773 *et seq.*

[61] This right of the panel was first granted in *United States – Shrimp*, in which the Appellate Body reversed the opposite ruling of the panel in this respect, WT/DS58/AB/R, 12 October 1998. In the decision *United States – and Bismuth III*, WT/DS138/AB/R, 7 June 2000, paras 39–42, a corresponding authority of the Appellate Body was also accepted. After the enactment of a provision for the presentation of *amicus curia briefs* of 8 November 2000 (WT/DS135/9) by the Appellate Body in *European Communities – Measures Affecting Asbestos and Asbestos-Containing Products*, WT/DS135/AB/R, 12 March 2001, para. 51, the Appellate Body was vehemently criticised by the majority of Members in the General Council. In the concrete case, the Appellate Body then declined to consider all *amicus curiae briefs*. But implicitly, it again confirmed the permissability of such statements in principle, *European Communities – Asbestos*, paras 50–57.

[62] The Appellate Body in *United States – Gasoline* rejected the idea that WTO law is in itself conclusive. WTO law must rather be seen in conjunction with other rules of international law, and not in "clinical isolation", *United States – Standards for Reformulated and Conventional Gasoline*, WT/DS2/AB/R, 29 April 1996, 17.

[63] Vienna Convention on the Laws of Treaties (VCLT), 23 May 1969, see Ch. 2 para. 2.

interpretation are codified. It is generally presumed that most of the rules mirror customary international law.[64] Art. 3.2 s.2 DSU does not explicitly refer to the Vienna Convention, because some of the Members of the WTO, especially the United States and France, do not belong to that international treaty.

1. *Subject Matter*

262 The subject matter of proceedings is specified in Art. 4.2, 6.2 and 7 DSU. According to the Appellate Body, a **"matter"** before the Panel (the DSB) consists of the measure(s) at issue and the claims relating to those measures, as set out in the request for establishment.[65]

263 Thus, the **determination** of the matter is mainly left to the parties – the **applicant** makes a first definition in its request for consultations, which must include arguments comprising information on the controversial **measures** and references to the **legal basis**. The request for the establishment of a panel, in accordance with Art. 6.2 DSU, must have corresponding reasoning and information.

264 If the disputing parties do not agree otherwise, this information serves as the basis for the **mandate of the Panel** in accordance with Art. 7.1 DSU.[66] The Panel's mandate is limited to "relevant provisions in any covered agreement or agreements cited by the parties to the dispute" (Art. 7.2 DSU). Other international agreements and treaties are excluded, and the Panel can rely on them only if they are relevant for the matter in hand.

265 The relatively unspecified rules about the subject matter and the fact that its determination is primarily based on information provided by the parties have more than once resulted in disagreements.[67] On the one hand, **identification of the measures** has led to problems. Generally, identification is carried out by referring to the underlying laws and regulations of the Member in question. This may cause problems where measures are not clearly prescribed in the laws and regulations or the laws and regulations may have a wider scope of application.

[64] See the arguments of the Appellate Body in *United States – Gasoline*, WT/DS2/AB/R, 10 *et seq.* with regard to Art. 31 VCLT.

[65] *Guatemala – Anti-Dumping Investigation regarding Portland Cement from Mexico*, WT/DS60/AB/R, 25 November 1998, para. 76.

[66] As a result, the determination of the matter in dispute is mainly the responsibilty of the claiming party: if the disputing parties are unable to agree on a different determination, the measure, identified by the complaining Member, is the measure in dispute, see above para. 23.

[67] See Appellate Body Reports *Argentina – Footwear Safeguards*, WT/DS121/AB/R, 14 December 1999, 73 *et seq.* and *United States – Certain EC Products*, WT/DS165/AB/R 11 December 2000, 68 *et seq.*

266 Also the **determination of the relevant agreements** (**"claims"**), which has the effect of limiting the mandate of the Panel to the rules included therein, has caused difficulties when Members wanted to rely on the provisions of other agreements in the course of proceedings.[68]

2. *The Legal Effect of the Reports of the Panel and Appellate Body*

267 Reports of the Panel and Appellate Body are **binding** for the parties involved once they have been adopted by the DSB.[69] The recommendations and rulings, included in the Reports, are basis for their enforcement.

268 The extent of the **binding effect** and the legal validity of these decisions is not easy to determine in cases where Members change the respective regulations or administrative practice. The situation can become even more complicated if these amendments give rise to **further and new complaints**. In this case, Art. 21.5 DSU provides for a new truncated panel procedure and the possibility of the participation of the original members of the panel ("compliance panel").

269 The binding effect of the accepted reports, however, is **limited to the recommendations and rulings**. The legal arguments and interpretations does not assume any binding force. In particular, decisions of the Appellate Body or the Panel do not have binding effect until they have been adopted by the DSB. However, unaccepted reports can serve as useful guidance.[70]

270 The Appellate Body has clarified that decisions under the dispute settlement system of the **GATT 1947** will not become part of the WTO in the sense of Art. 1. *lit.* b (iv) GATT 1994. The provision governs the transition of the GATT *acquis* into the WTO legal order, and provides in particular that the decisions of the contracting parties of the GATT 1947 should be adopted as a whole into the WTO legal order. But the Appellate Body argued that reports of the panel under GATT 1947 could not be seen as decisions in this sense, as they were binding on only the parties. Furthermore, the Appellate Body has also decided that adopted reports of the Panel are not to be considered as "subsequent practice" in the sense of Art. 31 para. 3 *lit.* b Vienna

[68] See Appellate Body Report in *EC – Bananas*, footnote 59 above, 23.

[69] The legally binding effect of these decisions was not undisputed, *Bello*, The WTO Dispute Settlement Understading: Less is More, AJIL 90 (1996) 3, 416 *et seq.* It is however now accepted that the decisions of the DSB are binding for the Members, see *Jackson*, The Dispute Settlement Understanding: Misunderstandings on the Nature of Legal Obligation, AJIL 91 (1997) 1, 60, 63 *et seq.* and *Jackson*, International Law Status of WTO Dispute Settlement Reports: Obligation to Comply or Option to "Buy Out"?, AJIL 98 (2004), 109–125.

[70] *Japan – Alcoholic Beverages*, WT/DS8/R, WT/DS10/R, WT/DS11/R, 11 June 1996, para. 6.10; *Japan – Alcoholic Beverages*, WT/DS8/AB/R, WT/DS10/AB/R, WT/DS11/AB/R, 4 October 1996, paras 13 *et seq.*

Convention of the Laws of Treaties, which have to be considered in interpreting the treaties.[71]

271 The rulings of the panel and the Appellate Body have no **stare decisis**, as in Anglo-American legal systems. However, earlier rulings will be taken into account in later proceedings in the sense of the aim, explicitly expressed in Art. 3.2 DSU, of the "security and predictability of the multilateral trading system".[72]

VI. *Implementation and Enforcement*

272 The Panel or Appellate Body report completes only one part of the dispute settlement procedure. It is followed by the **surveillance of the implementation** of the recommendations and rulings, for which the **DSB** is responsible.[73] A further part also includes the possible imposition of **trade sanctions**.

273 The starting point of the implementation procedure are the **recommendations and rulings** of the DSB. The recommendations are those of the Panel or Appellate Body according to Art. 19.1 DSU, which the DSB formally adopts as its own. Art. 19 DSU provides that the Panel or Appellate Body shall recommend that the Member bring the measure into conformity with the agreements of the WTO should the measure in dispute not comply with WTO law.

274 The Panel and Appellate Body can on their own authority make further **suggestions on** how a specific member can put the recommendations into effect (Art. 19.1 S.2 DSU). In practice, this has happened in a few cases,[74] although the dispute settlement institutions are very careful about the sovereignty of Members in making specific suggestions which can easily be understood as orders.

1. *Surveillance of Implementation and Setting of Time Limits*

275 According to Art. 21.1 DSU Members have an obligation to **implement recommendations and rulings promptly**. In respect of sur-

[71] See *Japan – Taxes on Alcoholic Beverages*, WT/DS8/AB/R, WT/DS10/AB/R, WT/DS11/AB/R, 4 October 1996, 13 *et seq.* and *United States – Shrimp/Turtle*, WT/DS58/AB/RW, 22 October 2001, paras 107, 109.

[72] *India – Patent Protection for Pharmaceutical and Agricultural Chemical Products*, WT/DS79/R, 24 August 1998, 7.25 *et seq.*

[73] See Art. 21.6.

[74] E.g. in the *Banana* case after Ecuador's request, WT/DS27/AB/R, para. 139; *European Communities – Sugar Subsidies*, WT/DS265/R, WT/DS266/R, WT/DS283/R, 15 October 2004, paras 8.6–8.8.

veillance of the implementation through the DSB, they must inform the DSB of their ideas for implementation within 30 days of the adoption of the Panel or Appellate Body report, Art. 21.3 s.1 DSU.

276 In practice, the exceptional rule in Art. 21.3 s.2 DSU is often used, whereby the Member in question may be granted a **reasonable period of time** for implementation, if it is impracticable for him to implement recommendations and rulings immediately. This reasonable period of time can be approved by the DSB on a proposal from the Member affected (Section 3 *lit.* a), it can be mutually agreed by the parties to the dispute within 45 days of the date of the adoption of the recommendations or rulings in question (Section 3 *lit.* b), or through binding arbitration within 90 days (Section 3 *lit.* c). A guideline for the arbitrator is contained in Art. 21.3 *lit.* c DSU, according to which the reasonable period for implementation should not be longer than 15 months from the date of adoption of a panel's or Appellate Body's report. However, the period can also be shorter or longer depending on the particular circumstances.[75]

277 The frequently used **arbitral decision on the period for implementation** has led to a variety of answers to the question of defining the "reasonableness" of the time-period. At the centre of these diputes have often been the reasons which can or should be taken into account in allowing delayed implementation. Amongst others, there have been cases concerning the time needed to implement a national legislative or administrative procedure, the time needed by national industries to adapt to changed general conditions, and the time needed for achieving political acceptance. In the ever more varied arbitrations, a formal view was at first used, under which the period of 15 months provided for in Art. 21.3 *lit.* c DSU became the rule. Later, awards corrected that development so that now in general only the shortest period possible provided for in the national legal system of the Member concerned for implementation of the changes is allowed.[76]

278 Where a Member is granted **time for implementation**, the DSB retains the right to oversee the implementation process. This detailed surveillance regulated by Art. 21.6. DSU even covers the question in which time intervals the issue shall be placed back on the DSB's agenda.

---

[75] For example *United States – OCTG Sunset Review*, WT/DS268/12, 7 June 2005 – 12 months; *Canada – Pharmaceuticals*, WT/DS114/13, 18 August 2000 – 6 months; *Australia – Salmon*, WT/DS18/9, 23 February 1999 – 8 months; see also *Monnier*, The Time to Comply with an Adverse WTO Ruling – Promptness within Reason, JWT 35 (2001) 5, 825 *et seq.*

[76] *EC – Hormones*, WT/DS26/15, WT/DS48/13, 29 May 1998, para. 26; See also *Stoll & Steinmann*, WTO: The Implementation Stage, Max-Planck Yearbook of United Nations Law, 3 (1999), 407 *et seq.*

279 In light of the complicated mechanisms of political trade measures which constitute the vast majority of subject matters under the DSU, Art. 21.5 s.1 anticipated that **disputes** over the question of compliance, namely whether a Member **has completely and effectively implemented the recommendations and rulings**, might arise. In such a case, Art. 21.5 DSU provides for a shortened panel procedure. The so-called "compliance panel" shall submit a report within 90 days after the date of referral and stipulates that the original members of the Panel shall again be appointed, if possible.[77] This procedure has its rationale in the interest in a speedy and competent solution of the follow-up dispute. Due to the cryptical guidance given on its substance, the further consequences of such a procedure and its concrete design are left unclear.[78] However, unlike the arbitration envisaged by Art. 22.6 DSU, such proceedings cannot be considered to bar the other party from resorting to countermeasures (para. 289).

2. *Countermeasures*

280 The high reputation of dispute settlement in the WTO is in particular due to the ability to impose **"trade sanctions"** – in form of the suspension of concessions or other obligations as provided for in Art. 22 DSU – in order to enforce the implementation of recommendations and rulings. Due to the great political and economic significance of such sanctions, the procedure is subject to strict control by the DSB.

281 A Member which seeks to suspend concessions must apply to the DSB to do so. It must give details of the extent to which it wants to suspend the concessions and must accompany such motion with substantiated reasoning (Art. 22.2 and 3 DSU).

282 In terms of a **"right to trade sanctions"**, the DSB must agree to the above mentioned application within 30 days, provided that there is no consensus among its members to the contrary ("negative consensus"), or, as a second possibility, the potentially responding Member makes a request for an arbitration. This procedure is foreseen if the Member concerned claims that the amount of the "sanctions" is not justified or the countermeasures are in any other way unlawful.[79] Finally, the arbitrator sets the amount of the sanstions, which, when adopted

[77] Art. 21.5 DSU points to a possible extension of this short time frame.

[78] For an excellent analysis on Art. 21.5 see *Kearns & Charnovitz*, Adjudicating Compliance in the WTO: A Review of DSU Article 21.5, JIEL (2002), 331–352. See for the issues in review below para. 287 *et seq.*

[79] In the arbitration procedure the applicant can only challenge the level of suspensions and a violation of the procedure under Art. 22.3 DSU (see Art. 22.6 DSU).

by the DSB, are justified until the rulings or recommendations have been implemented in full.[80]

283 The widely-used term "sanction" needs to be clarified. The restrictions on trade described above and regulated in Art. 22 DSU indeed have the aim of enforcing the implementation of rulings and recommendations, and the legal framework of the WTO. But their amount is limited to the **equivalent of** the level of the nullification or impairment suffered (Art. 22.4 DSU).[81]

284 The suspension of concessions and other duties is not limited to the agreement in question. If the prevailing party to the dispute is of the opinion that such action, namely the suspension of concessions under the same agreement under which the breach occurred, is impracticable or ineffective, it can, in accordance with the conditions specified in Art. 22.3 *lit.* c DSU, seek to suspend concessions or other obligations under another WTO Agreement (so-called **"cross retaliation"**). This opportunity is made use of in particular in conflicts where the Members have very different reciprocal trade volumes and levels of economic development. Thus, even a developing country whose absolute import volume and therefore potential threat is low may impose effective sanctions on a larger Members for infringement of WTO law.[82]

285 Besides the element of coercion in order to punish unlawful behaviour and to restore justice as the classical form of a sanction, the countermeasure under Art. 22 DSU also contains the idea of **compensation**. In this respect, the laws of the political economy become important: In a purely economic sense the impact of trade restrictions, whether lawful or not, is not limited to the Member involved. The member acting unlawfully harms not only other Members' national economies, but also its own, and the same applies in the case of trade sanctions. In the history of the GATT, this interrelation has more than once prevented countries from using authorized sanctions or even from applying for possible sanctions.[83]

---

[80] Art. 22.7 DSU last sentence.

[81] In *European Communities – Bananas* the equivalance between the level of nullification and impairment on the one hand and the suspension of concessions on the other hand was specified by the arbitrators not in the sense of proportionality, but as exact congruency between damage and countermeasure, WT/DS27/ARB, 9 April 1999, 19 *et seq.*

[82] Ecuador was, during the "Banana conflict" with the EU, authorised to suspend concessions and other duties to a total value of US$ 201,6 million. The suspension included concessions of the GATS with regards to "wholesale trade services (CPC 622) in the principal sector of distribution services" and the following TRIPS duties: "Section 1: Copyright and related rights, Art. 14 on Protection of performers, producers of phonograms (sound recordings) and broadcasting organisations; Section 3: Geographical indications; Section 4: Industrial designs", WT/DS27/ARB/ECU, 24 April 2000, 171 *et seq.* See also paras 513 *et seq.*

[83] See the single case under the GATT 1947 in which countermeasures were authorized by

286 The possibility of compensation is for the first time provided for under the WTO in Art. 22.1 DSU. Compensation must be given **voluntarily** and must be in accordance with WTO law. The rules on compensation are therefore relatively imperfect. In particular, it remains open what the subject of such compensation is and to what extent the winning Member's right to enforcement can be satisfied by it. In practice, the suspension of concessions plays the most important role, especially because of the automatic authorisation by the DSB and the resulting "right to sanctions".

3. *The Relationship Between Countermeasures and Implementation*

287 As has already been discussed, Art. 21.5 DSU provides for a special procedure clarifying whether a Member has correctly and completely implemented a recommendation or a ruling of the DSB. This question has repeatedly been disputed between the Members concerned and is – especially – problematic in cases in which the winning Member seeks trade sanctions immediately, and possibly without a parallel procedure under Article 21.5.

288 Its interest in enforcement of the law is juxtaposed by the interest of the burdened Member in being protected from trade sanctions after fullfilling its obligation to implement the rulings and recommendations of the DSB. However, the procedure in Art. 21.5 DSU does not have suspensive effect. It is therefore possible for a Member to be subjected to countermeasures which are later found to be unjustified due to correct implementation of DSB's recommendations or ruling.

289 This problem of proper **sequence** arose for the first time in the *Bananas* dispute between the EU and some Members from Latin America and the US. In particular, there was the question of the relationship between the procedure of Art. 21.5 DSU and the arbitration procedure of Art. 22.6 DSU, which, according to sentence 5, expicitly provides for suspensive effect. In this dispute, both procedures had been carried out and completed in parallel. In the Art. 22.6 DSU procedure, which dealt with the amount of the countermeasures, the arbitrators incidently examined to what extent steps taken towards implementation may reduce the allowable amount of countermeasures, and incidently examined the matter of compliance.[84]

---

the CONTRTACTING PARTIES, *Netherlands Action under Art. XXIII:2 to Suspend Obligations to the United States*, 8 November 1952, BISD 1S/32 (1953). However, even these countermeasures were never implemented due to their economic impracticability.

[84] *European Communities – Bananas* – Recourse to Arbitration by the EC under Article 22.6 of the DSU, WT/DS27/ARB, 9 April 1999. In parallel to this arbitration, Ecuador and the EU both requested compliance panels according to Art. 21.5, WT/DS27/RW/EEC and

290 This incidental **expansion of the competences of the arbitrators** has, in practice, led to the fact that the parties now agree in bilateral agreements attached to the requests for establishment that the procedure as set out in Art. 21.5 DSU shall precede the procedure on sanctions under Art. 22.6 DSU.[85] In the case of continuing disagreement, both procedures may be used in parallel, as in the *Banana* dispute, due to the contradictory provisions of the DSU. The legal uncertainty has increased after the Appellate Body's report. In the view of the Appellate Body, the resolution of the relationship between Art. 21.5 and 22 DSU is the duty of the Members, not of the dispute settlement bodies (see Art. IX:2 WTO Agreement).[86] Suggestions for amendments are being discussed since the Seattle ministerial conference (para. 296).

VII. *Special Provisions for Dispute Settlement in Specific Agreements*

291 A series of WTO Agreements contain special provisions for dispute settlement. They often concern consultation procedures, the participation of certain WTO organs and committees and experts in the procedure and govern in part individual questions on implementation. An overview of these special rules can be found in Appendix 2 DSU.[87] The WTO Agreement itself includes, with Art. XX GPA and especially Art. 4 of the Agreement on Preshipment Inspection (paras 327 *et seq.*), the first concrete provisions concerning rights for complaints by individuals. The Agreement on Preshipment Inspection provides for the establishment of **independent entities** (IE), which may supervise conflicts between an exporter and an entity for preshipment inspection on the application of one of the parties (Art. 4 *lit.* a). The subject of such proceedings is the question whether the parties applied the rules of the agreement during the course of the disputed preshipment inspection. These approaches show that the individual is not ignored, but – albeit marginally – integrated into the WTO framework.

WT/DS27/ECU. All three decisions were rendered on the same day thus finding a "logical way forward" to the dilemma of the formally differing time frames of the provisions.

[85] E.g. in the conflict between Canada and Brazil on subsidies for the aircraft industry, *Brazil – Aircraft* WT/DS46, the Agreement is contained in the Appendix to the document WT/DS46/13, 26 November 1999. See more recently the "Confirmed Procedures between Japan and the United States under Articles 21 and 22 of the Dispute Settlement Understanding in the Follow Up to the Dispute in Japan – Measures Affecting the Importation of Apples", WT/DS245/10, 30 June 2004.

[86] *United States – Import Measures on Certain Products from the European Communities*, WT/DS165/AB/R, 11 December 2000, para. 92.

[87] For special consultation clauses see Art. 19 Agreement on Agriculture; Art. 11.1, 12.2 SPS; Art. 8.4, 8.10 ATC; Art. 14.1 TBT; Art. 8 TRIMs; Art. 17.2 AD; Art. 19.2. SD; Art. 7 PSI; Art. 7 Agreement on Rules of Origin; Art. 6 Agreement on Import Licensing Procedures, Art. 30 SCM; Art. 14 Agreement on Safeguards; Art. XXII, XXIII GATS; Art. 64.1 TRIPS.

VIII. *Prospects – The Reform of the DSU*

292 The new dispute settlement system of the WTO has already achieved great significance. Some **major disputes** which remained unresolved under the GATT dispute settlement mechanism because of delays and political implications could now finally be resolved under the WTO dispute settlement mechanism.[88]

293 In a **large number of new cases**, the dispute settlement system has proved successful in the final and effective settlement of disputes and contributed significantly to the implementation of the WTO legal framework in the common interest of the Members. Furthermore, the panel and, in particular, the Appellate Body have further interpreted and clarified the extensive and complex new rules within a relatively short period of time.

294 Nevertheless, the Members have agreed on further negotiations on **reform of the DSU** on the basis of existing expertise and further suggestions from Members. According to a decision taken at the ministerial conference in Doha in November 2001, this review process, that should have been completed no later than May 2003,[89] still continues.[90]

295 The proposals for reform concern problems with the establishment of the **panel** for individual cases and its *ad hoc* composition. Despite the great effort made in the composition and establishment of the panel, the first instance in the dispute settlement procedure is somewhat unclear and intransparent. Furthermore, the Appellate Body lacks a possibility for remand[91] and the dispute settlement institutions are getting closer and closer to reaching the limits of its capacity.[92]

296 A further important review aspect is the relationship between implementation and imposition of countermeasures and therefore the clarification of the relationship of Art. 21.5 to Art. 22 DSU (**"sequenc-**

[88] Such as the *Hormones* case, *Bananas* case, *Japanese alcoholic beverages* case, and the *United States' Foreign Sales Corporations* case.

[89] This deadline was later prolonged to May 2004.

[90] "We agree to negotiations on improvements and clarifications of the Dispute Settlement Understanding. The negotiations should be based on the work done thus far as well as any additional proposals by Members, and aim to agree on improvements and clarifications not later than May 2003, at which time we will take steps to ensure that the results enter into force as soon as possible thereafter.", WT/MIN(01)/DEC/1 20 November 2001. On the Ministerial Conference of Doha, see also paras 795 *et seq.*; a comprehensive overview on the proposal made by WTO Members is given under <http://www.law.georgetown.edu/iiel/research/projects/dsureview/synopsis.html>.

[91] See *Palmeter*, The WTO Appellate Body Needs Remand Authority, JWT 32 (1998) 1, 41–44.

[92] A further aspect is the doubling of the time limit for the selection of the panelists from 30 days in 1996, to approximately 67 days in 2001.

ing").[93] In this regard, the EU has suggested inserting into the DSU provisions giving precedence to the procedure under Art. 21.5 and providing for an appeal.[94] A group of Members are in favour of making the compliance procedure an obligatory stage in the dispute settlement. In their opinion, the practice of "bilateral agreements" between the parties to a specific dispute does not promote legal certainty and the predictability of rulings within the scope of the DSU and also discriminates against smaller Members and developing countries.[95]

297 Finally, another point of discussion is the improvement of transparency of the dispute settlement proceedings in relation to the regulation of *amicus curiae briefs*.[96]

298 The high utilisation and success of the dispute settlement procedure and the sanctions imposed have clarified the **opportunities for and the limits of enforcement** under the WTO. In principle, the DSB allows the successful complaining Member legitimately to impose trade restrictions as **"compensation"** for the infringement of its rights by another Member. Economically, this procedure for implementation of rights is counterproductive, since trade restrictions, irrespective of whether they were originally unlawful or taken as a countermeasure, not only affect the other member but also economic interests in its own country.[97]

299 The form of countermeasures also has a constitutional law dimension for the Member subject to them by reason of its unlawful measures: As the sanctions against the EU show, countermeasures hurt specific sectors of the economy, which are in general not in any way connected with those sectors which are the subject of the unlawful measure. Since the countermeasures are considered measures of a foreign State, they actually cannot be challenged on the basis of national or European law.[98]

---

[93] Instructive suggestions by the EU, TN/DS/W/1, 13 March 2002, as amended by TN/DS/W/38, 23 January 2003, and by India TN/DS/W/5, 7 May 2002.

[94] TN/DS/W/1, 13 March 2002. See also the suggestions of the EU, its members, and other WTO Members at the Ministerial Conference in Doha for amending the DSU, WT/MIN(99)/8, 22 November 1999. An inclusion of an Art. 21 *bis* for the determination of compliance has also been proposed by Japan, TN/DS/W/32, 22 January 2003.

[95] Joint Concept Paper, JOB(02) 45, 31 May 2002 (restricted), see also WT/MIN(01)/W/6, 1 November 2001.

[96] See the explanation of transparency, paras 784 *et seq*.

[97] Under the GATT 1947 this resulted in the fact that countries did not use countermeasures, because they were of the opinion that they would harm themeselves more than the countries the meaures were adressed to. This problem also became clear under the WTO, as in the hearings in the United States about the countermeasures in the individual case. Both in the *Banana* dispute and in the Hormones case, hearings took place in the United States to lay down the countermeasures against European imports. In many cases, US importers also asserted serious economic loses, see International Trade Reporter, Vol. 15, No. 49, 16 December 1998, 2092.

[98] See para. 102.

300 Claims for compensation against a Member State by injured individuals have very little chance of success under national or European law, even if one attributes the imposition of countermeasures to the behaviour of the concerned Member. Thus, some sectors of a national economy are in danger of being subjected to arbitrary trade sanctions for the breach of WTO law or non-implementation of decisions of the DSB by their national governments, without any possibility of reimbursement or claim for damages.[99] In the EU the fact that WTO law has no direct effect in the national legal orders contributes to the fact that an infringement of WTO law cannot be alleged against the EU itself. (paras 677 *et seq.*)

301 The model of countermeasures is unsatisfactory, because it is limited to remedy measures *ex nunc*. A more rational and more effective system would be a realignment **towards monetary damages, including interest**. A starting-point may be seen in Art. 22.1 and .2 DSU, which provide for compensation and consultations. However, such compensation should be awarded voluntarily (Art. 22.1 s.3 DSU) and therefore this does not comform to the overall concept of a ruling awarding damages.

[99] In conjunction with the banana conflict, some other claims for damages were rejected by the European Court of First Instance, see T-18/99, T-30/99, T-52/99, Coll. 2001, II 913 *et seq.* – *Cordis a. o.* and most recently Judgment of the Court of First Instance of 3 February 2005, T-19/01, not yet reported – *Chiquita Brands International.*

CHAPTER FOUR

TRADE IN GOODS

Saul L. Sherman & Hinrich Glashoff, Custom Valuation: Commentary on the GATT Customs Valuation Code, 1988; *Maarten Smeets*, Tariff Issues in the Uruguay Round – Features and Remaining Issues, JWT 29 (1995) 3, 91–106; *Joseph A. LaNasa III*, Rules of Origin and the Uruguay Round's Effectiveness in Harmonizing and Regulating Them, AJIL 90 (1996) 4, 625–640; *Rosemary Fennell*, Community preference and developing countries, European Foreign Affairs Review 2 (1997) 2, 235–253; *Hans-Joachim Prieß & Ralph Pethke*, The pan-European rules of origin: the beginning of a new era in European free trade, CMLR 34 (1997) 4, 773–809; *Norio Komuro*, International harmonisation of rules of origin, in: *Philip Ruttley* (Ed.), The WTO and international trade regulation, 1998, 86–115; *Otfried Schwarz & Kurt Wockenfoth* & *Helmut Friedl* (Eds), Zollrecht, 3. Aufl., 1998 (loseleaf); *Peter-Tobias Stoll & Bernd Goller*, Electronic Commerce and the Internet, German Yearbook of International Law 41 (1998), 128–169; *Emily Rome*, The background, requirements, and future of the GATT/WTO Preshipment Inspection Agreement, Minnesota Journal of Global Trade 7 (1998) 2, 469–507; *Theodor Bail & Walter Schädel & Hans Hutter*, Zollrecht der Bundesrepublik Deutschland und Europäischen Gemeinschaften, (loseleaf); *Yukyun Shin*, Implementation of the WTO Customs Valuation Agreement in developing countries: Issues and recommendations, JWT 33 (1999) 1, 125–143; *Vinod Rege*, Developing country participation in negotiations leading to the adoption of the WTO Agreements on Customs Valuation and Preshipment Inspection: A public choice analysis, World competition 22 (1999) 1, 37–117; *Vinod Rege*, Developing country participation in negotiations leading to the adoption of the WTO Agreements on Customs Valuation and Preshipment Inspection, World Competition 22 (1999) 1, 37–117; *Philippe G. Nell*, WTO negotiations on the harmonization of rules of origin: A first critical appraisal, JWT 33 (1999) 3, 45–71; *Anwarul Hoda*, Tariff Negotiations and Renegotiations under the GATT and the WTO: Procedures and Practices, 2001; *Joseph Tasker*, The Information Technology Agreement: building a global information infrastructure while avoiding customs classification disputes, Brooklyn Journal of International Law 26 (2001) 3, 917–948; *Moshe Hirsch*, International Trade Law, Political Economy and Rules of Origin, JWT 36 (2002) 2, 171–188; *Matthew T. MacGrath*, Customs law, The International Lawyer 36 (2002) 2, 267–286; *Peter Witte* (Ed.), Zollkodex (Kommentar), 3rd ed., 2002; *Kyle Bagwell & Petros C. Mavroidis & Robert W. Staiger*, It's a question of market access, AJIL 96 (2002) 1, 56–76; *Mitsuo Matsushita & Thomas J. Schoenbaum & Petros C. Mavroidis*, The World Trade Organization, 2003; *Matthew T. McGrath & Cortney O'Toole Morgan*, Customs law, The International Lawyer 37 (2003) 2, 245–262; *Peter Witte & Hans-Michael Wolffgang*, Lehrbuch des Europäischen Zollrechts, 4th ed., 2003; *Paul Beynon*, Community mutual recognition agreements, technical barriers to trade and the WTO's most favoured nation principle, European Law Review 28 (2003) 2, 231–249; *Stefano Inama*, Trade preferences and the World Trade

Organization negotiations on market access, JWT 37 (2003) 5, 959–976; *Danesh Sarooshi*, Sovereignty, economic autonomy, the United States, and the international trading system, European Journal of International Law 15 (2004) 4, 651–676.

I. *Market Access – Art. II GATT 1994*

302 The duty raised on goods crossing borders is called a customs duty, or tariff. Depending on the direction of the flow of trade, it can be divided into import-, export- and transit duties. Customs have always been used for the protection of the domestic market against competition – and therefore against pressure on wages, prices and working conditions – (**Protection Tariffs**), as well as a source of internal taxation (**Finance Tariffs**).[1] While the fiscal function of tariffs plays only a minor role in most countries, the protective function is still of significance: customs duties are still a fundamental instrument for protection. The aim of binding these unilaterally defined and changeable customs duties as well as their gradual reduction were, together with the most-favoured-nation principle, **central elements of the GATT 1947**. Also after the coming into force of the WTO Agreement, the permanent lowering of customs duties remains – under the catchword of **market access** – one of the significant concerns of the WTO.[2]

303 **Art II:1 *lit.* b GATT 1994 has fundamental significance in this context.** It provides that products of a WTO Member on their importation into the market of another Member shall be assessed for duty according to the terms set out in the schedule of concessions. These **schedules of concessions** are components of the GATT 1994 (Art. II:7) and have considerable size.[3] They are composed of four parts: Part I contains the rate of duty applicable on the basis of general most-favoured-nation treatment. Part II contains the preferential customs duties given to the developing countries. Part III lists the non-tarif concessions, and Part IV the obligation of Members to limit subsidies on

[1] Customs duties are one of the traditional own resources of the EU. For 2005, the total amount of customs duties in the budget of the European Community was € 10,750 million (10.1%) plus € 1.613 million from agricultural duties and sugar levies (1,5%), in 2001 the respective figures have been € 1.665 million (13%) and 2.038 million (2,3%); see the final budget of the EU for the financial year 2005, OJ EC No. L 60/I 22, 8 March 2005.

[2] For market access after the Uruguay-Round, see the study of the WTO Secretariat, Market Access: Unfinished Business, Special Study No. 6, 2001, < http://www.wto.org/english/ res_e/ booksp_e/special_study_6_e.pdf>.

[3] Annexed to the Marrakesh Protocol are 89 schedules of concessions, which contain 23,226 pages and are spread over 31 volumes. In April 1995, 26 of the least developed countries submitted their schedules of concessions, which were summarised in three further volumes and were also annexed to the WTO Agreement.

agricultural production. While Members are obliged to grant concessions in Parts 1 and 4, they can be more selective with regard to preferential customs duties and concessions on non-tariff measures.

The rate of duty on a product set out in the schedule of concessions is the highest (maximum) duty the Member can raise. This is called a **bound tariff**. Members are free to apply a lower rate in practice (applied tariff). The listed goods are also, according to Art II:1 *lit.* b GATT 1994, exempt from all other duties and charges[4] imposed on or in connection with the importation.

304 The extent and nature of **obligations** accepted by the Members **vary considerably**. There are differences with regard to the absolute number of the bound tariff positions and their allocation among groups of products, as well as with regard to the percentage of products classified as duty-free. This last-mentioned relationship between bound duty-free products and the overall tariff positions serves as an indicator for the degree of freedom of trade of a country, which varies significantly between Members, especially in the area of industrial products.[5] There were also differences in the implementation periods – the Marrakesh Protocol of the GATT 1994 provides for the implementation of tariff reductions in five equal stages from January 1, 1995 until January 1, 1999. Some Members have prolonged these deadlines on the basis of specific provisions.

305 The schedules of concessions are the **result of negotiations** between the Members. They took place under the GATT in the trade rounds mentioned earlier (para. 15). In the WTO, negotiations on further lowering of tariffs take place in a negotiation group on market access for non-agricultural products (NAMA)[6] and in the newly launched Doha Round (paras 795 *et seq.*).

306 The **procedure** for these negotiations has **changed** several times. In the first five trade rounds after 1947, the rate of duty was negotiated **product by product**. The main exporting countries prepared a list of the desired rates (request list), which was submitted to the main importing countries. In order to negotiate specific concessions, the main exporting countries also prepared a list of (possible) concessions for the groups of goods in which the other parties had trade interests. If the

---

[4] As a result of the Understanding on the Interpretation of Article II:1 b GATT 1994, the "other duties or charges" are bound and are therefore recorded in the schedules.

[5] See WTO Secretariat, Market Access (above footnote 2) Table II.1, 8 *et seq.* For comparison: the percentage of bound duty-free tariff positions is 26.69% in the EU, 39.4% in the United States, 17.2% in Switzerland and 14% in the Czech Republic.

[6] See TN/C/1 4 February 2002 and most recently the Decision adopted by the General, Council on 1 August 2004, WT/L/579, 2 August 2004, Annex A, paras 27 *et seq.*

parties to the negotiations agreed on a duty rate for a product, the rate was incorporated in Part I of the schedule of concessions of the respective parties and, because of most-favoured-nation treatment, also applied in relation to all other contracting parties of the GATT.

307 In the negotiations of the Kennedy (1964–1967) and Tokyo Rounds (1973–1979) the strategy was altered, so that the countries now sought a **linear lowering** of tariffs for groups of goods, while excluding certain sensitive goods from this principle. Furthermore, there was the less successful attempt to negotiate on the lowering of tariffs for a whole sector, for example chemicals or steel.[7] The negotiations on customs in the Uruguay Round (1986–1994) were not conducted under a general negotiation method. The negotiations mandate provided only that the lowering of customs duties should meet the level of the Tokyo Round.[8] With its overall reduction of tariff levels of 38% the Uruguay Round eventually even surpassed the Tokyo-Round level of 34%.[9]

308 The concessions of Members can be temporarily suspended under the different exception provisions (paras 151 *et seq.*), but they can also be permanently withdrawn. Art. XXVIII GATT 1994[10] sets out a procedure based on the principles of negotiations and compensation. If a Member intends to withdraw a concession, it must start negotiations with the Members most closely concerned and has to compensate for trade disadvantages following the withdrawal of the concession by new concessions on other products.

309 Part IV of GATT 1994, which is dedicated to **trade and development**, provides for the implementation of unilateral customs advantages for developing countries, which are not subject to most-favoured-nation treatment, "for a rapid and sustained expansion of the export earnings" and with the aim of a significant increase in less-developed countries'

[7] A special success of this negotiating approach was reached at the Ministerial Conference of Singapore 1996 with the Ministerial Declaration on Trade in Information Technology Products, WT/MIN(96)/16 of 13 December 1996. This declaration, also known as the Information Technologies Agreement (ITA), provides for the full abolition of customs duties on certain information technology products. See *Stoll & Goller*, GYIL 41 (1998), 128, 132 *et seq.*

[8] See extensively on the negotiations of the Uruguay Round *Smeets*, Tariff Issues in the Uruguay-Round – Features and Remaining Issues, JWT 29 (1995) 3, 91 *et seq.*

[9] After the eight trade rounds since 1947, the average applied customs rate for industrial products is only 4.6% in the EU, 4.3% in the Untied States and 4.2% in Japan. However, these average rates depend mainly on the level of development of the economy in question. The average rate is 17.6% in Cameroon, 12.6% in Mexico and 8.2% in Hungary. (Source: WTO, Average for the years 1996–1999). For more details on the tariff negotiations, see *Hoda*, Tariff Negotiations and Renegotiations under the GATT and the WTO: Procedures and Practices, 2001.

[10] Art. XXVIII GATT 1994 has to be read in conjunction with the notes and supplementary provisions in Annex I to GATT 1994. The details of the procedure are governed by the Understanding on the Interpretation of Article XXVIII GATT 1994.

share in world trade.[11] For this purpose, industrialised countries and the European Union have introduced Generalized System of Preferences (GSP),[12] which allows developing countries to export their goods at reduced, or zero tariffs.[13] The reduced tariff rates are those contained in Part II of the schedule of concessions. Apart from the GSP, preferential customs are also granted on a regional and bilateral level, for example through associative agreements or as autonome measures.[14]

310 The **effectiveness** of this **system of preferences** is **impaired** by protection clauses, exceptive provisions for specific sensitive goods and groups of goods, especially in the agricultural and textile sectors, as well as by the withdrawal of concessions with the increasing economic success of the developing country concerned. The question of market access for developing countries has developed into one of the most crucial trade-political themes. The successful progress of negotiations for the lowering of customs duties will depend on the willingness of industrial countries to open their markets completely for goods in areas in which the developing countries are competitive.[15]

II. *Tariff Classification and Customs Valuation*

311 The levying of customs duties in practice demands a schematic classification of the goods in question and the determination of its customs value.

312 The **customs tariff** also sets out whether goods are subject to tariffs and, if so, how much that tariff should be. It is, together with the formal and material provisions, part of the customs law of a country or a customs union, and is the basis for the customs authorities to clear goods. The tariff is structured into duty rates and tariff schemes, i.e. the systematic listing of all imaginable goods (**nomenclature**). The basis for nearly all nomenclatures used worldwide is the **Harmonised**

---

[11] Art. XXXVI:2 and Art. XXXVII:1 *lit.* a and 1 *lit.* b GATT 1994.

[12] See on the treatment of developing countries in general paras 84 *et seq.* above.

[13] An example of "zero tariff" preferences is the so-called "Everything But Arms" Initiative (EBA) by the EU, which allows for least-developed countries to import all goods excluding arms and munitions into the EU without tariff payments or quantitative restrictions, Council Regulation (EC) 416/2001 of 26 February 2001, OJ EC No. L 60/1, 1 March 2001.

[14] E.g. the Partnership Agreement between the Members of the African, Caribbean and Pacific Group of States and the European Community and its Member States, signed in Cotonou on 23 June 2000, OJ EC No. L 317/3, 15 December 2000.

[15] See *Inama*, Market Access for LDCs, JWT 36 (2002) 1, 85 *et seq.*; compare – as an example – the Panel report in *European Communities – Export Subsidies on Sugar*, WT/DS265/R,WT/DS266/R, WT/DS283/R, 15 October 2004, paras 7.108 *et seq.*

System (HS) administered by the World Customs Organization (WCO).[16] The HS, which is based on an international treaty,[17] is a logical structure consisting of a six-digit code with annotations, which comprises 21 chapters with 96 sections and 1.200 headings, which covers over 5,000 groups of goods. The HS can be extended by the contracting parties to accommodate further digits. This flexibility is necessary, because the nomenclature is not only used for the imposition of customs duties but also for the purposes of compiling statistics, taxation, trade limitations and monitoring.

313 In the European Community, which is a Customs Union according to Art. 25 *et seq.* ECT, customs law is structured into the **customs code** and the **provisions for implementation** passed at Community and national levels.[18] One of the Community provisions for implementation contains the tariff scheme for the Community, the so-called **Combined Nomenclature** (CN).[19] The CN is part of the **Common Customs Tariff**, which contains the single tariff rates, preferential measures and other tariff measures of the Community.[20]

314 The Combined Nomenclature covers the nomenclature of the HS and further common sub-headings, as well as introductory provisions and additional annotations to the sections, chapters and footnotes, which refer to the sub-heading of the CN. These extensions are necessary so that measures other than customs rates can be taken into consideration by import clearance into the Common Market. These measures include import bans and restrictions, quotas and requirements for licences. Technically, they are administered by an expansion of the six-digit code by two further digits. Besides the CN, the European Commission has established the **Integrated Tariff of the European Community**

[16] The Harmonized Commodity Description and Coding System is used by more than 190 countries and economies and covers over 98% of the merchandise in international trade, see World Customs Organization, at: <http://www.wcoomd.org/ie/En/en.html>.

[17] The International Agreement on Harmonized Commodity Description and Coding of goods of 14 June 1993, OJ EC No. L 198/1, 20 July 1987. Art. 16 of this Agreement provides for a special procedure for changes, after which the Agreement can be adjusted to the development of the markets. The last amendment will enter into force on 1 January 2007, see G/MA/W/67, 2 February 2005.

[18] Council Regulation (EEC) No. 2913/92 for the determination of the Community Customs Code, OJ EC No. L 302/1, 19 October 1992.

[19] Commission Regulation No. 2454/93 of 2 July 1996, laying down provisions for the implementation of the Council Regulation (EEC) No. 2913/92 establishing the Community Customs Code, OJ EC No. L 253, 11 October 1993, 1, last amended by Regulation (EC) No 648/2005 of 13 April 2005, OJ EC No. L 117/13, 4 May 2004.

[20] Council Regulation No. 2658/87 of 23 July 1987 on the tariff and statistical nomenclature as well as the Common Customs Tariff, OJ EC No. L 256, 7 September 1987, 1, Appendix 1, last amended by Council Regulation (EC) No 493/2005 of 16 March 2005, OJ EC No. L 82/1, 31 March 2005.

(**TARIC**),[21] which is based on the Combined Nomenclature, and adds a ninth and tenth digit to the code number. The further sub-headings allow for the encoded registration of, for example, anti-dumping and countervailing measures (paras 463 *et seq.* and 492 *et seq.*), and customs duties and quotas.

315 *Example:*

Title HS	08	edible fruits, peel of citrus fruits and melons
Heading HS	0805	citrus fruits, fresh or dried
Sub heading HS	0805 30	lemons (citrus limon, citrus limonum) and limes (citrus aurantifolia)
Sub heading CN	0805 30 10	lemons (citrus limon, citrus limonum)
Sub heading TARIC	0805 30 10 05	fresh
Sub heading TARIC	0805 30 10 99	other

316 Customs duties can be imposed on different bases, namely as specific duties, *ad valorem* duty or mixed duties. For specific duties, the calculation is based on weight, volume, length, or quantity. For an ***ad valorem*** **duty**, the customs duty is a percentage of the value of the good. *Ad valorem* duties have the advantage that they are transparent, that they are charged on cheap and expensive goods in the same way and adjust to the price developments in the customs area concerned. Therefore, the *ad valorem* duty became the standard instrument in tariff systems. However, its application requires the determination of the underlying **customs value**.

317 The GATT in its **Art. VII** contains a provision which sets out some basic principles for assessment of the customs value. According to this provision the value for tariff purposes shall be calculated on the basis of the **actual value** of the imported merchandise or of like merchandise. Explicitly excluded as calculation basis are the value of comparable merchandise with origin in the importing country or the use of arbitrary or fictitious values (Art. VII:2 *lit.* a GATT 1994).

318 Based on principles and definitions as contained in the 1950 **Brussels Valuation Convention**,[22] the "actual value" was fixed as the normal

[21] The so-called Integrated Tariff of the European Community (Tarif Intégré de la Communauté, TARIC), see *Alexander*, in: *Witte* (Ed.), Zollkodex Art. 20, para. 10; TARIC available at: <http://europa.eu.int/comm/taxation_customs/dds/en/tarhome.htm>. An 11th digit serves for the encoding of national measures, such as national sales tax rates.

[22] The definitions, which are recognised as customs value norms, are based on the Brussels Valuation Convention of 15 December 1950, UNTS 157, 129, in force since 4 November

competitive price, i.e. the price the merchandise would achieve in an open market of independent vendors and consumers. The fixing of this "competitive price" as a fictitious value for all imaginable goods has proved itself to be hardly feasable. In addition, Canada and the United States used their own rules for valuation.

319 The problem of lacking unity was resolved by the **GATT "Customs Valuation Code"**, negotiated during the Tokyo Round in 1979, which was replaced after the end of the Uruguay Round by the almost identical **Agreement on the Implementation of Article VII GATT 1994**. The Agreement applies to the valuation of imported products for the purpose of the imposition of *ad valorem* duties and takes the **transactional value** as a basis for the determination of the value. The basis for calculation of the duty is therefore the actual price paid for the product being assessed for duty.[23] Furthermore, there are five further obligatory methods for calculation in cases in which the transactional value method is not sufficient. These six methods stand in a hierarchy to each other and have to be used step by step until the customs value of a product can be determined.[24]

III. *Rules of Origin*

320 Rules of origin determine the origin of goods. Clarification of origin is necessary if the origin **is relevant for the applicable rule for import**. This is the case for unilateral customs preferences, which apply only to specific nations and therefore exclude most-favoured-nation treatment (**preferential rules of origin**). Also, the origin of a product is important for the imposition of trade measures such as anti-dumping and countervailing measures, for the monitoring of quantitative restrictions and origin marks and labels (**non-preferential origin rules**). Furthermore, the rules of origin have statistical and public procurement functions.

321 The **determination of the country of origin** of a product is particularly difficult if products are processed, assembled, repackaged or transported on their way from the producer to the market of the importing country.

1952, and were negotiated under the umbrella of the Council for Cooperation in the field of customs. The organisation, also known as the Brussels Customs Council, changed its name to World Customs Organisation (WCO) after the founding of the WTO.

[23] Art. 1 and 8 of the Agreement.

[24] The European Community has implemented the Agreement in Art. 28 to 36 of the Community Customs Code (see note 18 above).

322 The necessity for clear and transparent rules of origin has never been in dispute. Nevertheless, there are still **no universal rules** in this area. The GATT 1947 did not manage to achieve more than a definition and recommendations.[25] Also the two so-called **"Kyoto Conventions"** of 1973 and 1977, negotiated under the umbrella of the Brussels Customs Council, contain only recommendations for the harmonization of rules of origin.[26] Detailed rules can be found in the framework of regional preferential Agreements, bilateral free trade Agreements and, finally, in form of autonomous origin rules.[27]

323 Basically, the rules of origin evince **four principles**: First, a product is considered to be of the origin of the country in which it is entirely produced. However, it is often difficult to determine the extent of the processing which may affect the origin. An origin change can – secondly – be presumed, if the processing or handling leads to another customs classification (tariff jump). It is also possible – thirdly – to determine the origin by the extent of value enhancement or – fourthly – to explicitly define specific processes of handling as causative for the determination of origin.

324 The **Agreement on Rules of Origin**, negotiated during the Uruguay Round and contained in Annex 1A to the WTO Agreement, has the aim of harmonizing the non-preferential rules of origin. It refers to rules of origin which apply for most-favoured-nation treatment, the imposition of anti-dumping and countervailing duties, the use of protective measures, requirements for labelling, discriminatory quantitative restrictions and quotas, and for trade statistics and the public procurement function. However, the Members still have a certain degree of discretion in the concrete determination of criteria that confer origin.[28] A **three-year work programme**, the so-called Harmonization Work Programme (HWP), was set out with the aim of drafting a proposal for harmonized rules of origin. The granting of customs preferences as an application of the rules of origin is not mentioned in the Agreement. However, it also applies to preferential rules of origin according to a common statement in Appendix II. Admittedly, rules of origin in preferential tariff regimes are not covered by the harmonization programme.

---

[25] BISD 2S/56, 5S/54 and 28S/12 Suppl. 18, see also the second supplementary note to Art. VIII in Annex I of the GATT 1994.

[26] International Agreement on Simplification and Harmonisation of Customs Procedure of 18 May 1973, OJ EC No. L 100/2, 21 April 1975, and Supplements, OJ EC No. L 166/1, 4 July 1977.

[27] For the autonomous rules of origin of the European Community, see Art. 22 to 27 of the Community Customs Code (see note 18 above) and Art. 35 to 140 of the Regulation (EEC) No. 2454/93 laying down provisions for the implementation of Community Customs Code.

[28] Compare *United States – Rules of Origin for Textiles and Apparel Products*, WT/DS243/R, 21 July 2003, paras 6.23 *et seq.*

325 To date, the HWP has not been **successfully concluded**. After an extension of the three-year period provided for in Art. 9.2 (c) of the Agreement by a further year and a half until the end of 1999, in total 486 points of positions, relating to specific products, were still left open. On the basis of a decision by the General Council, the negotiation mandate was repeatedly extended so that, by the new deadline of July 2005, the remaining 94 core policy issues shall be completed. Since this decision, the granting of a new mandate has been discussed. This development of the HWP is due to the hesitancy of the Members to agree on harmonized rules of origin in the sensitive sectors of agriculture and textiles. Instead, most sections of the nomenclature are negotiated product position by product position.[29]

326 The WTO is fundamentally linked to the **World Customs Organization** (para. 312) in the areas of customs classification and valuation as well as of rules of origin. According to Art 4.2 of the Agreement on Rules of Origin, a technical committee was established "under the auspices of the Customs Co-operation Council", which shall carry out the technical work and which shall ensure conformity with the HS.[30]

IV. *Preshipment Inspection*

327 The customs classification and valuation rules make demands on national administrations which – in their practical application – have not yet been fulfilled by all WTO Members. The lack of efficiency in customs administrations offers great potential for abuse, since products can be classified in more advantageous tariff classifications or the value for customs purposes is knowingly underestimated, without those fraudulent actions being discovered and sanctioned. A number of Members therefore employ the so-called preshipment inspection (PSI). This includes **inspection and control of products in the exporting country**, before they are transported to the importing country. Such inspection verifies (i) whether the goods meet the quantitative and qualitative requirements of the contract for sale as well as the requirements of the importing country, and (ii) whether the agreed price really corresponds

[29] The report by the Chairman of the Committee on Rules of Origin to the General Council, G/RO/52, 15 July 2002, is instructive for an overview of the negotiations on the HWP.

[30] After the foundation of the WTO, the Brussels Customs Council changed its name (see footnote 22). See also Art. 18 *et seq.* of the Agreement on Implementation of Article VII GATT 1994, which provides for the establishment of a technical committee, which also works under the auspices of the World Customs Organization.

to the actual value of the goods.[31] 39 Members from Asia, Africa and Latin America have implemented preshipment inspections, carried out by private firms specialized in this area.[32]

328 This preshipment inspection can considerably hinder international trade: it causes additional costs and delays transport. It can be misused for the purpose of exposing business secrets and has considerable potential for the arbitrary use of control methods and procedures. With the **Agreement on Preshipment Inspection** (PSI), an interntional framework of rights and duties has been agreed upon, which reduces the trade-limiting effects of preshipment inspection. The Agreement obliges those who use the preshipment inspection, as well as the exporting members, to not discriminate in the context of the control (Art. 2.1 and 3.1 PSI). Furthermore, it contains provisions for the execution of the procedure and formulates requirements in relation to transparency and the protection of confidential information.

329 The Agreement also lays down an **independent review procedure** (Art. 4) to deal with disputes, which deserves particular mention. Following an unsuccessful complaint (Art. 2.21 PSI), an independent entity (IE) deals with the dispute. The procedure provides for the establishment of a three-person panel, which must reach a decision within eight working days from the filing of the application. The peculiarities of this procedure are that, first, an independent entity constituted jointly by an organization representing preshipment inspection entities and an organization representing exporters is established[33] and, secondly, the parties are private persons: the controlling company, and the exporter.[34] A working group has submitted two reports, in which numerous proposals for the further development of the Agreement in this respect have been made.[35]

---

[31] In this case, inspections aim at controlling the covert out-flow of capital by the payment of excessive bills.

[32] The last investigation carried out by the WTO Secretariat was that of 30 July 2004, see G/VAL/W/63/Rev.5, 8 October 2004, with an overview of the WTO Members using preshipment inspection regimes and the employed Inspection Agencies.

[33] Following the decision of the General Council of 13 December 1995, this task is carried out by the International Chamber of Commerce (ICC), and the International Federation of Inspection Agencies (IFIA), WT/L/125/Rev.1.

[34] For settlement of disputes under the PSI, see also para. 211.

[35] G/L/214, 2 December 1997 and G/L/300, 18 March 1999.

CHAPTER FIVE

NON-TARIFF BARRIERS TO TRADE

Robert E. Baldwin, Nontariff Distortions of International Trade, 1970; *Hans A. Ohlinger*, Die Relevanz nicht-tarifärer Handelshemmnisse im internationalen Handel und ihre Wirkungen auf die Integration der Entwicklungsländer in der Weltwirtschaft, 1986; *OECD*, Indicators of Tariff and Non-tariff Trade Distortions, 1996; *Christian Tietje*, Normative Grundstrukturen der Behandlung nichttarifärer Handelshemmnisse in der WTO/GATT-Rechtsordnung, 1998; *Neela Mukherjee*, Non-tariff barriers and trade in services, World competition 21 (1998) 5, 79–91; *Bijit Bora & Aki Kuwahara & Sam Laird*, Quantification of non-tariff measures, 2002.

330 Tariffs and their reduction have played a significant role in the world trade order and its development because of their historical significance, as the rules described above have shown. There are other increasingly noticeable state measures which also limit trade. Because of their diversity, they are negatively classified as **non-tariff barriers to trade (NTB)**. These NTBs include quotas, which have the same aim as customs duties, which is to reduce imports through **quantitative restrictions** (paras 333 *et seq.*). As a result of the debatable economic effects, the lack of transparency, and in the interests of a unified body of rules for the liberalization of trade, the world trade order has laid out a strict **principle of tariffication** (para. 334), whereby all forms of quantitative restrictions are banned, that is to say, they are reconverted into tariffs. This principle is set out in GATT 1994 Art. XI. However, there are some exceptions to this. These clear rules of the GATT 1947 have barely become effective with respect to textile and agricultural products. In both areas members have reached special agreements, which set out limits on quantities. Following the WTO Agreements on both agriculture and textiles and clothing, these areas will gradually become governed by the general rules.

331 In addition to import restrictions on quantity, Art. XI GATT 1994 also includes bans and conditions concerning the composition of goods, the form of their sale and their origin, all in relation to import. There is also a very different category of non-tariff barriers to trade, namely **technical barriers to trade** (paras 381 *et seq.*). These, especially due to the increasing erosion of tariffs as the classical forms of protectionism, play an important role, because they question the achievement of the liberalization that is being striven for, and instead set out a new, more covert form of protection of goods produced in the domestic market.

332 The problems linked to these measures are fundamentally different from the quantitative restrictions discussed previously. In this case, it is not just about measures at the borders, which directly influence imports, but also rules which are concerned with the sale and marketing of goods on the domestic market. Furthermore, the clear rules of Art. XI GATT 1994 here apply only with significant restrictions. Rules which apply only to the internal market do not come within the scope of Art. XI, and must be judged in accordance with Art. III GATT 1994. In addition, the WTO legal system recognises the wide-ranging legitimate motives and interests of the Members in their laws, in relation to the exception rules of Art. XX GATT 1994. The critical tension between market-access interests and non-discrimination on the one had, and legitimate national interests in law on the other, is further clarified and expanded on in two special Agreements, the Agreement on Technical Barriers to Trade (TBT) and the Agreement on Sanitary and Phytosanitary Measures (SPS).

I. *The Prohibition of Quantitative Restrictions*

Frieder Roessler, Selective Balance-of-Payments Adjustment Measures Affecting Trade, JWT 9 (1975) 6, 622–653; *Richard Blackhurst*, The Economic Effects of Different Types of Trade Measures and Their Impact on Consumers, OECD, 1986; *Jan Tumlir*, GATT Rules and Community Law, in: Meinhard Hilf/Francis G. Jacobs/Ernst-Ulrich Petersmann (Eds), The European Community and GATT, 1986, 1–22; *Margaret Garritsen DeVries*, Balance of payments adjustment, 1945 to 1986: the IMF experience, (IMF-Studie) 1987; *Ernst-Ulrich Petersmann*, Constitutional Functions and Constitutional Problems of International Economic Law, 1991 *Frieder Roessler*, The Constitutional Function of the Multilateral Trade Order, in: Meinhard Hilf/Ernst-Ulrich Petersmann (Eds), National Constitutions and International Economic Law, 1993, 53–62; *Christian Koenig*, Die öffentlich-rechtliche Verteilungslenkung: Grund und Grenzen einer Deregulierung am Beispiel der Vergabe von Konzessionen, Kontingenten und Genehmigungen zur unternehmerischen Nutzung öffentlich verwalteter Güter, 1994; *Ernst-Ulrich Petersmann*, The Transformation of the World Trading System through the 1994 Agreement Establishing the World Trade Organization, EJIL 6 (1995) 2, 161–221; *Hans H. Glismann*, Wirtschaftliche Auswirkungen mengenmäßiger Importbeschränkungen, 1996; *Peter-Tobias Stoll*, Freihandel und Verfassung, ZaöRV 57 (1997) 1, 83–146; *Jai S. Mah*, Reflections on the balance of payments provisions in the WTO, World competition 21 (1998) 5, 139–148; *Chantal Thomas*, Balance-of-Payments Crisis in the Developing World: Balancing Trade, Finance and Development in the New Economic Order, American University International Law Review 15 (2000) 6, 1249–1277; *Robert Rowthorn*, De-industrialization and the balance of payments in advanced economies, 2004.

1. *General*

333 Tariffs and quotas (in other words: quantitative restrictions) serve, in their economic perspective, to limit the import of specific goods, and to protect domestic industries from competition. Both lead to economic costs, and to an increase in the price of imported goods: in the case of quotas due to higher costs where there is limited supply, in case of tariffs due to the increased import price. At any rate, viewed relatively, **quotas clearly cause higher overall social costs**. Quotas work differently from tariffs and lead to a decoupling of demands from the world market and annul the customs mechanisms of the free market. They also require administrative distribution, which causes expenditure and uncertainty. A further fundamental difference between import tariffs and quantitative restrictions is that, with tariffs, the artificial increase in price of the product is collected by the imposing state itself for the benefit of the public purse, while in the case of quantitative restrictions exporters or the particular exporting country benefit instead. From the point of view of foreign economic policy, quantitative restrictions are, however, often preferred, since their effects are less visible and, according to the constitutional framework of many states, such restrictions are much easier to introduce and, in some cases, can even be implemented without parliamentary control.[1]

334 The GATT 1994 **prohibits quantitative restrictions**, and instead expresses a preference for tariffs. While the GATT allows tariffs and attempts to reduce them by reciprocal commitments (Art. XXVIII*bis* GATT 1994), "no prohibitions or restrictions other than duties, taxes or other charges, whether made effective through quotas, import or export licences or other measures shall be instituted or maintained by any contracting parties" (Art. XI:1 GATT 1994). In the sense of a tariffication of trade barriers, this preference for tariffs has always found a policy-led political structure for further liberalization of trade.[2] The GATT 1994 thus prescribes a kind of proportionality in holding its Members to tariffs as a comparatively efficient means of protection. In this sense, the "constitutional" element of the strengthening of national foreign trade policy is often discussed.[3] The individual participant in

[1] See *Blackhurst*, The Economic Effects of Different Types of Trade Measures and Their Impact on Consumers, OECD 1986; *Tumlir*, GATT rules, 4; *Roessler*, The Constitutional Function of the Multilateral Trade Order, in: Hilf/Petersmann, National Constitutions and International Economic Law, 1993, 53 (54 ff.); for more in depth detail *Stoll*, Freihandel und Verfassung, ZaöRV 57 (1997) 1, 83, 101 *et seq.*

[2] The attempt made by the Uruguay Round to make critical areas of world trade subject to stronger control often utilizes the instrument of tariffication of non-tariff measures: see *Stoll*, Freihandel und Verfassung, 57 ZaöRV (1997) 1, 83, 121 *et seq.*

[3] *Petersmann*, Constitutional Functions, 230: "The GATT Principle of the Use of Uniform

the market place profits from the fact that the direct interference of the national state authority in the quantity of goods imported or the administrative distribution of quotas is limited, while the additional costs of indirect control are borne through tariffs. The **requirement of tariffication** thus remains the basis of transparency, accountability and negotiability of trade restrictions in the international trade order.

2. *Exceptions for Balance of Payments Purposes*

335 A **significant exception** to these rules is contained in **Art. XII GATT 1994**, which allows for restrictions of the quantity or value of imports to protect a Member's external financial position and balance of payments.[4]

336 In the **balance of payments** of a state, every economic transaction between nationals and foreigners in a particular period is summarized according to value. This balance of payments can be subdivided in the following: the current account, including the exports and imports of merchandise and investment income; the capital account measuring foreign investment; and the official reserve account including foreign exchanges, gold, special drawing rights and other assets. The current account gives an overview of a country's payments linked to economic transactions. In general, exports are linked to inward payments, and imports are linked to outward payments. Usually, imports are paid for in foreign currency, i.e. assets and claims in the currency of the exporting party. Difficulties with balance of payments occur when a national economy has higher expenditure on imports than it can earn by the production of domestic goods. Deficits up to a certain level can be covered by the gold and foreign currency supplies of the national central bank and its reserve credit balance at International financial institutions such as the International Monetary Fund, since it uses these reserves to supply money to the national business banks. These exchange stabilization reserves are, however, limited, so that the stabilization of these balances of payments must ultimately be funded from other sources. At present, difficulties with the balance of payments can be remedied either by a devaluation of the national currency, i.e. a reduction in value in relation to the foreign currency, or by a reduction in imports. If imports are reduced, less foreign currency is needed in the domestic economy and the deficit is reduced. As long as the fixed exchange rates of the Bretton-Woods System remained in place, nations could not unilater-

---

and Proportionate Policy Instruments." Fundamentally: *Tumlir*, International Economic Order and Democratic Constitutionalism, ORDO 34 (1983), 71, 80: "The international economic order can be seen as the second line of national constitutional entrenchment [. . .]".

[4] See also Art XVIII:2 GATT 1994, which contains a comparable rule for developing countries. For a comparison of both regulations, see GATT, Analytical Index, 377.

ally adopt the instrument of devaluation. As a consequence, the GATT had to find a manageable solution to this problem. A system of exceptions is thus found in Art. XII to XV GATT 1994.

337 According to **Art XII:2 lit a GATT 1994**, the institution, maintenance or intensification of import restrictions must be necessary in order "to forestall the imminent threat of, or to stop, a serious decline in its monetary reserves". If financial conditions improve, the restrictions must be progressively relaxed and finally eliminated (Art XII:3 *lit.* d s.2 GATT 1994). At the same time, Members are not obliged to change their economic policies for the purpose of removing limitations (Art XII:3 *lit.* d s.2 GATT 1994). This sovereignty-preserving provision is far from self-evident from an economic point of view, as a balance of payments deficit can only be eradicated through changes to economic policy over a long period.[5]

338 According to the **Declaration on Trade Measures Taken for Balance-of-Payments Purposes,**[6] which is part of the Tokyo Round, these rules may be used for the protection of the balance of payments relating to all trade policy measures. In addition, further prerequisites were formulated in this declaration: a limiting measure must be publicized, the measure with the least detrimental effect must be applied, it is inadmissible to use more than one measure in relation to the same product and, finally, a time limit for the removal of limitation measures must be set.

339 The **Understanding on the Balance-of-Payments Provisions of the GATT 1994**[7] clarifies and expands on these exception clauses and attempts to eliminate uncertainties. It contains rules relating to the form and implementation of restricting measures, and lays down a procedure for notification, documentation and consultation.

340 The **substantive rules** of the Understanding demonstrate the preference of the GATT for price-based measures. It expressly refers to the principles of the 1979 Declaration, and confirms that measures such as import surcharges are admissible on the basis of protection of the balance of payments (Art. 2). Furthermore, quantitative restrictions may

---

[5] See *India – Quantitative Restrictions*, WT/DS90/AB/R, 23 May 1999. This Appellate Body decision centred around Art. XVIII:11 GATT 1994, the equivalent regulation to Art. XII:3 *lit.* d for developing countries. The Appellate Body confirmed the decision of the Panel with the explanation that macro-economic measures for the removal of deficit of balance of payments must be entirely independent of a definite development policy (para. 126). This statement could be interpreted as pointing towards a narrow interpretation of the exception clause.

[6] BISD 26S/205. The Declaration remains applicable even after entry into force of the Understanding on Balance-of-Payments Provisions.

[7] LT/UR/A-1A/1/GATT/U/3, 15 April 1994.

be used only to rectify a critical balance of payments situation, thus triggering a duty of justification (Art. 3). The measures adopted may not exceed what is necessary, while the selection of the goods concerned must be justified and publicized (Art. 4). In summary, measures for the protection of the balance of payments must be limited to a specific period of time, price-based, proportionate and transparently applied.

341 **Procedurally**, consultations between Members should guarantee the transparent drafting and utilization of these measures, while the specifics are guided by a Decision of 28 April 1970.[8] Notification to the Council for Trade in Goods of the measures at least 30 days after their enactment is a fundamental principle of the consultation process. A general overview of all legislative and administrative measures must be notified annually to the Secretariat. At the request of a Member, the **Committee on Balance of Payment Restrictions** may review the notification (Art. 5 *et seq.* Understanding, Art. IV:7 WTO Agreement). To this extent, the Member concerned is obliged to produce documentation which gives a concrete overview of the restrictions, the adopted measures and the time limits for their abolition (Art. 11).

342 The regulations of the Understanding fall within the scope of Art. XXII and XXIII GATT 1994 as well as within the rules of the **Dispute Settlement Understanding**.

343 If quantitative restrictions are adopted, Members are obliged to use these measures in a **non-discriminatory** way (Art. XIII GATT 1994). The individual quotas must be divided among the importing states in accordance with the trade shares of the individual importers (Art XIII:2 GATT 1994). If the implementation of quotas is not possible the restrictions can also be implemented through the grant of import licences or permits in accordance with Art. XIII:2 lit b GATT 1994. Art. XIII:3 GATT 1994 lays down regulations for these situations regarding the information policies of members.[9]

344 The topic of balance of payments also comes under the responsibility of the **International Monetary Fund** (IMF). Art. XV GATT 1994 adjusts to this fact by obliging members to cooperate with the IMF and to pursue a coordinated overall policy.

---

[8] Procedures for Consultation on Balance of Payment Restrictions, BISD 18S/48–53.

[9] There are exceptions to the rules of non-discrimination in Art XV GATT 1994, which are drafted in accordance with Art. VIII and XIV of the Articles of Agreement of the International Monetary Fund. These provisions of the IMF have since become invalid following the introduction of floating exchange rates, see *Senti*, WTO, para. 832.

3. *Import Licenses*

345 Import licences are grants through an administrative procedure, which must be in place before the import of goods into the customs area of a Member takes place. **Licensing procedures** also serve as a sensible way in which to supervise the exports of goods, such as military goods. 90 Members have adopted respective laws, regulations and administrative procedures,[10] which play an important role in trade relating to agriculture as well as textiles and clothing. As a result, the dispute over the regulation of the internal banana market in the EU significantly dealt with issues relating to national licensing procedures.[11]

346 According to **Art. VIII:1 *lit.* c GATT 1994**, the formalities involved in the import and export of goods should be kept to a minimum and should be constructed as simply as possible. The number of accompanying documents required should be reduced and simplified.[12] Similarly, according to **Art. X GATT 1994**, Members are obliged to publish their legal and administrative principles, court and administrative decisions relating to provisions, limitations and bans relating to imports and exports. These duties are especially important in relation to import licences, as they allow for quantitative restrictions to be implemented.

347 These duties are specified in the **Agreement on Import Licensing Procedures**.[13] The procedures must be implemented in a transparent and non-discriminatory manner in order to avoid restrictions on trade. The Agreement differentiates between automatic (Art. 2) and non-automatic (Art. 3) import licensing. There are some general rules which apply to both categories: the relevant procedural and administrative rules must be neutral in application and administered in a fair and equitable manner, all relevant procedural rules and instructions must be notified within a specific time frame, and forms and procedures must be as simple as possible (Art. 1.3 *et seq.*). Furthermore, there are specific requirements for each category relating to their area of use and their period of use. The principles of transparency and non-discrimination are particularly important for the non-automatic import licensing procedure.

---

[10] Report of the Committee on Import Licensing to the Council for Trade in Goods (2004), G/L/715, 23 November 2004, para. 5.

[11] *European Communities – Regime for the Importation, Sale and Distribution of Bananas*, WT/DS27/AB/R 9 September 1997. *Jackson/Grane*, JIEL 4 (2001) 3, 581 *et seq.* gives an overview of the procedures involved in the banana conflict. Certain regulations of the Agreement were also part of the Panel decision in *India – Quantitative restrictions*, WT/DS90/AB/R (see above footnote 5).

[12] See also the obligation to publish trade regulations in Art. X GATT 1994.

[13] LT/UR/A-1A/5, 15 April 1994. The Agreement is based on the Import Licensing Code of the Tokyo Round.

348 A **Committee on Import Licensing** has been established in accordance with Art. 4, and is included in the institutional structure of the Council for Trade in Goods. The Committee is responsible for receiving notifications of the relevant regulations on import licences and every amendment thereof (Art. 1.4 *lit.* a, Art. 8.2 *lit.* b). The Members, under certain conditions, have the opportunity to notify any un-notified or amended regulations of other members, in accordance with Art. 5.5, so-called "reverse-notification". The Agreement on Import Licensing Procedures is within the scope of the Dispute Settlement Understanding (Art. 6).

II. *The Principle of Tariffication – Trade in Agricultural Products and in Textiles and Clothing*

349 The GATT has, for several decades, failed to claim validity in two important economic sectors: trade in agricultural products, and trade in textiles and clothing. In the negotiation of the Uruguay Round, an attempt was made to correct these faults. With the **Agreement on Agriculture (AoA)** and the **Agreement on Textiles and Clothing (ATC)** a legal framework was established which allowed for the step by step integration of the goods concerned into the general trade rules of the GATT.

1. *Trade in Agricultural Products and the Agreement on Agriculture*

Jai S. Mah, Reflections on the Special Safeguard Provision in the Agreement of Agriculture of the WTO, JWT 33 (1999) 5, 197–204; *Kenneth J. Thomson*, The CAP and the WTO after the Uruguay Round Agreement on Agriculture, European foreign affairs review 1 (1996) 2, 169–183; *Tashi Kaul*, The Elimination Of Export Subsidies And The Future Of Net-Food Importing Countries In The WTO, Fordham Journal of International Law, 24 (2000) 1/2, 383–409; *Silke Trumm*, Agrarhandel und Weltwirtschaft, 2001; *Kevin C. Kennedy*, Reforming Farm Trade in the Next Round of WTO Multilateral Trade Negotiations, JWT 35 (2001) 6, 1061–1079; *Joseph A. McMahon*, (ed.), Trade & Agriculture (2001); *James Rude*, Under the Green Box. The WTO and Farm Subsidies, JWT 35 (2001) 5, 1015–1033; *Fabian Delcros*, Le statut juridique de l'agriculture à l'OMC, Revue du Droit de l'Union Européenne 2001, 688–730 = JWT 36 (2002) 2, 353–403; *Melaku Geboye Desta*, The law of international trade in agricultural products, 2002; *Carmen G. Gonzalez*, Institutionalizing inequality: the WTO Agreement on Agriculture, food security, and developing countries, Columbia journal of environmental law 27 (2002) 2, 433–490; *Michael N. Cardwell* (ed.), Agriculture and international trade, 2003; *Alberto Valdés*, Special safeguards for developing country agriculture, World Trade Review, 2 (2003) 1, 5–31; *Kym Anderson* (ed.), The WTO and agriculture, 2004; *Clete D. Johnson*, A barren harvest for the developing world?, Georgia Journal of International & Comparative Law 32 (2004) 2, 437–472; *Ralf Peters*, Conference on Trade and Development: Shifting sands – searching for a compromise in the WTO negotiations on agriculture, 2004; *Merlinda D. Ingco* (ed.), Agriculture and the WTO, 2004.

a. *Development and Background*

350 Although agricultural products fall within the scope of the general rules of the GATT, exceptional measures and individual decisions have led to the formation of a special set of rules, counteracting the basic principles of the GATT, since the 1950s. On the basis of the exemption clause of Art. XI:2 *lit.* c GATT 1947, **quantitative restrictions on imports** in both the agricultural and fish sectors were widely used. As part of the use of the exception in accordance with Art. XVI:3 GATT 1947, the export of agricultural products was **continually subsidized**. Furthermore, many forms of **support for domestic production** were utilized which were difficult for the GATT to supervise, and which were therefore tolerated. Above all was the Common Agricultural Policy (CAP) of the EU, which was developed from the origins of the European integration in 1957. Finally, following the United States' defeat in a conflict with the Netherlands over milk production, an unlimited waiver was in place since 1955, allowing decisions to be made irrespective of the obligations under Art. II and XI of the GATT 1947.[14]

351 These protectionist policies, based on arguments of security of supply, stability of structure and multi-functionality (see para. 362), are linked to high social costs. The degree of protection of national agriculture can be measured in relation to the so-called **Producer Support Estimate (PSE)**. According to this, the estimated annual payments from consumers and taxpayers to agricultural producers between 2002 and 2004 in the EU amounted to 34%, in Canada and the United States to 20%, in Japan to 60% and in Norway and Switzerland to 70%, with an OECD average of 30%.[15]

352 Equally, these protectionist policies are accompanied by **strong restrictions on world trade**. Even today, national markets for agricultural products are protected even more strongly against imports than the markets for industrial goods: the average applied tariff rate in 2000 was 22.9% in Canada, 17.3% in the EU, 18.2% in Japan, and 11.0% in the United States.[16] At the same time, agricultural producers receive high levels of aid. These support measures for the Members of the Quad Group (the EU, Japan, Canada and the United States), amounted to 6.0 billion US$ for Canada, 35.6 billion US$ for the United States, 47.8 billion US$ for Japan and 118 billion US$ for the EU(15) in 2003.[17] On the other hand, agricultural trade, despite being of decreasing

[14] BISD 3S/32 *et seq.* Regarding the dispute between the United States and the Netherlands, *Dairy Products from the Netherlands*, BISD, vol. II (1952), 116.

[15] OECD: Agricultural Policies in OECD Countries: Monitoring and Evaluation, 2005.

[16] WTO Annual Report 2001, 30, note the correction of the statistical data as mentioned in the report.

[17] OECD, (see above footnote 15), Table 1.3, Producer Support Estimate by Country.

importance in world trade, is significant. In 2003, agricultural trade was valued at 674 billion US$, which was equivalent to 9,2% of world trade.[18]

353 In the Uruguay Round, the so-called Cairns Group,[19] the classical agricultural exporters, as well as many developing countries which rely on the proceeds of agricultural export, succeeded in having this sector included in the WTO rules. The **Agreement on Agriculture (AoA)**,[20] which was established despite much controversy, strives for the creation of a **fairer and more market-oriented** agricultural system with the long term aim of the gradual reduction of support and protectionist measures.[21] The Agreement includes special provisions for trade in agricultural products, which take precedence over those of other Agreements, in conjunction with Annex 1A of the WTO Agreement (Art. 21.1 AoA). The Agreement is based on three principles: market access, domestic support and export subsidies. Furthermore, it includes numerous special rules for developing countries.

b. *Market Access – Tariffication*

354 The central element of the concept summarized under market access is **tariffication**. Members have a duty to transform all non-tariff-based measures in relation to the import of agricultural products into tariffs (Art. 4 AoA). In the future, non-tariff-based measures may be neither maintained nor newly introduced (Art. 4.2 AoA).[22] At the same time, a tariff reduction of an average of 36% for industrial states over 6 years, and of an average of 24% for developing countries over 10 years has been agreed upon. Irrespective of the implementation of this average reduction obligation, individual tariffs are to be reduced by 10 and 15%, respectively for all goods, including sensible agricultural goods, within the given time limit. These obligations are contained in the schedules of concessions, which have been drawn up to include a tariff scheme for all classes of goods (see para. 303).

355 The concept of market access is supplemented by the idea of **minimum import quantities**, that is to say, a specific amount of each type of

---

[18] See the statistical results of the WTO International Trade Statistics 2004, 103, 104.

[19] 15 traditional agricultural exporters have come together to form the Cairns Group: Argentina, Australia, Brazil, Canada, Chile, Columbia, The Fijian Islands, Indonesia, Malaysia, New Zealand, Paraguay, the Philippines, South Africa, Thailand and Uruguay.

[20] LT/UR/A-1A/2, 15 April 1994.

[21] The second recital of the preamble to the Agreement on Agriculture adopted the formulation of negotiations mandate of the Uruguay Round, see also the formulation in Art. 20 AoA.

[22] Expressly, quantitative import restrictions, variable import levies, minimum import prices, discretionary import licensing, non-tariff measures maintained by state-trading enterprises, voluntary export restraints, and similar border measures other than ordinary customs duties are mentioned in Art 4.2 footnote 1 AoA. Exceptions to this principle of tariffication exist for grains, rice, fruit and vegetables.

agricultural product that minimally is to be imported into every WTO Member. The Agreement guarantees from 1 January 1995 the continuation of the minimum import quantities of the reference period from 1986 to 1988. Furthermore, further market access must be granted if the import of goods is at a level below 3% of national consumption.[23] This provision is to ensure that, from 2000, 5% of national consumption of a product must be sourced from imports.[24] Since these percentages are not included in the actual Agreement, the Members are bound by them only as they are applied in the schedules of concessions. The policy of minimum import quantities is to be replaced by **tariff quotas** after the tariffication of non-tariff-based measures. Then, imports within the set import quantity are regulated by the prescribed tariff, while all imports exceeding this quantity will be subject to higher, and perhaps prohibitive, tariffs. Following the completion of the tariffication process, agricultural products are only be protected by tariffs between WTO Members.

356 If measures have been converted into tariffs, Members can also rely on a **special safeguard provision** (**SSG**, Art. 5 AoA). However, to use this provision, the member must have designated the goods in question in its schedule of concessions as ones to which the SSG applies,[25] and the factual situation must fulfil one of the following criteria: it must have reached a volume trigger, by imports having reached levels above a set level, or a price trigger, whereby goods must have dropped below a set price. Protection measures as part of Art. 5.1 AoA may be used as additional tariffs, but must not be used in relation to quotas.

c. *Rules on Domestic Support and Export Subsidies*

357 The Agreement on Agriculture also includes numerous rules relating to domestic support measures and export subsidies, which must be seen as special concessions supplementary to the general WTO rules relating to subsidies. (see in this respect paras 517 *et seq.*).

d. *Further Rules, Institutions and Procedures*

358 According to Art. 17 AoA, a **Committee on Agriculture** has been established as part of the institutional structure for the Council for Trade

[23] See the Modalities for the Establishment of Specific Binding Commitments under the Reform Programme of 20 December 1993.

[24] According to Annex 5 AoA certain exceptions apply, which then trigger compensatory higher contingencies.

[25] It must label the product with "SSG" next to in the product name in the schedule of concessions. 39 WTO Members currently have 6,156 products listed for SSG treatment, see Committee on Agriculture, Special Session, Special Agricultural Safeguard – Note by the Secretariat, TN/AG/S/12, 20 December 2004.

in Goods. The Committee supervises the implementation of the Agreement, receives notifications from Members, and gives Members a forum for consultations.[26]

359 The express reference to the **SPS Agreement** in Art. 14 of the Agreement on Agriculture recognizes the rights of Members to apply their own standards of food and health safety (paras 420 *et seq.*).

360 The so-called **"peace clause"** on due restraint contained in Art. 13 AoA is of great significance. According to this provision so-called **"green box"** measures may not be subject to countervailing duties, an action under the Agreement on Subsidies and Countervailing Measures (ASCM), or a procedure under the Dispute Settlement Understanding until the end of the nine-year implementation period, ending on 31 December 2003. Similarly, the so-called "blue box measures" (paras 519 *et seq.*) may also be addressed only in a limited way. Countervailing tariffs may only be implemented where (the threat of) material injury has been determined in accordance with Art. VI GATT 1994 or Part V of the Agreement on Subsidies and Countervailing Measures. A subsidy is actionable only if it exceeds the levels agreed upon in 1992 in accordance with Art. 5 *lit.* f ASCM. While the peace clause formally expired nine years after the entry into force of the Agreement on Agriculture, the possibility of enacting special safeguards remains throughout continuing reform process (Art. 5.9, see paras 363 *et seq.*).

361 The Agreement on Agriculture contains **special and differential treatment** for developing countries, as well as further special rules for least developed and net food-importing countries (Art. 15 and 16). In addition to the extension of the implementation period and the reduced reduction commitments, measures were also introduced to assist with food aid, help for the development of agricultural industry, and cooperation with the World Bank and the International Monetary Fund. The detailed rules are contained in a Ministerial Decision on the basis of Art. 16.1 AoA.[27]

362 The Agreement on Agriculture protects the interests of its Members, in so far as they relate to environmental protection, food safety, land development, safety of income in agriculture, and protection against poverty.[28]

---

[26] Committee on Agriculture (Regular Meetings) General Council Overview of WTO Activities (2004), G/L719, 19 November 2004.

[27] Ministerial Decision on the Possible Negative Effects of the Reform Programme on Least-Developed and Net Food-Importing Developing Countries. See also the new Food Aid Convention (FAC) 1 July 1999. The aim of the FAC is to supply developing nations with sufficient levels of food, independently of local supply and prices in world markets, see also International Grains Council <http://www.igc.org.uk>.

[28] See in this respect e.g. Art. 33 ECT.

This element of the Agreement which can be summarized under the heading of **"multi-functionality of agriculture"** is one of the main objects of the **continuing negotiations**.

e. *Continuing Negotiations*

363 According to Art. 20 AoA, the negotiations on **continuation of the reform process** started in February 2000. These were to cover, amongst other things: (i) the experience gained from the introduction of measures following the reduction commitments, (ii) the effects of the Agreement on world agricultural trade, (iii) specific non-trade concerns such as multi-functionality, (iv) further necessary obligations for successful completion of the reforms. The agricultural negotiations on these topics have still not been completed and have dominated the negotiations during the Doha and Cancún Ministerial Conferences. It is fair to say that the current negotiations on agriculture have become the **key issue** for the WTO agenda and – as it seems – for the world trade order as a whole. Currently, the negotiations on agriculture are still underway, running parallel to the new world trade round (the "Doha Round") (paras 795 *et seq.*).[29]

364 While the negotiations started in 2000 based on the mandate of Art. 20 AoA, a new mandate for continued negotiations was agreed upon as part of the **Doha Ministerial Declaration**. It urged the Members to continue negotiations on the three main pillars of the Agreement on Agriculture, namely market access, domestic support and export subsidization. The Doha Declaration text reflects the difficulties and positions involved: while the text clearly refers to the "reductions of, with a view to phasing out, all forms of export subsidies", it also states that the aims are to be pursued "without prejudging the outcome of the negotiations".[30]

365 In view of this in itself contradictory mandate, it is not surprising that the **deadlines** foreseen in the Doha Round negotiations **could not be met**. Originally, the deadline for the production of numerical targets, formulas and other "modalities" for countries' commitments was to be March 2003, but at the Ministerial Conference in Cancún, no results were achieved. Finally, in July 2004 a General Council Decision now contains a "Framework Agreement" on agricultural negotiations in its Annex A.[31] However, even as this so-called **"July Package"** has

[29] A comprehensive summary of the negotiation process is given in a briefing document prepared by the WTO Secretariat, WTO Agriculture negotiations, December 2004, <http://www.wto.org/english/ tratop_e/agric_e/agnegs_bkgrnd_e.pdf>.

[30] WT/Min(01)/DEC/1, 20 November 201, para. 13.

[31] Doha Work Programme, Decision Adopted by the General Council on 1 August 2004, WT/L579, 2 August 2004.

been heralded as a "historic breakthrough",[32] it only sets outs the framework for establishing future negotiation modalities, and does not contain any concrete results.

366 The "July Package" stresses the single undertaking approach and emphasises the importance of special and differential treatment for developing countries. The main achievement of the "July Package" is the agreement on a so-called **"tiered formula"** approach, meaning that higher levels of support (or tariffs) will be subject to greater overall reductions.[33] Also, the text contains the idea of an "end point" for all scheduled export subsidies.[34] However, specific numerical targets are not contained in the framework and, similarly, a specific end date for export subsidies is lacking – rather, this end date is "to be agreed". Lastly, Members are allowed to designate an "appropriate" number as products as **"sensitive"**, and thus outside the tiered formula approach for market access.[35]

367 Taking into account the rather **divergent views of the negotiating parties**, it remains doubtful whether the modalities for further agricultural negotiations will be completed by thc Ministcrial Conference in Hong Kong in December 2005.

368 In the course of the negotiations, 15 traditional **agricultural exporters** and some developing countries in the Cairns Group (para. 353), have called for a phasing out of, or at least further reductions in, export subsidies, the expiry of "blue box measures",[36] and improved market access. These suggestions have been supported by the **United States** in the past. Furthermore, the export-orientated developing countries strove for further market access and the removal of export subsidies. On the other hand, the **EU**, supported by Japan, Switzerland and Norway has addressed the multi-functional character of agriculture.

369 A significant example for the conflicting interests and problems that have to be addressed is the treatment of cotton. During the agriculture negotiations Benin, Burkina Faso, Chad and Mali described the damage that has – from their point of view – been caused to them by **cotton subsidies** in industrialized countries ("Cotton initiative").[37] According to

---

[32] See the WTO News Item, 31 July 2004, <http://www.wto.org/english/news_e/news04_e/news04_e.htm>.

[33] Doha Work Programme (footnote 31), Annex A, para. 7 for overall reduction of domestic support, para. 9 for bound total AMS, and para. 28 *et seq.* for market access.

[34] *Ibid.*, paras 18 and 19.

[35] *Ibid.*, para. 31 *et seq.*

[36] See for a description of so-called "blue" and "green box" measures paras 519 *et seq.*

[37] Joint Proposal by Benin, Burkina Faso, Chad and Mali, Poverty Reduction: Sectoral Initiative in Favour of Cotton, TN/AG/GEN/4, 16 May 2003.

the "July Package" (para. 365), a sub-committee on cotton has now been set up to focus on this topic separately from the agriculture negotiations.[38]

2. *Agreement on Textiles and Clothing*

Niels Blokker, International regulation of world trade in textiles: lessons for practice, a contribution to theory, 1989; *Lane S. Hurewitz*, Textiles, in: Terence P. Stewart (ed.), The GATT Uruguay-Round – A Negotiating History (1986–1992), Vol. I (1993), 255–380; *idem*, International Regulation of World Trade in Textiles, 1989; *Claudia Jimenéz Cortés*, GATT, WTO and the regulation of international trade in textiles, 1997; *Xiaobing Tang*, The Integration of Textiles and Clothing into GATT and WTO Dispute Settlement, in: James Cameron (ed.), Dispute resolution in the World Trade Organisation, 1998, 171–203; *Kristine K. Dunn*, The Textiles Monitoring Body: Can it bring Textile into GATT?, Minnesota Journal of Global Trade 7 (1998) 1, 123–155; *Peter Berz*, Sektorielle Handelsbeschränkungen autonomer und vertraglicher Art: Textil, in: GH II/Krenzler (Eds), Recht der Europäischen Union, 2000 (loseleaf), E 11 paras 11 *Fabrizio Marrella*, L'Organisation Mondiale du Commerce et les textiles, Revue générale de droit international public 104 (2000) 3, 659–693; *Kenneth A. Reinert*, Give Us Virtue, But Not Yet; Safeguard Actions Under the Agreement on Textiles and Clothing, The World Economy 23 (2001) 1, 25–55; *Sung J. Kim*, The Agreement on Textiles and Clothing, JIEL 5 (2002) 2, 445–468; *Mark Williams & Kong Yuk-Choi & Shen Yan*, Bonanza or mirage? Textiles and China's accession to the WTO, JWT 36 (2002) 3, 577–591.

370 Trade in textiles and clothing is of great economic significance. The development of a textile industry with the aim of exporting the goods made plays an important part in industrial development. The textile sector in industrialized states is under immense pressure from competition, due to the considerable labour intensity and therefore also dependency on wage costs. Trade relating to textiles grew between 1985 and 1997 by 18.2% to a volume of approximately 155 billion US$; trade relating to clothing grew in the same period by 259% to a volume of approximately 177 billion US$. Among the main exporting nations are China, Korea, Italy, Germany and the United States, and among the main importing nations are the United States, Germany, Japan, Great Britain and France.

371 The GATT and its regulations have hardly applied to this sector. As a reaction to the strong growth in the export of cotton textiles and clothing from developing nations, and under the pressure of influential national interest groups, two so-called "Cotton Arrangements" were agreed upon in 1960, which were superseded by the by the so-called **Multifibre Arrangement (MFA)** in 1974.[39] The Multifibre Arrangement was a framework agreement which facilitated the continuing practice

[38] Doha Work Programme (footnote 31), Annex A, para. 4. The Sub-Committee was established by a decision of the Agriculture Committee, TN/AG/13, 26 November 2003; see the Sub-Committee's Work Programme, TN/AG/SCC/1, 29 March 2005.

[39] Arrangement Regarding International Trade in Textiles, GATT Doc. TEX.NG/1, BISD

of usage of import quotas through bilateral agreements or unilateral measures. The mechanism on the one hand relied on the implementation of quotas by the importing nations, which were aimed at rectifying any market disruptions,[40] and, secondly, on "voluntary export restraints" (VERs) on the part of the exporting countries.[41] With its final 44 GATT contracting parties, including China as a non-member of the GATT, the Multifibre Arrangement covered a large sector of the international textile market. This allowed and ensured, in practice, an effective protection from competition of markets of industrial Members, as well as enforcing discriminatory rules between the parties concerned in the administration of import quotas.

372 As a result of these special rules it did not seem excessive for the mandate of the **Uruguay Round** to speak merely of "eventually integrating" this sector entirely into the GATT.[42] A further liberalization lay and lies, above all, in the interests of the developing countries, whose approach during the negotiations was, however, not united. Some of these states could hope for a better chance of access to markets as a result of this liberalization. Other nations feared a loss of the limited, but guaranteed, market access opportunities granted by the Multifibre Arrangement.

373 The **Agreement on Textiles and Clothing (ATC)**, which was the result of the negotiation of the Uruguay Round, made provision for the **eventual, staged inclusion** of trade in textiles and clothing in the GATT regime.

374 Its scope includes the textile and clothing products which are listed in the Annex (Art. 1.7 ATC). The six-digit numbers of the harmonised system are again used for the classification and codification of the goods (see para. 312). Generally, the goods are primarily classified from the first level of production, that is to say that raw materials, such as cotton or raw silk, are not included.[43]

1S/3; as amended by the Protocol Amending The 1986 Protocol Extending The Arrangement Regarding International Trade in Textiles (com.tex/63) 20.7.1989, BISD 36S/8 (1989). The period of validity was extended by the Protocol Maintaining in Force the Arrangement Regarding Inter-national Trade in Textiles (L/7363) 9 December 1993, BISD 40S (1993)/4 until 31 December 1994.

[40] The protection clauses of the Multifibre Arrangement, along with the concept of market disruption, signify a deviation from the concessions for emergency measures relating to the import of specific goods in accordance with Art. XIX GATT 1994.

[41] In the wake of the Japanese accession to the GATT 1947, as many as 50 contracting parties declared they would not apply the rules of the GATT to Japan in relation to textiles and clothing trade according to the provision of Art. XXXV GATT, see GATT Analytical Index, 1035 *et seq.*

[42] The mandate of the Uruguay Round reads as follows: "Textiles and clothing. Negotiations in the area of textiles and clothing shall aim to formulate modalities that would *permit the eventual integration of this sector into GATT* on the basis of strengthened GATT-Rules and disciplines, thereby also contributing to the objective of further liberalisation of trade." Emphasis added.

[43] Annex I lists all textiles and clothing products which were subject to an MFA quota by at least one Member.

375 The staged inclusion of the Agreement on Textiles and Clothing in the GATT 1994 was governed by Art. 2.6 to 2.8 ATC. The 10-year time frame for inclusion was subdivided into 4 levels. In the first level, which ended on 31 December 1997, Members had to have textiles and clothing form at least 16% of their total imports on the basis of 1990 in the GATT 1994;[44] in stages 2 and 3 this level was increased to 17 and 18%. In the fourth stage, which began on **1 January 2005**, the remaining share of 49% was to be achieved. On that date, as transition was fully completed, the Agreement on Textiles and Clothing expired (Art. 9 ATC).[45] Members had wide discretion in the selection of the goods at each level. Following liberalization the goods are governed exclusively by the general provisions of the GATT. Safeguard measures are now possible only according to the general rules of the Understanding on Safeguards, while bilateral agreements on quantitative restrictions are prohibited.

376 Following the entry into force of the Agreement on Textiles and Clothing, no new restrictions were to be introduced. The **remaining import quotas** for goods which were not included in the ambit of the GATT 1994, but were governed by the rules of the Multifibre Arrangement, were to be raised in four steps (in parallel to the staged import increase). The four steps were governed by the following increases:

Transition period for the inclusion of the textile and clothing sectors in the GATT 1994

Stage Timeframe	Share of the total import to be transformed to the GATT	Share of the existing quotas per year to be transformed to the GATT (Increase rate 1994 = 6%)
Stage 1 1.1.1995–31.12.1997	16%	6,96%
Stage 2 1.1.1998–31.12.2001	17%	8,7%
Stage 3 1.1.2002–31.12.2004	18%	11,05%
Stage 4 from 1.1.2005*	49%	No quotas

* Full integration of textiles and clothing sector into GATT 1994 and termination of the ATC.

[44] The initial subordination of goods under the GATT 1994 was to be specifically notified in accordance with the Decision on the Notification of First Integration under Article 2.6 of the Agreement on Textiles and Clothing.

[45] There was no possibility of an extension.

377 The Agreement on Textiles and Clothing provided for the reduction of **further quantitative restrictions** which were not directly governed by the Multifibre Arrangement (Art. 3 ATC). These restrictions were to be notified and either brought into harmony with the GATT 1994 or removed within a period of 10 years.

378 During the transitional period Art. 6 ATC also contained a so-called **"transitional safeguard clause"**, which was to protect Members from increased import levels for goods which were not part of the GATT 1994. For this to happen, two prerequisites were to be fulfilled: first, the Members had to have proved that the increased levels of imports are seriously damaging (or threatening to damage) domestic industry producing like and/or directly competing products. To this end, the effects of import were to be tested against specific factors (Art. 6.3 ATC). Furthermore, the Member facing this danger was to notify other Members of these specific dangers. If the consultation between Members was unsuccessful, the Member at risk was allowed unilateral protection measures. Its identity would be made public and the measures supervized by the Textile Monitoring Body (TMB). Art. 5 ATC contained detailed rules on protection against **circumvention** by transfer or diversion of trade flows and the false declaration of certificates of origin.

379 The **Textile Monitoring Body** (TMB) was a special body for the supervision and implementation of the Agreement on Textiles and Clothing under the general umbrella of the Council for Trade in Goods. It was made up of a chairperson and 10 members, who were not representatives of WTO Members, but rather acting *ad personam*. The Textile Monitoring Body was to be balanced and representative, that is to say, it was to fulfil geographic and specific interest group requirements.[46] The Textile Monitoring Body supervized the functioning of the Agreement on the basis of notification and communications on the part of the Members, and had an interesting function in relation to dispute settlement. Before a Member could resort to the Dispute Settlement Body, the Textile Monitoring Body was to consider the issue, and make recommendations (Art 8.5 ATC).[47] Only then, after this pre-procedure had been decided upon, was a Member entitled to request the establishment of a Panel.[48]

---

[46] For the last composition of the Textile Monitoring Body see WTO Annual Report 2004, 40.

[47] Issues involving the ATC were the subject matter of four disputes: *United States – Cotton Yarn*, WT/DS192/AB/R 8 October 2001; WT/DS192/R 31 May 2001; *Turkey – Textiles*, WT/DS34/R, 31 May 1999; *United States – Shirts and Blouses*, WT/DS33/AB/R, 25 April 1997, WT/DS33/R, 6 January 1997; *United States – Underwear*, WT/DS24/AB/R 10 February 1997, WT/DS24/R 8 November 1997.

[48] See e.g. *Turkey – Textiles*, WT/DS34/R, 31 May 1999, paras 9.82 *et seq.*

380 All four transitional steps were completed by 1 January 2005. Thus, textile and clothing products are now governed by the **general rules** of the GATT 1994.[49] The sector continues to have great significance, as can be witnessed in the continuing discussions on special safeguards relating to Chinese textile imports, which are admissible on the basis of specific rules in the Chinese Protocol of Accession.[50]

III. *Technical Barriers to Trade*

Christian Tietje, Voluntary Eco-Labelling Programmes and Questions of State Responsibility in the WTO/GATT Legal System, JWT 29 (1995) 5, 123–158; *US National Research Council*, Standards, Conformity Assessment, and Trade: Into the 21st Century (1995); *Seung Wha Chang*, GATTing a green trade barrier: eco-labelling and the WTO Agreement on Technical Barriers to Trade, JWT 31 (1997) 1, 137–159; *Erik P. Bartenhagen*, The Intersection Of Trade And The Environment: An Examination Of The Impact Of The TBT Agreement On Ecolabeling Programs, Virginia Environmental Law Journal 17 (1997) 1, 51–81; *James H. Mathis*, Mutual Recognition Agreements: Transatlantic Parties and the Limits to Non-tariff Barrier Regionalism in the WTO, JWT 32 (1998) 6, 5–31; *Christian Tietje*, Normative Grundstrukturen der Behandlung nichttarifärer Handelshemmnisse in der WTO-GATT-Rechtsordnung, 1998; *Robert Howse & Donald Regan*, The Product/Process Distinction – An Illusory Basis for Disciplining 'Unilateralism' in Trade Policy, EJIL 11 (2000) 2, 249–289; *Raymond L. Tricker*, CE conformity marking and new approach directives, 2000; *Frederik Wiemer*, Produktsicherheit und freier Warenverkehr in GATT, WTO, 2001; *Gabrielle Marceau & Joel P. Trachtmann*, The technical barriers to Trade Agreement, the Sanitary and Phytosanitary Measures Agreement, and the General Agreement on Tariffs and Trade, JWT 36 (2002) 5, 811–881; *Irene McConnell*, The Asbestos case at the World Trade Organization, Tulsa journal of comparative & international law 10 (2002) 1, 153–182; *Sebastian Puth*, WTO und Umwelt – Die Produkt-Prozess-Doktrin, 2003; *Paul Beynon*, Community mutual recognition agreements, technical barriers to trade and the WTO's most favoured nation principle, European law review 28 (2003) 2, 231–249; *Terence P. Stewart*, A nexus of trade and the environment, Colorado journal of international environmental law and policy 14 (2003) 1, 1–52; *Spencer Henson & John S. Wilson* (Eds), The WTO and technical barriers to trade, 2005.

[49] The impact of phasing out the Agreement is discussed by *Nordås*, The Global Textile and Clothing Industry post the Agreement on Textiles and Clothing, WTO Discussion Paper 2005, 24 *et seq*.

[50] Background Statistical Information with Respect to Trade in Textiles and Clothing, WT/L/692, 20 September 2004; from the EU perspective see the press release of the European Commission of 24 April 2005, <http://europa.eu.int/comm/trade/ issues/sectoral/industry/textile/pr240405_en.htm>; compare also the Protocol of Accession of the People's Republic of China, WT/L/432, 23 November 2001, para. 9 and Annex 7.

1. *General*

381 Technical barriers to trade usually mean state measures which make import into or marketing in the domestic market subject to certain (technical) **conditions of the product**, or – and this is highly disputed – which relate to a product's **production methods**. Technical barriers to trade range from a specific individual measure to the more frequent wide ranging, abstract, technical standards and their application.

382 Technical standards increasingly **influence the development, production, trade or marketing** of goods and services. They facilitate marketing and trade by way of standardization, ensure inter-operability of technical products or aim at ensuring the safety of consumers and the environment. They are set in large part by private businesses, industrial groups and private and public standardization bodies on national, regional and international levels, but are also defined directly by national public authorities and government. Some of those regulations are enacted by public authorities and made mandatory for the import and marketing of the product in question, or are included in offers for government procurement.

383 Such standards and measures **limit trade** when they are not harmonized and when producers, exporters and importers are forced to determine certain standards for individual markets, and then to tackle the relevant conformity and recognition procedures, as well as to ensure that their products meet various demands. If the relevant certification that proves the conformity of the product with the technical standards of the importing country is missing, it is usually not allowed to enter that market.[51]

384 As the development of the internal market of the European Union has shown, such trade limitations can best be overcome by way of **harmonization**. Another issue is the **mutual recognition** of standards. Lastly, measures are subject to **case-by-case scrutiny** involving consideration of the interest in unrestricted trade on the one hand, and the objectives pursued by the regulation on the other.

385 The WTO itself does not have the competence to harmonize international standards for goods. Instead, the International Organisation for Standardisation, the International Electrotechnical Commission, the Codex Alimentarius Commission of the FAO, the World Health Organisation, and the Economic Commission for Europe are more

[51] For example, the CE Symbol signifies the conformity of an industrial product with the relevant secondary legislation of the EU, and is a prerequisite for the transportability of goods within the home market.

active in pursuit of international harmonization. It should not be overlooked, however, that work on harmonization, which considers and compares the ideas and practices of many states, is protracted and hindered when the states have different ideas on the type and intensity of regulation required.

386 As already stated (para. 382), technical restrictions cover more than just those imposed at national frontiers. They also include measures which are implemented and related to the internal market. In the WTO context, next to the fundamental prohibition on quantitative restrictions and other measures in accordance with Art. XI:1 GATT 1994, which, amongst others, concerns requests for conformity certificates, there is also the principle of national treatment according to Art. III:4 GATT 1994 to be considered. The legal admissibility of the abovementioned measures is finally guided by Art. XX GATT 1994.

387 These general rules include very few criteria or suggestions for the complex problem of technical barriers to trade. However, on the basis of these principles the much more detailed Agreement on Technical Barriers to Trade (TBT) and the Agreement on Sanitary and Phytosanitary Measures (SPS) were included in the legal order of the WTO.

2. *Agreement on Technical Barriers to Trade (TBT Agreement)*

388 Under the GATT specific rules in form of an **Agreement on Technical Barriers to Trade**, the so-called "Standards Code", were drafted as part of the **Tokyo Round**.[52] These were elaborated on during the Uruguay Round and implemented under the same name under the WTO. The Agreement applies to all products, including industrial and agricultural products (Art. 1.3), while purchasing specifications for government procurement purposes (Art. 1.4), as well as all sanitary and phytosanitary measures, are excluded (Art. 1.5).[53] The TBT Agreement contains regulations for the **preparation, adoption and application of technical regulations** (Art. 3) and **standards** (Art. 4), as well as **conformity assessment procedures** (Art. 5 *et seq.*), and relates to questions of harmonization (Art. 2.4 *et seq.* and Art. 9) and recognition (for instance Art. 2.7 and 6.1).

389 A specific aspect of the TBT in its form in the Uruguay Round is that it sets out regulations on **process and production methods (PPMs)**.[54] The legality of these PPMs under the rules of the GATT 1994, in particular under Art. XX GATT 1994, is doubtful. However, according

[52] BISD 26S/8 *et seq.*
[53] See Art. 1.4 SPS and also paras 420 *et seq.*
[54] Under the previous Agreement of the Tokyo Round, PPMs were excluded.

to the definitions contained in Annex 1, "product characteristics or their related product and production methods" are explicitly included as possible elements of technical regulations and standards under the TBT Agreement (No. 1 and 2).[55] PPMs are thus included in the scope of the Agreement to the extent that they are "related" to a specific product.

390 Otherwise, standards which lay down prerequisites for the product's production process must be considered in light of the general rules of the GATT. According to the majority opinion the GATT 1994 does not authorize Members to subject imported goods to domestic PPM standards. The fundamental idea in this discussion is the concept of "like products", which is contained in the GATT 1994, as well as in Art. 2.1 and 5 TBT.[56] In the Panel decisions under the GATT 1947, PPMs were not permitted as a criterion for differentiation, so that the differential treatment of physically "like products" was seen as a violation of the principle of non-discrimination.

391 This theme is one of the most disputed areas of WTO law, in which a final decision has not been reached. The leading decision in this area is that in the case of ***US-Shrimp/Turtle***. The subject matter of the case was a US trade-restricting measure for the import of giant shrimps, which were caught in a certain manner which endangered turtles. The Appellate Body decided that – in principle – such a PPM standard may be enforceable in accordance with Art. XX *lit.* g GATT 1994.[57]

a. *Rules for Binding Technical Regulations*

392 The Agreement first and foremost deals with binding **technical regulations**, which set certain product characteristics or their related processes and production methods, including the applicable legal and administrative provisions. Next to provisions on the preparation, adoption and application of these regulations through central government the TBT Agreement also contains corresponding obligations in relation to local government or administration, and non-state bodies (Art. 3)

393 Generally, Art. 2.1 TBT incorporates **most favoured nation** (corresponding to those in Art. I:1 GATT 1994) and **national treatment rules** (corresponding to those in Art. III GATT 1994).

---

[55] Annex 1 No.1 TBT: "Document which lays down product characteristics or their related processes and production methods, including the applicable administrative provisions, with which compliance is mandatory. It may also include or deal exclusively with terminology, symbols, packaging, marking or labelling requirements as they apply to a product, process or production method." It is not completely obvious whether the word "related" is missing from No. 1 s.2 as an editorial fault, see *Chang*, JWT 31 (1997) 1, 137, 141 *et seq.*, *Appleton*, Environmental Labelling Programmes, 1997, 93.

[56] For the use of this concept in the GATT 1994 see paras 123 *et seq.* and 138 *et seq.*

[57] *United States – Import Prohibition of Certain Shrimp and Shrimp Product*, WT/DS58/AB/R, 12 October 1998, paras 134 *et seq.* see also in relation to this issue, paras 187 and 733 *et seq.*

394 Art. 2 TBT operates in a structure similar Art. XX GATT 1994 in referring to **Members' rights**, but with more concrete and far-reaching rules in relation to the preparation, adoption and application of technical regulations, and the limitations that may apply.

395 The TBT Agreement in Art. 2.2. s.3 refers to **"legitimate objectives"** which the Members can pursue through the implementation and use of these technical regulations. This list, although not exhaustive, includes national security requirements (see Art. XXI GATT 1994), the prevention of deceptive practices (Art. XX *lit.* d. GATT 1994), the protection of human health or safety, animal or plant life or health and the environment (see Art. XX *lit.* b and g GATT 1994). This catalogue thus incorporates the aims of Art. XX GATT 1994, but deviates from it in form and content.

396 On the other hand, Art. 2.2 s. 1 TBT stipulates that "Members shall ensure that technical regulations are not prepared, adopted or applied with a view to or with the effect of creating unnecessary obstacles to international trade."

397 This limitation, which corresponds to the *chapeau* of Art. XX GATT 1994 (para. 192) is **specified** in light of the abovementioned aims. According to Art. 2.2 s. 2 TBT, these technical regulations may not be more trade-restrictive than is necessary to achieve the goals, taking into account the risk of non-fulfilment. This provision does not aim at completely balancing the legally protected interests, as is the case in, e.g., European law, where it is part of the idea of **proportionality**. However, it comes closer to this idea than the rules of Art. XX GATT 1994.

398 Furthermore, Art. 2.2 s. 4 TBT contains a limiting **methodical specification**, namely that in the **risk assessment** the "available scientific and technical information, related processing technology or intended end-uses of products" are to be considered as relevant elements of consideration. Art. 2.3 TBT limits the validity and use of regulations in a **temporal dimension** in relation to changing circumstances. Art. 2.8 contains the well known principle that technical regulations should be used in terms of performance rather than in terms of design or descriptive characteristics, to give research and development the **freedom** to search for the best technical solution.

399 In many respects the rules relate to **international harmonization**. Members have a duty cooperate, as far as possible, in the attempt to develop international norms through the existing international bodies (para. 385) when implementing or planning such regulations. Furthermore, these international norms should be used as the basis for national technical regulations, save for cases in which these international regulations "would be an ineffective or inappropriate means for the fulfilment of

the legitimate objective pursued, for instance because of fundamental climatic or geographical factors or fundamental technological problems" (Art. 2.4). Furthermore, Members have a duty to adapt and optimize their technical regulations using international standards.[58]

400 If one of the legitimate goals is achieved through Art. 2.2 TBT by the preparation, adoption or application of a technical regulation which is in accordance with the relevant international standards, it shall be "**rebuttably presumed** not to create an unnecessary obstacle to international trade" (Art. 2.5).

401 The Agreement does not contain a definition of an "international standard", nor does it set out which organisations may work towards or establish one. During the second triennial review of the TBT,[59] the Members decided on **principles for the development of international standards**. These include transparency, openness, impartiality, consensus, effectiveness, usefulness and coherence.[60] During the third triennial review these issues were further discussed and several recommendations were adopted in this respect.[61]

402 Art. 2.7 TBT states that Members should give "positive consideration" to the recognition of equivalent technical restrictions of other members, even where they differ from their own, and thus includes the element of **mutual recognition**.

403 The TBT Agreement contains far-reaching **information obligations starting with the drafting phase** of a technical regulation, in cases in which no appropriate international standards exist, or when the draft deviates from the existing international standards and the measure may have significant effects on international trade. As a consequence, as early as at the drafting phase of such technical regulation or conformity assessment Members (i) are subject to an early publication date, (ii) must reveal the purpose and reasons for their methods to other WTO Members via the Secretariat, (iii) must produce copies of the conformity assessments on demand, and (iv) they must also allow a period for comments by other Members, which must be discussed (Art. 2.9 TBT). A protection clause allows deviation from certain aspects; however, a minimum level of transparency is always demanded (Art. 2.10 TBT).

---

[58] *European Communities – Trade Description of Sardines*, WT/DS231/R, 29 May 2002, para. 7.78.

[59] G/TBT/9, 13 November 2000.

[60] Decisions of the Committee on Principles for the Development of International Standards, Guides and Recommendations with relation to Articles 2 and 5 of and Annex 3 to the Agreement, G/TBT/9 Annex 4, 13 November 2000.

[61] G/TBT/13/, 11 November 2003.

b. *Rules for Technical Standards*

404 The TBT Agreement differentiates between the abovementioned technical regulations and technical standards. **Technical standards** are understood as rules, directives, and criteria for goods and their related production processes and methods which, in contrast to the technical regulations, have no binding character.[62] To an extent, the Agreement goes off at a tangent with regard to these standards. It opts for the idea that the standard-setting organization of Members conform to rules contained in a "Code of Good Practice" (Art. 4), which is part of the Agreement as Annex 3: it includes the principle of most-favoured-nation treatment, national treatment, and proportionality, and also recommends cooperation between the standard-setting organization and the international standardization bodies. The Code also includes, as does Art. 2, corresponding informational obligations. The central government is under an international legal obligation to take reasonable measures available to ensure that the Code is observed.[63]

c. *Conformity Assessment Procedures*

405 **Conformity assessment procedures** include those processes which are directly or indirectly used to determine that relevant requirements in technical regulations or standards are fulfilled.[64] The procedure of conformity assessment is to be set out so that neither discrimination (Art. 5.1.1 TBT) nor unnecessary restrictions on trade occur, that is to say, the procedures may not be stricter or be applied more strictly than is necessary to give the importing Member adequate confidence that products conform with the applicable technical regulations or standards (Art. 5.1.2 TBT). In general, the requirements of the conformity assessment procedures are based on the rules relating to technical regulations.

406 As far as conformity assessment procedures are concerned, the TBT Agreement follows the need to stimulate Members to recognize the results of foreign procedures. This **mutual recognition** necessitates trust in the implementation of qualitative and quantitative procedures. An important aspect of this goal is reasonable and enduring technical expertise in the process. Members are encouraged by Art. 6.3 TBT to enter into mutual recognition agreements (MRAs) as far as possible.

---

[62] As for technical regulations, technical standards may include specifications relating to terminology, symbols, packaging and labelling requirements as applicable to a product, process or production method, see Annex 1, No. 2.

[63] Therefore, the European Commission is seen as part of the Central Government of the EU, Annex 1. No. 6.

[64] The legal definition of these ideas is contained in Annex 1. No. 1 to 3 of the TBT. The Agreement returns to the general ideas and definitions of the ISO/IEC handbook, deviations are noted in the "explanatory notes" in Annex 1.

This possibility has indeed been widely used. It is important to note that the rules incorporated in these bilateral agreements do not have to conform to the principle of most-favoured-nation treatment. Members may use private organizations for conformity assessment procedures only if these comply with the rules of the Agreement (Art. 8). Finally, the obligation to develop this system on international levels, and to cooperate in such an international process is also applicable in relation to the development of conformity assessment procedures (Art. 9).

d. *Further Procedural Issues and Institutions*

407 Every Member has a duty to establish a national **enquiry point** which must answer all questions relating to the regulations, standards and procedures, as well as provide all requested documentation (Art. 10 TBT).[65] Additional transparency is added by the **Committee on Technical Barriers to Trade**, which is to administer the functioning of the Agreement under the supervision of the Council on Trade in Goods (Art. 13).[66]

408 The TBT Agreement also includes regulations on **technical assistance** for the implementation of the Agreement and the establishment of national standardization organisations (Art. 11 TBT). Furthermore, **special and differential treatment** is provided for developing countries, including regulations on technical assistance and longer implementation periods (Art. 12 TBT).

409 The rules of the TBT Agreement fall within the scope of Art. XXII and XXIII GATT 1994, as well as the **Dispute Settlement Understanding** (Art. 14 TBT). The possibility of the establishment of technical expert groups in dispute settlement cases for the clarification of technical questions is expressly mentioned and Annex 2 TBT contains procedural rules in this respect.[67]

e. *Dispute Settlement, and Relationship with the GATT*

410 The rules of the TBT Agreement were only seldom the subject matter of dispute settlement cases.[68] In ***United States – Gasoline***, the complaining parties (Venezuela and Brazil) brought an action against the

---

[65] The national enquiry points are referred to in the Note by the WTO Secretariat, National Enquiry Points, G/TBT/ENQ/26, 7 March 2005.

[66] The note by the WTO Secretariat G/TBT/1/Rev.8, 23 May 2002 reproduces the decisions and recommendations adopted by the Committee concerning its rules of procedure and the interpretation, implementation and administration of the TBT Agreement.

[67] For the alternative consultation of individual experts see *European Communities – Asbestos*, WT/DS135/R, 18 September 2000, para. 5.19.

[68] A statistical overview of dispute settlement is given in a Background Document of the WTO Secretariat, G/TBT/12, 21 February 2003, 14.

United States' import rules for fuels, and alleged a breach of the TBT Agreement. However, in light of the Panel's finding of a violation of Arts. I and III of the GATT, it declined to rule on the alleged breach of the TBT Agreement for reasons of judicial economy.[69] In ***European Communities – Asbestos***, the Appellate Body qualified the disputed French decree, which banned the use of asbestos and goods containing asbestos, as a technical regulation. However, a review of this regulation, especially in light of Art. 2 TBT Agreement, was not undertaken for procedural reasons. As there were no material findings by the Panel relating to the TBT Agreement, the Appellate Body was not able to review any legal questions of interpretation in accordance with Art. 17.6 DSU.[70]

411 The **relationship of the TBT Agreement to the GATT 1994** has yet to be fully explored by the dispute settlement organs of the WTO. The preamble to the TBT Agreement aims at furthering the goals of the GATT 1994. For this purpose, the TBT includes a series of rules which have limited and special scope. The abovementioned rebuttable presumption of Art 2.5 TBT, which stipulates that no unnecessary obstacle to international trade is to be presumed if the regulation in question is in accordance with the relevant internationally agreed standards, must be emphasized. The Appellate Body has held that Members' obligations under the TBT Agreement appear to be different from those under the GATT, so that they could be seen as additional requirements.[71] This indication of the Appellate Body supports the concept of the TBT as a parallel Agreement to the GATT 1994.

412 This idea is also supported by the decision in ***European Communities – Sardines***.[72] Following the arguments of the Appellate Body in *European Communities – Bananas III*, which found that Panels must make findings in relation to specific agreements before general agreements,[73] the compatibility of the relevant measures with the TBT Agreement was tested. As the TBT Agreement related more specifically and in more detail to technical barriers, compatibility with the GATT was to be analyzed only at the second stage.[74]

413 However, in general, technical regulations and standards which relate to the production methods or processes used in the manufacture of goods must conform with the rules of the GATT 1994.

---

[69] *United States – Gasoline*, WT/DS2/R, 29 January 1996, para. 6.43.

[70] *European Communities – Asbestos*, WT/DS135/AB/R, 12 March 2001, paras 80 *et seq*. the Appellate Body concluded that it could not complete the legal analysis, because the Panel had not made findings on the substantive claims under the TBT Agreement.

[71] See *European Communities – Asbestos* (see above footnote 70), paras 82 *et seq.*

[72] *European Communities – Trade Descriptions of Sardines*, WT/DS231/R, 29 May 2002.

[73] *European Communities – Bananas* (see above footnote 11), para. 204.

[74] *European Communities – Sardines* (see above footnote 72), paras 7.15 *et seq.*

3. *Agreement on the Application of Sanitary and Phytosanitary Measures (SPS)*

Steve Charnovitz, The World Trade Organization, Meat Hormones, and Food Safety, International Trade Reporter 14 (1997), 1781; *idem*, Environment and Health under the WTO Dispute Settlement, The International Lawyer 32 (1998) 3, 901–921; *David Hurst*, Hormone: European Communities – Measures Affecting Meat and Meat Products, EJIL 9 (1998) 1, 182–183; *Hiranya Fernando Senadhira*, Appellate Body Report of the Beef Hormones Case: A Brief Analysis, Bridges 2 (1998) 9; *Barbara Eggers*, Die Entscheidung des WTO Appellate Body im Hormonfall, EuZW 9 (1998) 5/6, 147–151; *Joost Pauwelyn*, The WTO Agreement On Sanitary and Phytosanitary (SPS) Measures As Applied In The First Three SPS Disputes, JIEL 2 (1999) 4, 641–664; *Terence P. Stewart*, The SPS Agreement of the World Trade Organization and plant pest infestations. – American University international law review 14 (1999) 4, 1107–1127; *Peter-Tobias Stoll*, Controlling the Risks of Genetically Modified Organisms: The Cartagena Protocol on Biosafety and the SPS Agreement, Yearbook of International Environmental Law 10 (1999), 82–119; *Terence P. Stewart & David S. Johanson*, The SPS-Agreement Of The World Trade Organization And International Organizations: The Roles Of The Codex Alimentarius Commission, The International Plant Protection Convention, And The International Office Of Epizootics, Syracuse Journal of International Law and Commerce 26 (1999) 1, 27–54; *Terence P. Stewart & David S. Johanson*, The SPS-Agreement Of The World Trade Organization And The International Trade Of Dairy Products, Food and Drug Law Journal 54 (1999) 1, 55–72; *David L. Devernoe*, Substantial Equivalence: A Valid International Sanitary and Phytosanitary Risk Assessment Objective For Genetically Modified Foods, Case Western Reserve Law Review 51 (2000) 2, 257–296; *David G. Victor*, The Sanitary And Phytosanitary Agreement Of The World Trade Organization: An Assessment After Five Years, New York University Journal of International Law and Politics 32 (2000) 4, 865–937; *Gerald G. Sander*, Gesundheitsschutz in der WTO – eine neue Bedeutung des Codex Alimentarius im Lebensmittelrecht?, ZEuS 3 (2000) 3, 335–375; *Robert Howse*, Democracy, Science, and Free Trade: Risk Regulation On Trial At The World Trade Organization, Michigan Law Review 98 (2000) 7, 2329–2357; *Kevin C. Kennedy*, Resolving International Sanitary and Phytosanitary Disputes In The WTO: Lessons and Future Directions, Food and Drug Law Journal 55 (2000) 1, 81–104; *Regine Neubauer*, Fine-Tuning WTO Jurisprudence And The SPS-Agreement: Lessons From The Beef Hormone Case, Law and Policy in International Business 31 (2000) 4, 1255–1284; *Denise Prévost*, The SPS Agreement as a bottleneck in agricultural trade between the European Union and developing countries, Legal issues of economic integration 29 (2002) 1, 43–59; *Heather D. Heavin*, The Biosafety Protocol and the SPS Agreement, Journal of environmental law and practice 12 (2003) 3, 373–421; *Terence P. Stewart*, A nexus of trade and the environment, Colorado journal of international environmental law and policy 14 (2003) 1, 1–52; *Wayne Jones*, Organisation for Economic Co-operation and Development: The impact of regulations on agro-food trade – the technical barriers to trade (TBT) and sanitary and phytosanitary measures (SPS) agreements, 2003; *Graham Mayeda*, Developing disharmony?, JIEL 7 (2004) 4, 737–764; *Markus Böckenförde*, Grüne Gentechnik und Welthandel. Genetic engineering and world trade, 2004.

a. *Introduction and Legal Basis*

414 One of the main aims of the Uruguay Round was to bring trade in agricultural goods under the jurisdiction of the GATT (para. 353). This trade was not only limited by unbound tariffs and quantitative restrictions on the basis of waivers. It also included numerous restrictions regarding demands and procedures serving the aims of sanitation and phytosanitation. There is evidence of a tendency towards stricter regulation in this area, with relevant trade-limiting effects which may also lead to **great potential for conflict** in relation to trade policies. This tendency is based on, amongst others, the increasingly critical attitude of consumers, the industrialization of food production and the renewed significance of cultural and traditional aspects of food and agriculture.

415 The **Agreement on the Application of Sanitary and Phytosanitary Measures (SPS)** is relevant to this sector. The Agreement, while guaranteeing the rights of Members to implement relevant measures (Art. 2.1 SPS), serves to minimize their negative effects on trade (Preamble, para. 4 SPS), as well as to exclude arbitrary or unjustified discrimination between Members where identical or similar conditions prevail, "which could constitute a disguised restriction on trade" (Art. 2.3 SPS).

416 To this end, Members have a duty to use SPS-relevant measures only to the extent necessary to protect human, animal or plant life or health (Art. 2.2 SPS). Save for the possibility of provisional measures contained in Art. 5.7, measures should be based on scientific principles and may not be maintained without sufficient **scientific evidence.**[75]

417 Thus, the SPS Agreement concretizes the relevant articles of the GATT 1994, especially Art. XX *lit.* b. It includes the presumption that measures applied in accordance with the rules of the SPS Agreement are also in accordance with the GATT 1994 (Art. 2.4 SPS).

418 Furthermore, the Agreement encourages the **harmonization and mutual recognition** of such measures between Members.

419 The Agreement has played a fundamental role in a series of highly public and controversial **disputes,**[76] including the *Hormones* case,[77] *Japan – Agricultural Products,*[78] *Australia – Salmon*[79] and *Japan – Apples.*[80]

---

[75] There are, however, no limits to the scientific mainstream. A divergent minority opinion is also sufficient as the basis for SPS relevant measures to be used by Members, as long as the opinion is well founded and comes from reliable sources, *European Communities – Measures Affecting Meat and Meat Products (Hormones)*, WT/DS26/AB/R and WT/DS48/AB/R, 16 January 1998, paras 121 and 194.

[76] An overview of the trade and political meanings of SPS relevant measures of individual Members is offered by the report of the WTO Secretariat, Specific Trade Concerns, G/SPS/GEN/204/Rev.5, 25 February 2005.

[77] *European Communities – Hormones*, (see footnote 75 above).

[78] *Japan – Measures Affecting Agricultural Products*, WT/DS76/AB/R, 22 February 1999.

[79] *Australia – Measures Affecting Importing of Salmon*, WT/DS18/AB/R, 20 October 1998.

[80] *Japan – Measures Affecting Importation of Apples*, WT/DS245/AB/R, 26 November 2003.

b. *Scope of Applicability*

420 The SPS has a precisely defined scope. It is based on the concept of "sanitary and phytosanitary measures", and is **limited in light of the objectives and aims pursued by the measures** (Art. 1.1, Annex A, para. 1 SPS). Annex A, para. 1 SPS, which contains definitions, differentiates between various risks and subjects of protection and provides for four different combinations in its *lit.* a–d.

421 Measures which protect human, animal or plant life or health from **pests** or which prevent or limit other damage caused by their entry or establishment are listed in *lit.* a, c and d. Dangers to human, animal or plant life or health from **"additives, contaminants, toxins or disease-causing organisms in foods, beverages or feedstuffs"** are contained in *lit.* b. Furthermore, dangers to animal and plant life or health from **diseases, disease-carrying or disease-causing organisms** (*lit.* a), as well as dangers to human health or life from diseases carried by animals, plants or goods (*lit.* c) are named.

422 These definitions, common to the vocabulary of the relevant international instruments for sanitary and phytosanitary measures, are very technical and require careful **interpretation**. For example, it is uncertain whether measures relating to **genetically modified organisms (GMOs)** fall within the regulations of the SPS Agreement.[81]

423 In the final paragraph of Annex A para. 1 SPS various regulative forms of such measures are cited. The wide range includes, *inter alia* "end product criteria; processes and production methods; testing, inspection, certification and approval procedures". Thus, the SPS also includes **production-related** measures.

424 "Relevant requirements associated with the transport of animals or plants, or with the materials necessary for their survival during transportation" are also cited, thus incorporating **animal welfare** ideals.

425 Finally, even the **packaging and labelling** requirements directly relating to food safety are expressly mentioned.

426 Provided that these measures can either directly or indirectly affect international trade, their development and application are covered by the SPS Agreement (Art. 1.1 SPS). Measures which do not fall within this definition can be covered by the TBT Agreement (Art. 1.4 SPS), and

[81] *Stoll*, Controlling the Risks of Genetically Modified Organisms: The Cartagena Protocol on Biosafety and the SPS Agreement, Yearbook of International Environmental Law 10 (1999), 82 *et seq.*

may also be covered by the general provisions of the GATT 1994.[82] It is for this reason that, for example, the Appellate Body rejected the applicability of the SPS Agreement due to the inorganic character of asbestos and the related dangers to health in ***EC – Asbestos***.[83]

427 The **temporal scope** of the Agreement in not limited to measures which were implemented after its entry into force on 1 January 1995. The Panel and the Appellate Body have both agreed that they may pass judgment on measures which were already in force before that date.[84]

c. *Harmonization and Mutual Recognition*

428 In relation to its significant importance (para. 302), which has already been discussed, the **harmonization** of sanitary and phytosanitary measures is extensively covered by the SPS Agreement.

429 Members must base their measures on international standards, guidelines and recommendations (Art. 3.1 SPS). Annex A para. 3 SPS names the **relevant standard-setting international organizations** for the respective subject matters.[85]

430 If national measures conform to such international standards, guidelines and recommendations, they shall be deemed necessary and **presumed** to be consistent with the provisions of the SPS and GATT 1994 (Art. 3.2 SPS).

431 Under certain prerequisites **national measures** which provide for a higher level of sanitary or phytosanitary protection than international standards may be justified (Art. 3.3 SPS). There must be scientific justification available for the higher level, or the higher level must be determined in accordance with the provisions set out in Art. 5.1 to 5.8 SPS Agreement.[86] Furthermore, these measures may not contradict other provisions of the Agreement.

---

[82] For the similarities and differences of the TBT and SPS Agreement, see *Rege*, GATT Law and Environment-Related Issues Affecting the Trade of Developing Countries, JWT 28 (1994) 3, 95, 103 *et seq.*

[83] *European Communities – Asbestos* (see above footnote 70), para. 167.

[84] *European Communities – Measures Affecting Meat and Meat Products*, WT/DS26/R/USA, paras 8.24–8.28, and WT/DS48/R/CAN, paras 8.27–8.31 as well as WT/DS26/AB/R, WT/DS48/AB/R 13 February 1998, paras 128–30.

[85] According to Annex A. para. 3, questions of food safety are to be dealt with by the Codex Alimentarius Commission. In relation to animal safety and *zoonoses*, questions must be referred to the Office International des Epizooties. For matters of phytosanitation and the corresponding international standards, one must refer to the International Plant Protection Convention and the relative regional organizations. Annex A Nr. 3 also includes an opening clause, wherein the norms, directives and recommendations of other international organisations may be referred to.

[86] See *European Communities – Hormones* (see above footnote 75), paras 176 *et seq.*

432 With reference to continuing harmonization, with the aim of the development and regular supervision of internationally agreed standards, guidelines and recommendations, Members have an explicit obligation, in accordance with Art. 3.4 SPS, to participate, as far as possible, in the work of the relevant international organizations. These organizations include the **Codex Alimentarius Commission**, which is administered by the World Health Organisation (WHO) and the United Nations Food and Agriculture Organisation (FAO), which work for standards for safety in food; the **Office International des Epizooties** (IOE)[87] which deals with animal diseases; and the organizations of the **International Plant Protection Convention (IPPC)**, concerned with pest control.

433 The Committee for Sanitary and Phytosanitary Measures, set up in accordance with Art. 12.1 SPS, has the aim of designing a process for the supervision of international harmonization, and to **coordinate** related efforts with other international organizations.[88]

434 Thus, the SPS Agreement refers to the standardization of **other International Organizations.** Despite their supervisory and coordination efforts the WTO itself and the Committee have only limited influence on the process of standardization itself. Deficits and shortcomings in the drafting of these standards can therefore lead to tension within the WTO. For example, the *Hormones* case dealt with an often criticised decision of the Codex Alimentarius Commission in relation to the feeding of hormones to promote the growth of calves, which had been decided by only a narrow majority in the respective organization. Also, as a result of blockades, the Commission was unable to deal with the long debated topic of genetically modified organisms (GMOs).

435 As well as harmonization, the SPS Agreement contains provisions for **mutual recognition** of measures and standards. Art. 4.1 SPS talks of a clear duty for recognition even if such measures differ from a Member's own or from those used by other members trading in the same product, provided that the exporting nation can prove objectively that its measures allow for the appropriate level of protection of the importing Members (**equivalence principle**). According to Art. 4.1 s.2 SPS, the importing Member should be allowed access for control, testing and other relevant procedures. Art. 4.2 SPS encourages WTO Members to enter into consultations, with the aim of entering into bilateral and multilateral agreements in relation to the recognition of equivalence. In practice, Members are often not satisfied with the idea of equivalence. Rather, they demand identical controls, especially in relation to devel-

---

[87] The IOE is also known as the World Animal Health Organisation.
[88] See Art. 3.4 and 12.4 SPS.

oping countries.[89] The idea of mutual recognition, mentioned in Art. 4 SPS, has still not achieved great significance.

d. *The Admissibility of Measures in Individual Cases*

436 Art. 5 SPS is of greater significance, as it covers the prerequisites which relate to the admissibility of **Members' measures** in individual cases and irrespective of harmonization and mutual recognition. This provision contains three general regulations: (i) it prescribes that all measures must be based on a **risk assessment**, (ii) it specifies the elements of non-discrimination, and (iii) it contains a rule on provisional measures in Art. 5.7 SPS.

437 Art. 5.1 SPS demands that there must be an **assessment of the risks** to the life or health of humans, animals or plants, and therefore sets procedural requirements of rationality for such measures.

438 Art. 5.1 and 5.3 SPS describe which factors must be taken into account in such risk assessment. In the sense of international harmonization not of the standards themselves, but rather of the assessment *procedures*, the **procedures as developed by the relevant International Organizations** are to be considered (Art. 5.1 SPS).

439 Furthermore, such risk assessment must be based on **scientific evidence** as prescribed in detail in Art. 5.2 SPS. These include various production methods and procedures, inspection, testing and sampling and checking methods, the existence of certain diseases or pests and certain disease- or pest-free areas, as well as other environmental conditions. As these factors show, the assessment of risk is not limited to biological contexts, but also contain regulatory technical contexts (related production methods and procedures), as well as the corresponding regulatory instruments (such as inspection procedures).

440 The standards of risk assessment are not just limited to factors open to scientific appraisal, such as biological observations or the occurrence of certain illnesses or pests, but also take the actual **usage and technical procedures** into account. The scientific references contained in Art. 5 SPS thus do not limit the circle of possible factors. Rather they define methodical approaches to risk assessment procedures.

441 In relation to the health of animals and plants, **relevant economic factors** of the Members are also taken into consideration. Potential damage in term of loss of production, cost of control or eradication and the relative cost-effectiveness of alternative methods to limiting risks all fall under this heading (Art. 5.3 SPS).

[89] Committee on Sanitary and Phytosanitary Measures, SPS Agreement and Developing Countries, G/SPS/GEN/128, 16 July 1999.

442 Art. 5 SPS demands that a measure must be **based on** the risk assessment. The Panel in the ***Hormones*** case interpreted this as a procedural obligation and decided that the risk assessment must have been considered in the drafting and implementation of the measure.[90] This would have had the effect of making it impossible to supply the scientific evidence only during a dispute settlement procedure.[91] However, the Appellate Body did not follow this interpretation of the wording of Art. 5.1 SPS. Instead, it accepts it as sufficient if the measure, at the time of the dispute settlement procedure, can be based on some scientific evidence.[92] The basis for this decision was that new or recent scientific discoveries could otherwise support the same measures if immediately implemented again (and thus irrespective of the outcome of a dispute settlement procedure).

443 If, at the end of the risk assessment, it is deemed that there is a risk, the Member must take further steps to **determine a suitable level of protection** (Art. 5.4 to 6 SPS). With this differentiation of individual procedural steps, the SPS Agreement follows the belief that the scientific risk assessment is not sufficient on its own as a basis for appropriate measures. Art. 5.4 to 6 SPS contains a relevant and noteworthy list of criteria and rationales for limiting risks.

444 Members should ensure that, when setting protection levels, negative effects on trade are kept to a minimum (Art. 5.4 SPS). The measures should "not be more trade-restrictive than required to achieve their appropriate level of sanitary or phytosanitary protection, taking into account technical and economic feasibility" (Art. 5.6 SPS). A footnote makes it clear that this is not the case if "there is another measure, reasonably available taking into account technical and economic feasibility, that achieves the appropriate level of sanitary or phytosanitary protection and is significantly less trade-restrictive".[93] In the cases of ***Australia – Salmon*** and ***Japan – Agricultural Products***, a three-step test of the criteria of necessity was developed. A sanitary or phytosanitary measure is not necessary in the sense of the SPS Agreement, when an alternative measure is available, which (i) is technically and economically feasible and available (ii), offers the same level of protection in the given situation and (iii) is less restrictive on trade than the

[90] *European Communities – Hormones*, WT/DS26/R, 18 August 1997, para. 8.113 (US), para. 8.116 (Canada).

[91] See *Hurst*, Hormones: European Communities – Measures Affecting Meat and Meat Products, EJIL 9 (1998) 1, 182 *et seq.* <http://www.ejil.org/journal/Vol9/No1/sr1g.html>.

[92] *European Communities – Hormones* (see above footnote 75), paras 189–93.

[93] See the legal definition in the footnotes of Art. 5.6 SPS.

measure in question.[94] This test can be seen as a further step towards a test of proportionality.[95]

445 Further, Art. 5.5 SPS is of great significance. The provision aims for a strengthening of the principle of non-discrimination and the limitation of disguised restrictions on trade. Members are to avoid arbitrary or unjustified distinctions in levels of protection, even when these arise from different situations.[96] These rules are of great importance, since they enforce a requirement for **consistency** with reference to similar political areas, which is hardly provided for in national legislation. One example of the use of this principle is the conflict between the EU and the United States with regard to the import of beef treated with hormones. The Panel and the Appellate Body criticized the EU for its strict stance on the ban on the feeding of growth-promoting hormones in the beef sector, while, at the same time, the addition of antibiotics to animal feedstuffs was acceptable.[97] A further example is the limitation of Australian imports on fresh and frozen salmon, in ***Australia – Salmon***, which was seen as unjustified, since comparable or even more severe health risks were evident in other kinds of fish.[98]

446 The regulation also includes instructions for the development of guidelines to further the practical implementation of Art. 5.5 SPS. The instructions are qualified, in that all relevant factors, including the exceptional character of human health risks to which people voluntarily expose themselves, must be taken into account.

447 Finally, the **precautionary rules** contained in the SPS are of special significance, even if they are not expressly referred to as such in Art. 5.7 SPS.[99] The Members have the right provisionally to implement measures on the basis of pertinent information, even in cases in which the relevant scientific evidence is not sufficient. In these cases there is an underlying obligation to collect additional information necessary for a more objective assessment of risk, and to review the measures within a reasonable period of time.[100]

---

94 *Australia – Salmon*, WT/DS18/AB/R, 20 October 1998, para. 194; *Japan – Agricultural Products*, WT/DS76/AB/R, 22 February 1999, para. 123.

95 See *Hilf/Puth*, The principle of proportionality on its way into WTO/GATT law in v. Bogdandy/Mavroidis/Mény (Eds), Studies in transnational economic law in honour of Claus-Dieter Ehlermann, 2002, 199 *et seq.*; see para. 397 for similar developments under the TBT Agreement.

96 See the fundamental provision Art. 2.3 and the special provision of Art. 5.5 SPS.

97 *European Communities – Hormones* (see above footnote 75).

98 *Australia – Salmon* (see above footnote 94), paras 154 and 227 *et seq.*

99 To date, only Japan has relied – unsuccessfully – on Art. 5.7 SPS, see *Japan – Agricultural Products* (see above footnote 94), paras 86–94 and *Japan – Apples*, WT/DS245/AB/R, 26 November 2003, paras 161–188.

100 In relation to the permissible relevant measures, the Members may look to other international organisations, as well as the measures used by other Members.

448 In general, this provision is understood to be an expression of the **precautionary principle**, which has gained increased significance in the area of environmental and consumer protection.[101] In the ***Hormones* case** the EU did not rely on Art. 5.7 SPS, but rather based its claims on the more general application of the precautionary principle. The Appellate Body refused to accept the validity and content of this principle. It decided that, in the framework of the SPS Agreement, a general principle could not displace the specific provisions of Art. 5.7 SPS.[102]

449 The SPS includes the idea that a **regional** epidemic of a disease or pest is not necessarily a sufficient basis for applying a measure to the entire area, even though it could be (Art. 6 SPS). Consequently, a general ban on imports of an exporting nation is not valid if a disease or pest is contained only within a region of that nation. In assessing the conditions of a region, the exporting nation must supply information on the prevalence of the disease or pest, the existence of eradication or control programmes, and appropriate criteria and guidelines by the relevant international organizations.[103] If a Member wants to continue with the export of goods, it must prove that a certain area is free from pests or diseases, or subject to only low pest prevalence.[104]

e. *Further Procedural and Institutional Provisions*

450 The observance of sanitary or phytosanitary provisions in imports and exports presupposes a knowledge and availability of the rules of the importing Member (**transparency**). According to Art. 7 SPS, Members are under the obligation to notify any changes to SPS measures and to indicate any changes as regulated in Annex B. Every Member must promptly publicize any SPS measures and must establish national inquiry points to answer any questions of exporting nations with advice and facts.[105]

451 In an institutional sense, the **Committee on Sanitary and Phytosanitary Measures** completes the Agreement. The aim of the Committee is to provide the Members with a discussion forum for coordination, cooperation and harmonization in the area of the SPS Agreement. Decisions are taken by consensus, as is the usual GATT practice.[106]

---

[101] See observations of the Commission of Applicability of the Precautionary Principle (2000) 1, 2 February 2000 and the Decision of the EFTA High Court of 5 April 2001, published in EuZW 12 (2001) 18, 573 *et seq.; Alemanno*, Le principe de précaution en droit communautaire, Revue du Droit de l'Union Européenne 2 (2001) 4, 917 *et seq.*

[102] *European Communities – Hormones* (see above footnote 75), para. 124.

[103] Art. 6.1 s.2 SPS.

[104] Art 6.3 SPS.

[105] See the Handbook of the WTO Secretariat for details <http://www.wto.org/english/tratop_e/sps_e/spshand_e.pdf> and *Japan – Apples*, WT/DS245/R, 15 July 2003, paras 8.305 *et seq.*

[106] Art. 12.1 s.3 SPS.

452 Concurrently, the Committee functions as an **interface** between the WTO and the related international organizations in the area of SPS measures, especially the Codex Alimentarius Commission, the Office International des Epizooties, and the secretariat of the International Plant Protection Convention (para. 432). This is to secure the availability of the best possible scientific and technical information and to avoid parallel activities.[107]

453 The SPS Agreement is similar to the TBT Agreement in that it provides for Panels for **dispute settlement** under the rules of the DSU, as well as an advisory technical experts group to provide answers to scientific and technical questions (Art. 11.2 SPS).

[107] For the activities of the individual organizations, see the Report (2004) on the Activities of the Committee on Sanitary and Phytosanitary Measures, G/L/709, 8 November 2004.

CHAPTER SIX

FAIR TRADE AND REMEDIES – ANTI-DUMPING, SUBSIDIES AND GOVERNMENT PROCUREMENT

Jacob Viner, Dumping: A Problem of International Trade, 1923; *Johannes-Friedrich Beseler & A. N. Williams*, Anti-dumping and Anti-subsidy law: the European Communities, 1986; *Martin Nettesheim*, Ziele des Antidumping- und Antisubventionsrechts, 1994; *Gary Horlick & Eleanor C. Shea*, The World Trade Organization Antidumping Agreement, JWT 29 (1995) 1, 5–31; *Alan O. Sykes*, The economics of injury in antidumping and countervailing duty cases, International review of law and economics, 16 (1996) 1, 5–26; *David A. Palmeter*, A commentary on the WTO Anti-dumping Code, JWT 30 (1996) 4, 43–69; *Kofi Oteng Kufuor*, The developing countries and the shaping of GATT/WTO antidumping law, JWT 32 (1998) 6, 167–196; *Alicia Cebada Romero*, Antidumping, countervailing duties, and safeguard measures: comparison between the Agreements of the European Community and European eastern countries and NAFTA, Arizona journal of international and comparative law 16 (1999) 2, 437–479; *Marco C. Bronckers & Natalie McNelis*, Rethinking the "like product" definition in WTO antidumping law, JWT 33 (1999) 3, 73–91; *Paul C. Rosenthal & Robert T. C. Vermylen*, The WTO antidumping and subsudies agreements: did the United States achieve its objectives during the Uruguay Round?, Law and policy in international business 31 (2000) 3, 871–895; *Michael Rodi*, Die Subventionsrechtsordnung, 2000; *Richard O. Cunningham*, Commentary on the first five years of the WTO Antidumping Agreement and Agreement on Subsidies and Countervailing Measures, Law and policy in international business 31 (2000) 3, 897–905; *Brink Lindsey*, The US antidumping law: rhetoric versus reality, JWT 34 (2000) 1, 1–38; *Martin Lukas*, Antisubventionsrecht, in: GH II/*Krenzler*, E 7 (2000); *Fritz-Harald Wenig*, in: *Manfred Dauses* (Ed.), Handbuch des EU-Wirtschaftsrechts, 2000 (loseleaf), K II; *Wenxi Li*, Anti-dumping law of WTO/GATT and EC: gradual evolution of anti dumping law in global economic integration, 2001; *Marc Bénitah*, The law of subsidies under the GATT/WTO system, 2001; *Pierre Didier*, The WTO anti-dumping code and EC practice, JWT 35 (2001) 1, 33–54; *Michael Sánchez Rydelski*, EG und WTO Antisubventionsrecht, 2001; *James P. Durling & Matthew R. Nicely*, Understanding the WTO anti-dumping agreement: negotiation historiy and subsequent interpretation, 2002; *Alexander Polouektov*, Non-market economy issues in the WTO anti-dumping law and accession negotiations, JWT 36 (2002) 1, 1–37; *Christian Tietje*, Current developments under the WTO agreement on subsidies and countervailing measures as an example for the functional unity of domestic and international trade law, 2004; *Edwin Vermulst & Folkert Graafsma*, WTO disputes: anti-dumping, subsidies and safeguards, 2004; *Judith Czako & Johann Human & Jorge Miranda*, A handbook of anti-dumping investigations, 2004; *Peggy A. Clarke & Jacques Bourgeois*, WTO Dispute Settlement practice relating to subsidies and countervailing measures, The WTO dispute Settlement System 1995–2003, 2004, 353–379; *William A. Kerr*, Anti-dumping in the Doha negotiations: Fairy tales at the WTO, JWT 38 (2004) 2, 211–244; *Arandhna Aggarwal*, The WTO Anti-Dumping Agreement: possible reform through the inclusion of a public interest clause, ICRIER 142 (2004); *Douglas R. Nelson & Hylke Candenbussche* (eds), The WTO & anti-dumping, 2005.

454 Undercutting prices, subsidies and public procurement at the regional and national level often fall within the scope of competition policy and related regulations. Unlike the ill-fated Havana Charter (para. 13),[1] however, the GATT does not include such concepts. Instead, dumping (paras 458 *et seq.*) and subsidies (paras 489 *et seq.*) are dealt with by Art. VI, which is based on a quite different concept: whereas competition policy concerns fair competition in the market place, Art. VI GATT 1994 is often considered as applying a concept of "fair trade". Such concept can be considered to apply a measure of fairness which relates to States and their interests and relations, as ruled upon by the world trade order.[2]

455 **Art. VI** GATT 1994 includes regulations on dumping and subsidies, making it clear that these practices are to be "condemned" under certain circumstances. Unlike competition law concepts, however, the focus of Art. VI is solely **trade-related**. Thus, this regulation does not rule on the legality of dumping or subsidies, but rather authorizes Members to counteract these practices by levying additional tariffs in certain limited circumstances.

456 Special and more detailed rules on these topics were agreed upon during the Tokyo Round. During the Uruguay Round these rules were further elaborated on, now forming the **Agreement on Implementation of Art. VI GATT** (the so-called Anti-Dumping Agreement – ADA) and the **Agreement on Subsidies and Countervailing Measures** (the so-called SCM Agreement – ASCM), as part of the WTO order.

457 The establishment of the WTO also led to the entry into force of the **Agreement on Government Procurement (GPA)**, which deals with similar questions of fair trade.

---

[1] The entire Chapter V of that Charter was devoted to competition or, as the heading reads, "Restrictive Business Practices".

[2] The need to include more competition or anti-trust regulations at the WTO level has, however, been voiced repeatedly. See, e.g. *Petersmann*, The international competition policy of the EC and the need for an EC initiative for a "Plurilateral Agreement on Competition and Trade" in the WTO, in: *Syder*, (ed), Constitutional dimensions of European Economic Integration, 1996, 289 *et seq.*; *Ehlermann & Ehring*, WTO dispute settlement and competition law: views from the perspective of the Appellate Body's experience, Fordham International Law Journal 26 (2003) 6, 1505 *et seq.*; *Weinrauch*, Competition Law in the WTO: the rationale for a framework Agreement, 2004.

I. *Anti-dumping*

458 Historically, national anti-dumping rules first evolved in the United States and Canada, and were then incorporated into the national laws of many, mainly industrialized states.[3] National anti-dumping laws emerged to protect national businesses against aggressive practices of driving out competition by exporting under cost, or above cost, but nevertheless under the prices for the product in the exporters home market.

459 While condemning the practice of dumping under certain circumstances, the aim of GATT and WTO regulations on dumping is not limited to combating these unfair trade practices. The more fundamental interest in firm rules on dumping and subsidies lies in the **curbing of the protectionist tendencies** of Members. Fear of possible abuses of the system stems from the fair amount of discretion left to the acting Members states, inherent in the calculation of dumping and the causal injury determination which may well be used specifically to target foreign competitors. This tendency has significantly increased with the continuous lowering of tariffs and the greater stress of competition that the opening of markets has brought about.[4] Therefore, the work on international anti-dumping rules and disciplines must be understood as a quest to balance two (opposed) objectives: to maintain mechanisms to counteract unfair trade practices on the one hand, and to limit the protectionist application of this instrument in circumvention of the stricter rules on safeguards (see above paras 162 *et seq.*) on the other hand.

460 Over recent decades, the originally small number of states with national anti-dumping legislation and the number of anti-dumping procedures have considerably increased. Until 1980 such proceedings took place mainly in the European Union, the United States, Australia, Canada, New Zealand, and South Africa. In the 1980s, the number of proceedings doubled to 1,600; from 1990 to 1999 2,483 such proceedings were notified. It is to be observed that recently anti-dumping measures have increasingly been initiated by "non-traditional" Members such as Mexico, Brazil, Argentina, Korea, and India. In 2004 the WTO received 76 notifications by Members concerning national anti-dumping legislation.[5] While between 1990 and 1994 31% of proceedings were attributed to developing and transition countries, the percentage for the period of 1995 to 1999 rose to 47%. The **main target countries** of anti-dumping

[3] As for the recent tendency of developing states to use this instrument see para. 460.
[4] *Blonigen & Presa*, Antidumping, Working Paper of the National Bureau of Economic Research, July 2001, at <http://www.nber.org/papers/w8398>.
[5] WTO, Report (2004) of the Committee on Anti-dumping Practices, G/L/707, 4 November 2004, 2.

measures in the year 1999/2000 were the EU, China, Korea, Indonesia, Taiwan, Thailand, India, Russia, Japan, and the United States. Metal and especially steel are the sectors most targeted by anti-dumping proceedings.[6]

461 As the official name of the Anti-Dumping Agreement already indicates, the central rule on anti-dumping can be found in **Art. VI GATT 1994**, which makes it clear that the introduction of a product into the commerce of another country at less than normal value is to be condemned if it causes or threatens material injury to an established industry in the territory of that Member. However, Art. VI **does not contain a prohibition** on the practice of dumping. Such a prohibition would not be easy to enforce, as dumping – in contrast to the grant of a subsidy[7] – is not a government-driven practice. Rather, it is a business practice which is commonly accepted as long as it does not produce unwanted negative effects, and thus distorts trade. Instead of prohibiting dumping, Art. VI GATT 1994 authorizes member states to take national measures to counteract the trade distortion. According to Art. VI:2 GATT 1994 a contracting party is allowed to levy an additional duty on the dumped product (**"anti-dumping duty"**) in order to offset the trade-distorting effects of the dumping.

In addition to this general statement **Ad Art. VI GATT 1994**[8] contains some clarifications on the determination of dumping and on currency conversions. Ad Art. VI:1 No. 2 also recognizes that special difficulties exist in determining the normal value of a product imported from a country where all prices are fixed by the state, and that a comparison with domestic (market-based) prices may not be appropriate. This recognition serves as the basis for the differential treatment of products from market and **non-market economies**, inherent in most national anti-dumping laws.

Art. VI GATT 1994 itself does not give much guidance on the circumstances under which Members are to be allowed to impose countermeasures against these unfair trade practices. Nor does the provision include any procedural safeguards to ensure that this instrument is not used in a protectionist manner. However, significant regulations and clarifications in this respect were included in the so-called **Tokyo Code**, which was negotiated during the Tokyo Round.[9] The ADA builds on the general statement contained in Art. VI GATT 1994 and on the

---

[6] The numbers are taken from an UNCTAD study analysing the 2,483 anti-dumping procedures between 1990 and 1999, "Impact of Anti-Dumping and Countervailing Duty Actions", TB/B/COM.1/EM.14/2, 24 October 2000, at <http://www.unctad.org/en/docs/c1em14d2.en.pdf>.

[7] See below paras 496 *et seq.*

[8] See Annex 1 of the GATT 1994, Notes and Supplementary Provisions.

[9] Agreement on Implementation of Article VI GATT, BISD 26S/171, which entered into force on 1 January 1980. See also the Agreement on Interpretation and Application of Art. VI, XVI and XXIII GATT, BISD 26S/56, which entered into force on 1 January 1980.

Tokyo Code by specifying the conditions under which Members are authorized to act against dumped imports. To this end the **ADA** contains numerous and detailed rules for national anti-dumping investigation procedures and stipulates methods for defining the phrases used in Art. VI, such as "dumping", "normal value", "export price" and "injury". Art. 1 ADA makes it clear that national anti-dumping measures shall be adopted only pursuant to investigations initiated and conducted in accordance with the provisions of the ADA.

462 The ADA consists of three parts and two annexes. While parts II and III of the Agreement contain institutional provisions and provisions on dispute settlement (part II), as well as final provisions (part III), the main material standards on anti-dumping procedures are contained in part I (Art. 1–15). This main part of the Agreement contains rules on the definition of dumping (Art. 2) and on the definition of injury (Art. 3), as well as multiple procedural provisions on national anti-dumping investigation, determinations and measures. Lastly, Annex I covers on-the-spot investigations, while Annex II imposes constraints on the use of best information available in cases in which better information cannot be obtained owing to the parties failure to cooperate.

1. *Dumping and the Determination of Dumping*

463 Dumping refers to a **comparison of two prices** of a product, namely the real, or "normal", price for a product (the products **"normal value"**) on the one hand, and the price at which the product is exported into the market of a foreign country (the **"export price"**) on the other hand. Dumping within the meaning of WTO law occurs when the export price is **significantly less** than the products normal value (Art. 2 ADA). "Anti-dumping" refers to national measures by an importing Member to counteract the process of dumping, namely the levying of an **anti-dumping duty**. Through this additional duty the price of the product in the importing Members market is raised to what is believed to be the products normal (i.e. fair) value.

464 In these calculations of normal value and export price, certain factors such as the wage structure and social costs of production are not to be taken into account. The idea of free trade is essentially based on differences in this respect and the respective **"comparative advantages"** – social or environmental problems which are caused by this comparative advantage are not to be solved by the imposition of anti-dumping duties, but are the subject of other regimes within the WTO order.[10]

[10] Imports can also be subject to measures applied as safeguard measures in accordance with Art. XIX GATT 1994, see above paras 162 *et seq.*

465 In principle this price comparison in dumping investigations seems rather simple. However, Members have spent considerable time agreeing on ways to calculate and construct such prices in situations in which it was felt that either the normal value or the export price could not simply be calculated according to the normal methods. Building on these **uncertainties**, Art. 2 ADA contains elaborate and often complex standards for dumping determinations, covering methods for the evaluation of the normal value of the product (Art. 2.2), the construction of the export price (Art. 2.3), the comparison between the two (Art. 2.4), the concept of like product (Art. 2.6), as well as special rules for non-market economies (Art. 2.7).

466 The starting point for the determination of the **normal value** of the product is the **sale price, in the ordinary course of trade**, in the exporting (home) country (Art. 2.5).[11] However, in cases in which there is no "ordinary course of trade" this price is not seen to be an adequate basis for the determination of the normal value and the methods of calculation become more complicated. Art. 2.2 ADA deals specifically with the notion of the absence of an "ordinary course of trade" and allows alternative calculation methods for two distinct cases: where there are no significant sales of a like product in the domestic market of the exporter (less than 5% of the exports),[12] or where there is a "particular market situation" or a low volume of sales in the domestic market of the exporting country.

467 For these situations, Art. 2.2 ADA and Art. VI GATT 1994, contain two alternative methods for price calculations "in the absence of such domestic price" (**constructed normal value**): the export price to a third country on the one hand, or the actual cost of production on the other. In the calculation of normal value according to the cost of production, Art. 2.2 stipulates that a reasonable amount for **administrative, selling and general costs (so-called "SGA costs")**, as well as for profits, must be added, and contains further specifications to this end.

468 As with the determination of the normal value, the ADA distinguishes between the normal situation and alternative methods for calculation of the **export price**. Normally, the export price is the price actually paid by the importer and is evidenced in the trading documents (**bill of lading**). However, in certain situations this price is believed to be unreliable, namely where the exporter and importer are "related", i.e. part of the same enterprise or otherwise closely linked by association or Agreement. In this case Art. 2.3 allows the use of an **alternative export price** consisting of the price of first sale to an independent buyer. If

[11] Or, in transhipment cases, the country of origin of the product.
[12] The so-called "5% representative test rule", see footnote 2 to Art. 2.2 ADA.

there is no such sale, or if the product is no longer in the same condition as at the time of export (i.e. it has been altered), a second alternative method may be used. This calculated export price then is similar to the calculated normal value, allowing for SGA costs and profits.[13]

469 In order to ensure a **fair comparison** between the normal value and the export price, Art. 2.4 ADA contains detailed provisions on allowances. As generally the comparison is to be made **"at the same level of trade"**, normally ex-factory, allowances must be made for differences which affect the price comparability, such as taxes, costs, profits, quantities, physical characteristics, and currency conversions.[14] In highly prominent cases the dispute settlement institutions of the WTO have clarified that the practice of **"zeroing"**, namely the exclusion of non-dumped products in the calculation, is contrary to Article 2.4.2 ADA. Thus, products which are not dumped must also be considered when calculating the weighted average of all export transactions concerning the same product.[15]

The result of this calculation is the so-called **dumping margin**. This margin defines the level of dumping and also represents the maximum level of anti-dumping measure that may be implemented. However, the ADA finds that it is desirable for the amount of the dumping duty to be less than the dumping margin (Art. 9.1).[16]

As far as imports from **non-market economies (NMEs) are concerned**, Art. 2.7 ADA states that the aforementioned provisions are without prejudice to the second Supplementary Provision to paragraph 1 of Article VI in Annex I to GATT 1994 (Ad Art. VI).[17] Thus, special rules contained in national legislation concerning dumped imports from NMEs still apply in addition to the rules set out in the ADA. In the United States' and the European Union anti-dumping legislation the normal value of a product from a NME exporter is calculated according to the cost of production in a **third ("analogous") country**.[18]

---

[13] Cases that have dealt with questions relating to normal value and export price calculations include: *United States – DRAMS*, WT/DS99/R, 29 January 1999; *Thailand – H-Beams*, WT/DS122/R, 28 September 2000, para. 7.95 *et seq.*; *European Communities – Bed-linen from India*, WT/DS141/R, 30 October 2000, para. 6.119 *et seq.* and WT/DS141/AB/R, 1 March 2001, para. 45 *et seq.; Guatemala – Grey Portland Cement*, WT/DS156/R, 24 October 2000, para. 8.180 *et seq.*; *United States – Stainless Steel Plate*, WT/DS179/R, 22 December 2000, para. 6.106 *et seq.*; *United States – Hot-rolled Steel Products*, WT/DS184/AB/R, 24 July 2001, para. 131 *et seq.*; *Argentina – Ceramic Flow Tiles*, WT/DS189/R, 28 January 2001, para. 6.106 *et seq.*

[14] As for currency conversions see *United States – Stainless Steel Plate*, WT/DS179/R, 22 December 2000, para. 3.1.

[15] *European Communities – Bed-Linen from India*, WT/DS141/R, 30 October 2000; WT/DS141/AB/R, 1 March 2001 and *United States – Dumping Determinations on Softwood Lumber from Canada*, WT/DS264/R, 13 April 2004; WT/DS/264/AB/R, 11 August 2004.

[16] See also para. 8.

[17] See para. 461 above.

[18] See the special rules for China and Russia in EU anti-dumping legislation, Council

2. *Determination of Injury*

470 Under Art. VI GATT 1994, as well as under the ADA, dumping itself does not lead to the authorization of national anti-dumping measures. Both Art. VI GATT 1994 and Art. 1 ADA clearly state that dumping is to be condemned only if it causes an **injury to the domestic industry**. Thus, the ADA contains specific rules on when national authorities may make findings of "injury".

471 As to the definition of the concept of injury, footnote 9 to Art. 3 ADA makes it clear that injury is to mean three different kinds of damage: material injury to domestic industry, the threat of material injury, and material delay in the establishment of a national industry. While injury, i.e. damage itself is quantifiable, the concept of "material" injury is unclear. However, Art. 3 formulates prerequisites for the national authorities under which such **"material injury"** may be found. For one, the finding of an injury according to Art. 3 must relate to clear evidence and include an objective investigation of "both *(a)* the volume of the dumped imports and the effect of the dumped imports on prices in the domestic market for like products, and *(b)* the consequent impact of these imports on domestic producers of such products." The ADA further lists 15 factors that are to be evaluated during such investigation.[19]

472 In the case of a **threat of injury** national authorities may not rely on allegations or remote possibilities – the circumstances causing injury must be clearly foreseen and imminent. In the evaluation of this issue the national authorities are to consider specific factors, such as the rate of increase of the dumped imports (Art. 3.7).

A further prerequisite for anti-dumping measures is the **causal link** between the dumping and the material injury caused to domestic industry. Again, this causation must be substantially evidenced, and Art. 3.5 lists alternative factors that must be taken into consideration as a cause for the injury. The national authority shall take these factors into con-

Regulation (EC) No 905/98 of 27 April 1998 amending Regulation (EC) No 384/96, OJ No L 128/18, 30 April 1998. According to this legislation, market economy status may be granted to individual producers if they can show that they manufacture under market economy conditions (in a "bubble of market economy"). The EU and Russia agreed on market economy status for Russian producers during a summit on 29 May 2002.

[19] The non-exhaustive list of Art. 3.4 ADA covers the following economic factors: actual and potential decline in sales, profits, output, market share, productivity, return on investments, or utilization of capacity; factors affecting domestic prices; the magnitude of the margin of dumping; actual and potential negative effects on cash flow, inventories, employment, wages, growth, and the ability to raise capital or investments. See, e.g. *Thailand – H-Beams*, WT/DS122/AB/R, 12 March 2001, paras 125 *et seq.* and 7.231; *Mexico – High Fructose Corn Syrup*, WT/DS132/R, 28 January 2000, para. 7.128. The cumulative evaluation of imports from several countries all subject to anti-dumping investigations falls under the *de minimis* rule (Art. 3.3 ADA).

sideration in its decision, ruling out the causality of these factors for the injury found.

Clearly, the finding of causal injury depends largely on the definition of the **domestic industry**. In this respect Art. 4.1 states "that the term 'domestic industry' shall be interpreted as referring to the domestic producers as a whole of the like products or to those of them whose collective output of the products constitutes a major proportion of the total domestic production of those products". It is important to note that Art. 2.6 ADA includes a definition on the concept of **"like products"** which differs considerably from its use in other Agreements. For the purposes of the anti-dumping investigation the definition given is rather narrow and does not include directly competitive products.[20]

Art. 4 ADA also contains rules for certain **specific situations**. Where a producer is related to the importer or exporter of the product, or where he himself is the importer of the product, such producer may be omitted from the group making up the "domestic industry". In certain circumstances a regional domestic industry may be treated as the whole domestic industry, so that the internal market of a member state may be divided into a number of competing markets for the purposes of anti-dumping measures (Art. 4.1 (ii) ADA).[21] Where there is **regional economic integration** of several Members according to Art. XXIV GATT 1994, the integrated markets as a whole shall be the "domestic" market of these member states. Accordingly, the domestic industry of the EU generally is comprised of the industry of all of the member states.[22]

3. *Procedural Rules on Initiation and Investigation*

473 The decision whether or not to take anti-dumping measures must be based on a **formal investigation** by the competent national authorities. This national investigation procedure must fulfil certain minimum requirements relating to its initiation and implementation. At the same time as it sets requirements for national procedures, the ADA seeks to harmonize national standards and procedural principles in relation to so-called **"interested parties"** – meaning the governments and industries concerned.

474 The national investigative procedure regularly begins with the submission of a written complaint (the application) "by or on behalf of the **domestic**

[20] As does Art. 4.1 *lit.* c of the Safeguards Agreement, see paras 162 *et seq.*

[21] In this case anti-dumping duties will be levied only on products destined for certain regions of the domestic industry (see Art. 4.2 ADA). This regulation is subject to the constitutional law of the importing Member.

[22] As with other internal markets, the regional markets of economically integrated Member states may also be subdivided in accordance with Art. 4.1 (ii) ADA.

industry" producing the dumped or a like product. This application must contain evidence of the dumping, the injury and the causal link, and must be supported by 25% of the producers concerned (relating to total production).

475 A national investigation may be initiated or continued only in cases in which either the volume of the dumped imports or the dumping margin crosses a certain threshold. This so-called ***"de minimis"*** **rule** stipulates that a dumping margin must be considered negligible if it is less than 2% of the export price. The volume of dumped imports is seen to be negligible where it accounts for less than 3% of the imports of the like products, unless several *de minimis* imports from different countries combined account for more than 7% of the total imports. Where an application is filed in a *de minimis* case scenario the national authority must immediately terminate the procedure.

476 The prerequisites set out by the ADA for the national procedure deal with the rights of the national authorities to seek and obtain **information** from the parties concerned, as well as with the safeguarding of rights of due process for the parties concerned and the other "interested parties". In particular, the ADA contains elaborate rules on the gathering of evidence and access to information, as well as rules on procedure in the case of non-cooperation or the submission of false information by the governments or industries concerned (Art. 6 and Annex II). Also, the ADA contains a **right to be heard** and the rights to present evidence and of access to the file, confidentiality and information rights. Importantly, the transparency of the procedure is stipulated by Art. 12, which obliges national authorities to **publish** and explain the initiation of an investigation, as well as all determinations.

477 As for the duration of the procedure, Art. 5.10 ADA makes it clear that a national procedure should be concluded within **one year**, and should last no longer than 18 months, after its initiation.[23]

4. *National Measures and Review*

478 Where the national authorities determine that all the prerequisites for the imposition of measures are fulfilled they may act against the unfair dumping practice. By using the word "may" the ADA clarifies that there is **no obligation** on a Member to impose any measure once a finding of injurious dumping has been made – again, the ADA gives authority to the Member to act against dumping if all the prerequisites

[23] See also Art. 6.1.1 and 7.3 ADA.

are fulfilled and the procedural rules have been followed, however, without creating an obligation to counteract dumping under WTO law.[24]

479 The ADA provides for certain possible measures to counteract dumping: **anti-dumping duties, provisional measures and price undertakings**. This list of proposed measures is **conclusive** – further measures by national authorities or courts are contrary to WTO law (see also Art. 18.1 ADA).[25]

480 Following the investigation the national authorities may impose an **anti-dumping duty** on imports of the dumped product. Collection of the duty is to be non-discriminatory, with all imports of the product from all sources found to be injuriously dumped being affected. The amount of the duty may not be higher than the dumping margin. However, a lower duty is to be preferred, as the ADA is based on the idea that a dumping duty should be just high enough to counteract the injury to the domestic industry, and not necessarily counteract the dumping practice as a whole (Art. 9.1 ADA).[26] According to Art. 11.3 ADA the definitive anti-dumping duty is to be terminated **no later than five years** from its imposition unless continuing or recurring dumping and injury are to be expected.

481 In order quickly to offset the negative effects of dumping, i.e. the injury during the investigation, national authorities may resort to **provisional measures**. They may be applied 60 days after the beginning of the investigation and take the form of provisional anti-dumping duties or, preferably, a security paid by the alleged dumper. Provisional measures may be taken only in the case of a preliminary finding of dumping and injury to domestic industry and may be imposed for up to four months in normal proceedings, with the possibility of extension for up to nine months in special situations.[27]

482 An alternative way to suspend or even terminate the anti-dumping investigation is a so-called **"price undertaking"**, to be agreed upon between the government authority and the exporter. In a price undertaking the exporter agrees to revise his price or not to export products to the area

[24] In contrast, the US anti-dumping legislation calls for mandatory imposition of anti-dumping duties in case of a finding of dumping and causal injury.

[25] This was expressly stated by the Appellate Body in *United States – Anti-Dumping Act of 1916*, WT/DS136/AB/R and WT/DS162/AB/R, 28 August 2000, paras 133 *et seq.* More recently, the conclusiveness of measures was upheld in *United States – Continued Dumping and Subsidy Offset Act of 2000 (Byrd Amendment)*, WT/DS217/AB/R, WT/DS234/AB/R, 16 January 2003, para. 265.

[26] The EU has applied this preference in the form of the so-called "lesser duty rule", see para. 488.

[27] Both provisional and definitive anti-dumping measures have retroactive effect, see Art. 10 ADA.

in question. Price undertakings are to be voluntary and should be no higher than the dumping margin Art. 8.1 ADA.

483 All measures imposed by national authorities must be **reviewed** at fixed intervals in order to ensure that anti-dumping measures are not imposed for a longer period than that for which they are justified.[28] To this end, the Anti-dumping Agreement contains reviews in three different circumstances. During the time of imposition of the anti-dumping measure the national authority on its own behalf, as well as upon request by interested parties, shall review the measure in accordance with Art. 11.2 ADA in order to "examine whether the continued imposition of the duty is necessary to offset dumping, whether the injury would be likely to continue or recur if the duty were removed or varied, or both" (**"interim review"**). Positive information substantiating the review is to be submitted by the party and the measure is to be terminated immediately if the duty is found to be unwarranted.

As stated, definitive anti-dumping measures are to be continued for a maximum of five years from its imposition. However, Art. 11.3 ADA contains the possibility of continuing measures where the expiry of the measure is likely to lead to recurring or continued dumping and injury. On an application by domestic industry within a reasonable time of the expiry of the measure the national authorities review whether this may be the case (**"expiry review"**).[29]

Finally, in cases of a so-called "newcomer", i.e. a producer that did not import into the area at the time of the original anti-dumping investigation, an accelerated review is to be carried out by the national authorities during which no anti-dumping duty is to be levied from this importer (**"newcomer review"**).

5. *Institutions and Dispute Settlement*

484 The Anti-dumping Agreement introduces a **Committee on Anti-Dumping Practices** which is integrated into the institutional structure of the Council for Trade in Goods. It is composed of representatives from each of the Members. One of the main responsibilities of the Committee is the administration of and reporting on anti-dumping measures of the individual Members. All Members are required to notify

---

[28] See *United States – DRAMS*, WT/DS99/R, 29 January 1999, paras 6.22 *et seq.*

[29] In US anti-dumping law this review is referred to as a "sunset" review. The US legislation on this matter was the subject of a WTO dispute settlement proceeding, see *United States – Sunset Review of Anti-Dumping Duties on Corrosion-Resistant Carbon Steel Flat Products from Japan*, DS/244/AB/R, 15 December 2003 in which the US practice was found to be in violation of WTO rules (Art. 11.3 ADA).

their laws and regulations on anti-dumping procedures and to report all measures. This **notification and reporting obligation** follows a two-fold motive: to discipline the behaviour of the Members and to create the empirical basis for the further evolution of the anti-dumping regime.[30]

485 The breach of obligations stemming from Art. VI GATT 1994 or the Anti-dumping Agreement generally falls within the applicability of the Dispute Settlement Understanding. By way of deviation from the normal dispute settlement rules, the Anti-dumping Agreement contains an **important restriction on the Panels standard of review** and rules of interpretation. Regarding the interpretation of the Agreements, the Panel is bound by the national authority's interpretation, as long as it rests on one of the possible interpretations, irrespective of whether the Panel had favoured a different method of interpretation. More importantly, the competence of the Panel in anti-dumping cases is limited to an evaluation of whether the conclusion reached by the national authorities was **objective and unbiased and based on the proper facts**. Even if the Panel comes to a different overall conclusion on the dumping questions, an unbiased and objective conclusion reached by the national authorities is not to be overruled. Thus, the Panel is not allowed to make its own separate determination of dumping or injury ("*de novo*" review). Instead, it is limited to reviewing whether, in reaching its determination, the national authority followed the procedural steps laid down by the Anti-dumping Agreement in an objective and unbiased manner.

486 By imposing these strict limitations on the Panel's authority of review, which was a concession made to include mandatory dispute settlement in the field of anti-dumping, it has become evident from recent cases that review of the material legality of the anti-dumping measures, i.e. whether dumping or injury actually existed, is substituted by a **review of the procedural requisites** for the application of the measure.[31]

---

[30] The Committee is also responsible for the establishment of new uniform rules on anti-circumvention, following the Ministerial Decision on this topic. For this purpose an informal group on anti-circumvention was established. The examples cited in a statement by the WTO Secretariat clearly depict the many facets of the problem: G/ADP/IG/W/29, 18 April 2001.

[31] The EU has prepared for the inclusion of WTO DSB findings into its national law by Council Regulation (EC) No 1515/2001, 23 July 2001, on the measures that may be taken by the Community following a report adopted by the WTO Dispute Settlement Body concerning anti-dumping and anti-subsidy measures, OJ No L 201/10, 26 August 2001.

6. *Anti-dumping Legislation in the EU and the United States*

487 The US law on anti-dumping is contained in **Title VII of the Tariff Act of 1930**,[32] which was recently the subject of a Panel proceeding.[33] The Tariff Act is implemented by measures laid down by the US Department of Commerce (DOC)[34] and the US International Trade Commission (USITC).[35] While the DOC is responsible for the determination of dumping, the USITC performs the investigation on dumping and injury (injury test). In addition, the US authorities refer to the **Antidumping Act of 1916**,[36] which was held in a dispute settlement case not to be in conformity with the WTO[37] and which is in the process of being repealed by the US.[38] The Subsidies Enforcement Office (SEO) is responsible for complaints concerning foreign subsidies.[39] Where the USITC finds that there has been dumping and injury, the DOC is under an obligation to impose anti-dumping measures. The amount of anti-dumping duties to be levied must be identical to the margin of dumping found.

488 The EU has implemented the Anti-dumping Agreement by **Council Regulation (EC) No. 384/96** on protection against dumped imports from countries not being members of the European Community, as amended.[40] The regulation authorizes the European Commission to take provisional, and the Council of the European Union to take definitive, anti-dumping measures on an application from the Community industry. In contrast to the United States, the EU legislation implements provisions recommended in Art. 9.1 ADA in the form of a so-called **"lesser duty rule"**, and thus links the level of anti-dumping duty to the level of injury sustained by the Community industry, not to the margin of dumping.[41] Also, it makes the imposition of anti-dumping duties subject to their being in the **Community interest**. Thus, automatic adoption

---

[32] 19 U.S.C. §§ 1671 *et seq.*

[33] *United States – Measures Treating Export Restraint as Subsidies*, WT/DS194/R, 29 June 2001.

[34] 19 C.F.R. Part 351.

[35] 19 C.F.R. Part 200.

[36] 15 U.S.C. §§ 71–74.

[37] *United States – Anti-Dumping Act of 1916*, WT/DS136/R, 31 March 2000, WT/DS162/R, 29 May 2000; WT/DS136/AB/R, WT/DS162/AB/R, 28 August 2000.

[38] See the status report on implementation of 11 November 2004, WT/DS136/14/Add.32, WT/DS162/17/Add.32.

[39] See for an in-depth description of these institutions concerning subsidies the joint annual report of the USTR and the DOC to the Congress, Subsidies Enforcement Report (2004), at <http://www.ustr.gov/assets/Trade_Agreements/Monitoring_Enforcement/Subsidies_Enforcement/asset_upload_file596_5700.pdf>.

[40] Council Regulation (EC) No 461/2004 of 8 March 2004 amending Regulation (EC) No 384/96 on protection against dumped imports from countries not members of the European Community and Regulation (EC) No 2026/97 on protection against subsidised imports from countries not members of the European Community, OJ EC No L 77/12, 13 March 2004.

[41] See para. 480.

of definitive measures is not laid down in EU law. The investigation and determination of anti-dumping measures are administered by Directorates B and C of the **Directorate General Trade** of the European Commission. Directorate B is involved in the determination of injury and of community interest, while Directorate C is concerned with the dumping aspects of the investigation.[42]

II. *Subsidies and Countervailing Measures*

489 In parallel to the rules on anti-dumping, the WTO also contains rules on subsidization by Members. In a more competitive international environment WTO Members are often willing to help their national industries compete by granting financial assistance in the form of subsidies. For instance, the European Union granted subsidies in the amount of € 90 billion, mainly to the manufacturing sector, railway lines, agriculture, and coal during the period from 1997 to 1999.[43] In light of this **economic importance** the rules on subsidization follow the aim of disciplining and regulating the national practice of subsidization, with even more specific rules and prohibitions relating to subsidies that are felt to be most trade-distorting and unfair, such as export subsidies and subsidies containing local content rules.

490 Originally, **Art. XVI GATT 1947** contained but one paragraph on subsidization, allowing for a notification requirement for trade-distorting subsidies. Following further negotiations, additional amendments to Art. XVI GATT 1994 were incorporated into the Agreement, mainly pertaining to export subsidies, i.e. subsidies that are dependent upon export performance. Mirroring anti-dumping situations, **Art. VI:3 GATT 1994** contains the opportunity for Members to apply so-called "countervailing duties" in case of material injury attributed to subsidies.

491 As with the rules on anti-dumping, neither Art. XVI nor Art. VI GATT 1994 contain any clear guidance on the procedural issues of national subsidization. Owing to the need for additional and more comprehensive rules, a framework Agreement on subsidies was drafted during the Tokyo Round (**"Subsidies Code"**), which served as the basis for the

---

[42] See on the activity of the EU in anti-dumping and anti-subsidy matters the 22nd Annual Report from the Commission to the European Parliament on the Communities Anti-Dumping, Anti-Subsidy and Safeguard Activities, Overview of the Monitoring of Third Country Anti-Dumping, Anti-Subsidy and Safeguard Cases (2003), COM (2004) 828 final, 27 December 2004. Recent statistics can be found at <http://europa.eu.int/comm/trade/issues/respectrules/anti_dumping/stats.htm>.

[43] See the Ninth Survey on State Aid in the European Union, COM (2001) 403 final, 18 July 2001, para. 56.

discussion during the Uruguay Round.[44] While comprehensive in scope, the additional amendments to Art. XVI, as well as the Subsidies Code, were adopted by only a few, mainly industrialized Members.

492 The Uruguay Round **Agreement on Subsidies and Countervailing Measures** (the so-called SCM Agreement – ASCM) incorporated the body of the Tokyo Subsidies Code and expanded on these rules. Thus, the significance of the new Agreement is the broadening of the scope of the Agreements rules not only in a substantive sense, but also in membership. Following the Uruguay Round's single undertaking approach, the rules of the Agreement on Subsidies and Countervailing Measures have now become binding for all WTO Members.

493 While the basic structure of the Agreement on Subsidies and Countervailing Measures is **similar** to that of the Anti-dumping Agreement – it also gives guidance on procedural issues that bind national subsidization procedures and addresses possible counter-measures – in its rules on remedies the ASCM must be clearly **distinguished** from the parallel rules on anti-dumping.

494 The Antidumping Agreement understands dumping as a private practice by industry for which the Members cannot be made directly responsible (see above para. 461). The Agreement thus does not need to make a statement on the legality of the dumping practice itself. In contrast, subsidization is a trade distortion practised **directly by the governments of the Members**. Therefore, the Agreement on Subsidies and Countervailing Measures also includes rules on specific forms of subsidies which Members must refrain from using altogether ("prohibited subsidies") as well as on subsidies which may have negative effects on other Members' industries ("actionable subsidies"). Thus, the Agreement on Subsidies and Countervailing Measures contains not only an authorization for Members individually to act against the trade distortion, but also **rulings on the legality of certain forms of subsidization**.

495 As a consequence, the Agreement's remedies include not only rules on possible national measures in the form of countervailing duties against subsidization, but also the possibility of **directly invoking the breach of the Agreement** on Subsidies and Countervailing Measures against the subsidizing Member under a WTO Panel procedure under the authority of the Dispute Settlement Body.[45] However, these two remedies can be utilized only under certain distinct conditions relating to the type of effect of the trade distortion on the importing Member.[46]

---

[44] BISD 26S/56, which entered into force on 1 January 1980. See also footnote 9 above.

[45] In the Subsidies Code established during the Tokyo Round these two possibilities for action were referred to as "track I" (unilateral) and "track II" (multilateral).

[46] See below paras 509 *et seq.*

While broad in scope, the Agreement on Subsidies and Countervailing Measures generally does not cover agricultural subsidies. These are dealt with in the **Agreement on Agriculture**, which contains specific disciplines on them. The importance of agricultural subsidies for the further development of the WTO cannot be understated. Even though the failure of the last Ministerial Conference in Cancun was attributed to developing Members' boycott of discussions on competition and investment rules, the underlying differences concerning the EUs and United States' unwillingness substantially to reduce their agricultural subsidies was the driving force for the collapse of negotiations. The special rules on agricultural subsidies will therefore be discussed separately below (see paras 517 *et seq.*). Apart from the Agreement on Subsidies and Countervailing Measures, additional rules on subsidies are also contained in the plurilateral **Agreement on Trade in Civil Aircraft**[47] as well as in an **OECD Shipbuilding Agreement**.[48]

Over recent years and in parallel to developments in the anti-dumping field, a larger number of Members have enacted **national instruments on foreign subsidization**. While as of 31 December 2000 only 52 Members had notified such national regulations, this number has almost doubled to 96 Members as of 4 November 2004.[49] Such regulations are often enacted in relation to anti-dumping legislation. However, anti-subsidy measures are far less common than anti-dumping measures: between July 2002 and June 2003 there were a total of 103 national measures in force, with 13 new investigations initiated.[50]

1. *Definition of a "Subsidy" in the ASCM*

496 The Agreement on Subsidies and Countervailing Measures in its Art. 1 defines the term **"subsidy"** and thus defines the applicability of its rules to national measures. The Agreement uses a **broad definition** containing two prerequisites for a subsidy: first, a financial contribution by a government or public body, or any form of price support in the sense of Art. XVI ASCM, and, secondly, the "conferring of a benefit".

[47] The Agreement on Trade in Civil Aircraft has 30 signatories and 30 observers, of which two are international organizations (IMF and UNCTAD). See the recent Annual Report of the Committee on Trade in Civil Aircraft (2004), WT/L/591, 11 November 2004.

[48] Agreement Respecting Normal Competitive Conditions in the Commercial Shipbuilding and Repair Industry, signed on 21 December 1994 between the EU, Finland, Japan, Korea, Norway, Sweden, and the United States. Owing to the failure of the United States to ratify the Agreement, it has not entered into force. The full text can be downloaded from the OECD website, at <http://www.oecd.org/dataoecd/2/5/1880215.pdf>.

[49] The EU is counted as a single Member. See the Report of the Committee on Subsidies and Countervailing Measures (2004), G/L/711, 9 November 2004, para. 10, 3 and Annex C. For the data on the year 2000, see the WTO Annual Report (2001), 63 *et seq.*

[50] WTO Annual Report 2004, 45.

497 In addition to all forms of income or price support in the sense of Art. XVI GATT 1994, Art. 1 ASCM includes a **broad range of national support practices** in its definition of a subsidy. It includes not only the direct transfer of funds, like grants and loans as the most obvious example of financial contribution, but also other, indirect forms of contributions. Art. 1 mentions government revenue that is otherwise forgone or not collected and a government provision or purchase of goods and services other than general infrastructure.

498 Art. 1 defines **"government"** action as action by a government or public body within the territory of a member, and thus includes all levels of government, be it at the federal, state, or regional level. Art. 1(a)(1)(iv) further makes clear that these actions are also "government" actions in cases in which a private body is entrusted with or directed to carry out the contribution instead of the government. Thus, the common former practice of redirecting public funds through private enterprises in order to circumvent the applicability of the rule on subsidies has been curbed.

499 The second prerequisite to be fulfilled is the **"conferring of a benefit"** according to Art. 1 (b) ASCM. As in anti-dumping law, where one of the problems involves the determination of dumping through the calculation of several, constructed prices, in subsidies law one practical problem involved in the determination of a subsidy is the conferring of a benefit. The two differing approaches to this problem advocated (mainly) by the European Union and the United States have been sufficiently clarified by the Appellate Body. While the United States had argued that the conferring of a benefit necessarily entails some sort of "cost of the government", the Appellate Body has now stated that the "benefit" must be determined from the view point of the recipient. If the recipient is "better off", i.e. "he has received a financial contribution on terms more favourable than those available to the recipient in the market", then he has received a "benefit" (the so-called **"commercial benchmark" test**).[51]

500 Art. 14 ASCM gives further guidance on the **calculation of the benefit**, which, in turn, serves as the basis for the determination of the amount of subsidy. Art. 14 ASCM states that all national methods for calculation of the benefit must be provided for in national legislation and shall be transparent and adequately explained. In addition, all calculation methods must be consistent with the guidelines given in Art. 14, which include disciplines for certain situations. For instance, Art. 14 (b)

[51] *Canada – Measures affecting the Export of Civilian Aircraft*, WT/DS70/AB/R, 20 August 1999, para. 157 *et seq.*

ASCM stipulated that a loan by a government should be considered as conferring a benefit only when there was a difference between the amount the firm receiving the loan paid on it and the amount the firm would pay on a comparable commercial loan which the firm could actually obtain on the market, in which case the benefit should be the difference. Art. 14 (b) ASCM serves as an example of the "commercial benchmark" test used for the calculation of a benefit.

501 The Agreement on Subsidies and Countervailing Measures thus covers a wide range of government action. It limits the application of parts III and V (the so-called "countervailable" subsidies, i.e. subsidies against which Members can impose countervailing duties) to **"specific"** subsidies. Thus, the prerequisite of specificity acts as a **filter** to reduce the wide range of subsidies covered under the Agreement to those that distort trade.[52]

502 Art. 2 ASCM defines four types of subsidies as specific, depending on the **target** on the one hand (specific enterprise, specific industry, or specific region), and on the **contingent** (export performance and domestic input) on the other. In general, subsidies for which the authority or legislation establishes objective criteria or conditions governing eligibility and amount shall not be specific, provided that the eligibility is automatic and the criteria and conditions are strictly adhered to. The criteria and conditions must be clearly spelled out in law and must be neutral, in that they do not favour certain enterprises, economic and horizontal in application.

In addition to this "specificity in law" (or **"*de jure*" specificity**), a subsidy may be considered to be specific in fact (**"*de facto*" specificity**). Factors which may lead to such "*de facto*" specificity include the predominant use of the subsidy programme by a limited number of enterprises, the grant of a disproportionately large amount to certain enterprises and the manner in which discretion has been exercised by the national authorities. In sum, it is the **actual effect** of the subsidy, not its form, that is considered to be relevant.

2. *Categories of Subsidies in the Agreement on Subsidies and Countervailing Measures*

503 The Agreement on Subsidies and Countervailing Measures establishes three types of subsidies, namely prohibited subsidies (part III), actionable subsidies (part IV), and non-actionable subsidies (part V). In a symbolic

[52] In this respect Art. 2.3 makes it clear that those subsidies that are expressly prohibited under the ASCM (Art. 3) are also deemed to be specific.

description this categorization has been referred to as the "traffic-light" categorization, with the prohibited subsidies referred to as "red-light", the actionable as "yellow-" or "amber-light", and the non-actionable as "green-light" subsidies. However, the provisions regarding non-actionable ("green-light") subsidies remained in force only until December 1999, as no consensus was reached among the WTO Members on their extended application according to Art. 31.1 ASCM. The two categories remaining in force to date are the **prohibited** and the **actionable subsidies**. As stated, subsidies falling under the Agreement on agriculture are not covered by the Agreement on Subsidies and Countervailing Measures.

504 Part II deals with **prohibited ("red-light")** subsidies, which are deemed to be specific according to Art. 2.3 ASCM. According to Art. 3.2 ASCM Members are not allowed to grant or maintain such subsidies. Art. 3 defines prohibited subsidies as:

(a) "subsidies contingent, in law or in fact, whether solely or as one of several other conditions, upon export performance, including those illustrated in Annex I;
(b) subsidies contingent, whether solely or as one of several other conditions, upon use of domestic over imported goods".

505 As to the first type of prohibited subsidies Annex I contains a list of 12 different types of subsidies which are contingent on **export performance**, including a full or partial exemption from taxes or charges (Annex I, *lit.* e),[53] currency retention schemes (Annex I, *lit.* b), or export credit guarantees or insurance programmes (Annex I, *lit.* k). Annex I lists 11 types of subsidies that are considered export subsidies, but this list is illustrative, and not conclusive.[54] Another type of subsidy defined in Art. 3 relates to those which require the use of local products and thus act as import substitution subsidies (so-called **"local content" requirements**). The Appellate Body has held that – even though not expressly mentioned in the provisions – *de facto* local content requirements are also covered by Art. 3.[55]

506 The second remaining category of subsidy is that of an **"actionable" subsidy** in accordance with part III of the Agreement on Subsidies and Countervailing Measures. In contrast to a prohibited subsidy, which is forbidden solely by reason of its content and allows for remedies to all Member irrespective of any negative effects, an "actionable" subsidy

---

[53] See in this respect the controversial case *United States – Tax Treatment for "Foreign Sales Corporations"* (FSC), WT/DS108/AB/R, 24 February 2000.

[54] See more generally *Kleiner*, Bananas, airplanes and the WTO: prohibited export subsidies, International and Comparative Law Review 10 (2002), 129 *et seq.*

[55] *Canada – Certain Measures Affecting the Automobile Industry*, WT/DS139/AB/R, WT/DS142/AB/R, 31 May 2000, para. 142.

is a subsidy which – irrespective of its specific content – **causes "adverse effects"** to the interests of other Members. Art. 5 defines three distinct types of "adverse effects" which are in turn important for the scope and type of remedy available. Adverse effect according to Art. 5 ASCM thus entail:

(a) "injury to the domestic industry of another Member;
(b) nullification or impairment of benefits accruing directly or indirectly to other Members under GATT 1994 in particular the benefits of concessions bound under Article II of GATT 1994;
(c) serious prejudice to the interests of another Member.

507 While the notion of a "nullification and impairment of benefits" is used in parallel to Art. XXIII GATT 1994 (see para. 208) and the concepts of "injury" and "like products"[56] in Art. 15 ASCM are used in parallel to the WTO's anti-dumping rules, Art. 5 (c) ASCM includes a category of adverse effect unique to the rules on subsidies, namely **"serious prejudice"**. Art. 6 ASCM in this respect serves as a clarification of Art. XVI GATT, which uses this term, but gives no guidance on its scope. **Art. 6.1 ASCM** defines several situations of such serious prejudice and thus served to clarify certain situations in which a member state could surely rely on taking action against a subsidy. However, according to Art. 31.1 ASCM, this provision is **no longer in force**. As with the "green-light" subsidies, member states could not agree on the continuation of this provision and its applicability ceased in December 1999.

508 In addition to the clear-cut, but no longer applicable provision of Art. 6.1, in which effects causing serious prejudice were positively defined, **Art. 6.3 ASCM** describes situations in which serious prejudice "may" be deemed to arise, namely cases in which the effect of the subsidy is to displace or impede imports into the market of the subsidizing Member (a) or exports from a third country market (b), the increase in world market share of a product of the subsidizing Member (d), or significant price undercutting by the subsidized product (c). Art. 6 contains elaborate criteria for the calculation and specification of procedures in these situations, as well as exceptions. As with injury determinations in anti-dumping proceedings, the method for determination of serious prejudice according to Art. 6.3 allows for considerable discretion.

3. *Remedies*

509 In its rules on remedies the Agreement on Subsidies and Countervailing Measures must be **clearly distinguished** from the parallel rules on

---

[56] See above paras 72 *et seq.*

anti-dumping, which are otherwise similar in methodology. As the Agreement on Subsidies and Countervailing Measures contains rules on the legality of the granting of certain subsidies by Members, it offers **two distinct remedies** to affected Members: the invocation of the dispute settlement procedures of the WTO against another Member for breach of the Agreement (**"multilateral track"**) on the one hand, and the enactment of counter-measures to offset the effects of the subsidization (**"unilateral track"**) on the other.

510 The multilateral track as stipulated in the Agreement on Subsidies and Countervailing Measures is in essence a fast-track equivalent of the "normal" dispute settlement procedures set out in the Dispute Settlement Understanding. Access to the so-called multilateral track is foreseen for **both** types of subsidies, namely for prohibited subsidies in Art. 4 ASCM and for actionable subsidies in Art. 7 ASCM. Both provisions contain procedures for Panel proceedings including consultation, and in this respect set **strict and short time limits** for the completion of these disputes. The time limit for actionable subsidies in Art. 7 stipulates the establishment of a Panel within 75 days, the circulation of the report within 120 days, and the adoption of the report within 150 days, with the possibility of a further appeal. The time limits for the prohibited subsidies laid down in Art. 4 are even stricter. In the case of a complaint against a prohibited subsidy a Panel is to be established within 30 days, the Panel report circulated in 90, and adopted within 120 days, with the possibility of an appeal. According to Art. 4.5 ASCM the Panel may request assistance from the so-called "permanent group of experts" in deciding whether the subsidy in question is in fact prohibited.

511 In the case of prohibited subsidies, the multilateral track is open to all Members, irrespective of any negative effects of the subsidization – the **existence** of such prohibited subsidy alone is enough to enable the triggering of the remedy procedure. With actionable subsidies, **all adverse effects** give access to the multilateral track in accordance with Art. 7.1 ASCM.

While access to the multilateral track is fairly unrestricted, the Agreement on Subsidies and Countervailing Measures sets out elaborate prerequisites for Members before they can resort to unilateral measures. The unilateral instrument used in anti-subsidy law is the so-called **"countervailing duty" (CVD)**, which may be implemented in order to offset the effect of the subsidy up to the amount of the subsidy (see Art. 19.4 ASCM and Art. VI:3 GATT 1994). Should a Member seek to implement unilateral action in the form of a countervailing duty, further requirements in accordance with part V ASCM must be fulfilled. Most importantly, the implementation of a countervailing duty is subject to a **finding of "injury"** as defined by Art. 15 ASCM in the course of a national investigation. The link of unilateral measures to a finding of injury mirrors the general rule of Art. VI:6 GATT 1994 and therefore corresponds to the methodology of the rules on anti-dumping (paras 470 *et seq.*).

4. *Rules for National Investigations and Measures*

512 The rules for **national investigation** largely mirror those on national anti-dumping procedures. They set out specific requirements pertaining to the initiation of the proceedings, the use of evidence, a *"de minimis"* rule, due process rights of the parties involved, rules on review of national measures, and requirements of transparency and notification.[57]

513 The Agreement on Subsidies and Countervailing Measures differs from the corresponding rules on anti-dumping in particular in the duration of provisional measures (only four months, Art. 17.4 ASCM), the possibilities for exporters and subsidizing governments to enter into voluntary obligations (Art. 18.1) As in anti-dumping proceedings the **duration of the countervailing duty** is to be five years, unless the expiry of the measure would lead to recurrence or continuation of the subsidy and injury (Art. 21.3).

5. *Special and Differential Treatment for Developing Countries*

514 Developing countries in the WTO can make use of special rules incorporated in Art. 27 ASCM which contain substantial deviations from the "normal" regime. By incorporating these so-called **"special and differential" rules** the WTO order accepts that subsidies play an important role in the development of national industries and that full application of the rules set out in the Agreement on Subsidies and Countervailing Measures would not be reasonable. The Agreement accepts three categories of developing countries: (i) the group of least developed countries (LDC) as designated by the United Nations, (ii) the developing countries listed in Annex VII *lit.* b when the GNP per capita has reached US$ 1,000 per annum, and (iii) all other developing countries.

515 The basic principle governing the special and differential treatment rules is that the more a country's industry is developed and competitive, the less deviation from "normal rules" is permitted. Most importantly, developing Members are granted **longer periods** for the implementation of specific obligations. Thus, prohibited subsidization regimes may be kept in force for as long as eight years from entry into force of the Agreement on Subsidies and Countervailing Measures (Art. 27.2, .3 and .5) or may

[57] See above paras 76 *et seq.*

remain in place until certain economic criteria are fulfilled.[58] Also, Members must adhere to different and **higher *"de minimis"* thresholds** regarding imports from developing Members (Art. 27.10).

6. *Institutions*

516 The Agreement on Subsidies and Countervailing Measures is administered by a special **Committee on Subsidies and Countervailing Measures** which is composed of representatives of each Member. Its main function is to receive and oversee **notification** of national subsidization and countervailing measures and laws (Art. 24.1 ASCM). The Agreement also provides for the establishment of a subsidiary body, the **Permanent Group of Experts (PGE)**, to be composed of five independent and highly qualified persons (Art. 24.2). The PGE shall assist the Panels in deciding on prohibited subsidies – when requested – and provide advisory opinions to Members on the existence and nature of subsidies. However, the PGE has so far not been asked by a Panel to assist in its decision-making process. Lastly, a Working Party on Subsidy Notifications has been established, to work on facilitation of the notification process.[59]

7. *Agricultural Subsidies*

517 The ASCM's definition of subsidies generally also includes agricultural subsidies, even though the application of the substantive rules of the Agreement on Subsidies and Countervailing Measures is excluded for agricultural subsidies in most cases. The rules governing these subsidies are found in parts IV and V of the **Agreement on Agriculture (AoA)**. Following the difficult negotiations on agriculture, the inclusion of special rules was the only way to bring this highly contentious area back under the auspices of the WTO rules. In the legal vacuum prior to the Uruguay Round Agreements many specific practices such as strict allocations and technical barriers, as well as a high level of subsidization, had developed in this sensitive sector, many of them firmly countering the overall ideals of free trade.

---

[58] The criteria refer to the $US 1,000 per capita GNP benchmark. para. 10.1 of the Doha Ministerial Decision on Implementation-Related Issues and Concerns ("Implementation Decision"), WT/MIN(01)/17, 20 November 2001, has clarified the conditions for graduation from the special regime set out for certain members in Annex VII *lit.* b. The new methodology for calculation is included in G/SCM/38, Appendix 2, 26 October 2001. The Committee has agreed on Procedures for Extensions under Article 27.4 for Certain Developing Country Members, G/SCM/39, 20 November 2001.

[59] See generally the Report of the Committee on Subsidies and Countervailing Measures (2004), G/L/711, 9 November 2004.

518 The Agreement on Agriculture in this respect contains specific rules according to which agricultural subsidies may be continued with a view to phasing them out. In doing so the Agreement differentiates between so-called measures of "domestic support" and the more problematic agricultural export subsidies. In order to incorporate the special rules of the Agreement on Agriculture into the system of the Agreement on Subsidies and Countervailing Measures the latter contains several exceptions to the benefit of the former regulations. Agricultural subsidies therefore are categorized neither as prohibited nor as actionable under the Agreement on Subsidies and Countervailing Measures.[60] However, as agricultural subsidies also fall within the scope of the Agreement on Subsidies and Countervailing Measures, all agricultural subsidies must be **notified** under its provisions, and a breach of provisions of the Agreement on Agriculture regarding subsidies could be brought within the remedy procedures of the Agreement on Subsidies and Countervailing Measures.

a. *Domestic Support*

519 Members have agreed in general to a **reduction** of domestic support measures. The starting point for this commitment is a **classification system** of all measures in force **in terms of trade-distorting effect or effect on production**. As with the different subsidies the Agreement on Agriculture distinguishes between different classifications of support measures so that certain symbols for the different measures have evolved: the "green", "blue", and "amber" boxes (paras 503 *et seq.*).

520 Domestic support measures that have no or no significant effect on trade or production are **exempt** from this reduction commitment. Specifically this relates to the measures listed in **Annex II** to which two basic principles apply: that support is effected by public funds that do not involve a transfer of funds from consumers, and that the measure may not have the effect of a price support on the part of producers. The different measures are grouped into 13 categories, which in turn contain further prerequisites. As an example, nos. 5 to 13 include direct payments to producers, while nos. 2 to 4 deal with indirect payments. These domestic support measures which are exempt from a commitment to reduce are also commonly referred to as **"green box" measures**.

521 So-called **"blue box" measures** are also exempt from the reduction commitment according to Art. 6 AoA. These measures refer to special measures taken by developing Members, *"de minimis"* product-specific

[60] See the relevant exceptions in Arts. 3.1 and 5 ASCM.

measures (Art. 6.4), and direct payments aimed at reducing production (Art. 6.5).

522 All other domestic support measures – the **"amber box" measures** – are subject to the **reduction commitment**. These commitments are contained in lists for each individual Member. Pursuant to a specific calculation method all measures add up to the **"aggregate measure of support" (AMS)** for each product, in order to make a percentage reduction workable.[61] Currently 34 Members have entered into such commitments.[62]

The industrialized Members have committed themselves to an annual reduction of 20% for six years, while developing countries were to reduce their support by 13% annually over ten years. Least developed countries were exempt from commitments. Members which have not made commitments are nevertheless obliged to remain within the *"de minimis"* levels of "blue box" measures.

b. *Export Subsidies*

523 The Agreement on Agriculture also addresses agricultural **export subsidies** which are subject to the provisions of part V AoA. Subsidies for the export of agricultural products generally are consistent with the GATT according to **Art. XVI:3**. Agricultural products are thus treated differently from industrial goods, for which Art. XVI GATT 1994 contains a prohibition on export subsidies.

524 Members have committed themselves to grant only the subsidies contained in their national lists. Also, agricultural subsidies are to be **notified** and are included in a **general reduction commitment**. Art. 9. a–f AoA defines the most common subsidization practices, including direct subsidization (a), sale of non-commercial stock at a lower price (b), subsidization to reduce the cost of marketing exports (d), and subsidies on agricultural products contingent on their incorporation in export products (f). The reduction commitment is based on the amount of payments and the amount of the subsidized exports. Industrialized Members were committed to reduce the amount of subsidized exports by 21% a year for six years, and the corresponding payments by 36%. For developing members these reductions are 14 and 24% over a period of ten years. According to Art. 9.4 AoA developing countries were allowed to make use of special rules during the six year implementation period, during which they were not obliged to enter into commitments for specific export subsidies.

[61] A Member's AMS is calculated on the basis of national support measures in the years from 1986 to 1988. The calculation method is set out in Art. 1 *lit.* a and Annex III.

[62] For details compare WTO Secretariat, Domestic Support, TN/AG/S/4, 20 March 2002.

Circumvention of these rules is made more difficult by linking potential circumventive practices such as the declaration of agricultural exports as **international aid** to specific requirements. Lastly, Members undertake to work toward the development of internationally agreed disciplines to govern the provision of export credits, export credit guarantees or insurance programmes (Art. 10.2 AoA).

c. *Ongoing Negotiations*

525 Following the completion of the reductions as contained in the Agreement, negotiations as foreseen in Art. 20 AoA commenced on a further reduction of domestic support measures and export subsidization. In parallel to the negotiations on market access, the negotiations on reduction on support measures are at the heart of the ongoing Doha Round (see paras 795 *et seq.*). The current "July Package"[63] now contains modalities for the negotiations and calls for a "tiered approach" to be used in reducing higher levels of support by a greater margin than lower levels. However, as for export subsidies, while the framework agreement now contains the aim of the negotiations to set an end date for the phasing out, this end date is "to be agreed" in the ongoing negotiations.[64]

III. *Government Procurement*

Bernard Hoekman & Petros C. Mavroidis (Eds), Law and Policy in Public Procurement: The WTO Agreement on Government Procurement, 1997; *Gerhard Kunnert*, WTO-Vergaberecht: Genese und System sowie Einwirkungen auf das EG-Vergaberegime, 1998; *Christopher MacCrudden*, International economic law and the pursuit of human rights: a framework for discussion of the legality of "selective purchasing" laws under the WTO Government Procurement Agreement, JIEL 2 (1999) 1, 3–48; *Arie Reich*, International public procurement law: the evolution of international regimes on public purchasing, 1999; *Susan L. Arrowsmith & John Linarelli & Don Wallace*, Regulating public procurement: national and international perspectives, 2000; *Martin Dischendorfer*, The existence and development of multilateral rules on government procurement under the framework of the WTO, Public procurement law review 9 (2000) 1, 1–38; *Christoph Spennemann*, The WTO Agreement on Government Procurement – A Means of Furtherance of Human Rights?, ZeuS 4 (2001) 1, 43–95; *OECD*, The Size of Government Procurement Markets, 2002; *C. Koenig & A. Haratsch*, Grundzüge des deutschen und europäischen Vergaberechts, NJW 2004, 2637–2642; *S. Arrowsmith*, Transparency in government procurement, JWT 37 (2003) 2, 283–303.

526 The **Agreement on Government Procurement (GPA)** opens the public procurement markets to competition by providing for most-

[63] Doha Work Programme, Decision Adopted by the General Council on 1 August 2004, WT/L579, 2 August 2004.

[64] *Ibid.*, paras 18 and 19.

favoured-nation and national treatment as well as transparency for these transactions. It thus closes the gap left in the GATT 1994, which exempts government procurement of goods from the principle of national treatment (Art. III:8). The Agreement on Government Procurement is a plurilateral Agreement and thus does not apply to all WTO Members, while being open for membership to all interested Members.

527 The Agreement accounts for the fact that Members function not only as regulators, but **also as demanders of traded products and services**. The economic importance of public (government) procurement has continued to be of significance in recent years notwithstanding the progressive liberalization of former state monopolies, especially in the telecommunications sector. According to the OECD the government procurement market in 1998 had reached 19.6% of the gross domestic product (GDP) of OECD member states, which corresponded to 4,733 billion US$. For non-OECD members the figure was calculated at 14.48% of GDP 816 billion US$.[65] In the EU government procurement reached an average of 13.9–14.6% of GDP between 1993 and 1998. In 1998 this percentage corresponded to 1,054 billion €.[66]

528 Due to the high volumes at stake and the limited funds available, public authorities have an interest in tenders being awarded to the lowest bidder. In this respect it must be stated that governments also pursue other, mostly structural and socio-political, aims in procurement tenders (so-called **"secondary policies"**).[67]

529 For this reason the GATT 1994 contained an **exemption** for this sector and a similar provision is now found in Art. XIII GATS. According to Art. III:8 *lit.* a GATT 1994 the principle of national treatment (paras 139 *et seq.*) does not apply to "regulations or requirements governing the procurement by governmental agencies of products purchased for governmental purposes".[68] As far as services are concerned, the principles

---

[65] OECD, The Size of Government Procurement Markets (2002), 20.

[66] European Commission, Measuring the Impact of Public Procurement Policy: First Indicators, Single Market News No. 20 (March 2000), at <http://europa.eu.int/comm/internal_market/smn/smn20/s20mn18.htm>.

[67] These secondary policies of procurement regulations in the state of Massachusetts were the subject of a dispute settlement procedure initiated by the EU and Japan against the United States. The state law limited the ability of any government agency or authority to purchase goods or services from entities having business connections with Burma. Bids by these entities, as identified on a "restricted purchase list", were considered only after 10% had been added to their bid, thus making a successful bid almost impossible. See *United States – Measures Affecting Government Procurement*, WT/DS88 and WT/DS95. The authorization for establishment of a panel has lapsed (see Art. 12.1 DSU). See for an overview *Fitzgerald*, Massachusetts, Burma, and the World Trade Organization, Cornell International Law Journal 34 (2001) 1, 1 *et seq.*

[68] Discriminatory treatment is also possible according to the regulations concerning state trading enterprises (Art. XVII:2 GATT 1994).

of most-favoured nation and market access do not apply to government procurement actions (Art. XIII GATS).

530 However, some Members realized as early as the 1960s that government procurement represented a large proportion of the markets which was effectively exempt from competition under the general rules. Following preparatory work by the OECD, the EC and EFTA the Tokyo Round established a first international Agreement on this subject which supplied a framework for international public procurement.[69] The Agreement was enacted as a **Plurilateral Agreement**, not binding on all GATT contracting parties, but on the signatory states. Following the Uruguay Round the revised Tokyo Round Agreement is now in force as the Agreement on Government Procurement. Contrary to other plurilateral Agreements under the GATT it was not possible to "multilateralize" the Agreement. Rather, it is still only plurilateral, with 38 Members at the moment. Nine Members are negotiating accession; 20 other States and four other international organizations (the IMF, the ITC, UNCTAD and the OECD) have observer status.[70]

531 The Agreement on Government Procurement applies to procurement of goods and services by any contractual means by governments or other entities as listed in **Appendix I** of the Agreement (Art. I). While goods are completely covered by the Agreement, Members may include or exclude certain services or construction services in positive and negative lists (Annexes 4 and 5 to Appendix I). The inclusion of regional and communal government entities, which was first agreed upon in the new Agreement on Government Procurement, is of particular importance as 65% of all public procurement is affected by authorities at this level.

532 The Agreement on Government Procurement covers only procurement over a certain **threshold**. This threshold is determined by the individual Members and is set out in the Annex to Appendix I according to Art. I:4 GPA. The thresholds currently agreed upon are as follows:

[69] Tokyo Round Agreement on Government Procurement, BISD 26S/22 *et seq.*, amended 1987, BISD 34S/177 *et seq.*

[70] Contracting parties are: Canada, European Communities (including its 25 Member States), Hong Kong China, Iceland, Israel, Japan, Korea, Liechtenstein, Netherlands with respect to Aruba, Norway, Singapore, Switzerland, United States; countries negotiating accession are: Albania, Bulgaria, Georgia, Jordan, the Kyrgyz Republic, Moldavia, Oman, Panama, and Chinese Taipei; see also the Report (July 2003–November 2004) of the Committee on Government Procurement, GPA/82, 26 November 2004.

Summary table of thresholds in Annexes 1, 2 and 3 of Appendix 1 to the GPA (expressed in SDR:[71])[72]

COUNTRY	ANNEX 1			ANNEX 2			ANNEX 3		
	Goods	Services except con-struction services	Construc-tion services	Goods	Services except construc-tion services	Construc-tion services	Goods	Services except construc-tion services	Con-struction services
Canada	130,000	130,000	5,000,000	355,000	355,000	5,000,000	355,000	355,000	5,000,000
European Communities (and its 15 member States)	130,000	130,000	5,000,000	200,000	200,000	5,000,000	400,000	400,000	5,000,000
Hong Kong, China	130,000	130,000	5,000,000	200,000	200,000	5,000,000	400,000	400,000	5,000,000
Iceland	130,000	130,000	5,000,000	200,000	200,000	5,000,000	400,000	400,000	5,000,000
Israel	130,000	130,000	8,500,000	250,000	250,000	8,500,000	355,000	355,000	8,500,000
Japan	130,000	130,000	4,500,000	200,000	200,000	15,000,000	130,000	130,000	15,000,000
			Architectural services: 450,000			Architectural services: 1,500,000			Architectural services: 450,000
Korea	130,000	130,000	5,000,000	200,000	200,000	15,000,000	450,000	450,000	15,000,000
Liechtenstein	130,000	130,000	5,000,000	200,000	200,000	5,000,000	400,000	400,000	5,000,000
Netherlands-Aruba	130,000	130,000	5,000,000	n.a.	n.a.	n.a.	400,000	400,000	5,000,000
Norway	130,000	130,000	5,000,000	200,000	200,000	5,000,000	400,000	400,000	5,000,000
Singapore	130,000	130,000	5,000,000	200,000	200,000	5,000,000	400,000	400,000	5,000,000
Switzerland	130,000	130,000	5,000,000	200,000	200,000	5,000,000	400,000	400,000	5,000,000
United States	130,000	130,000	5,000,000	355,000	355,000	5,000,000	250,000 or 400,000	250,000 or 5,000,000	400,000

Annex 1 refers to central government entities, Annex 2 to sub-central government entities, and Annex 3 to all other entities which procure in accordance with the Agreement, in general public enterprises or public authorities such as utilities.

533 The central aim of the GPA is to extend the scope of the principle of **non-discrimination** to the government procurement sector and to assure a high level of transparency in national tendering procedures. Such transparency is to be safeguarded by specific guidelines on tendering procedures as well as on notification and documentation of the modalities of the selection procedure. As for non-discrimination, all par-

[71] SDR (Special Drawing Rights) are units used for calculation by the IMF, which are based on the individual members' entitlement to the IMF' assets. The value of the SDR is calculated on a day-to-day basis and is based on the combined and averaged values of different national currencies, such as Yen, Euro, Sterling and US$.

[72] From the WTO-website at http://www.wto.org/english/tratop_e/gproc_e/thresh_e.htm.

ties shall provide immediately and unconditionally for the same treatment as is accorded to (i) domestic products, services and suppliers (national treatment), and (ii) products, services and suppliers of any other Party (most-favoured nation) in accordance with Art. III:1 GPA. Further, the regulations in Art. III:2 GPA are to ensure that government entities do not discriminate against or otherwise treat less favourably local suppliers on the basis of foreign ownership or foreign country of production.

534 Most Members have notified **exceptions to Art. III**, which are listed in the respective Annexes to Appendix I. These exceptions relate to the provision of goods and services by certain other member states and are based in the lack of reciprocity in the level of concessions granted by party in question.

535 Particular mention must be made of the special rules on **dispute settlement**. According to Art. XXII GPA, disputes between the parties may be submitted to the normal dispute settlement procedures of the DSU, allowing for some specific deviations due to the plurilateral character of the GPA. Additionally, Art. XX GPA commits the member states to providing for national "challenge procedures", enabling suppliers to challenge alleged breaches of the GPA. Challenges are to be heard by an impartial and independent review body (Art. XX:6 GPA), while the remedies include rapidly imposed interim measures as well as compensation.[73]

536 In addition to the Committee on Government Procurement, the government procurement sector is also dealt with in two multilateral working groups. The Singapore Ministerial Conference in 1996 set up a **Working Group on Transparency in Government Procurement**, which is to evaluate the rules in the various member states and which is to work towards a future agreement on transparency.[74] Also, Art. XIII:2 GPA itself provides for multilateral negotiations on government procurement of services, which started in a second working party two years after the entry into force of the agreement. The reports of the second working party have clearly shown that the regulations currently included in the GPA mirror the current consensus of member states.[75]

---

[73] This compensation may be limited to the costs of tender preparation or protest (Art. XX:7 *lit.* c GPA).

[74] WT/MIN(96)/DEC, 18 December 1996, para. 21; Report (2003) of the Working Group on Transparency in Government Procurement, WT/WGTPT/7, 15 July 2003. See also the renewed mandate of the Doha Ministerial Declaration, WT/Min(01)/DEC/1, 20 November 2001, para. 26. According to this mandate, negotiations on this "Singapore Issue" were to be re-launched on the basis of a positive and explicit consensus by Members at the Fifth Ministerial in Cancún. After the failure to reach consensus on this matter at Cancún, the negotiations have been officially halted and no longer form part of the Doha Round negotiations, see the Doha Work Programme, Decision Adopted by the General Council on 1 August 2004 ("July Package"), WT/L/579, 2 August 2004, para. 1 *lit.* g.

[75] See Annual Report of the Working Party on GATS Rules to the Council on Trade in Services (2004), S/WPGR/14, 25 November 2004.

CHAPTER SEVEN

RULES FOR TRADE IN SERVICES

Raymond J. Krommenacker, World-Trade Services: The Challenge for the Eighties, 1984; *Werner Zdouc*, WTO dispute settlement practice relating to the GATS, JIEL 2 (1999) 2, 295–346; *Joel P. Trachtman*, Trade in financial services under GATS, NAFTA and the EC: a regulatory jurisdiction analysis, Columbia Journal of Transnational Law 34 (1995) 1, 37–122; *Ansgar M. Wimmer*, The impact of the General Agreement on Trade in Services on the OECD Multilateral Agreement on Investment, World Competition 19 (1996) 4, 109–120; *Patrick Low & Aaditya Mattoo/Arvind Subramanian*, Government procurement in services, World Competition 20 (1996) 1, 5–26; *Yi Wang*, Most-favoured-nation treatment under the General Agreement on Trade in Services and its application in financial services, JWT 30 (1996) 1, 91–124; *Rachel Frid*, The Telecommunications Pact under the GATS – another step towards the rule of law, Legal issues of European integration 24 (1997) 2, 67–96; *Aaditya Mattoo*, National treatment in the GATS: corner-stone or Pandora's box?, JWT 31 (1997) 1, 107–135; *Eva Carceles Poveda & Susanne Dröge*, International trade in financial services: an assessment of the GATS, Aussenwirtschaft 52 (1997) 4, 603–635; *Marco C. Bronckers & Pierre Larouche*, Telecommunications services and the World Trade Organization, JWT 31 (1997) 3, 5–48; *Neela Mukherjee*, Non-tariff barriers and trade in services: A comparative assessment of capital and labour mobility in the GATS under the World Trade Organization, World Competition 21 (1998) 5, 79–91; *Friedl Weiss*, Dispute settlement under the General Agreement on Trade in Services, in: James Cameron (Ed.), Dispute resolution in the World Trade Organisation, 1998, 148–170; *Philip Chang*, GATS, the modes of supply and statistics on trade in services, JWT 33 (1999) 3, 93–115, *John Gaffney*, The GATT and the GATS: should they be mutually exclusive Agreements?, Leiden Journal of International Law 12 (1999) 1, 135–153, *Matthias Köhler*, Das Allgemeine Übereinkommen über den Handel mit Dienstleistungen (GATS): Rahmenregelung zur Liberalisierung des internationalen Dienstleistungsverkehrs unter besonderer Berücksichtigung des grenzüberschreitenden Personenverkehrs von Dienstleistungsanbietern, 1999; *André Sapir*, The General Agreement on Trade in Services: From 1994 to the year 2000, JWT 33 (1999) 1, 51–66; *Pierre Sauvé*, Developing countries and the GATS 2000 Round, JWT 34 (2000) 2, 85–92; *Roger Kampf*, in: GH II/Krenzler (Eds), Kommentar EU-Recht (loselaef), 2000, Finanzdienstleistungen E 26; *Andrew D. Mitchell*, Towards Compatibility: The Future of Electronic Commerce within the Global Trading System, JIEL 4 (2001), 683–723; *Byung-il Choi*, Treatment of autonomous liberalization in the WTO new service round, JWT 35 (2001) 2, 363–378; *Mahmood Bagheri*, Optimal level of financial regulation under the GATS, JIEL 5 (2002) 2, 507–530; *Christoph Beat Graber*, Handel und Kultur im Audio-visionsrecht der WTO, 2003; *Leonard Alan Winters*, Liberalising labour mobility under the GATS, Commonwealth Secretariat, 2002; *Raymond Saner & Sylvie Fasel*, Negotiating trade in educational services within the WTO/GATS context, Aussenwirtschaft 58 (2003) 2, 275–308; *Johan Leon Steenkamp*, The impact of e-commerce on the balance of commitments in the GATS Financial Services Agreement, in: M. Nettesheim/G. Sander (Eds), WTO-Recht und Globalisierung, 2003, 189–222; *Markus Krajewski*, National regulation and trade liberalization in services, 2003; *Rudolf Adlung*, GATS and democratic legitimacy, Aussenwirtschaft 59 (2004) 2, 127–149; *WTO Secretariat*, Handbook on the GATS Agreement, 2005.

I. *The General Agreement on Trade in Services (GATS) – development and overview*

1. *History*

537 With the introduction of the General Agreement on Trade in Services, which entered into force on 1 January 1995, trade in services was added to the world trade order, which had previously been applicable only to goods. With this new agreement, the steady growth in trade in services, its significant volume[1] and the lack of international regulation up to that point were addressed.

538 The inclusion of trade in services in the negotiations at the Uruguay Round was not without controversy. The initiative for an enlargement of the GATT system came from the United States,[2] and was later supported by other industrialized countries.[3] In contrast, the developing countries saw dangers for the development of their own economies through substantial liberalization and feared the erosion of state control in this sector. This controversy led to the fact that the negotiations on trade in services were not commenced as part of the negotiation of the eighth GATT Round in Punta del Este, later named the Uruguay Round. Rather, negotiations were triggered by a separate Ministerial Decision, which set out a special and individual basis for negotiation on trade in services. Differences of opinion also existed regarding the form, content and scope of the new rules. Trade in services had, hitherto, not been regulated internationally. Many important service sectors, such as telecommunications, energy provision and transport were subject to strong national

---

[1] In 2003, commercial services at a value of 1,795 billion US$ were exported, of which 823 billion US$ were exported to the EU, 330 billion US$ to North America, and 352 billion US$ to Asia, WTO International Trade Statistics, 2004, 18; <http://www.wto.org/english/res_e/statis_e/its2004_e/its2004_e.pdf>.

[2] The US Trade Act 1974, which was signed in conjunction with the Tokyo Round, included trade in services. In the Tariff Act 1984 the inclusion of trade barriers and distortions with reference to trade in services was named as an aim of bilateral and multilateral trade negotiations; detailed information on the origin of the GATS is provided by *Croome*, Reshaping the world trading system, 2nd ed., 1999, 102, 243 *et seq.*

[3] In April 1985 the OECD-States agreed with the US-position and furthered the inclusion of services in the negotiations; compare also the OECD Codes of Liberalisation of Capital Movements and of Current Invisible Operations, <http://www.oecd.org/dataoecd/14/13/1935919.pdf>.

regulation or state monopoly. Owing to the limited scope of internationally liberalized areas and the problematic negotiations in the GATS framework, this agreement – in contrast to the more "developed" GATT – addresses service sectors individually and contains mere basic principles and mandates for continuing liberalization negotiations for some sectors, where a full and comprehensive liberalization could not be agreed upon.

2. *Overview*

539 The special and individual mandate, the lack of a tradition of liberalization in this sector and the complexity of the matter have led to an **independent and individual regime for the trade in services**. The new GATS, contained in Annex 1B to the WTO Agreement, now contains a comprehensive set of rules which are structurally similar to the GATT. It includes all the rules previously contained in the GATT, however often in a different form to suit the conditions of trade in services.

540 As with the GATT, the GATS also includes **schedules of commitments** which, in contrast to GATT concessions, also contain important material provisions for the complex subject mater. The concessions list is categorized into a list of 12 service provision sectors, which follows the United Nations Central Product Classification (CPC) System.[4]

541 Furthermore, the GATS also contains several **sector-specific Annexes**, which include additional rules and procedures for the specific sector and for further negotiations.

542 In some sectors, Members have collated the results of such sector-specific negotiations in **additional supplementary Protocols**.[5] Seen from a purely formalistic standpoint, the GATS thus has a stronger hierarchical structure than the GATT with its supplementary Agreements.

543 Following an introductory Article with definitions and clarification of the scope of the Agreement (Part 1), the **GATS** contains the material rules in its second and third parts. Part 2 covers "General Obligations and Disciplines", while Part 3 is concerned with "Specific Commitments".

---

[4] See Services Sectoral Classification List of the GATT Secretariat, MTN.GNS/W/120, 10 July 1991. These 12 sectors are: (1) business (including professional and computer) services, (2) commercial services, (3) construction and related engineering services, (4) distribution services, (5) educational services, (6) environmental services, (7) financial (insurance and banking) services, (8) health-related and social services, (9) tourism and travel-related services, (10) recreational, cultural and sporting services, (11) transport services, (12) other services not included elsewhere.

[5] Such supplementary protocols have, for instance, been used in the areas of telecommunications and financial services, see paras 592 *et seq.*

This differentiation already makes it clear that the GATS treats these two areas separately – on the one hand the general obligations applicable to all GATS related activities, and on the other hand specific and additional obligations only applicable to the specific commitments entered into in the different sectors. In particular, Art. XVI–XVIII GATS include specific commitments which apply only in cases where concessions have been made. Part IV (Art. XIX–XXI) addresses further liberalization through mandatory and periodic negotiations, while parts V (Art. XXII–XXVI) and VI (Art. XXVII–XXIX) consist of institutional and final provisions.

3. *GATS Institutions and References to Other WTO Institutions*

544 The **central organ** of the GATS is the Council for Trade in Services, which is open to all Members,[6] comparable to the General Council of the GATT (para. 26). The GATS Council has made use of the competence established by Art. XXIV:1 s.2 GATS and has established four sub-organs: the Committee on Financial Services, the Committee on Specific Commitments, which is working for the improved classification of the specific commitments in all areas,[7] the Working Party on domestic regulation, which is working towards improvements in licensing and qualification standards, as well as the Working Party on GATS Rules, which is concerned with the state measures for acquisition and subsidies. Special competence is given to the Council on Trade in Services respect of technical assistance to developing countries. This technical assistance is to be decided on by the GATS Council, before it is provided for by the WTO Secretariat according to Art. XXV GATS. However, cooperation with other international institutions in questions of services is not within the authority of the GATS Council, but rather within that of the General Council.

545 As the GATS is a completely self-contained system, independent of the GATT, it has its own provisions for **consultation** (Art. XXII), **dispute settlement** and **enforcement** (Art. XXIII), which in general refer to the DSU (paras 198 *et seq.*).

4. *The Relationship with the GATT 1994*

546 As stated, trade in services has – with the GATS – been individually and specifically addressed, outside and in parallel to the framework of the

[6] This is governed by Art. IV:5 WTO Agreement, see the Annual Report of the Council for Trade in Services to the General Council (2004). S/C/22, 2 December 2004.

[7] This committee was formerly known as the "Working Party on Professional Services".

GATT 1994. In reality, however, many activities cannot be separated into either a GATT or a GATS context. The most common example of the **interrelationship between the two regimes** is simple repair work. The repair itself is qualified as a service, but cannot be delivered without an object, the product in question. In this scenario the question concerning the relationship of GATT to GATS rules arises. However, neither the GATT, nor the GATS, nor the WTO Agreement itself contains any provisions on a possible conflict.

547 In the so-called ***Periodicals* case** between the United States and Canada, which was one of the first cases to refer also to GATS provisions, the relationship between the GATS and the GATT 1994 was explicitly addressed. The subject of the dispute was the Canadian practice of higher taxation of advertisements in so-called "split run" periodicals, as compared with national periodicals. "Split-run" periodicals are periodicals which are produced exclusively for an export market – in this case the magazine in question was the Canadian version of the US-American "Sports Illustrated". As Canada had not entered into any GATS obligations in the relevant sector, the United States claimed a violation of GATT provisions. In its defence, Canada argued that the agreements were mutually exclusive. As the subject matter of the case related not to taxation, but mainly to GATS issues for which Canada had made no concessions, the GATS – according to Canada – must be exclusively applied, precluding a recourse to GATT provision. However, in its findings the Panel, as well as the Appellate Body, referred to Art. II:2 WTO Agreement, which states that all Annexes are "integral parts" of the WTO Agreement as a whole and, as such, are binding on all Members. Accordingly, the dispute settlement authorities saw room for applying the GATT and thus seem to have favoured an overlap of the scopes of both agreements.[8]

548 In the ***Bananas* dispute**[9] the United States, in addition to the GATT violations, also claimed a violation of GATS provisions. Specifically, the United States claimed breaches of GATS obligations in relation to the sale and distribution of the bananas in the EU, for which the EU had made concessions under the GATS ("distribution services"). The EU – similarly to Canada in the *Periodicals* case – argued that the agreements were *a priori* mutually exclusive: as the arguments of the United States related to goods, namely bananas, only the GATT provisions could be addressed in dispute settlement proceedings. Furthermore, as the EU

[8] *Canada – Certain Measures Concerning Periodicals*, WT/DS31/AB/R, 30 June 1997, *Canada – Certain Measures Concerning Periodicals*, WT/DS31/R, 14 March 1997, 3.35 *et seq.*

[9] *European Communities – Bananas*, WT/DS27/R/ECU, 22 May 1997; *European Communities – Bananas*, WT/DS27/AB/R, 9 September 1997.

had secured a "waiver" from its GATT obligations for the special treatment of bananas from the former colonies under the Lomé Agreement, no further provisions of other agreements could be brought into play against the regime.

549 The Panel and the Appellate Body did not follow the EU's restrictive interpretation.[10] On the contrary, by using the general rules of treaty interpretation the dispute settlement authorities assumed that both agreements must **stand next to each other on an equal footing**, thus making overlaps inevitable. In their view, the implementation of the GATS did not limit the applicability of the GATT. The decisions were based on the evident lack of any rules of conflict, as, for example, Art. XVI:3 WTO Agreement or the rules on interpretation in Annex 1A. Thus, it is now clear that the absence of any collision-type provisions leads to both agreements being applicable on the same level and in their own right. Where there is an inevitable overlap in the provisions, a violation of both agreements can be claimed. If Members want to safeguard their practice by means of "waivers" then these waivers must contain all the obligations of the different agreements.

550 The differentiation between GATT and GATS rules also plays an important role in the field of **E-Commerce**. The GATS clearly deals with services, such as tourism, which are offered and purchased via the Internet. However, goods such as books, CDs and videocassettes, which can be ordered online, fall within the jurisdiction of the GATT. Even more uncertain is the regulation of so-called "e-products" in their narrowest sense: are the rules of the GATT applicable to a book in its electronic version or does the GATS provide the relevant means of regulation? Since the levels of protection against discrimination under the GATT are much stronger than those under the GATS, the decision has very real and practical consequences.[11] Not surprisingly, the United States and Japan have argued for the applicability of GATT rules in view of their dominating e-commerce industries,[12] while the majority of WTO Members seemingly favours the applicability of GATS.[13] The

[10] *European Communities – Bananas*, WT/DS27/R/ECU, para. 285 and *European Communities – Bananas*, WT/DS27/AB/R, paras 217 *et seq.*

[11] In the framework of the GATT, the ideas of most favoured treatment and of national treatment are not restricted. The GATS anti-dumping rules and the limitations on subsidies are still relatively uncertain. On the other hand, customs duties are applicable only to goods.

[12] Work Programme on Electronic Commerce, submitted by the United States, WT/GC/16, 12 February 1999; Preparations for the 1999 Ministerial Conference, Electronic Commerce, Communication from Japan, WT/GC/W/253, 14 July 1999.

[13] See Preparations for the 1999 Ministerial Conference, WTO Work Programme on Electronic Commerce, Communication from the European Communities and their Member States, WT/GC/W/306, 9 August 1999; for E-Commerce and the WTO see *Mitchell*, Towards Compatibility: The Future of Electronic Commerce within the Global Trading System, JIEL 4 (2001) 4, 683 *et seq.*, specifically for classification, see para. 690 *et seq.*

majority can refer to the decision of the Appellate Body in the aforementioned *Canada – Periodicals* case. In it the Appellate Body expressly stressed the importance of the "physicality" of the periodical itself, and thus concluded that the GATT rules applied.[14] In contrast, products in electronic form are not material objects. In practice, the Members have agreed in the Ministerial Declaration on Global Electronic Commerce of 1998 not to levy tariffs on digital products.[15] Members have reaffirmed this position and have also agreed to further negotiate on the status on electronic commerce in the ongoing Doha-Round.[16]

II. *Applicability and Scope: Trade in Services*

551 The definition of the applicability and scope of the GATS is of great significance to the rules for international trade in services. Art 1:3 *lit.* b GATS sets out what should be understood as a **service**: the GATS includes all services with the exception of those supplied in the exercise of governmental authority.[17] The broad definition of the concept of a "service" is largely due to the fact that it was felt by the negotiating parties that a definition of a "service" was hardly possible, as it is not countable or tangible.[18]

552 Thus, in general, all possible services are included in the scope of the GATS, save for two exceptions. On the one hand, air traffic services are not covered by the general rules of the GATS, but are rather dealt with in the specific annex on this subject. More importantly, services provided for by the government on a non-commercial basis are excluded from the application of the GATS. Art. I:3 *lit.* c GATS makes it clear in this respect that such services are to be understood as "any service which is supplied neither on a commercial basis, nor in competition with one or more service suppliers." The main examples of this kind of service are health, social security and education services provided by governments which are not supplied under market conditions or are even free of charge.

---

[14] *Canada – Certain Measures Concerning Periodicals*, WT/DS31/AB/R, 30 June 1997, 17. Canada argued that the higher taxation of periodicals on the basis of printed announcements was aimed at the provision of services, and that therefore their legality was to be judged only according to the rules of the GATS.

[15] WT/MIN(98)/DEC/2, 25 May 1998 ("without prejudice to [. . .] the rights and obligations of Members under the WTO Agreements").

[16] See para. 34 of the Doha Ministerial Declaration, WT/Min(01)/DEC/1, 20 November 2001.

[17] These are defined as non-commercial, for example, the central bank or welfare state, or not subject to competition, see Art. 1:3 *lit.* c GATS.

[18] See *Köhler*, Das Allgemeine Übereinkommen über den Handel mit Dienstleistungen (GATS), 1999, 30 *et seq.*

553 As seen, the scope of the GATS is not effectively limited by the definition of the services included. However, the GATS as a trade policy instrument does not cover services in general, but, according to its title, **"trade in services"**. While the understanding of trade in goods is relatively easy, namely cross-border delivery of a specific product, the notion of "trade in services" needs further definition, to be found in Art. I:2 *lit.* b–d GATS. Art. I:2 describes **four** possibilities for trade in services, called **"modes of supply"**.

554 Art. I:2 *lit.* a GATS covers trade in services at a **cross-border supply** level. This type of supply of services is in line with the classical understanding of GATT trade regulation of transborder trade flows.[19]

555 Due to the peculiarities of the services sector, Art. I:2 GATS also includes three other modes of supply: according to *lit.* b the Agreement also applies to services which are consumed abroad by a consumer of one Member, after being provided by a supplier of another Member. In this mode, there is no cross-border supply of the service itself, which is supplied fully in the territory of one Member. However, the cross-border element is satisfied here by the crossing of the border by the recipient of the service. Thus, this mode is referred to as the **"consumption abroad"** mode.

556 Lastly, Art. I:2 also includes modes of supply in which not the recipient, but the supplier, crosses the border in order to supply the service in the territory of another Member – either by **commercial presence** or by the **presence of natural persons** (modes *lit.* c and d). These modes address the supply of a service through subsidiaries of a company and by foreign specialists. This specific subject is further clarified by special rules and specific concessions for individual member states.

557 In sum, the GATS provides for almost full coverage of all possibilities of trade in services. The four modes of supply do not effectively limit the already broad understanding of the term "services" under the GATS. All different cross-border movements, of the service itself, the supplier and the recipient, are addressed by Art. I:2. As a consequence of these broad rules the GATS **also covers transactions which take place entirely within the territory and economic order of a single Member**. The GATS therefore heavily influences the national regula-

[19] For an example see *Mexico – Measure Affecting Telecommunication Services*, WT/DS204/R, 2 April 2004, paras 7.25 *et seq.* concerning voice telephony, circuit-switched data and facsimile services between the United States and Mexico.

tory powers of the Members in this sector, which had hitherto been left largely to individual national governments. In particular, it must be noted that the differentiation between cross-border and internal measures, common in the framework of the GATT, is eliminated in the framework of the GATS.

III. *The Rules of the GATS*

1. *Basis and Overview*

558 As stated, the GATS functions as an individual, coherent and **separate set of rules** for the service sector. As a new agreement, it builds on the experiences of the GATT and uses common principles, such as non-discrimination and market access. However, owing to the specifics of the service sector and its difficult negotiations, the GATS framework differs substantially in its application of these common principles.

559 The very ambitious (on account of its broad scope) legal framework of the GATS **touches matters traditionally embedded into national economic and legal systems**, and therefore have far-reaching provisions for national regulation. The GATS contains provisions and standards not only for trade in services and for monopolies and competition procedures, but also on financial transactions, establishment and entry.

560 In this context it is important to keep in mind that the GATS is the first attempt to establish a coherent framework agreement on the services sector in international trade. International liberalization in this field therefore is only at its beginning and often touches sensitive matters of national economies, such as telecommunications and financial services. In order to achieve agreement on a broad framework the GATS negotiators had to make certain important compromises which are mirrored in the structure of the material rules. As a consequence of these difficulties, the GATS first and foremost contains **minimum standards** applicable to all trade in services. In addition, for sectors and services for which Members have entered into specific commitments, the GATS contains **additional rules** set out in part III (Art. XVI *et seq.*). These additional commitments come into play when Members enter into special commitments during the continuing liberalization negotiations in the relevant sector.

Overview: minimum standards and additional obligations

Minimum Standard	*Additional Obligation*
Non Discrimination	
Most Favoured Nation, Art. I	National Treatment, Art. XVII
Market Access	
	Legally binding commitments, Art. XVI: Prohibition of certain national measures, Art. XVI:2 Unrestricted financial transfers, Art. X
Transparency and Rule of Law	
Publication obligation, Art. III:1	Impartial operation of law, Art. VI:1–3 Specific Reporting Obligations, Art. III:
Standards and Requirements	
Possibility for mutual recognition and with access for third parties, preference for multilaterally agreed criteria, Art. VII	Harmonization through negotiated disciplines, Art. VI:4

2. *Non-Discrimination*

561 The basis for the GATS order is the principle of **most-favoured-nation** (**MFN**) treatment as contained in Art. II:1. In parallel to the scope of the Agreement, this principle provides for the equal treatment of all foreign services and service suppliers. However, in contrast to Art. I GATT 1994, which applies unconditionally, the most-favoured-nation obligation in the GATS is **qualified by the possibility of derogation** according to Art. II:2. Thus, in GATS, a cornerstone of the multilateral trading order applies only subject to the qualification that no exemption has been notified under the Annex to Art. II. However, this seemingly important deviation from the general principles is itself limited by several prerequisites. The provisions contained in the Annex to Art. II make it clear that deviations were accepted only at the time of entering into the Agreement – the possibility of an exemption was thus a "one-off" possibility at the entering into force of the agreement. Only in the sectors that are still under negotiation, such as transport, are additions to the list of exemptions still allowed. Any further deviations from the most-favoured-nation treatment must be obtained by the normal WTO procedure of a so-called "waiver".[20] Also, any exemption

[20] In relation to the specific sectors of financial services, sea transport and telecommunica-

listed should "in principle" not remain in force for more than 10 years according to No. 6 of the Annex and is subject to a review by the Services Council after five years according to Nr. 3 of the Annex. Most importantly, however, it must be noted that the possibility of deviating from most-favoured-nation treatment is not meant in a negative, but in a "positive", sense – thus, a Member may list an exemption relating to Art. II only if it wishes to treat another, specified Member's services or service suppliers better, i.e. preferentially to all other foreign services or service suppliers. Even under the exemption clause of Art. II:2 GATS it is therefore not possible to discriminate against certain Members in contravention of the most-favoured-nation principle. More than 70 Members have made use of this provision of the GATS.[21]

562 Apart from this deviation from a general principle of the WTO order, the GATS also contains another unique speciality: **national treatment is not a general obligation** applicable to all trade in services. There is no general guarantee of national treatment, as there is in Art. III GATT 1994.

563 Rather, it is **applicable only in light of specific commitments** according to Art. XVII GATS. This speciality of the GATS again is the effect of the difficult negotiations in this field and must be seen as a trade-off for the broad scope of the Agreement. Members are now obliged to treat all foreign services or service suppliers equally, but these do not have a general right to be treated equally to domestic services or service suppliers.

564 The scope of national treatment is **specified** in Art. XVII:2 and 3 GATS. According to Art. XVII:2 GATS Members may secure national treatment by treatment which is formally identical to or formally different from that given to domestic services or suppliers. Art. XVII:3 GATS further specifies that treatment is to be regarded as less favourable only where it changes the conditions of competition in favour of domestic services or service suppliers.

3. *Market Access and Further Provisions*

565 The GATS does not grant market access to all services as a general right – rather, market access-related rights are subject to specific commitments being made in a specific service sector. According to Art. XVI:1

tions, the possibility of extensions of the list of exceptions is allowed until the completion of negotiations. Furthermore, the regional economic areas also have, as in Art. XXIV GATT 1994, the chance of weakening the principle of most-favoured-nation.

[21] With this, the preferential system was to be provisionally maintained, so-called "grandfathering", para. 14.

GATS Members are **bound** by these commitments and are obliged to grant access as specified to all Members' services and service suppliers.

566 As a result of further much more complex material rules, the GATS contains extra provisions which aim at protecting the preconditions of trade in services and guarantee that market access is not encroached upon by other state influences. These include **limitations in quantity** in relation to the number of suppliers, the total value, the number of service operations and the number of people (work force) involved. Also prohibited are limitations referring to the type of legal entity and the **participation of foreign capital**.[22]

567 Finally, except for a balance-of payments situation according to Art. XII GATS, any restriction on the **international transfer and payment of capital** relating to a specific commitment shall be prohibited according to Art. XI:1 GATS.

4. *Transparency and Rule of Law*

568 Art. III:1 GATS stipulates an **obligation of transparency**, which is also contained in Art. X:1 GATT 1994, and ensures that the Members have a duty to publicise national measures and international agreements. It obliges the Members by the time of entry into force to publish all measures of general application which pertain to the operation of the GATS. In addition, Art. III:4 GATS contains an obligation on the Members promptly to respond to requests for specific information on any of their measures. The general obligation to provide information has been strengthened by an institutional requirement – all Members are required by Art. III:4 GATS to institute so-called "national inquiry points" through which information is to be provided.[23] The scope of the notification obligation is limited by the express protection of confidential information, as regulated in Art. IIIbis.[24] Lastly, Art. III:5 GATS introduces a new form and scope of notification requirement by allowing Members to notify to the Council in Trade in Services measures taken by another Member which in their opinion affect the operation of the agreement.

569 Once a Member has entered into a specific commitment, more **specific notification requirements** are contained in the GATS. For instance, according to Art. III:3 GATS each Member must at least annually

---

[22] Such restrictions were discussed in the framework of negotiations on investment measures and goods, but were not accepted by the TRIMS.

[23] The EU has made an inquiry point available on the internet <http://gats-info.eu.int/index.html>.

[24] This relates to information the publication of which might impair the imposition of a law or in other ways might run counter to the public interest, or might impair the legitimate commercial interests of certain public or private enterprises.

inform the Council for Trade in Services of the introduction of any new, or any changes to existing, laws, regulations or administrative guidelines which significantly affect trade in services covered by its specific commitments under this Agreement.

570 The obligations contained in Art. X:2 and 3 of the GATT, relating to the **rule of law** and the objective and impartial application of national measures, are not part of the general obligations of the GATS. However, Art. VI GATS provides for obligations pertaining to national regulation which apply to sectors in which specific commitments were undertaken. Once specific commitments are undertaken, the rules contained in Art. VI GATS relating to **domestic regulation** apply.[25]

571 For these sectors Art. VI:1 GATS sets out the general understanding that national measures of general application should be administered in a reasonable, objective and impartial manner. In this respect each Member is obliged to institute national judicial, arbitral or administrative tribunals through which national decisions may be challenged by the foreign service supplier.[26] According to para. 2 *lit.* b the Members do not have an obligation to implement judicial proceedings or procedures which do not fit with their own constitutional systems or the provisions of their legal systems. According to para. 3, in cases when the provision of services requires approval, the applicant must make a submission for a decision within a set time and, on the basis of the application, notify the situation of the approval procedure. In sum, Members are subject to wide-reaching obligations with regard to the establishment and administration of national procedures.[27]

5. *Competition and Restrictive Business Practices*

572 It has already been discussed in chapter 6 that the WTO includes important regulations against the distortion of competition by private or state actors (paras 454 *et seq.*). The GATS in its Art. XV contains rules for **subsidies** which mirror the general obligation in the GATT context as elaborated on in the Agreement on Subsidies and Countervailing Measures (see paras 492 *et seq.*). However, no further agreement could be reached during the Uruguay Round negotiations and Art. XV:1

[25] While these rules belong to the general obligations of the second part they apply only in "sectors where specific commitments are undertaken". The scope of the obligations is similar to that of Art. X:1 GATT 1994.

[26] Provided that such procedures are not separate and independent from the corresponding decision on judicial unity, the Members must make sure that they carry out an objective and impartial test, para. 2 *lit.* a s.2.

[27] Similar wide-reaching duties are also mentioned in the TRIPS Agreement, see paras 654 *et seq.*

GATS therefore calls for further multilateral negotiations on this matter. These negotiations are continuing in the so-called "Working Group on GATS Rules". The only "remedy" laid down in Art. XV:2 GATS consist of a request for consultation between affected Members concerning specific subsidization, a request which is to be given "sympathetic consideration".

573 However, the GATS does contain rules on **monopolies** (Art. VIII) and so-called **"restrictive business practices"** (Art. IX GATS). With regard to monopolies and exclusive service suppliers, each Member is required to ensure that such suppliers do not act in a manner inconsistent with that Member's specific commitments and the general obligations of Art. II GATS (most-favoured-nation) in accordance with Art. VIII:1. Members are further required to ensure that monopolies do not abuse their monopoly rights outside the scope of this right and when in competition with other service suppliers according to Art. VIII:2 GATS. If a Member is of the opinion that another Member's monopoly is acting inconsistently with the specific commitments the Council on Trade in Services will demand specific information on the relevant operations.

574 The GATS in its Art. IX also contains specific rules on "business practices". In contrast to the GATT which, in relation to **trade restrictions from private parties**, contains only rules on (anti-)dumping, the GATS in its Art. IX includes more far-reaching provisions on the practices of private entities, similar to national competition (or anti-trust) rules. Art. IX:1 GATS recognizes that certain business practices of service suppliers may limit competition and thereby restrict trade. To be able to appreciate this declaration, it is important to consider that some states have only recently lowered their resistance to the negotiation of questions of competition in the General Council of the WTO (paras 716 *et seq.*).

575 In para. 2 there are provisions for the **consultation** of Members in relation to the successful elimination of such practices. It is envisaged, on the basis of existing national law, that an acceptable standpoint will be found for the protection or maintenance of secrets and confidential information.

6. *National Regulation: Standards and Requirements*

576 As a result of the significance of individual national measures for the provision of services, the possibility of **mutual recognition** of qualifications for services suppliers is addressed in Art. VII GATS. The provision contains rules for the **recognition of foreign employment qualifications, requirements** and certifications, as far as is necessary for the authorization, licensing or certification of a service provider, Art. VII:1 GATS. Such recognition is to be achieved by harmonization or otherwise and may be based on an agreement or arrangement with the country concerned. As a general guideline, Art. VII:2 and 3 GATS specifies the requirements of such recognition arrangements and focuses primarily on the safeguarding of the principle of non-discriminatory application.

577 Art. VII:3 GATS includes a formulation on the basis of Art. XX GATT 1994, on the requirement that **recognition may not constitute** a means of **discrimination** between states in the application of its standards or criteria for the authorization, licensing or certification of services suppliers, or a disguised restriction on trade in services.

578 According to Art. VII:2 GATS, Members should, when there is an agreement between them on mutual recognition, **offer similar opportunities to Members** not parties to this agreement, for entry into the agreement, or for the provision of a new Agreement. Provided that an individual Member has entered into an agreement for recognition, it should give other Members the opportunity for recognition of their training, employment practices, acceptance and certification procedures.

579 According to Art. VII:5 GATS, recognition should, as far as possible, be based on mutually accepted criteria. For this purpose, the Members should work together and with the international governmental and non-governmental organizations concerned towards the introduction and establishment of **common international standards** and the criteria for the recognition of general international standards for the practice of relevant services trades and professions. This provision for harmonization runs parallel to the problem of technical barriers to trade in the GATT 1994 (paras 381 *et seq.*).

580 Furthermore, the Members are also under an obligation to notify **and inform** (Art. VII:4 GATS) the Council for Trade in Services of new developments. This obligation is not concerned only with unilateral or multilateral recognition practices and the corresponding agreements, but also with information on the establishment of negotiations on questions of recognition, to allow other Members to take part.

581 In fields in which such harmonized standards exist and in which Members have entered into specific commitments, Members have to respect such harmonized standards according to Art. VI:5 GATS. In this sense the Council on Trade in Services is mandated by Art. VI:4 GATS to develop international disciplines to ensure that such measures are not used as unnecessary barriers to trade (para. 579). In relation to mutual recognition, there is a mechanism for **harmonization**, which prescribes goals and criteria (*lit.* a–c). According to Art. VI:5 GATS Members may make restrictions in areas in which they have made concessions in relation to the introduction of admission and qualification requirements, as well as technical norms.

582 In 1995, the **"Decision on Professional Services"** introduced a Working Party on Professional Services, to work on multilateral rules and possible restrictions on trade through qualification, licensing and technical standards.[28] It has established the "Disciplines on Domestic Regulation" for the accountancy sector, which are binding and introduce specific obligations in this sector. In addition to these disciplines a standstill agreement was signed, which maintains the *status quo* and restricts the introduction of new admission provisions until after the complete incorporation of the "Disciplines" into the GATS.[29] Under its new title the "Working Party on Domestic Regulation" was called on by the Council on Trade in Services to draft binding rules for the entire services field, and to present its final report to the Council of Ministers at the Ministerial Conference at Cancún.[30] However, owing to the failure of the entire Conference, no binding rules were adopted.

7. *Exceptions*

583 The GATS system itself, like the GATT, includes exceptions covering all sectors, which the Members can refer to in order to derogate from their duties. **Safeguard measures** in the national interest are contained in Art. X GATS in parallel to Art. XIX GATT 1994, and in relation to balance of payments in Art. XII GATS.

584 Furthermore, the GATS includes in its Art. XIV a regulation corresponding to Art. XX GATT 1994, for general **exceptions**,[31] and in its Art. XIV*bis* a regulation for exceptions in relation to national security (which corresponds to Art. XXI GATT 1994).

585 In addition, the principles of most-favoured-nation treatment, market access and national treatment do not apply to **government procurement** measures in accordance with Art. XIII GATS. In this sense, all procurement by governmental agencies or services purchased for governmental services, and not with a view to commercial resale, are

---

[28] Decision on Professional Services, adopted by the Council for Trade in Services on 1 March 1995, S/L/3, 4 April 1995, see also LT/UR/D-5/7, 15 April 1994.

[29] Decision on Disciplines Relating to the Accountancy Sector, S/L/63, 14 December 1998.

[30] Decision on Domestic Regulation, WT/S/L/70, 26 April 1999.

[31] See *United States – Measure Affecting the Cross-Border Supply of Gambling and Betting Services*, WT/DS285/AB/R, 7 April 2005, paras 291 *et seq.*: "Article XIV of the GATS, like Article XX of the GATT 1994, contemplates a 'two-tier analysis' of a measure that a Member seeks to justify under that provision."

covered. Further specific rules on government procurement are to be drafted in a "Working Party on GATS rules" instituted by the Council on Trade in Services.[32]

8. *Ongoing Liberalization*

586 The GATS addresses matters concerning continuing liberalization more directly than the GATT 1994. Therefore, the notion of a need for progressive liberalization is expressly included in Art. XIX GATS. This provision, often referred to as the "built-in agenda" of the GATS, mandates new rounds of negotiations on the further liberalization of the entire sector every five years. Art. XIX addresses the **aims** and the **guiding principles** of these negotiations (paras 1 and 2), as well as some **procedural** and **preparational** matters (paras 3 and 4). In these negotiations, which are aimed at enhancing market access, Members' policy objectives and development are to be taken into consideration. The Council on Trade in Services is obliged to establish guidelines for negotiations and negotiation procedures.

587 Art. XIX *et seq.* GATS provide the institutional basis and procedures for **negotiations on specific concessions**. The schedules of commitments linked to this are described further in Art. XX GATS, which differentiates between the various service sectors. They comprise information on limitation and conditions of market access, conditions and specific rules for national treatment and further admissions according to Art. XVIII GATS. Furthermore, there is a time limit for the implementation of such commitments. Art. XXI GATS sets out how the individual lists may be amended. If a Member intends to undertake a new commitment, modify or withdraw a scheduled commitment specific procedures, adopted by the Council for Trade in Services, have to be used.[33]

588 In February 2000, negotiations started as provided for in Art. XIX GATS, followed by a decision in March 2001 on guidelines and procedures.[34] The negotiations were included in the Ministerial Declaration at Doha on the basis of a request-offer-approach.[35] As the negotiations

[32] See, e.g., S/WPGR/1, 30 October 1996. For government procurement in general see paras 526 *et seq.*

[33] Procedures for the Implementation of Article XXI of the General Agreement on Trade in Services (GATS) – Modification of Schedules, S/L/80, 29 October 1999; Procedures for the Certification of Rectifications or Improvements to Schedules of Specific Commitments, adopted by the Council for Trade in Services on 14 April 2000, S/L/84, 18 April 2000.

[34] Guidelines and Procedures for the Negotiations on Trade in Services, Adopted by the Special Session of the Council for Trade in Services on 28 March 2001, S./L/93, 29 March 2001.

[35] Ministerial Declaration, adopted on 14 November 2001, WT/MIN(01)/DEC/1, 20 November 2001, para. 15.

had been linked to the new world trade round, they were to completed by 1 January 2005 at the latest.[36] The negotiations are still underway and – so far – a successful termination is not foreseeable.[37]

9. *General Provisions*

589 The GATS includes provisions on **economic integration** (Art. V), which correspond to the rules of Art. XXIV GATT 1994 with reference to customs unions (para. 8 *lit.* a)[38] and free trade areas (para. 8 *lit.* b).[39]

590 Art. VIII is concerned with monopolies and providers, and refers to Art. XVII GATT on **state-owned companies**.

591 Reference to the interests of **developing country Members**, which is often discussed in negotiations, has been included in Art. IV GATS. According to para. 1, these interests should be considered primarily through specific concessions in accordance with Parts III and IV GATS. The concessions relate to three different objectives: according to *lit.* a, special concessions should serve to strengthen capacity for domestic services, the effectiveness and competitiveness of developing nations, and achieve access to technology on commercial levels. According to *lit.* b, access to distribution channels and information networks should be improved and, finally, according to *lit.* c, this should be governed by the liberalization of market access and the possibility of export in the interest of developing nations. According to the provisions of Art. IV:2 GATS developed country Members should establish contact points to facilitate access by developing nations and their service providers to information in relation to the corresponding markets.

IV. *Specific Areas of Liberalization and their Rules*

592 As stated above, the ambitious project of establishing a coherent legal order on all trade in services led to the need to allow for special treatment in certain sectors in which the agreement of all Members could not be reached. Specific rules negotiated for these sectors mirror the special negotiating situation and contain definitions and certain modifications of the GATS. In addition to the Annex on Art. II containing

---

[36] For negotiations in the framework of the new World Trade Round, see paras 795 *et seq.*

[37] Compare Special Session of the Council for Trade in Services, Report by the Chairman to the Trade Negotiations Committee, TN/S/19, 24 March 2005.

[38] Compare *Canada* – Certain Measures Affecting the Automotive Industry, WT/DS139, 142/R, 11 February 2000, paras 10.265–10.272.

[39] See also para. 114.

the exemptions from most-favoured-nation treatment, at the time of ratification the GATS contained seven Annexes on five different sectors.[40]

593 Following further negotiations on these topics, **four** more Annexes, called **Protocols**, were added which embody specific commitments for particular sectors. With regard to these specific areas of liberalization which were under continuing negotiation, the Members were again allowed to add to their Exemptions from Art. II for these sectors.[41] The fundamental difference between Annexes and Protocols thus lies in the fact that Protocols contain concessions and exceptions to the principle of most-favoured-nation, whereas the Annexes – with the exception of the Annex to Art. II GATS – contain general rules for the various service sectors. According to Art. XXIX GATS all Annexes, and therefore also all Protocols, are integral parts of the GATS Agreement.

1. *Telecommunications*

Patrick Low & Aaditya Mattoo, Reform in basic telecommunications and the WTO pronouncements: the Asian experience, 1997; *Miriam Gonzalez-Durántez*, Telecommunications and GATS 2000, International Profit Law and Regulation, 1999, 155–157; *Dietrich Barth*, The Prospects of International Trade in Services Friedrich Ebert Foundation, Strategic Planning Department, 1999, Part VII; *Krista Schwarting Rose*, Changing Frequencies: The Federal Communications Commission Globalizes the Telecommunications Industry with the Adoption of the WTO Agreement, Minnesota Journal of Global Trade 8 (1999) 1, 161–196; *Sabine von Schorlemer*, Globale Telekommunikation und Entwicklungsländer: Die Liberalisierung von Telekommunikationsdiensten in GATT/WTO, 2000; *Cowhey Peter F. & Mikhail M. Klimenko*, The WTO Agreement and telecommunication policy reforms, World Bank, Development Research Group, Trade, 2001; *Richard Senti*, Die Welthandelsordnung der Telekommunikation, Aussenwirtschaft 2001, 43–68; *Peter Holmes & Alasdair R. Young*, Liberalizing and Re-Regulating Telecommunications in Europe: A Common Framework and Persistent Differences, HWWA Discussion Paper 159, 2002; *Bobjoseph Mathew*, The WTO Agreements on Telecommunications, 2003.

594 The GATS includes an Annex on Telecommunications, which contains no material concessions, but instead sets out the basic rules for the

[40] These are the Annex on Movement of Natural Persons Supplying Services under the Agreement, the Annex on Air Transport Services, the Annex on Financial Services, the Second Annex on Financial Services, the Annex on Negotiations on Maritime Transport Services, the Annex on Telecommunications and the Annex on Negotiation on Basic Telecommunications.

[41] Second Protocol to the GATS, S/L/11, adopted 21 July 1995, entry into force 1 September 1996; Third Protocol to the GATS, S/L/12, adopted 21. July 1995, entry into force 30 January 1996; Fourth Protocol to the GATS, S/L/20, adopted 30 April 1997, entry into force 5 February 1998; Fifth Protocol to the GATS, S/L/45, adopted 11 November 1997, entry into force 1 March 1999. There is no "first protocol" – it was to contain special concessions for developing country Members, which were eventually incorporated into the Uruguay Round schedules, so that there was no need for a separate protocol.

specialized sector of telecommunications. According to para. 4 the duty of **transparency** according to Art. III GATS is strengthened for the technical specifications for information networks and services. Para. 5 includes special provisions on **market access**, which refer in particular to access to information networks. In ***Mexico – Telecommunication Services*** the Panel found that "the Annex applies to measures of a Member that affect access to and use of public telecommunications transport networks and services by basic telecommunications suppliers of any other Member." However, the obligations in the Annex "are aimed at facilitating the exploitation of scheduled commitments, and do not create a right to supply a service where no commitments exist."[42] Para. 5 *lit.* d addresses data protection.[43] Finally, para. 6 includes a provision on state **cooperation** in this area, which provides for the participation of international organizations, in particular the International Telecommunications Union, the United Nations Development Program and the World Bank.

595 In general, many Members were cautious about telecommunications during the Uruguay Round. As a result, while many states made some concessions in their general concession lists for the telecommunications sector, the area of **basic telecommunication services**, which is involved in the pure transmission of information,[44] was left for future negotiation.[45] Consequently, the GATS, in its "Annex on Negotiations on Basic Telecommunications", set forth a negotiations mandate for the Members, to work on specific concessions in this area, and makes an exception to the principle of most-favoured-nation for these negotiations. The negotiations mandate was fulfilled with the negotiation of the so-called **fourth protocol**.[46] As with other protocols, the Members were able to exempt the principle of most-favoured-nation in relation to the Annex to Art. II GATS.

596 Apart from binding new commitments, the fourth Protocol also has one other speciality – it includes a so-called **"Reference Paper on Basic Telecommunication"** which contains specific definitions and principles

[42] *Mexico – Affecting Telecommunication Services*, WT/DS204/R, 2 April 2004, paras 7.274 *et seq.*

[43] *Kirby*, Legal aspects of transborder data flows, Computer Law Journal 11 (1991), 233 *et seq.*

[44] Basis telecommunications services (such as voice telephony, fax, telex, etc.) must be differentiated from the so-called "value added services", in which the service provider does some work, such as saving or duplication. This type of service provision was not discussed in the negotiations. However, many members have made concessions in this area.

[45] It should not be forgotten that in many nations telecommunications networks are controlled by monopolies or state-run businesses, and therefore immediate liberalisation was not desirable.

[46] See the "Fourth Protocol to the GATS", WT/S/L/20, 30 April 1996, which was finally implemented on 5 February 1998.

for the sector which were adopted by many Members.[47] In the main, the Reference Paper deals with rules on privatisation of state monopolies and access to their telecommunication networks.

2. *Maritime transport*

Dietrich Barth, The Prospects of International Trade in Services Friedrich Ebert Foundation, Strategic Planning Department, 1999, Part IX; *Carsten Fink & Aaditya Mattoo & Ilena Cristina Neagu*, Trade in International Maritime Services: How Much Does Policy Matter?, World Bank Working Paper 2522, 2001, *Benjamin Parameswaran*, The liberalization of maritime transport services, 2004.

597 The **"Annex on Negotiations on Maritime Transport Services"** relates to international maritime transport,[48] and refers to "international shipping, auxiliary services and access to and use of port facilities". Importantly, the Annex states that the principle of most-favoured-nation treatment does not apply to this sector and calls for further negotiation. A "Negotiating Group on Maritime Transport Services" was set up and at the end of the negotiating Round and 29 Members had made commitments in international shipping services. Moreover, on 28 June 1996 the **Decision on Maritime Transport Services** was adopted.[49] The Council for Trade in Services decided to suspend the negotiations and to resume them with the commencement of comprehensive negotiations on services, which started in the year 2000 (paras 586 *et seq.*).[50]

598 The negotiations underway are embedded in the special framework conditions of this service sector. The basic international instrument governing maritime transport with commercial vessels is the **liner conference system**. Already since the end of the 19th century, liner shipping has been organised by associations of maritime carriers providing cargo transportation of scheduled, advertised services upon uniform or common rates on particular geographical routes. Most OECD countries recognize the liner conference system and have granted some form of anti-trust immunity.[51] In 1974, the United Nations Conference on Trade and Development (UNCTAD) adopted the **Code of Conduct for**

[47] The incorporation of this duty occurred as the result of unusual and obscure means: the states referred to the reference paper when making their lists of concessions, and accepted additional concessions, although the reference paper included no sector-specific concessions.

[48] *Abrahamsson*, International Shipping: Developments, Prospects and Policy Issues, Ocean Yearbook 8 (1989), 158 *et seq.; Mukherjee*, Multilateral Negotiations and Trade Barriers in Service Trade – A Case Study on U.S. Shipping Services, JWT 26 (1992) 5, 45 *et seq.*

[49] S/L/24, 3 July 1996.

[50] Joint Statement from the European Communities and their Member States; Hong Kong, China; Japan; Republic of Korea; Norway and Singapore, S/CSS/W/8, 6 October 2000.

[51] E.g. United States: Ocean Shipping Reform Act (OSRA); Australia: Trade Practices Act 1974 (Part X).

Liner Conferences to meet the aspirations of developing countries for greater participation of their carriers in the transportation of liner cargoes. In the ongoing WTO negotiations "offers" – for example by the EU – were based on the understanding that the Liner Code is an applicable instrument.[52]

3. *Financial Services*

Dilip K. Das, Trade in financial services and the role of the GATS: Against the backdrop of the Asian financial crisis, JWT 32 (1998), 79–114; *Brian Woodrow*, The 1997 World Trade Organization accord on financial services: its impact on and implications for the world insurance industry, Geneva papers on risk and insurance 25 (2000), 78–103; *Julian Arkell*, International investment, profit liberalization and freedom from rules: some issues for the insurance sector to consider, Geneva papers on risk and insurance 25 (2000), 104–115; *Aaditya Mattoo*, Financial services and the WTO: Liberalization Commitments of the Developing and Transition Economies, World Economy 23 (2000) 3, 351–386; *Andrew Cornford*, The WTO negotiations on financial services, UNCTAD Discussion Paper 172, 2004.

599 Rules on financial services were highly controversial during the Uruguay Round negotiations. According to No. 5 of the Annex on Financial Services such services are defined as insurance and insurance-related services and **banking** and other **financial services**. The Annex also contains some important exceptions to the services definitions of the GATS (Art. I:3 GATS) in respect of services supplied in the exercise of governmental authority. It excludes all financial activities conducted by central banks, activities forming part of a statutory system of social security or public retirement plans and other activities conducted by a public entity with the guarantee or using the financial resources of the government (No. 1 *lit.* b). Financial services provided by public institutions are therefore totally excluded from the GATS. According to para. 1 *lit.* d, the limitations set out in Art. I:3 *lit.* c for the public provision of services, namely, the commercial competence of public authorities in financial services, do not apply. This means that the provision of services by public institutions is unregulated.

600 With regard to **national regulations**, certain measures for "prudential reasons", and the protection of investors, depositors and those taking insurance, as contained in para. 2 *lit.* a, are allowed. Furthermore, measures for the protection of the integrity and stability of the financial system are allowed. According to this, those responsible for national decisions on sensitive political and economic areas are allowed some scope.

[52] *Taylor*, Evaluating the Continuing GATS Negotiations Concerning International Maritime Transport Services, Tulane Maritime Law Journal 27 (2002), 129 *et seq.*

601 According to para. 2 *lit.* b information on businesses and accounts of individual customers is treated as **confidential**, like commercially valuable information of public institutions, and is therefore protected.

602 A **second Annex** on Financial Services concerned the time limits within which Members were allowed to add to the Annex on Art. II Exemptions or modify their commitments.[53]

603 As stated and shown by the material rules contained in the Annexes, many Members had difficulty in entering into substantial commitments. In order nevertheless to reach a certain level of liberalization in this sector, the **"Understanding on Commitments in Financial Services"** was agreed upon as part of the Uruguay package.[54] It contains alternative rules on the specific commitments and included a "standstill" agreement according to which the signatories were not allowed to add additional exemptions to the most-favoured-nation principle. The commitments entered into by the United States, the EU and Japan followed this set of rules.[55]

604 Since 1995 the specific commitments of Members in this sector have been further negotiated. As early as 1995 a **"Second Protocol to the GATS"** was agreed upon by some, but not all, Members.[56] In particular, the United States introduced wide-reaching new exemptions from the principle of most-favoured-nation, so that in 1997 a new and improved package was introduced, as a result of which the United States revoked its exceptions. These specific concessions were named the **fifth protocol**, and were implemented in 1999.[57] With this, 95% of financial services are covered by special duties for the Members.[58]

605 The Annex on Financial Services also includes special disciplines on the recognition of foreign service suppliers. The recognition of qualifications and licences was further elaborated on in the **"Disciplines on Domestic Regulation in the Accountancy Sector"** which also introduced another "standstill" agreement for new qualification requirements.

[53] According to the Decision on Financial Services, Members are granted a special deadline of six months after the implementation of the Agreement for the retraction or modification of their own commitments.

[54] See the ministerial decision "Understanding on Commitments in Financial Services", which was adopted during the ministerial conference in Marrakesh, Doc LT/UR/U/1, 15 April 1999.

[55] See *Trachtman*, Trade in Financial Services under GATS, NAFTA, and the EC: A Regulatory Jurisdiction Analysis, Columbia Journal of Transnational Law 34 (1995) 1, 37, 69.

[56] Second Protocol to the GATS, 24.7.1995, WT/S/L/11, 1 September 1996.

[57] Fifth Protocol to the GATS, 3.12.1997, WT/S/L/45, 1 March 1999.

[58] See WTO Focus No. 37, January/February 1999. 8.

4. *Air Transport*

Christopher Findlay & Deunden Nikomborirak, Air Transport, 1999; *Ruwantissa Abeyrathne*, Emerging Trends in Aviation Competition Laws in Europe and North America, World Competition 23 (2000), 141–176; *Ruwantissa Abeyrathne*, Competition and Liberalisation in Air Transport, World Competition 24 (2001), 607–637; *Wolfgang Hubner & Pierre Sauvé*, Liberalization Scenarios for International Air Transport, JWT 35 (2001), 937–987; *Ruwantissa Abeyrathne*, Trade in Air Transport Services Emerging Trends, JWT 35 (2001), 1133–1168.

606 The Annex on Air Transport[59] mainly defines the applicability of the GATS: according to para. 2 of the Annex it does not apply **to traffic rights** and services directly related to the exercise of traffic rights. This sector is still mainly governed by bilateral agreements between individual Members.[60] The existing rules of international air transport, as a result of the IATA and the allocation of lines, are protected.

607 According to para. 3 of the Annex, the Agreement should apply to the following services: **repair and servicing** of aircraft, and the **sale and marketing** of air transport services and services for **computer reservations**. According to para. 5, there are provisions for the review of rules by the Council for Trade in Services, to take place at least every five years.

5. *Movement of Natural Persons*

Matthias Köhler, Das Allgemeine Übereinkommen über den Handel mit Dienstleistungen (GATS): Rahmenregelung zur Liberalisierung des internationalen Dienstleistungsverkehrs unter besonderer Berücksichtigung des grenzüberschreitenden Personenverkehrs von Dienstleistungsanbietern, 1999; *Elspeth Guild*, The movement of natural persons and the GATS: a UK perspective and European dilemmas, European foreign affairs review 4 (1999) 3, 395–415; *Sumanta Chaudhuri & Aaditva Mattoo & Richard Self*, Moving people to deliver services, JWT 38 (2004) 3, 363–393.

608 Supply by the movement of natural persons (mode 4, para. 555) was another contentious topic during the negotiations. The developing Members in particular sought the broad liberalization of this mode in order make use of their comparative advantage of low labour costs. This mode is now dealt with in the **"Annex on the Movement of Natural Persons"**, which contains few, but important, rules.

[59] See *v. Zabinsky*, European Union external competence and external relations in air transport, 1996 and *Haanappel* (Ed.), EEC air transport policy and regulation, and their implications for North America, 1990.

[60] See, for example, the Open-Sky Agreement between the USA and Germany: Protocol between the United States of America and the Federal Republic of Germany to Amend the Air Transport Agreement of July 7, 1995, with its related Route Schedule, signed on 23 May 1996 in Milwaukee, published in: 46 ZLW (1997), 3, 33 *et seq.*

609 For instance, No. 2 of the Annex makes it clear that the GATS does not market of another Member, nor does it apply to measures regarding citizenship, residence or employment on a permanent basis. Further, No. 4 of the Annex and the accompanying footnote expressly allow for border measures and visa requirements.[61] The Annex makes it clear that only **temporary** rights of aliens will be protected – a idea similar to the EU's rule on free movement of workers is expressly excluded. No. 3 of the Annex includes a negotiations mandate for the Members to discuss specific concessions in this area. With the negotiation of the Third Protocol, specific concessions in this area were finally established.[62]

[61] See the footnote to para. 4 of the Annex.
[62] Third Protocol to the GATS, S/L/12, adopted 21 July 1995, entry into force 1 January 1996.

CHAPTER EIGHT

THE PROTECTION OF INTELLECTUAL PROPERTY AND THE TRIPS

Friedrich-Karl Beier & Gerhard Schricker (Eds), GATT or WIPO? New Ways in the International Protection of Intellectual Property, 1989; *Giorgio Sacerdoti* (Ed.), Liberalization of services and intellectual property in the Uruguay Round of GATT: proceedings of the Conference on the Uruguay Round of GATT and the Improvement of the Legal Framework of Trade in Services, 1990; *Thomas Cottier,* The Prospects for Intellectual Property in GATT, CMLR 28 (1991), 383–414; *Peter-Tobias Stoll,* Technologietransfer – Nationalisierungs- und Internationalisierungstendenzen, 1994; *idem*, Stichwort: "155. WIPO – World Intellectual Property Organization", in: *Rüdiger Wolfrum* (Ed.), United Nations: Law, Policies and Practice, 1995, 1431–1440; *Friedrich-Karl Beier & Gerhard Schricker* (Eds), From GATT to TRIPs – The Agreement on Trade-Related Aspects of Intellectual Property Rights, 1996; *Michael Blakeney*, Trade-Related Aspects of Intellectual Property Rights: A Concise Guide to the TRIPs Agreement, 1996; *Jerome H. Reichman*, From Free Riders to Fair Followers: Global Competition under the TRIPs-Agreement, New York University Journal of International Law and Politics (JILP) 29 (1997) 2, 11–94; *Marco Bronckers*, The Exhaustion of Patent Rights Under WTO Law, JWT 32 (1998) 5, 137–159; *Daniel Gervais*, The TRIPS agreement, drafting history and analysis, 1998; *Carlos M. Correa & Abdulqawi A. Yusuf*, Intellectual Property and International Trade: The TRIPs Agreement, 1998; *B. K. Keayla*, TRIPs Agreement on Patent Laws: Impact on Pharmaceuticals and Health for All, 1998; *Julie S. Sheinblatt*, The WIPO Copyright Treaty, Berkeley Technology Law Journal 13 (1998), 535–550; *Hanns Ullrich*, International Exhaustion of Intellectual Property Rights: Lessons from European economic integration, in: Mélanges en hommage à Michel Waelbroeck, 1999; *Rudolf Busse & Alfred Keukenschrijver & Klaus Schwendy & Thomas Baumgärtner* (Eds), Patentgesetz, 5. Aufl. 1999; *Matthijs Geuze & Hannu Wager*, WTO Dispute Settlement Practice Relating to the TRIPs-Agreement, JIEL 2 (1999) 2, 347–384; *Frederick Abbott & Thomas Cottier & Francis Gurry*, The International Intellectual Property System, Commentary and Materials, Part One and Two, 1999; *Michael Doherty & Ivor Griffiths*, The Harmonisation of European Union Copyright Law for the Digital Age, EIPR 22 (2000) 1, 17–23; *Panos Kanavos*, WTO and Patents: The Impact on the Pharmaceutical Industry, 2000; *Shanker A. Singham*, Competition policy and the stimulation of innovation: TRIPS and the interface between competition and patent protection in the pharmaceutical industry, Brooklyn Journal of International Law 26 (2000) 2, 363–416; *Vincent Chiappetta*, The Desirability of Agreeing to Disagree: the WTO, TRIPS, International IPR Exhaustion and a Few Other Things, Michigan Journal of International Law 21 (2000) 3, 333–392; *Bess-Carolina Dolmo*, Examining global access to essential pharmaceuticals in the face of patent protection rights: the South African example, Buffalo Human Rights Law Review 7 (2001), 137–163; *Muria Kruger*, Harmonizing TRIPs and the CBD: a proposal from India, Minnisota journal of global trade 10 (2001) 1, 169–207; *Rainer Schulte*, Patentgesetz mit Europäischem

Patentübereinkommen, Kommentar, 6. Aufl., 2001; *Jörg Reinbothe & Silke von Lewinski*, The WIPO Treaties 1996, Commentary and Legal Analysis, 2002; *Nuno Pires de Cavalho*, The TRIPs regime of patent rights, 2002; *Duncan Matthews*, Globalising intellectual property rights: the TRIPS Agreement, 2002; *Frederick M. Abbott*, The Doha Declaration of the TRIPS Agreement and Public Health, JIEL 5 (2002) 2, 469–505; *Carmen Otero García-Castrillón*, an approach to the WTO Ministerial Declaration on the TRIPS Agreement and public health, JIEL 5 (2002) 1, 207–211; *Andrew Evans*, Taming the counterfeit dragon: the WTO, TRIPs and Chinese amendments to intellectual property laws, Georgia journal of international & comparative law 31 (2003) 3, 587–618; *Daniel Gervais*, The TRIPS-Agreement: drafting history and analysis, 2nd ed., 2003; *Luigi Palombi*, Patentable subject matter, TRIPS and the European Biotechnology Directive, University of New South Wales law journal 26 (2003) 3, 782–792; *Haochen Sun*, Reshaping the TRIPs Agreement concerning public health, JWT 37 (2003) 1, 163–197; *Biswajeet Dhar*, Implementing Convention on Biological Diversity and agreement on TRIPs, Doha development agenda 2003, 282–295; *Frederick M. Abbott*, Are the competition rules in the WTO TRIPS Agreement adequate?, JIEL 7 (2004) 3, 687–703; *Karen Kaiser*, Geistiges Eigentum und Gemeinschaftsrecht, 2004; *Duncan Matthews*, WTO decision on implementation of Paragraph 6 of the Doha Declaration on the TRIPS Agreement and Public Health, JIEL 7 (2004) 1, 73–107; *Ruth Rikowski*, Globalisation, information and libraries: the implications of the World Trade Organisation's GATS and TRIPS Agreements, 2004; *Hanns Ulrich*, Expansionist intellectual property protection and reductionist competition rules: a TRIPS perspective, JIEL 7 (2004) 2, 401–430; *Haochen Sun*, The road to Doha and beyond: some reflections on the TRIPs Agreement and public health, EJIL 15 (2004) 1, 123–150; *Laurence R. Helfer*, Regime shifting: the TRIPs Agreement and new dynamics of international intellectual property law making, Yale journal of international law 29 (2004) 1, 1–83; *Robert Weissmann*, A long strange trips: the pharmaceutical industry drive to harmonize global intellectual property rules and the remaining WTO legal alternatives available to Third World countries, JIEL 25 (2004) 3, 1079–1132; *Mitsuo Matsushita*, Appellate body jurisprudenz on the GATS and TRIPS agreements, WTO dispute settlement system 1995–2003, 2004, 455–474; *Aaron X. Fellmeth*, Secrecy, monopoly and access to pharmaceuticals in international trade law: protection of marketing approval data under the TRIPs, Agreement, Harvard international law journal 45 (2004) 2, 443–502; *Gregory Shaffer*, Recognizing public goods in WTO dispute settlement: Who participates? Who decides?, JIEL 7 (2004) 2, 459–482; *Frederick M. Abbott*, Toward a new era of objective assessment in the field of TRIPS and variable geometry for the preservation of multilateralism, JIEL 8 (2005) 1, 77–100.

I. *Overview*

610 With the Agreement on Trade-related Aspects of Intellectual Property Rights – **TRIPS** – the WTO establishes detailed rules of its own next to the conventional system of intellectual property rights protection which unifies protection standards at a high level and considerably facilitates the enforcement of these rights. The protection of intellectual property rights has long been provided for at the international level by means of special conventions,[1] which are administered by the World Intellectual Property Organization – **WIPO**.

611 The extensive TRIPS, according to its wording and systematic position in Annex 1C to the WTO Agreement, applies not only to **trade in goods**, but **also** to **trade in services**. It contains three different sets of regulations:

612 It first establishes an **organizational and procedural framework** for the inclusion in the WTO of questions regarding the protection of intellectual property (Part VII). Apart from a special council, the Council for Trade-related Aspects of Intellectual Property Rights pursuant to Art. 68 TRIPS (Council for TRIPS), this framework involves transparency and notification duties (Art. 63:1, s. 2 TRIPS) and general regulations on the settlement of disputes between the Members (Part V), which essentially refer to the Dispute Settlement Understanding (Art. 64 TRIPS). Finally, there is an exception clause for national security matters (Art. 73 TRIPS).

613 On this basis, the Agreement – secondly – provides for **substantive protection standards** which are superimposed on and take priority over the law set out in the existing conventions. (Part I: General Provisions and Basic Principles and Part II: Standards concerning the Availability, Scope and Use of Intellectual Property Rights).

614 In its Part III, the Agreement contains – third – a novel rule on the **private enforcement of intellectual property rights** which describes in a sophisticated manner the procedures and remedies to be put in place by the individual Members for this purpose.

[1] The existing conventions administered by the WIPO include: Paris Convention for the Protection of Industrial Property of 20 March 1883, last revised in Stockholm on 14 July 1967 (UNTS Vol. 828, No. I-11851, 305), the Berne Convention for the Protection of Literary and Artistic Work of 9 September 1886, last revised in Paris on 24 July 1971 (UNTS Vol. 1161, No. I-18338, 3), the International Convention for the Protection of Performers, Producers of Phonograms and Broadcasting Organizations of 26 October 1961 (UNTS Vol. 496, No. I-7247, 43, Rome Convention), the Madrid Agreement Concerning the International Registration of Marks of 14 April 1891, last revised in Stockholm on 14 July 1967 (UNTS Vol. 828, No. I-11852, 389), the Madrid Agreement for the Repression of False or Deceptive Indications of Source on Goods of 14 April 1891, last revised in Lisbon on 31 October 1958 (UNTS Vol. 828, No. I-11848, 163), the Hague Agreement Concerning the International Deposit of Industrial Designs of 6 November 1925, last revised in Geneva on 2 July 1999 (WIPO-Doc. H/DC/40), the Patent Cooperation Treaty of 19 June 1970 (UNTS Vol. 1160, No. I-18336, 232) and the Budapest Treaty on the International Recognition of the Deposit of Micro-organisms for the Purposes of Patent Procedure of 28 April 1977 (ILM 17 (1978), 285).

II. *History and Origins*

615 In the context of international economic relations, new technologies and other innovations play an increasingly important role. Just as the global market has fostered technological development, it has received input from the latter. The loss of the technological supremacy of industrialized countries and the industrialization and development of technological potential in several states with industries in transition have caused competition to intensify. Thereby, the relevance of intellectual property protection has increased. Particularly in the eyes of the industrialized countries, the conventional international system for the protection of intellectual property rights was no longer able to control **this increase in importance**. Subject to criticism were, in particular, varying membership levels, the considerable leeway given to individual states in the design of their respective protection systems, and the non-existence of effective enforcement measures. A further development of the system for the protection of intellectual property rights at the international level was also severely obstructed by the fact that its rules had become an issue in the context of the North-South conflict and were in this regard partly subjected to lengthy and unsuccessful negotiations for revision.

616 The industrialized countries were no longer ready to accept these **structural deficits**. The United States, in particular, made it clear that, besides an agreement on trade in services, an agreement on intellectual property rights protection would have to be a precondition for a new world trade order on the basis of the GATT. This met with grim opposition from the developing countries which tried to prevent the inclusion of intellectual property rights with reference to the negotiation structure of the world trade order and with its established system of economic and political bargaining and reciprocal relationships. Apart from the reference to the negotiations which were abandoned early in the Tokyo Round, several points in the GATT 1947 and the dispute settlement practice served as a justification for the negotiation and regulation of such questions within the world trade order.

617 Of great importance in this context was a dispute settlement procedure initiated by the EU against the United States, the subject of which was § 337 of the Tariff Act of 1930.[2] Based on these starting points and

[2] See *United States – Imports of Certain Automotive Spring Assemblies*, 26 May 1983, L/5333, BISD 30S/107; *United States* – Section 337 of the Tariff Act of 1930, 23 November 1988, BISD 36S/345 *et seq.* This case concerned a US exclusion order with respect to the Dutch E.I. du Pont de Nemours and Company (Akzo N.V. v. USITC, 808 F.2d 1471 (Fed.Cir. 1986) of 22 December 1986; Court of Appeals (Akzo N.V. v. USITC, 107 Supreme Court Reporter 2490 of 1 June 1987).

an approach initially limited to clear cases of product piracy, the TRIPS, in the course of negotiations, developed as a very extensive regulation of substantive intellectual property rights and their enforcement, whose relationship with the further existing conventions under the WIPO is still difficult to determine.

III. *Basics, Objectives and Principles*

618 The TRIPS in its part I contains general regulations. Art. 1.2 TRIPS defines the **term** "intellectual property" through the inclusion of all categories of rights stipulated in part II. The provision to that extent refers to the intellectual property rights mentioned in sections 1 to 7 of part II TRIPS, and thus includes copyright and related rights (Art. 9 *et seq.*, paras 627 *et seq.*), trademarks (Art. 15 *et seq.*, paras 632 *et seq.*), geographical indications (Art. 22 *et seq.*, para. 634), industrial designs (Art. 25 *et seq.*, paras 635 *et seq.*), patents (Art. 27 *et seq.*, paras 637 *et seq.*), topographies of integrated circuits (Art. 35 *et seq.*, para. 651), and the protection of undisclosed information (Art. 39, para. 652).

619 Fundamental objectives of "the protection and enforcement of intellectual property rights" are addressed in Art. 7 TRIPS. The provision refers to the promotion of technological innovation, the transfer and dissemination of technology, and the mutual advantages of producers and users of technological knowledge, and points to the social and economic welfare as well as to a balance of rights and obligations. The interests in the protection of individual and personal rights which, next to these economically oriented protection objectives, continue to be valid and important, are not addressed by the TRIPS but are, rather, as is shown by Art. 9.1 s. 2 TRIPS, excluded. In short, only the economic aspects of intellectual property rights are regulated by the TRIPS.

620 The TRIPS refers frequently to regulations in **conventions for the protection of intellectual property rights** which have already existed for a long time, and which were not meant to be substituted or supplanted by parallel and fundamentally new and comprehensive rules in a WTO Agreement. On the other hand it must be mentioned that the membership level of these conventions varies considerably and has many times been unsatisfactory as far as the global protection of intellectual property rights is concerned. During the negotiations on TRIPS it did not however appear to be a realistic option to fill the membership gaps of individual conventions for the protection of intellectual property rights up to the WTO level by means of obligations of accession and ratification of these individual agreements.

621 The TRIPS avoids these problems by means of **substantive cross references**. It obliges its Members, independently of their membership of the respective conventions, to apply and abide by particular substantive regulations under the conventions. This substantive connection between different treaty regimes is laid down in Art. 2.1 TRIPS for large parts of the Paris Convention in its 1967 version,[3] and in Art. 9.1. TRIPS for the Berne Convention in its 1971 version.[4]

622 The above-mentioned commitment undertaken by TRIPS Members by way of substantive cross references however additionally requires a special regulation on the **eligibility of the individual right holders**. While membership obligations in the classical area of the world trade order are tied to the goods of another Member, the commitment to guarantee intellectual property rights must refer to the individual right owners and thus to natural and legal persons. Art. 1.3 TRIPS clarifies that all nationals of other WTO Members are entitled to be accorded the treatment provided for in the TRIPS regardless of the membership status of their own country in the intellectual property conventions.[5] Art. 1.3 TRIPS defines "nationals of other Members" in order to determine the persons to whom Members shall accord such treatment, which includes national treatment. These individual substantive norms for the protection of intellectual property rights, which have been made binding for all WTO Members through substantive cross references and the expanded definition of individual eligibility, are further detailed and substantiated in Part II of the TRIPS. According to Art. 1.1 TRIPS, Members are in principal free to implement more extensive standards of protection, while they are at the same time at liberty to determine the appropriate form and legal arrangement with which to assure protection.[6]

623 In addition, the TRIPS in its Art. 3 and 4 contains a **general provision on national treatment and most-favoured-nation treat-**

[3] See for example the decision by the Appellate Body in *United States – Section 211 Omnibus Appropriations Act of 1998*, WT/DS176/AB/R, 21 February 2002, paras 322 *et seq.*, that trade names are covered by the TRIPS.

[4] See for example *United States – Section 110(5) of the US Copyright Act*, WT/DS160/R, 15 June 2000, para. 6.42 *et seq.* for the incorporation of Art. 11 and 11*bis* of the Berne Convention.

[5] Several of the substantive regulations in the conventions referred to in the TRIPS are designed in such a way that they grant rights to the nationals of the Members which are parties to the conventions concerned. These rights must be extended in view of the desired applicability of the rules between all WTO Members. This is now assured by Art. 1.3 TRIPS in that it creates the fiction that all WTO Members are also parties to the convention in question. Concerning "EC nationals" compare *European Communities – Protection of Trademarks and Geographical Indications for Agricultural Products and Foodstuffs*, WT/DS290/R, 15 March 2005, paras 7.191 *et seq.*

[6] Compare *European Communities – Trademarks and Geographical Indications*, (footnote 5), paras 7.762 *et seq.*

ment which adds to the particular regulations on non-discrimination in individual conventions.[7] The unchecked extension of the principle of most-favoured-nation treatment to intellectual property rights could have the final consequence that citizens of WTO Members benefit from the highest standard of protection of all international treaties for the protection of intellectual property rights, even if only one WTO Member is party to that treaty. To avoid this "free rider effect", Art. 4 s. 2 TRIPS – in contrast to the most-favoured-nation clause of the GATT 1994 (para. 119) – provides for exceptions from the most-favoured-nation principle.[8]

624 Finally, the TRIPS in Art. 6 addresses the most controversial question of the **exhaustion** of intellectual property rights. According to the principle of exhaustion, the holder of an intellectual property right has exhausted his exclusive rights with respect to a product or service which incorporates the intellectual property at the time that he himself, or someone else on his authorization, puts the product or service into circulation.[9] Art. 6 TRIPS stipulates that the issue of the exhaustion of intellectual property rights shall not be made the subject of WTO dispute settlement proceedings with the exception of Art. 3 and 4 TRIPS, and thus the questions of national treatment and most-favoured-nation treatment. The TRIPS therewith does not itself separately regulate the international exhaustion of intellectual property rights.

625 Furthermore, Art. 8 TRIPS addresses possible **limitations on intellectual property rights** which concern, on the one hand, limitations on intellectual property rights in the public interest, in particular with respect to health and nutrition. This aspect is taken up again in Art. 30 and 31 TRIPS regarding exceptions to patent rights and forms of use without the authorization of the right holder (para. 646). The other aspect which is addressed in Art. 8.2 TRIPS concerns the possible abuse of intellectual property rights in order to foster anti-competitive measures. This aspect is again dealt with in Art. 40 TRIPS which addresses antitrust law in relation to intellectual property rights (para. 653).

---

[7] *United States – Section 211 Omnibus Appropriations Act of 1998* (see footnote 3), paras 233, 353 *et seq.*

[8] The rights under the Treaty establishing the European Community and the Agreement establishing the European Economic Area are not subject to the most-favoured-nation clause since the European Commission had both Treaties notified to the TRIPS Council as an exception according to Art. 4 s. 2 *lit.* d., IP/N/4/EEC/1, 29 January 1996.

[9] See on the controversial issue of exhaustion, e.g., *Rinnert*, Die Erschöpfung von Markenrechten und das TRIPS, 2000; *Chiappetta*, The Desirability of Agreeing to Disagree: the WTO, TRIPS, International IPR Exhaustion and a Few Other Things, Michigan Journal of International Law 21 (2000) 3, 333 *et seq.*; *Bronckers*, The Exhaustion of Patent Rights Under WTO Law, JWT 32 (1998) 5, 137 *et seq.*

IV. *The Substantive Standards of Protection*

626 The second Part of the TRIPS contains substantive protection standards with regard to individual intellectual property rights.

1. *Copyright and Related Rights*

627 Among these are, first, the **copyright and related rights** in respect of which Art. 9.1 s. 1 TRIPS refers to Art. 1 to 21 of the Berne Convention. This cross-reference is at the same time limited by Art. 9.1 s. 2 TRIPS which exempts from the abovementioned obligation the rights conferred under Art. 6bis of the Berne Convention on essential guarantees of the personal rights of an author.

628 The following provisions detail and substantiate the scope of the copyright protection which is regulated in less concrete provisions in the Berne Convention (the so-called "Bern-Plus-Elements"). Art. 10.1 TRIPS makes it clear that **computer programs**, whether in source or object code, are to be considered as literary works in the sense of the Berne Convention. Similarly, Art. 10.2. TRIPS stipulates that compilations of data or **data banks** enjoy copyright protection even if the collected material itself is not subject to copyright protection. However, according to Art. 10.2 s. 1 – and as supplementation to Art. 9.2 TRIPS – copyright protection under the TRIPS requires that the collections "by reason of the selection or arrangement of their contents constitute intellectual creations". The TRIPS does not contain any special protection of contents on the **Internet** and in the **multimedia sector**.[10]

629 However, rules on **rental rights** (Art. 11 TRIPS) and on so-called **"related rights"**, i.e. rights of performance artists with respect to their performance and rights of producers of phonograms and broadcasting organizations are included (Art. 14 TRIPS).

630 Art. 12 TRIPS determines the **term of copyright protection** corresponding to common standards in international and national law to be no less than 50 years. The term begins either with the death of the author or with the first authorized publication of the work. The term of protection of the related rights is set out in Art. 14.5 TRIPS.

631 Under certain conditions, Art. 13 TRIPS permits **limitations on and exceptions to exclusive rights** of the author. As in the "three steps

[10] Such protection of programs and data banks is provided for, since its entry into force on 6 March 2002, by the WIPO Copyright Treaty of 1996 (WCT, OJ EC L 89/8 of 11 April 2000) in Art. 4 s. 1 and 5, which, together with the WIPO Performances and Phonograms Treaty of the same year, and effective as of 20 May 2002, (WPPT, OJ EC L 89/15 of 11 April 2000) also contains regulations for the multimedia sector.

test" of Art. 9 para. 2 of the Berne Convention, the limitations on and exceptions to the exclusive rights of the author must, first, be confined to "certain special cases" and, secondly, not "conflict with a normal exploitation of the work" or, thirdly, "prejudice the legitimate interests of the right holder".[11]

2. *Trademarks and Geographical Indications*

632 The second and third sections of TRIPS include regulations on trademarks (Art. 15 *et seq.*) and geographical indications (Art. 22 *et seq.*). Art. 15.1 s. 1 TRIPS contains a uniform international **definition** of a trademark for goods and services. Tying in with this are regulations on the **registrability** (Art. 15.1 s. 1 TRIPS)[12] and the content and scope of the rights conferred by the trademark (Art. 16 TRIPS). In *European Communities – Section 211* the Appellate Body stated that Art. 16 TRIPS confers "on the *owner* of a registered trademark an internationally agreed minimum level of **'exclusive rights'** that all WTO Members must guarantee in their domestic legislation. These exclusive rights protect the owner against infringement of the registered trademark by unauthorized third parties."[13]

633 Limited **exceptions** are permitted in accordance with Art. 17 TRIPS. Pursuant to the principle adopted in Art. 18 TRIPS which results from the particularities of the protection of marks, the registration of a trademark shall be renewable indefinitely. The **minimum term** of the original registration and of each further renewal is seven years. Other provisions address the purpose of maintaining the registration of a trademark (Art. 19 TRIPS), prohibit unjustified interference with its use (Art. 20 TRIPS)[14] and regulate **compulsory licensing** (Art. 21 TRIPS). Apart from compulsory licensing, the WTO Members may however lay

[11] See in this respect *United States – Section 110 (5) of the US Copyright Act*, WT/DS160/R, 15 June 2000. Accordingly, section 110 (5) (B) US Copyright Act (the so-called business exemption), which exempted from copyright infringements the broadcasting of music via radio or television in smaller businesses, in particular bars, shops and restaurants, is not compatible with the TRIPS. With regard to the related rights, Art. 14.6 s. 1 TRIPS refers to the Rome Convention.

[12] The Appellate Body made it clear in *United States – Section 211 Omnibus Appropriations Act of 1998* (see footnote 3), paras 155 *et seq.*, that the provision only stipulates which signs and combinations of signs are registrable at all. WTO Members are however not obliged actually to register such registrable signs as trademarks. National law can stipulate additional conditions for registration beyond those named in Art. 15.1 TRIPS.

[13] *United States* – Section 211 Omnibus Appropriations Act of 1998 (see footnote 3), para. 186.

[14] Such endeavours have taken place in particular in developing countries. Art. 20 TRIPS played a subordinate role in the Panel Report *Indonesia – Certain Measures affecting the Automobile Industry*, WT/DS54/R, WT/DS55/R, WT/DS59/R, WT/DS64/R, 2 July 1998, paras 14.275 *et seq.*, where the Panel eventually denied that there had been an infringement.

down conditions for the granting of licences as long as they do not violate Art. 20 and other basic principles of the TRIPS.

634 The international **protection of geographic indications** is provided for in Art. 22 *et seq.* TRIPS. It is however less standardized. The **protection of geographical indications for wines and spirits** is the most extensive in this respect. Art. 23.1 TRIPS obliges Members to prohibit the use of such indications if the goods concerned do not originate from the place indicated.

3. *Industrial Designs*

635 The fourth section of TRIPS is dedicated to the protection of industrial designs and thus of **design patents.**[15] Without giving a binding definition of industrial designs, Art. 25.1 s. 1 TRIPS obliges WTO Members to protect independently created industrial designs as long as these are new (patent approach) or original (copyright approach).

636 The rights of the owner to the **protection** of his industrial designs are listed in Art. 26.1 TRIPS, while Art. 26.2 TRIPS allows for **limited exceptions**. According to Art. 26.3 TRIPS, **protection lasts for** at least ten years.

4. *Patents*

637 Of great importance are the regulations of the fifth section (Art. 27 *et seq.* TRIPS) on patents. The protection of patents at the international level has long been disputed as such. The TRIPS regulations far exceed the previous international regulations in the Paris Convention for the Protection of Industrial Property, but also those of the Convention on the Grant of European Patents (EPC) of 5 October 1973[16] and aim at a **high standard of protection**, which in particular demands on many newly industrialising countries and developing countries a considerable amount of legislation to implement the legal obligations. This applies particularly to the regulations laid down in Art. 27 TRIPS. The provision governs which items should be patentable and repeats the generally accepted **conditions for patents**, such as new inventions, inventive steps and industrial application (Art. 27.1 s. 1).

---

[15] The TRIPS does not differentiate between design patents and utility patents. As a matter of fact, however, it regulates the design patent, without excluding the protection of utility patents.

[16] UNTS Vol. 1065, No. I-16208, 199, last amended by amending decision of the Administrative Council of the European Patent Organisation of 10 December 1998, OJ EPO January 1999; which came into force on 1 January 1999; see *Schulte*, Patentgesetz mit Europäischem Patentübereinkommen, Kommentar, 6th ed., 2001.

638 Art. 27.1 s. 1 TRIPS also states that patents should be available **in all fields of technology**. The provision therefore limits the longstanding practice of countries to exclude from patent protection certain areas of technology, such as the sectors health, nutrition and agriculture.[17] In addition, the provision makes it clear that protection must extend to products as well as to processes.

639 Art. 27.1 s. 1 TRIPS exceeds and strengthens the common level of patent protection by introducing a **principle of non-discrimination**. Apart from special provisions governing the implementation phase[18] and the special provision of Art. 27.3 TRIPS, the grant of patents and the exercise of the following rights shall be ensured "without discrimination as to the place of invention, the field of technology and whether products are imported or locally produced". Besides the requirement to grant patent protection in all fields of technology, this provision addresses two other points, which played an important and very disputed role in international patent protection. First, the principle of non-discrimination in Art. 27.1 s. 2 TRIPS applies to the place of invention and therefore prevents countries from refusing to grant patents to inventions which were brought to fruition in foreign countries. Of more importance is the question of the exercise of a patent. In the history of international patent protection, this aspect has repeatedly played a decisive and disputed role. In the past, numerous countries attempted to link patent protection and the exercise of the rights flowing from the patent to an advantageous economic activity in the country itself.[19]

640 Less controversial is the possibility of ruling out **patentability to protect the *ordre public***, stipulated by Art. 27.2 TRIPS. This limitation can be found in national, regional and international patent law and allows Members to refuse patent protection with respect to individual, particularly circumscribed public interests. Art. 27.2 therefore mentions *ordre public* and morality as potential barriers to the patent protection. Beyond this, this provision includes the protection of human, animal or plant life or health and the avoidance of serious damage to the environment.[20] It must be emphasised that a further precondition for such exclusion of patent protection is that it is "necessary" to protect the public interest and that – more important – "such exclusion is not made

[17] Existence, Scope and Form of Generally Internationally Accepted and Applied Standards, Norms for the Protection of Intellectual Property, Document Prepared by the International Bureau of WIPO, MTN.GNG/NG11/W/24 Rev.1, WO/INF/29, September 1988, Annex II.

[18] Art. 65.4 and Art. 70.8 TRIPS.

[19] Art. 27.1 is applicable to the exceptions granted under Art. 30 TRIPS, see *Canada – Patent Protection of Pharmaceutical Products*, WT/DS114/R, 17 March 2000, para. 7.91 *et seq.*

[20] This provision, by referring to the environment, extends the usual enumeration of subjects of protection according to Art. XX *lit.* b GATT 1994 – see para. 179.

merely because the exploitation is prohibited". There must therefore be a close relationship between the purpose of protection of the public interest and the exclusion of patentability.

641 Art. 27.3 TRIPS contains a further provision excluding the granting of patents in certain, especially enumerated areas. This highly contentious provision in the broadest sense affects the fields of medicine and biotechnology. According to Art. 27.3 *lit.* a TRIPS, the Members can first exclude the patentability of **diagnostic, therapeutic and surgical methods** for the treatment of humans or animals.

642 Art. 27.3 *lit.* b TRIPS governs exclusion with regard to different items of biotechnology. Sentence 1 makes it clear that micro-organisms cannot be excluded from patent protection. The patentability of micro-organisms has long been accepted in the legal orders of the majority of industrialized countries.[21] Apart from that, Art. 27.3 *lit.* b s. 1 TRIPS allows for the exclusion of patents in relation to **plants and animals**. This formulation must be interpreted in a narrow sense, so that the provision applies only to the patenting of plants and animals as such.

643 Art. 27.3 *lit.* b sentence 1 TRIPS allows Members to exclude **biological processes for the production of plants or animals** and therefore allows regulations as used widely in national legal systems. But this exception contains a restriction which excludes non-biological and microbiological processes. This means mainly biotechnological and biogenetic processes.

644 The results of plant breeding, new plant varieties, are not patentable in many countries but are protected by variety protection laws. Art. 27.3 *lit* b s. 2 stipulates such **protection of plant varieties**. In contrast to the previous exceptions in Art. 27.3 *lit* b s. 1 TRIPS, this is a positive principle for protection. In view of the different national legal frameworks, Members can choose the form of protection. It must "either be by patents or by an effective *sui generis* system or by any combination thereof". The TRIPS Council held several formal meetings during the period January 1999 to March 2002 in order to conduct the mandated review of the provisions of Art. 27.3 *lit.* b TRIPS. One general issue that was discussed is the issue of providing patent protection for plant and animal inventions, especially from a development perspective. Another issue that was raised is concerned with the scope of the exceptions, including the definition of the terms used in Art. 27.3 *lit.* b. It was argued that the absence of clear definitions could pose

[21] On the international level this is taken into account by the Budapest Agreement, which governs the deposit of such micro-organisms for purposes of patent application.

problems of legal uncertainty as regards the scope of patentability. The specific concerns that should be taken into account included those relating to public health, restrictions on research materials, limitations on competition as in the case of "gene-use restriction technologies" (GURTs), human rights, agricultural security, bio-piracy, traditional knowledge and farmers' rights.[22] Despite its limited content, Art. 27.3 *lit.* b plays a great role in the politically influenced dispute about the extent of patent protection in the biotechnology field.[23]

645 Besides the provisions on patentability and the requirements for patent applications in accordance with Art. 27 and 29 TRIPS, Art. 28 and Art. 30–34 TRIPS govern the rights conferred by a patent and therefore its **scope, limits and procedural requirements**. Art. 28 applies, according to its title, to the rights conferred by patents and especially the owner's exclusive rights.

646 According to Art. 30 TRIPS, the Members may "provide **limited exceptions** to the exclusive rights conferred by a patent". The criterion is that such "exceptions do not unreasonably conflict with a normal exploitation of the patent and do not unreasonably prejudice the legitimate interests of the patent owner" in which it is made clear that "legitimate interests of third parties" must be taken into account.

647 Art. 31 TRIPS contains extensive regulation on the **use of a patent without the authorisation of the right holder** which basically governs the allocation of compulsory licences and user rights to a state or private third parties. Art. 31 TRIPS links the allocation of compulsory licences and other forms of usage without the consent of the right holder to preconditions in respect of procedural requirements. The provision contains only limited conditions for the allocation of compulsory licences. It addresses the preconditions (*lit.* a, b, f), scope (*lit.* c, d, e and g), remuneration and legal protection (*lit.* h, i and j) and also contains special provisions on assignment of compulsory licences, on anti-competitive practices (*lit.* k) and on the exploitation of a dependant (second) patent (*lit.* l). The allocation of compulsory licences can also be restricted by other provisions of the TRIPS, so that the prohibition of discrimination between the different fields of technology in Art. 71.1 can come under consideration. This provision became very important in the attempt of individual developing countries to import or to produce pharmaceuticals for HIV therapy to – from their point of view – acceptable conditions (paras 672, 802).

---

[22] WTO Secretariat, Review of the Provisions of Article 27.3(B), Summary of Issues Raised and Point Made, IP/C/W/369, 8 August 2002.

[23] See para. 670.

648 For the special case of the grant of a compulsory licence for the removal of an **anti-competitive** situation, Art. 31 *lit.* k TRIPS provides for special, more relaxed rules.

649 On the subject of time limits for patent rights, Art. 33 TRIPS states that protection shall end no sooner than **twenty years** from the filing date.[24]

650 Art. 32 TRIPS addresses the **revocation or forfeiture** of a patent as a drastic national measure, but provides for judicial review in such cases as a minimum standard.[25]

5. *The Protection of the Topography of Integrated Circuits*

651 A special section 6 of the second part of the TRIPS is dedicated to the protection of topographies or the **"layout designs" of integrated circuits**. Art. 35 enforces the essential regulations of a treaty concluded in 1989 on intellectual property in integrated circuits, which never came into force (the IPIC Treaty).[26]

6. *Protection of Undisclosed Information and Know-How*

652 Part II of TRIPS contains a regulation which seems to have little to do with the protection of intellectual property. Art. 39.1 TRIPS includes an obligation on Members to protect **know-how** as a measure for effective protection against unfair competition. Thereby, an explicit reference is made to Art. 10bis Paris Convention. Art. 39.3 TRIPS protects **data submitted to governments or government agencies** in the context of approving the marketing of pharmaceutical or of agricultural chemical products.

7. *Measures for the Abolition of Anti-Competitive Practices*

653 Art. 40 addresses the important question of anti-competitive practices in relation to the use of intellectual property rights. It is closely related to the basic principle of Art. 8.2 TRIPS (para. 625) and makes it clear

[24] The wording allows for a longer protection period. It is also possible to extend the protection with additional rights after the expiry of the period.

[25] In case of the first rescission of a European patent by the decision of a board of appeal of the European Patent Office as a court of final appeal, according to a decision of the grand board of appeal of 10 December 1999, OJ 2000, 307–397, no further protection from a court shall be necessary, because such protection is not necessary in accordance with the earlier version of' Art. 62.5 TRIPS. See also the High Court of Justice, Queen's Bench Division London, GRUR Int. 1997, 1010 *et seq.*

[26] Treaty on Intellectual Property in Respect of Integrated Circuits, adopted at Washington on 26 May 1989.

that some licensing practices or conditions pertaining to intellectual property rights which **restrict competition** may have adverse effects on trade and may impede the transfer and dissemination of technology. In this regard, certain respective **measures of the Members are legitimised**, and these are set out in detail in Art. 40.2 TRIPS. Art. 40.3 and 4 TRIPS contains provisions on co-operation between Members in this field.

V. *Procedural Standards: Enforcement, Acquisition and Maintenance*

654 Besides substantive standards, the TRIPS in parts III and IV contains standards for proceedings for the acquisition and enforcement of intellectual property. The **enforcement** of intellectual property was one of the main concerns of the Uruguay Round. Related to this is a detailed regulation, which addresses civil and administrative procedures, measures at the borders and the criminal procedure on the national level. According to the fundamental provision of Art. 41 TRIPS Section 1, the regulations of part III serve two aims: On the one hand, the protection of intellectual property is to be developed in an effective and economic way. On the other hand, measures for the enforcement of rights of intellectual property must be prevented from interfering with legitimate trade. This task is set out in Art. 41.1 TRIPS, which also contains some basic principles for the procedure.

655 In the second section of this part, provisions on the **civil and administrative procedures** (Art. 42 *et seq.* TRIPS)[27] as well as general principles for procedures including the protection of confidential information (Art. 42 s. 4 TRIPS), rules on evidence, burden of proof, rights of information (Art. 43 TRIPS), damages, injunctions and reimbursement of costs can be found. The third section in its Art. 50 governs minimum standards, to which the **provisional measures** procedure must apply.

656 The fourth section covers detailed rules on **border measures** (Art. 51 *et seq.* TRIPS), which basically follow the mechanism that has been introduced by the Council Regulation of the EU on pirated goods[28] and the national laws established thereupon in recent years. They impose an obligation on Members to make available a procedure which enables the right holder, who has valid grounds, to lodge an application for the suspension of the release into free circulation of such goods by the

[27] *United States* – Section 211, (footnote 3), paras 203 *et seq.*

[28] Council Regulation (EC) No 3295/94 of 22 December 1994 laying down measures to prohibit the release for free circulation, export, re-export or entry for a suspensive procedure of counterfeit and pirated goods, EC OJ L 97/38, 18 April 1996, amended by Council Regulation (EC) No 241/1999 of 25 January 1999, EC OJ L 27/1, 2 February 2002.

customs authorities (Art. 51 s. 1 TRIPS). According to its wording, this provision refers only to "counterfeit trademark or pirated copyright goods" which are defined in a footnote to Art. 51 TRIPS. But the parties are free to provide such procedures for other infringements of intellectual property rights (Art. 51 s. 2) as well as for goods destined for export from their territories (Art. 51 s. 3).

657 With regard to **penalties** under criminal law, Art. 61 TRIPS stipulates that Members shall provide for penalties at least in cases of wilful trademark counterfeiting or copyright piracy on a commercial scale which include imprisonment and fines. Moreover, seizure, forfeiture and destruction of infringing goods and of any materials are included in this provision.

658 In the context of a separate fourth part of the TRIPS, Art. 62 addresses the **acquisition and maintenance of intellectual property rights** and the related *inter-partes* procedure. According to paragraph 1, Members are allowed to regulate reasonable procedures and formalities as a condition of the acquisition or maintenance of the intellectual property rights provided for under Sections 2 to 6 of part II.[29]

659 In view of the often far-reaching changes in national law demanded by the TRIPS, there are extensive provisions which govern retroactivity (Art. 70 TRIPS) and **transitional arrangements** for application (Art. 65, Art. 70.8 TRIPS).

660 Art. 65 TRIPS provides for a **transitional period of one year** until the Agreement has to be fully applied (Art. 65.1), which could be extended for developing countries for a further four years (Art. 65.2). This privilege is linked to the precondition that the developing countries which are in the process of transformation from a centrally-planned into a market, free-enterprise economy face special problems in undertaking structural reform of their intellectual property systems (Art. 65.3). A further time limit of five years was granted to those developing countries in which to introduce product patents in areas of technology not currently protectable in their territory (Art. 65.4).[30]

661 In the case a Member had to newly introduce the legal possibility to **protect pharmaceutical and agrochemical products** in accordance with Art. 27 TRIPS (para. 638), even in the extended transition period under Art. 65 *et seq.* TRIPS, they had to provide a means by which

[29] Excluded are copyright and related trademark rights, which are governed by Section 1 of part II, see paras 604 *et seq.*

[30] On this issue compare the proposals by the African Group, Council for TRIPS, Special and Differential Treatment Proposals Referred to the TRIPS Council, IP/C/36, 20 July 2005, Annex I.

applications for patents for such inventions could be filed (Art. 70.8 *lit.* a) to preserve priority (*lit.* b) and provide patent protection (*lit.* c).[31]

662 A ten-year period for transition (Art. 66 TRIPS) additional to the one-year time limit under Art. 65.1 applies to least-developed countries. These time limits are supplemented by an obligation on developed Members to provide incentives to enterprises and institutions in their territories for the purpose of promoting and encouraging **technology transfer** (Art. 66.2) and a general rule for **technical cooperation** (Art. 67).

VI. *Institutional Provisions, Dispute Settlement and Special Exemptions*

663 Because of its special position, the TRIPS has an organ with wide competences, the **Council for Trade-Related Aspects of Intellectual Property Rights** (Art. 68 TRIPS). It has the authority and obligation to monitor and review Members' compliance with their obligations and has the competence to consult with and seek information from any source it deems appropriate (Art. 68 s. 3) as well as a mandate to establish appropriate arrangements for cooperation with the WIPO (Art. 68 s. 1 TRIPS).[32]

664 Provisions for the **prevention and settlement of disputes** can be found in a special part V. Art. 63 TRIPS contains the principle of transparency, which first provides obligations of publication (para. 1) and notification (para. 2) and, secondly, of exchange of information (paras 3 and 4).

665 Art. 64 TRIPS generally refers to Art. XXII and XXIII GATT 1994 as the basic norms for **consultation and dispute settlement**. But according to subparagraphs 1 *lit.* b – the non-violation complaint – and *lit.* c – the situation complaint – of Art. XXIII of GATT 1994 was not to apply for a period of five years from the date of entry into force of the WTO Agreement. During this period, the Council for TRIPS was to examine the scope and modalities for non-violation and situation complaints and submit its recommendations to the Ministerial Conference for approval. The TRIPS Council has agreed that Members shall not initiate **non-violation complaints** under the TRIPS Agreement and

---

[31] See *India – Patent Protection for Pharmaceutical and Agricultural Chemical Products*, WT/DS50/R, 5 September 1997, WT/DS50/AB/R, 19 December 1997 and WT/DS79/R, 24 August 1998.

[32] The Council fulfilled this function with the conclusion of the Agreement between the World Intellectual Property and The World Trade Organisation of 22 December 1995, ILM 35 (1996), 754 IP/C/6.

has, since the time limit has expired, continued its examination of the scope and modalities for non-violation complaints.[33] In May 2003, a proposal with four options was tabled, from which the recommendation to ban non-violation complaints or to extend the moratorium received the support of a majority. However, as some other Members argued, that "creative legislative activity" will enable other Members to circumvent their obligations, no consensus was reached so far.

666 Art. 73 TRIPS contains **exemptions** which refer to the protection of the national security of a Member and are similar to those in Art. XXI GATT 1994. It must be emphasised that the Members have only a slightly limited wide range of discretion in this respect, as in Art. XXI GATT 1994 (paras 197 *et seq.*)

VII. *New Developments and Prospects*

667 The protection of intellectual property has been strengthened with the TRIPS. But it was also developed on the basis of the historical background within the framework of the existing international system and now faces very controversial **problems and challenges**.

1. *Further Development of the International System for the Protection of Intellectual Property*

668 The TRIPS certainly aims at the correction of deficiencies **of the historically grown international system** of protection of intellectual property of the conventions under the umbrella of the WIPO. However, it has not replaced, but rather has **strengthened** this system. The further development of the protection of intellectual property in international perspective is clearly subject to the work carried out by the WIPO and its specialised fora. Since the entry into force of the TRIPS important negotiations have taken place on this level, which have been partially completed. Examples are the Trademark Law Treaty of 1994, the WIPO Copyright Treaty and the WIPO Performances and Phonograms Treaty 1996, the Geneva Act of the Hague Agreement Concerning the International Registration of Industrial Designs of 1999 as well as the Patent Law Treaty of 2000. These new international regulations specify in parts existing standards comprising those of the TRIPS. In individual cases they extend these marginally, but so far, no discrepancies have arisen.

[33] Ministerial Conference, Implementation-Related Issues and Concerns, Decision of 14 November 2001, WT/MIN(01)/17, 20 November 2001, para. 11.1.

2. *New Problems and Controversies*

669 The protection of intellectual property on the international level is subject to tension due to conflicting interests – these **tensions** have now surfaced in the ongoing TRIPS negotiations.

a. *Intellectual Property and the Convention on Biological Diversity*

670 An often discussed problem is the relationship between TRIPS and the **Convention on Biological Diversity**.[34] This Agreement reinforces the sovereign rights of states to its genetic resources, i.e. to biological material that contains genetic information and can serve as the starting point for biotechnological research and development. Linked to this are regulations which ensure that the states take part in research, development and possible economic success (Access and Benefit Sharing, ABS). Patent law is criticised, as the user of such a patent based on genetic material has an absolute power of disposal, whereas the person (or state) who originally had the power of disposal over the genetic material has no substantive legal position. On the other hand, it is proposed that proof of origin of the genetic material used be required, so that the owner of rights to such material can enforce his power of disposal and claim to participate ("paper trail").[35] Recital 27 of Directive 98/44/EC on the legal protection of biotechnological inventions (para. 644) contains such an idea. The Committee on Trade and Environment of the WTO has discussed this issue, but has not come up with concrete results.

b. *Rights to Traditional Knowledge*

671 A further regulation of the Agreement on Biological Diversity, Art. 8 *lit.* g TRIPS, discusses a right of the local and indigenous groups to use their **traditional knowledge**. Such knowledge, often concerning medical questions, plays an important role in biotechnology as further developments can arise out of such knowledge. Based on the existing legal basis such knowledge is, however, protectable only in a limited manner. Discrimination and the lack of legal advice can further complicate enforcement. The protection of a respective right of disposal or, *vice versa*, a communal right to patent inventions is being discussed within the WIPO with regard to the general improvement of the legal position of such groups.[36]

---

[34] See *Wolfrum & Stoll & Klepper & Franck*, Genetische Ressourcen, traditionelles Wissen und geistiges Eigentum im Rahmen des Übereinkommens über die biologische Vielfalt, 2001.

[35] See WIPO Draft Intellectual Property Guidelines for Access and Equitable Benefit-Sharing – http://www.wipo.int/edocs/mdocs/tk/en/wipo_grtkf_ic_7/wipo_grtkf_ic_7_9.doc; Convention on Biological Diversity, Conference of the Parties, Decision VII/19, Access and benefit-sharing as related to genetic resources (Article 15), under E 7: "[. . .] disclosure of origin of genetic resources and associated traditional knowledge in applications for intellectual property rights, [. . .]"

[36] See http://www.wipo.int/tk/en/.

c. *Access to Essential Medicines*

672 The international system for the protection of intellectual property is massively criticised in the light of the urgent need for life-saving pharmaceuticals to control the threat of epidemics, especially in Africa. This problem, which came to public notice through proceedings before the South African High Court, concerns, on the one hand, the grant of compulsory licences and the interpretation of Art. 31 TRIPS (para. 647). On the other hand, it raises the issue of compulsory licensing in light of Art. 31 *lit.* f TRIPS which holds that such licenses "shall be authorised predominantly for the supply of the domestic market". Thus, production by third parties would not be possible in most cases. In this respect there are many unresolved questions which concern *inter alia* the exhaustion of the right (see Art. 6 TRIPS). These issues are addressed by the **Ministerial Declaration on the TRIPS Agreement and Public Health**, adopted by the Ministerial Conference on 14. November 2001[37] (paras 799 *et seq.*), and by the decision implementing this declaration, adopted by the General Council on 30 August 2003.[38] In the Ministerial Declaration it is made clear that Art. 31 TRIPS must be interpreted in light of the basic provisions of Art. 7 and 8 TRIPS.[39] Furthermore, the Council for TRIPS is requested to find a solution to the problem of the lack of capacity for local production.[40] In the decision of the General Council, the obligations of an exporting Member have been waived with respect to the grant of a compulsory licence to the extent necessary for the purposes of production of pharmaceuticals and their export to importing Members.[41]

[37] Ministerial Conference, Declaration on TRIPS Agreement and Public Health, adopted on 14 November 2001, WT/MIN(01)/DEC/2, 20 November 2001; see also *Abbott*, The Doha Declaration of the TRIPS Agreement and Public Health, JIEL 5 (2002) 2, 469 *et seq.*

[38] General Council, Implementation of Paragraph 6 of the Doha Declaration on the TRIPS Agreement and Public Health, Decision of 30 August 2003, WT/L/540, 2 September 2003. See in this respect *Hestermeyer*, Flexible Entscheidungsfindung in der WTO, GRUR Int. 2004, 194 *et seq.*

[39] WT/MIN(01)/DEC/2, (footnote 37), para. 5 *lit.* a: "In applying customary rules of interpretation of public international law, each provision of the TRIPS Agreement shall be read in light of the object and purpose of the Agreement as expressed, in particular, in its objectives and principles."

[40] WT/MIN(01)/DEC/2, (footnote 37), para. 6: "We recognize that WTO Members with insufficient or no manufacturing capacities in the pharmaceutical sector could face difficulties in making effective use of compulsory licensing under the TRIPS Agreement. We instruct the Council for TRIPS to find an expeditious solution to this problem and to report to the General Council before the end of 2002."

[41] WT/L/540, (footnote 38), para. 2.

3. *Intellectual Property in Context of the WTO Dispute Settlement: Intellectual Property Rights as the Subject of Sanctions*

673 As stated, one reason for the inclusion of intellectual property in the World Trade Order was the aim of establishing an effective instrument of enforcement between states through the applicability of the DSU in this field. However, the inclusion of intellectual property also has had other, not necessarily anticipated effects on dispute settlement procedures. Now – through the possibility of cross-retaliation – a trade sanction involving the **suspension of obligations of the TRIPS** has become possible, as can be seen in the course of the EU – Banana conflict (para. 284). After Ecuador and other Members had succeeded with their claims, they applied for authorisation to suspend concessions made in the sectors of copyright, rules of origin and utility patents.[42] In the arbitration, which was requested by the EU in accordance with Art. 22.6 DSU, this approach was seen as permissible, albeit with some limitations.[43] The arbitrators confirmed that possibilities to suspend concessions or obligations provided for in Art. 22.3 DSU under certain conditions also allow the recourse to other WTO Agreements, and therefore also to the TRIPS.[44] On the basis of this arbitration, Ecuador made a new application[45] which was then granted by the Dispute Settlement Body.[46]

[42] *European Communities – Bananas*, Recourse by Ecuador to Article 22.2 of the DSU, WT/DS27/52, 9 November 1999.

[43] *European Communities – Bananas*, Recourse to Arbitration by the European Communities under Article 22.6 of the DSU, WT/DS27/ARB/ECU, 24 March 2000.

[44] *European Communities – Bananas, (see footnote 43)*, (Footnote 43), paras 69 *et seq.* and 139 *et seq.* This also follows from Art. 22.3 *lit.* f iii) and *lit.* g iii) TRIPS.

[45] *European Communities – Bananas*, Recourse by Ecuador to Article 22.7 of the DSU, WT/DS27/54, 8 May 2000.

[46] Dispute Settlement Body, Minutes of Meeting on 25 April 2000.

CHAPTER NINE

THE WTO AND DOMESTIC LEGAL SYSTEMS

Eberhard Grabitz & Armin von Bogdandy (eds), U.S. Trade Barriers: A Legal Analysis, 1991; *Asif H. Qureshi*, The World Trade Organization: implementing international trade norms, 1996; *José Maria Beneyto*, The EU and WTO: Direct Effect of the New Dispute Settlement System? EuZW 7 (1996) 10, 295–299; *John H. Jackson. & Alan O. Sykes* (eds), Implementing the Uruguay-Round, 1997; *Peter-Tobias Stoll*, Freihandel und Verfassung, ZaöRV 57 (1997) 1, 83, 125 *et seq.; Piet Eeckhout*, The domestic legal status of the WTO Agreement: interconnecting legal systems, CMLR 34 (1997) 1, 11–58; *Thomas Cottier*, Dispute settlement in the World Trade Organization: characteristics and structural implications for the European Union, CMLR 35 (1998) 2, 325–378; *Georg M. Berrisch & Hans-Georg Kamann*, Die Handelshemmnis-Verordnung: Ein neues Mittel zur Öffnung von Exportmärkten, EuZW 10 (1999) 4, 101–106; *Mary Farell*, EU and WTO regulatory frameworks: complementarity or competition?, 1999; *Geert A. Zonnekeyn*, The Legal Status of WTO Panel Reports in the EC Legal Order: Some Reflections on the Opinion of Advocate General Mischo in the Atlanta Case, JIEL 2 (1999), 713–722; *Geert A. Zonnekeyn*, The status of WTO law in the EC legal order, JWT 34 (2000) 3, 111–125; *Carlos María Correa*, Implementing national public health policies in the framework of WTO Agreements, JWT 34 (2000) 5, 89–121; *Joseph H. Weiler*, The EU, the WTO and NAFTA (2000); *Meinhard Hilf & Frank Schorkopf*, WTO und EG: Rechtskonflikte vor den EuHG?, EuR 35 (2000) 1, 74–91; *Armin von Bogdandy*, Rechtsgleichheit, Rechtssicherheit und Subsidiarität im transnationalen Wirtschaftsrecht, EuZW 12 (2001) 12, 357–365; *Gráinne de Búrca & Joanne Scott* (eds), The EU and the WTO: legal and constitutional issues, 2001; *Stefan Ohlhoff & Hannes Schloemann*, Transcending the Nation State? Private Parties and the Enforcement of International Trade Law, in: *Jochen A. Frowein* & *Rüdiger Wolfrum* (eds), Max Planck Yearbook of United Nations Law 5 (2001), 675–734; *Gabrielle Marceaue & Cormelis Reiman*, When and How Is a Regional Trade Agreement Compatible with the WTO?, Legal Issues of Economic Integration 28 (2001) 3, 297–336; *Gráinne De Burca* (ed.) The EU and the WTO, 2001; *Allan Rosas*, Implementation and enforcement of WTO dispute settlement findings, JIEL 4 (2001) 1, 131–144; *M. Gregg Bloche*, WTO deference to national health policy, JIEL 5 (2002) 4, 825–848; *Jochem Wiers*, Trade and environment in the EC and the WTO, 2002; *Dapo Akande*, International adjudication on national security issues, Virginia journal of international law 43 (2003) 2, 365–404; *Steve Charnovitz*, The World Trade Organization and law enforcement, JWT 37 (2003) 5, 817–837; *Ernst-Ulrich Petersmann* (ed.), Transatlantic economic disputes, 2003; *Xin Zhang*, Implementation of the WTO Agreements, Northwestern journal of international law & business 23 (2003) 2, 383–431; *Heike Holbig* (ed.), China's accession to the World Trade Organization, 2003; *Geert A. Zonnekeyn*, EC liability for non-implementation of WTO dispute settlement decisions, JIEL 7 (2004) 2, 483–490; *Karen Kaiser*, Geistiges Eigentum und Gemeinschaftsrecht, 2004; *Sebastiaan Princen*, EC compliance with WTO law, EJIL 15 (2004) 3, 555–574.

674 The WTO and its legal order are subject to international law. Its activities and effects are, however, closely related to the regimes of its Members. Representation, the competence to negotiate and the **competence to conclude agreements**, as well as the **binding force** of those agreements, are substantially based on the national rules of international representation and the conclusion and adoption of international treaties. These rules play a great role in the continuing trade rounds and their future results. Which bodies have to give their consent in the course of proceedings depends on these (national) rules, and this fact in some cases, heavily influences the prospects for success of future negotiations from a political point of view.

675 Above all, rules and requirements set at the international level must have an effect on the national regimes of the Members and on the regime of the European Union, if such bodies want to enter into private trade transactions and economic subjects to which the WTO chiefly applies. Thus, the question of **applicability and implementation** of WTO rules and obligations is critically important.

676 The domestic regimes of Members regulate not only the binding nature and applicability of WTO law but also its **enforcement**. They govern legal remedies and the legal basis on which individuals – domestic or foreign natural or legal persons – can take **action against national or regional trade authorities**. Often, these rules of enforcement are based on the principles of the rule of law and legal protection as contained, amongst others, in Art. X GATT 1994. Besides this, national regimes often provide for other opportunities for individuals to sanction measures and the behaviour of **other Members**. This is usually a procedure whereby such sanctions can be examined on request and whereby the appropriate authority can be obliged to pursue such sanctions on a trans-national basis, especially by dispute settlement.

I. *Negotiations and Ratification*

677 The representation of Members in the WTO is governed by the general constitutional rules of each domestic legal order. The same rules apply to the negotiation process and the conclusion of new agreements that require ratification as a precondition for entering into force. The constitutional rules often provide for a power of representation by the government or the President and for the consent to as well as the enactment of corresponding measures for implementation by the parliament.

678 In the **European Union**, there is also the question of competence in relation to the Member States. According to Art. 133 ECT, the European Community has the competence for the **common commercial policy**.

Following from this, the Commission is responsible for representation and the Council concludes corresponding agreements.

679 A Committee appointed by the Council, the so-called **133 Committee**, supports the Commission in its negotiations. The 133 Committee is concerned with suggestions and working papers from the Commission for the implementation of the common commercial policy and sets out the standpoint of the EU. It is also responsible for the formulation and granting of mandates to the Commission for the negotiation of trade agreements. Every EU Member State has a permanent representative as well as a deputy on this Committee, and they are sent by the national ministry responsible for trade policy. At member level, the Committee meets monthly. Furthermore, the Committee as constituted by the deputies sits weekly. The Council has also established sectoral 133 Committees for the textiles, services, mutual recognition and motor vehicle sectors.

680 This competence in trade policy excludes parallel action by the EU Member States. But with the GATS and TRIPS, EU Member States still have competences in services and intellectual property rights (para. 703). The European Court of Justice confirmed this in its fundamental **Opinion 1/94**[1] on the joint competence of the Community for the conclusion of agreements in relation to the WTO Agreement. From the Community law point of view, the WTO Agreement is a mixed agreement.[2] Therefore, it was signed both by representatives of the EU and its Member States. The EU ratified the WTO Agreement and its Annexes by decision of the Council of 22 December 1994.[3]

681 The constitution of the **United States** assigns to Congress in the field of foreign trade, amongst others, the competence to collect duties (Article I, Section 8, Clause 1) and to regulate trade with foreign states (Clause 3, "commerce clause"). Competence is shared between the federal and state governments in the fields of services, capital investment, protection of intellectual property, and public procurement. The President represents the United States and can enter into negotiations with foreign countries. Moreover, he also has a series of implicit competences, which are signi-ficant for foreign trade policies. In this field, the Congress has delegated extensive legislative competences to the President.[4]

---

[1] ECJ opinion 1/94, ECR 1994, I-5267, para. 35 *et seq.* – *WTO Agreement.*

[2] Detailed *Rosas*, The European Union and Mixed Agreements, in: Dashwood & Hillion (eds), The General Law of E.C. External Relations, 2000, 200 *et seq.* See also the new wording in Art. 133 para. 6 subparagraph 2 EGV, OJ EC No. C 80/16 of 10 March 2001.

[3] Decision of the Council, 22 December 1994, relating to the adoption of the agreement in the framework of multilateral negotiations of the Uruguay Round (1986–1994), in the name of the European Community with regard to the areas falling within their jurisdiction (94/800/EU), OJ EC No. L 336/1 of 23 December 1994.

[4] See *Schüler*, in Grabitz & von Bogandy (eds), US Trade Barriers: A Legal Analysis, 7, 12 *et seq.* with further references.

682 The constitutional requirements for the completion of trade agreements depend on the type and content of the treaty in question. In general, international **treaties** can be concluded and ratified only by the President with the consent of a two-third majority of the Senate ("by and with the Advice and Consent of the Senate" Art. II, Section 2, Clause 2). There are also agreements which have been negotiated and concluded by the executive, which either have to be submitted to the Congress or need a simple majority in both Houses (**Congressional-Executive Agreements**), or which are concluded solely by the President (Presidential or Sole Executive Agreements). Since "Presidential or Sole Executive Agreements" are used almost exclusively in the military and diplomatic field, "Treaty" and "Congressional-Executive Agreements" are interchangeable instruments.[5] It is for the President to chose and initiate one of these procedures.

683 As a result of its special constitutional position in relation to the power to conduct foreign relations and in connection with the traditionally critical stance against contractual obligations on the basis of international law, the two-thirds majority needed for the ratification of treaties is often not achievable in the Senate. Since trade policy agreements such as the North American Free Trade Agreement (NAFTA) and the WTO Agreement have a high potential for political conflicts, they are often treated as Congressional-Executive Agreements.[6]

684 The Congress grants a **fast-track mandate** to the President to negotiate trade agreements in the majority of cases.[7] In other words, the Congress, for a limited time, commits itself to ratifying the results of negotiations without any amendments or to refusing them as a whole. This voluntary creation of a "ratification situation" is accompanied by increased participation and influence of Congressmen in the negotiating process.[8] The Omnibus Trade and Competitiveness Act of 1988[9] granted the President a fast-track mandate to negotiate the Uruguay Round. Furthermore, it gave the executive the competence to implement the obligation to reduce customs duties.

[5] See Restatement Third of Foreign Relations Law of the United States, § 303, Comment e, for an overview of international agreements in US law, see *Kirgis*, International Agreements and US Law, at: <http://www.asil.org/insights/insigh10.htm>.

[6] For the legal position in the United States and the implementation of the WTO Agreement, see *Leebron*, in: Jackson & Sykes (eds), Implementing the Uruguay-Round, 175 *et seq.*

[7] The Bush Administration uses the term "Trade Promotion Authority, TPA".

[8] The granting of a new fast track mandate limited to 1 October 2005 by the Export, Expansion and Reciprocal Trade Agreements Act 1998, in the run up to the "Millenium Round", failed to achieve a majority in the Congress. For the Doha Round following the ministerial conference in Doha (paras 795 *et seq.*), the President was granted a mandate by a majority of 215 to 214 in the House of Representatives and 66 to 33 in the Senate.

[9] Publ. L. No. 100–418, 102 Stat. 1107 (1988).

685 The formulation and execution of the President's competence in trade policy lies in the hands of particular authorities and institutions, of which the **United States Trade Representative** (USTR) is the most important. The USTR is a member of the Executive Office of the President and has the function of developing and coordinating US American trade policy, observing trade policies of other countries and conducting negotiations: All issues relating to the WTO are within the USTR's mandate. The USTR also relies on a system of advisory committees staffed by representatives of the American industry. Furthermore, some branches of the Trade and Agriculture Ministry take part in the enforcement of the WTO Agreement. Also, it has to be mentioned the US **International Trade Commission**, which is in charge for procedures on protective, anti-dumping and anti-subsidy-measures (para. 489).

686 The WTO Agreement was ratified by means of the extensive Uruguay Round Agreement Act 1994.[10] It includes some remarkable rules. For example, it contains a specific procedure for the cases in which it is decided in dispute settlement proceedings that the United States have breached WTO law.[11]

II. *Implementation and Applicability*

687 The rules and regulations of the WTO require corresponding drafting and amendment of the national laws and regulations of its Members (**implementation**). These require great regulatory efforts by the Members. The adaptation of Community laws in their relative areas of applicability in relation to specific agreements is carried out by a variety of acts, which are too numerous to mention.[12] Developing countries in particular continue to have problems in tackling the administrative and legal difficulties in implementing WTO obligations, despite the longer time limits for implementation granted in many agreements. For this reason, difficulties in implementation continue to be an important aspect of the Doha Round negotiations (see paras 795 *et seq.*).

688 Furthermore, the new rules have often faced **strong political resistance**. The new TRIPS rules in particular were highly disputed in many countries. Mistrust of effective implementation has, without a doubt, influenced

[10] Publ. L. No. 103–465, 108 Stat. 4809 (1994) = 19 U.S.C.A. §§ 3511 *et seq.* For the origin of the URAA see *Reams & Schultz*, Uruguay Round Agreements Act – A Legislative History, 1996.

[11] Loc. cit., 19 U.S.C.A. § 3533.

[12] A list of the WTO Documents which name all the implementation acts and duties of the EU is included in the report by the WTO Secretariat in relation to the mechanism for supervision of trade policies (TPRM), WT/TPR/S72, 14 June 2000, 163 *et seq.*

the US American Uruguay Round Agreement Act (URAA), by which the WTO Agreement and its Annexes where implemented in the United States. In this Act, the implementation of unilateral trade measures in accordance with Section 301 of the Trade Act 1974 was hardly limited,[13] although the conclusion of the Agreement on Safeguard Measures was primarily motivated by the intention to confine such kind of measures.[14] Section 102(a)(2) URAA[15] formulates a general reservation, which expressly determines that certain procedures of US law are not altered by the URAA.[16]

689 Questions of complete and effective implementation have been the subject of a series of disputes in the WTO. But one must also ask another question: how far can the **rules of the WTO be applied in national or EC law**, and does this application entail a duty of the respective governments to observe the law in a form which may even grant individuals a right **to rely directly** on WTO provisions?

690 According to the constitutional and legal rules of many Members, the rules of international agreements *become part of their legal order* upon ratification. The significance of this binding effect on respective state organs, states in a federal system, existing legislation, and the effects of international rules on individuals differ considerably among Members and their legal systems.

691 The European Court of Justice clearly affirmed the **internationally binding nature of GATT 1947** rules for the European Community in the *International Fruit Company* case.[17] The Court made it clear that the Community had assumed the authority of its Member States in the framework of the GATT. The WTO Agreement is now seen as an international treaty and binds the Community organs as well as those of its Member States (Art. 300(6) ECT).

692 In conjunction with the enforcement of Community law by the German authorities, some **German courts** have disputed the conformity of Community law with the provisions of the WTO.[18] The parts of the WTO Agreement which overlap with the jurisdiction of the Union and

---

[13] 19 U.S.C.A. § 2411.

[14] See *Horlick*, WTO Dispute Settlement and the Dole Commission, JWT 29 (1995) 1, 45 *et seq*.

[15] 19 U.S.C.A. § 3512.

[16] The provision says "Construction. – Nothing In This Act Shall Be Construed – (A) To amend or modify any law of the United States, including any law relation to – (i) the protection of human, animal, or plant life or health, (ii) the protection of the environment, or (iii) worker safety, or (B) To limit any authority conferred under any law of the United States, including section 301 of the Trade Act 1974, Unless specifically provided for in this Act."

[17] ECJ, joined cases 21–24/72, ECR 1972, 1219 paras 14 and 18.

[18] See the German case from a lower court in relation to the ECJ Decision, C-307/99 P, ECR 2001, I-3159 – *OGT Fruchthandelsgesellschaft* and C-104/97 P, ECR 1999, I-6983 – *Atlanta*.

the related trade agreements have a significant effect on Germany, since the German authorities have to apply Community law as influenced by the WTO legal order. Therefore, courts have repeatedly made references for a preliminary ruling to the European Court of Justice in accordance with Art. 234 EUT.[19]

693 Another question to be answered is whether the WTO Agreement and its related agreements confer rights which may be enforced directly before national or Community courts. In US and Italian law, such **direct effect** was allowed in individual cases in the past. It has been argued that some provisions of the GATT 1994 are sufficiently clearly drafted to be directly applied even without a further specifying implementing act by the Member concerned. However, such direct effect of the WTO Agreement and its accompanying provisions is explicitly ruled out in specific legal orders, such as those of the United States, Canada and Japan.[20]

694 Similarly, the ratification decision of the **EU Council** (para. 680) includes a clause whereby "its nature, the Agreement establishing the World Trade Organization, including the Annexes thereto, is not susceptible to being directly invoked in Community or Member State courts".[21] The Community based this decision on the lack of reciprocity, since the USA, Canada and Japan did not provide for direct applicability, and the EU would lose a vital negotiating position in allowing unilateral direct applicability.

695 The **ECJ** had already declined to give direct effect to the GATT 1947, on the basis that the GATT, whose fundamental idea was that of trade on the basis of reciprocity, was significantly characterized by the flexibility of its rules and decisions, especially those which allowed for deviation from obligations.[22]

696 This adjudication has the result that in general, **neither natural nor legal persons nor Member States** can challenge acts of the Community relating to the WTO before national courts or the ECJ. Even following the entry into force of the WTO Agreement, the ECJ has maintained this opinion, albeit with slightly amended reasoning.[23]

---

[19] See Bundesverfassungsgericht, Decision of 7 June 2000, – Bananenmarktordnung, BVerfGE 102, 147 = EuGRZ 2000, 328.

[20] See *Stoll*, Freihandel und Verfassung, ZaöRV 57 (1997) 1, 83, 128 *et seq.*

[21] 94/800/EC: Council Decision (of 22 December 1994) concerning the conclusion on behalf of the European Community, as regards matters within its competence, of the agreements reached in the Uruguay Round multilateral negotiations (1986–1994), EC OJ No. L 336/1 of 23 December 1994.

[22] ECJ, C-280/93, ECR 1994, I-4973 para. 106 – *Germany/Council*; also *Everling*, CMLR 33 (1996), 401 *et seq.*; ECJ, C-469/93, ECR 1995, I-4533 paras 26 *et seq.* – *Chiquita Italia.*

[23] ECJ, C-149/96, ECR 1999, I–8395 *et seq.* paras 36 *et seq.* – *Portugal/Council*, also *Hilf &*

697 The ECJ now bases its opinion on three main arguments: firstly, the WTO Agreement, while different from the GATT 1947, still maintains the same idea of a reciprocal negotiation-based framework between its Members; secondly, direct application by the courts would rob the WTO Members of the chance of agreeing on a mutually acceptable solution to a conflict, especially in light of the possibility provided for in Art. 22.2 DSU for payment of compensation; and, thirdly, the main trading partners of the EU also decline to give direct effect to WTO rules, so that unilateral direct application would run contrary to the aim of reciprocal application of the WTO agreements.

698 Similarly, a **claim for damages** by the parties concerned against the Community as a result of an infringement by the Community Organs of rules of the WTO order has, to date, not been supported by the European Court of Justice.[24] Such liability was suggested for cases where the Community was not making use of the options available in the GATT for a mutually accepted solution, and instead was opted for the decision of a neutral organ (the Panel), but eventually refused to follow this decision.[25]

699 The European Court of Justice has allowed for **two exceptions** which permit the **indirect testing** of Community acts and their conformity with GATT or WTO law. The Court will test the legality of a Community act with regard to the provisions of the GATT and the WTO if and when the act (1) is enacted to fulfill a specific obligation within the framework of the GATT/WTO order, or (2) the community act specifically refers to the GATT/WTO order.[26]

700 Special conditions also apply in relation to the TRIPS, whose conclusion and implementation depends on the jurisdiction of the EU Member States, as discussed above. The TRIPS forms part of Community law, but its provisions are just as rarely directly applicable within the legal order of the European Community as those of any other agreement of

Schorkopf, EuR 35 (2000) 1, 74, 82 *et seq*. See also ECJ, C-300/98 and C-392/98, ECR 2000, I-11307 para. 25 – *Dior*. In this decision, the ECJ leaned towards the judgment in Case C-149/96 *Portugal/Council* on the direct applicability of the TRIPS, see also *Hermes*, EuR 36 (2001) 2, 253 *et seq*. See also ECJ, C-307/99, ECR 2001, I-3159 paras 22 *et seq*. – *OGT Fruchthandelsgesellschaft*.

[24] See ECJ, C-104/97 P, ECR 1999 I-6983 paras 17 *et seq*. – *Atlanta* and ECJ, C-93/02 P, ECR 2003 I-10497 paras 51 *et seq*. – *Biret International*.

[25] According to Advocate General *Lenz* in his opinion in C-469/93, ECR 1995, I-4533 (4543) – *Chiquita Italia* and the opinion of Advocate General *Alber* in C-93/92 P (see footnote 24 above), paras 47 *et seq*.

[26] ECJ, C-352/96, ECR 1998 I-6937 para. 19 – *Italy/Council*. The first example of this exceptional situation was recognised by the ECJ judgment in *Nakajima*, C-69/89, ECR 1991 I-2069 para. 31, the second possible exception situation arose out of the judgment in *Fediol III*, C-70/87, ECR 1989, 1781 paras 19 *et seq*.

the WTO (paras 693 *et seq.*). The TRIPS is, however, characterized by particularities which allow for the **direct application** of its provisions **in the national legal orders of the EU Member States**.

701 The TRIPS is a mixed agreement[27] which falls partly within the external competence of the EC and partly within the competences of its Member States.[28] In Opinion 1/94, the European Court of Justice decided that the EC possessed an exclusive external competence only with regard to Art. 51 to 60 TRIPS and, as secondary Community law in the field of intellectual property, could be affected if the Member States were to participate in the conclusion of the TRIPS.[29]

702 On the question of the limited external competence of the EU, the Court ruled in the **Dior case** that Community law "in a field in which the Community has not yet legislated and which consequently falls within the competence of the Member States" does not forbid the direct application of the TRIPS provisions in the national legal orders of the Member States.[30] Community law does not rule out the possibility of a national legal order giving direct effect to Art. 50.6 TRIPS or allowing courts to use this provision *proprio motu*.[31]

703 As a result of this ruling, **Member States are allowed to make their own decisions** concerning the direct applicability of those TRIPS provisions which fall within their external competence.[32] Since these provisions do not become part of the legal order of the EU, it is not for the Community courts in interpretation of Community law, but for the competent organs in the national legal orders of the Member States to decide on direct applicability.[33] In **Austria, Germany and Ireland, direct applicability** has been confirmed by the highest civil courts.[34]

---

[27] The Treaty Establishing a Constitution for Europe of 19 October 2004 contained a different legal construction. Under the Constitutional Treaty, exclusive competence for a common commercial policy would have been extended to the commercial aspects of intellectual property, OJ EC 2004 C 310/1. The term "common commercial aspects of intellectual property" directly refers to the TRIPS.

[28] On the distribution of external competences in the field of intellectual property, *Kaiser*, Geistiges Eigentum und Gemeinschaftsrecht, 2004, 116 *et seq.*

[29] ECJ, Opinion 1/94, ECR 1994, I-5267, paras 71 and 180 – *WTO Agreement.*

[30] ECJ, Joined cases C-300 and 392/98, ECR 2000, I-11307, para. 48 – *Dior.*

[31] ECJ, (see footnote 30 above), para. 48.

[32] For an example of the legal basis authorizing the direct application of the TRIPS, see Deutscher Bundestag, printed matter No. 1277655 (new), 344.

[33] See *Epiney*, Zur Stellung des Völkerrechts in der EU, EuZW 10 (1999) 1, 5.

[34] Austrian High Court, GRUR Int. 1999, 279, 281, with regard to Art. 13 TRIPS; BGHZ (German Federal Court of Appeal, Civil Law Reports) 141, 13, 35, with regard to Art. 9 and 13 TRIPS, Irish High Court, GRUR Int. 1998, 339, with regard to Art. 27.1 TRIPS. The direct applicability of Art. 27.1 TRIPS in Ireland is made possible by s. 46(3) Patents Act 1964. According to this provision, no order shall be made in pursuance of any application under the Act which would conflict with any treaty, convention, arrangement or engagement applying to the State and any convention country.

704 Which TRIPS provisions exactly fall within the exclusive external competence of the EU or have remained part of the external competence of the Member States is not entirely clear. The amendments of Art. 133 ECT by the Treaties of Amsterdam and Nice have further complicated the issue.[35]

705 It was established by the European Court of Justice in its Opinion 1/94 that the exclusive external competence of the EC for the common commercial policy according to Art. 133(1) ECT encompasses Art. 51 to 60 TRIPS. The external competence for the commercial aspects of intellectual property in accordance with Art. 133(5) ECT is, however, concurrent and only exclusive insofar as the implied external competence that is derived from Art. 95(1) s. 2 ECT is exclusive, too. With this, **consistency between external and internal competences** is preserved. As a result of the "ERTA" ruling of the Court,[36] the implied external competence is exclusive insofar as the secondary Community law, which the EC adopted on the basis of Art. 95 (1) s. 2 ECT, could be affected if the Members States were to participate in the conclusion of an international agreement.

706 While this can regularly be presumed for EC regulations,[37] the European Court of Justice considers international agreements as not affecting EC directives if both international agreements and directives contain a minimum standard which does not bar the **Member States** from providing **stricter provisions** in their national legal orders.[38] Although the directives in the field of intellectual property are generally limited to minimum rules, the EC can, in exceptional cases, lay down concrete rules which the Member States must not deviate from.[39]

707 Lastly, it has also been discussed whether **decisions in WTO dispute settlement proceedings** should have direct effect or some binding force in national or Community legal systems.[40]

[35] On the Nice amendment, e.g., *Herrmann*, The Common Commercial Policy After Nice, CMLR 39 (2002), 7 *et seq.*

[36] ECJ, Case 22/70, ECR 1971, 263, paras 17/19 – *ERTA*.

[37] See, e.g., the various EC regulations on Community industrial property rights, <http://europa.eu.int/comm/internal_market/indprop/index_en.htm>.

[38] ECJ, Opinion 2/91, ECR 1993, I-1069, para. 18 – *ILO Convention*.

[39] On the exclusive external competence of the EC for concrete rules in directives see *Kaiser*, Geistiges Eigentum und Gemeinschaftsrecht, 2004, 154 *et seq.*

[40] In ECJ, T-254/97, ECR 1999, II-2743 para. 30 – *Fruchthandelsgesellschaft Chemnitz*, this question was relevant but was not discussed by the Court. According to the Court, the plaintiff had not sufficiently proved, that the criterion for direct effect had been fulfilled; for this question see *Zonnekeyn*, The Status of Adopted Panel and Appellate Body Reports in the European Court of Justice and the European Court of First Instance, JWT 34 (2000) 2, 93 *et seq.*

III. *Enforcing the Rules in Relation to Third Parties*

708 The lack of direct effect of WTO law has negative consequences for both natural and legal persons in relation to the EU Member States. They are unable to bring these issues to the attention of a court of the EU. However, in relation to other WTO Members, the EU provides an effective instrument for the indirect implementation of their rights.

709 The so-called **Trade Barriers Regulation**[41] creates a mechanism by which the Member States as well as the industry and businesses resident in the Community can cause EU organs to take action against the practices of third parties. This mechanism is aimed at barriers to trade (i) which cause damage to the Community market (Art. 1 *lit.* a) or (ii) take effect on the market of a third party and have detrimental effects on trade (Art. 1 *lit.* b).

710 On the basis of an application from a Community industry (Art. 3), a Community enterprise (Art. 4), or a Member State (Art. 6), proceedings will be initiated by the Commission. If the necessary evidence of the existence of the obstacles to trade and of the adverse trade effects is presented, the Commission will, after consultation with Member States, take a decision within 45 days of the application regarding the initiation of a formal **investigation procedure** against the respective third party (Art. 5 para. 4). The investigations of the Commission must be completed within a time limit of five to seven months, and must be reported to the Council (Art. 8). The Council then decides on any further steps which depend on whether the activities of the third party have hindered trade, and whether the Community interest has been interfered with. If both prerequisites are fulfilled, a dispute settlement procedure may be initiated in the WTO.[42] If the Dispute Settlement Body decides in favour of the EU and the third party does not accept the suggestions made, then the Trade Barriers Regulation provides for the facultative imposition of trade policy measures (Art. 12). If the third party takes sufficient measures in the course of the procedure to eliminate

---

[41] Council Regulation (EC) No. 3286/94 of 22 December 1994 laying down Community procedures in the field of the common commercial policy in order to ensure the exercise of the Community's rights under international trade rules, in particular those established under the auspices of the World Trade Organization, EC OJ No. L 349/71 of 31 December 1994, as amended by Council Regulation (EC) No. 356/95 of 20 February 1995, EC OJ No. L 41/3 of 23 February 1995 a detailed commentary is provided by *Berrisch & Kamann*, in: GH II/Krenzler (eds), Recht der Europäischen Union, E 9; *Bronckers & MacNelis*, The EU trade barriers regulation comes of age, JWT 35 (2001) 4, 427 *et seq.*

[42] The action brought against the Commission's decision not to take action against the retaliatory measures taken by the United States in relation to "prepared mustard" imported from France was dismissed by the Court of First Instance, compare Court of First Instance, ECJ, T-317/02, Judgment of the Court of First Instance of 14 December 2004, not yet reported, paras 89 *et seq.* – *Fédération des industries condimentaires de France (FICF).*

any obstacles to trade, or agrees to a mutually acceptable solution, then the procedure will be halted for the duration of the implementation of measures or consultations. If the prerequisites are not fulfilled, the procedure will be terminated (Art. 11). Within the scope of applicability of the WTO Agreement and its Annexes, trade policy measures can be decided upon only when the WTO dispute settlement procedure has been completed. If measures are implemented, they must be in line with the recommendations of the Dispute Settlement Body (Art. 11 para. 2).

711 The role model for the EU Trade Barriers Regulation is **Section 301 of the Trade Act of 1974** of the United States.[43] The provision puts the US Trade Representative under the obligation to implement unilateral measures in certain cases of unfair trade policies of third parties. The United States has been criticized for the use of the economic policy of Sections 301–310 of the Trade Act 1974. In a Panel decision, parts of the mechanism were held to be in breach of rules of the Dispute Settlement Understanding, the GATT 1994 and the WTO Agreement itself.[44]

712 From the perspective of individuals, the mechanism of the Trade Barriers Regulation has the disadvantage that the EU must pursue measures only if the Community agencies consider, that the interest of the Community is at stake. This entails a certain degree of discretion. It is a part of the **market access strategy** of the Community, with which the effective access of European Union businesses to world markets is to be achieved.[45] The mechanism is used with increasing intensity, and has, to date, led to a series of procedures of which several finally resulted in WTO dispute settlement.[46]

713 In conjunction with these formalized procedures at Community level, national trade associations and businesses are attempting to minimize the negative effects of the trade policies of other States by exerting **influence on their national governments**. These situations are made public to the other Member States and the European Commission during the

---

[43] 19 U.S.C.A. § 2411.

[44] *United States – Sections 301–310 of the Trade Act of 1974*, WT/DS152/R, 22 December 1999.

[45] Fundamental to this is the Announcement of the Commission, World Trade as a Global Advancement: Market Access Strategy of the European Union, COM (96) 53 14 February 1996, Decision of the Council 24 September 1998, OJ No. L 265/31 of 30 September 1998. The Commission has compiled a database, which gives information on restrictions on market access in third party nations, at: <http://mkaccdb.eu.int>.

[46] See *Argentina – Measures Affecting the Export of Bovine Hides and the Import of Finished Leather*, WT/DS155/R, 19 December 2000 and *United States – Anti-Dumping Act of 1916*, WT/DS136/AB/R, 28 August 2000; *Korea – Measures Affecting Trade in Commercial Vessels*, WT/DS273/R, 7 March 2005, 7.

sessions of the 133 Committee. Following an internal exchange of information, the Commission attempts to resolve differences of opinion through informal discussions. This line of action can then be a starting point for the formal dispute settlement procedure of the Dispute Settlement Understanding.

CHAPTER TEN

NEW ISSUES AND PROBLEM AREAS

714 The WTO and its substantive regulations have brought about a comprehensive system of international trade regulation. They develop a **progressive dynamic** which is not confined to the field of genuine economic regulation, but also touches upon other policy areas, such as, in particular, international environmental policies as well as the questions of international social standards and human rights. The fact that the whole system includes a built-in agenda (paras 23, 586) for further development contributes to this kind of dynamic.

715 The WTO and its activities exert strong attraction within the international system. The options for reconciling interests by linking issues over a broad spectrum and the effective enforcement mechanism make the WTO appear to be the best forum for other regulatory areas too. The WTO is therefore often in a **tense relationship with other international arrangements** and regulatory systems. It is increasingly drawn into the **public controversy about globalization**, in which it has become the subject of fierce criticism. Moreover, the WTO faces immense challenges due to these political dynamics and, even more so, due to the economic dynamics generated by liberalization.

I. *The WTO's Dynamic Development as an Economic Order*

1. *Complementing the WTO by Rules on Competition?*

Wolfgang Fikentscher, Collaborative activities among industrial competitors: in German, European, and U.S. antitrust law, and in the Draft International Antitrust Code in the GATT/WTO system, in: *Cheng, Chia-Jui* (ed.), International harmonization of competition laws, 1995, 109–126; *Maria-Chiara Malaguti*, Restrictive business practices in international trade and the role of the World Trade Organization, JWT 32 (1998) 3, 117–152; *Jürgen Basedow*, Weltkartellrecht, 1998; *Arwel Davies*, Tackling private anticompetitive behaviour in public contract awards under the WTO's Agreement on Government Procurement, World competition 21 (1998) 5, 55–77; *Mark A. A. Warner*, International aspects of competition policy: possible directions for the FTAA, World competition 22 (1999) 1, 1–36; *Frieder Roessler*, Should principles of competition policy be incorporated into WTO law through non-violation complaints?, JIEL 2 (1999) 3, 413–421; *Dimosthenis Papakrivopoulos*, The role of competition law as an international trade remedy in the context of the World Trade Organization, World competition 22 (1999) 3, 45–64;

Roger Zäch (ed.), Towards WTO competition rules: key issues and comments on the WTO report (1998) on trade and competition, 1999; *Ernst-Ulrich Petersmann*, Legal, economic and political objectives of national and international competition policies: constitutional functions of WTO "linking principles" for trade and competition, New England Law Review 1999, 145–162; *Friedl Weiss*, From World Trade Law To World Competition Law, Fordham International Law Journal 24 (2000) 2, 250–273; *Mark A. A. Warner*, After Seattle: is there a future for trade and competition policy rule-making?, Brooklyn journal of international law 26 (2000) 2, 307–362; *Daniel K. Tarullo*, Norms and institutions in global competition policy, AJIL 94 (2000) 3, 478–504; *Andrew D. Mitchell*, Broadening the vision of trade liberalization: International competition law and the WTO, World competition 24 (2001) 3, 343–365; *Bhagirath Lal Das*, Danger of negotiating investment and competition rules in the WTO, 2001; *Terry Winslow*, OECD competition law recommendations, developing countries and possible WTO competition rules, OECD journal of competition law and policy 3 (2001) 1, 116–137; *Kevin C. Kennedy*, Competition law and the World Trade Organization: the limits of multilateralism, 2001; *Sandeep Chauhan*, GATT to WTO: Gandhian alternative to new international economic order, 2001; *Claus D. Ehlermann & Lothar Ehring*, WTO dispute settlement and competition law: views from the perspective of the appellate body's experiences, 2002; *Bernard Hoekman & Petros C. Mavroidis*, Economic development, competition policy and the WTO, 2002; *Mitsuo Matsushita*, Basic principles of the WTO and the role of competition policy, Journal of world investment 3 (2002) 4, 567–584; *Mitsuo Matsushita*, Competition policy in the framework of WTO, European integration and international co-ordination 2002, 305–316; *Christoper R. Milner & Robert Read* (eds), Trade liberalization, competition and the WTO, 2002; *Joel Davidov & Hal Shapiro*, The feasibility and worth of a WTO competition agreement, JWT 37 (2003) 1, 49–68; *Hunter Nottage*, Trade and competition in the WTO: pondering the applicability of special and differential treatment, JIEL 6 (2003) 1, 23–47; *Philip Masden*, A competition policy for the WTO, 2003; *Amad K. Masa'deh*, Investment and competition in international policy: prospects for the WTO law, 2003; *Josef Drexl*, International competition policy after Cancun: placing a Singapore issue on the WTO development agenda, World competition 27 (2004) 3, 419–457; *Rafigul Islam*, A WTO mulitlateral framework for competition policy and trade-induced development, Journal of world investment & trade 5 (2004) 3, 491–508; *Roland Weinrauch*, Competition law in the WTO: the rationale for the framework agreement, 2004; *Bernard Hoekman & Kamal Saggi*, International Coorperation on domestic policies: lessons from the WTO competition policy debate, 2004; *Christian Tietje & Karsten Nowrot*, Forming a centre of transnational economic legal order?, EBOR 5 (2004), 321–351.

716 Academics and politicians have long discussed the idea of supplementing the WTO legal order by rules on competition. This idea is supported by the fact that the surge in liberalization triggered by the WTO has brought about a need for coordination in terms of competition law, which cannot satisfactorily be solved by national or European regulations on competition alone. The liberalization of trade was considerably advanced by the WTO. It made an important contribution to international economic interdependence and the emergence of a world market. As a result, there emerged multinational enterprises and international business practices which are in **need of adequate control of competition**.

717 Such need is becoming especially clear when considering the growing number of cross-border mergers, the development of dominant positions on world markets and transnational horizontal and vertical trade restrictions imposed by private entities.[1] Despite the difference in requirements and circumstances, clear **parallels** are apparent with the **development of the European Common Market**. The liberalization and opening of national European markets triggered a need for regulations on competition which was met as early as with the establishment of the European Economic Community in 1957 in the form of European rules on competition which now are contained in Art. 81 and 82 ECT. These competition rules played an important role in the formation of the Common Market. One may surely assume that the readiness of European states to consent to the accession to the European Union of less developed economies or to agree to a further opening of the market has been considerably enhanced by the fact that European competition law organizes and controls the influence of enterprises from other Member States.

718 **On the international level**, there is no legal regulation comparable to the system of Art. 81 and 82 ECT. In the context of the North-South conflict, questions concerning the regulation of competition have played an important role. Considering the largely absent regulation of competition, especially in developing countries, the UNCTAD in 1980 adopted a comprehensive codex on trade-restrictive competition practices.[2] The codex applies to all enterprises, states, regional organizations and services and transactions involving goods. It is, however, not legally binding and today should no longer play an important role in practice. The OECD, in 1986, adopted analogous regulations. These, however, were later dropped, again by reason of the differing opinions of the States on competition policy.[3]

719 Today, competition control at the international level is essentially based on the **extensive extraterritorial application of national competition rules**. In addition, **forms of bilateral cooperation** between

[1] According to US American Trade Law tolerance of anticompetitive behavior by a public authority can also be considered an unfair trade practice, § 1301 of the Omnibus Trade and Competitiveness Act of 1988, amends Chapter 1, Title III Trade Act 1974 – Section 301 as follows: "(d) (3) (B) Acts [. . .] that are unreasonable include [. . .] practices which (i) deny fair and equitable (III) market opportunities, including the toleration by a foreign government of systematic anticompetitive activities by private firms or among private firms in the foreign country that have the effect of restricting, on a basis that is inconsistent with commercial considerations, access of United States goods to purchasing by such firms [. . .]".

[2] UN Conference on Restrictive Business Practices, UN Set of Multilaterally Agreed Equitable Principles and Rules for the Control of Restrictive Business Practices, TD/RBP/CONF/10 UN (1980), adopted by resolution of the General Assembly, 5 December 1980, GA Res. 35/63, UN. GAOR, 35th Sess., Supp. No. 48, 123, UN. Doc. A/35/48 (1980).

[3] OECD, Council Recommendation Concerning Restrictive Business Practices Affecting International Trade, C (86) 44 (final) of 5 June 1986, reprinted in: ILM 25 (1986), 1629 *et seq.*

competition authorities, in particular of the big industrial countries, have developed, the significance of which must not be underestimated.[4] Of central significance is the agreement between the EU and the United States.[5] Big merger proposals are regularly reviewed in the framework of such co-operation by the competition authorities of all countries concerned with regard to their compatibility with the various national standards of competition law. Certain conditions may then be imposed or amendments requested. These procedures provide for the coordination of national competition law. These forms of coordination are, however, limited to the procedural level. The competition authorities therefore continue to apply national or European competition law. They thus largely focus on national markets and corresponding competition policy objectives. The competitive situation on the world market is not considered for its own sake but primarily with regard to the influence it may have on the national or European market.

720 When looking at the history of the world trade order, one notices that the question of international control of competition was by no means raised only recently. The **Havana Charter** (paras 13 *et seq.*) proved to be extremely far-sighted in relation to competition. It contains, in its Chapter V, a regulation on competition-restricting behaviour which consists of eight Articles.

721 The **GATT**, which developed out of the Charter, did not continue these regulations. It contains, just as European Community law did later, the beginnings of regulations against competition-distorting *state* interventions in the form of subsidies. Restrictive behaviour of *private parties* is, in contrast, addressed only at a single point in relation to dumping (Art. VI GATT 1994). However, this provision also does **not pursue a competition law approach** in the sense of establishing criteria for the prohibition of low price offers and providing for measures against improper conduct. Art. VI GATT 1994 rather focuses on state and trade policy. The provision contains an authorization of Members, which is specified in another agreement, to levy anti-dumping duties in such cases, in order to compensate for undue price undercuttings (para. 461).[6]

---

[4] See *Mozet*, Internationale Zusammenarbeit der Kartellbehörden, 1991.

[5] Agreement between the Government of the United States of America and the Commission of the European Communities regarding the application of their competition laws – Exchange of interpretative letters with the Government of the United States of America of 23 September 1991, OJ L 95/47 of 27 April 1995 = EuZW 3 (1992), 201 *et seq.*, extended by OJ L 173/26 of 18 June 1998.

[6] An analysis of WTO law with respect to competition law can be found in the document by the OECD working group Trade and Competition, COM/TD/DAFFE/CLP(98)26/Final, 29 January 1999.

722 In contrast, the "new" regulations on the protection of intellectual property and on services contain a much more complete approach to competition. **Art. 40 TRIPS**, for example, addresses questions of competition law with regard to licensing practices pertaining to intellectual property rights and affirms the authority of Members as regards regulation and enforcement (para. 653). In addition, with regard to procedure, it provides for consultations between the Members involved. In this sense, restrictive business practices are also addressed in **Art. IX GATS** (para. 573). In the field of the liberalization of services, this development has, however, gone further than was the case with goods. The special regulations and concessions for liberalization of the telecommunications markets,[7] for example, contain a number of very specific competition rules restricting the market power of market dominating enterprises – in particular of the currently privatised, formerly state-owned telecommunication enterprises.

723 Proposals to exceed these points of reference and to adopt general rules on competition in the framework of the WTO were first made within the academic community.[8] At the Ministerial Conference of Singapore in 1996, Germany and the EU, despite considerable resistance, then achieved the establishment of a **WTO Working Group on the Interaction between Trade and Competition Policy** (WGTCP), which was to deal with the relationship between trade and competition policy and to identify sectors for which legal regulation under the umbrella of the WTO appeared to be promising.[9] The **reports of the working party reveal** an in-depth analysis of the problem but remain reluctant to recommend a further regulation within the WTO.[10] In contrast, the Ministerial Conference in Doha in 2001 (para. 799) adopted a very far-reaching decision.[11] It states that there were good reasons for the establishment of a multilateral framework, in order to improve the contribution of competition policy to the promotion of international trade and development.[12] The Ministerial Conference furthermore decided

---

[7] Agreement on Telecommunication Services (Fourth Protocol to the GATS) of 15 February 1997, see para. 595 *et seq.* The provision was added to the list of obligations of the Members in accordance with Art. XVIII GATS.

[8] Draft International Antitrust Code as a GATT-WTO-Plurilateral Trade Agreement, International Antitrust Code Working Group, BNA Antitrust & Trade Regulation Report 64, No. 1628, 19 August 1993.

[9] Declaration of the Ministerial Conference of Singapore, 13 December 1996, WT/MIN/(96)/DEC, para. 20. The mandate of the working group included a limitation with regard to negotiations on possible international agreements. Negotiations should be initiated only upon clear consensus of the Members.

[10] See the reports to the General Council 1997–2000 of the Working Group on the Interaction of Trade and Competition Policy, WT/WGTCP/1 to 4 of 30 November 2000 and the last Report, WT/WGTCP/7, 17 July 2003.

[11] WT/MIN(01)/DEC/1, 20 November 2001, paras 23 *et seq.*

[12] Loc. cit., para. 23 1st. half sentence reads: "Recognizing the case for a multilateral framework to enhance the contribution of competition policy to international trade and development, [. . .]."

that negotiations should take place on this issue. These negotiations were envisaged to start after the 5th Meeting of the Ministerial Conference, depending on a decision on the modalities of the negotiations to be taken by explicit consensus.[13] However, rather than determining such modalities, the Cancún Draft Declaration called on the Working Group for further clarification "[. . .] including consideration of possible modalities for negotiations."[14] As the Declaration altogether failed to achieve consensus (para. 804), the Working Group did not resume its work.[15] In December 2004, the General Council decided to withdraw the issue from the work programme of the Doha Round.[16]

724 The scope, subject, and content of a regulation on competition at the level of the WTO remain **extremely contentious**. Some Members consider the existing extraterritorial application of national rules on competition and the existing coordination of procedures sufficient.[17] Furthermore, a multilateral regulation may be difficult to achieve. Ideas on competition policy and the competition law of the individual Members sometimes differ considerably. Differences are apparent even with regard to their fundamental objectives. In this regard, it is especially controversial whether the control of anti-competitive practices may take into account industry and structural policy aspects, including, for example, the support of small and medium-sized enterprises. There is further debate on the extent to which such control should serve the promotion of economic development and how this should be achieved.

2. *The WTO and Rules on Investment*

Todd S. Shenkin, Trade-Related investment measures in bilateral investment treaties and the GATT: moving toward a multilateral investment treaty, University of Pittsburgh law review 55 (1994), 541–606; *OECD*, Towards multilateral

---

[13] Loc. cit., para. 23 last half sentence reads: "[. . .] we agree that negotiations will take place after the Fifth Session of the Ministerial Conference on the basis of a decision to be taken, by explicit consensus, at that Session on modalities of negotiations."

[14] Draft Cancún Ministerial Text, Second Revision, JOB(03)/150/Rev.2 of 13 September 2003, para. 15.

[15] The last state of affairs is reflected in a Note by the Secretariat on Revised Tables Summarizing Contributions to the Working Group on Elements Included in Paragraph 25 of the Doha Ministerial Declaration, WT/WGTCP/W/246, 22 January 2004.

[16] Decision Adopted by the General Council on 1 August 2004, WT/L/579, 2 August 2004, para. 1, *lit.* g.

[17] It has been proposed that the development of market domination by a "global player" can be effectively prevented. For example, the acquisition by Boeing of the aircraft manufacturer and defence corporation McDonnell Douglas was successful after further conditions were imposed by the European Commission, and the projected merger of General Electric and Honeywell failed as a result of the European Commission's objection, see the report of the Commission on the application of the agreement between the EU and the United States and Canada (para. 719 above), 29 January 2002, COM (2002) 45 final.

investment rules, 1996; *Seymour J. Rubin*, Regional trade and investment in the era of the World Trade Organization, in: *Hungdah Chiu* (ed.), Proceedings of the International Law Association first Asian-Pacific Regional Conference, 1996, 424–431; *Pierre Sauvé*, Qs and As on trade, investment and the WTO, JWT 31 (1997) 1, 55–79; *Pierre Sauvé*, Regional versus multilateral approaches to services and investment liberalization: anything to worry about?, in: *Paul Demaret & Jean-Francois Bellis & Gonzalo Garcia Jiménez* (eds), Regionalism and Multilateralism after the Uruguay Round: Convergence, Divergence and Interaction, 1997; *Eric M. Burt*, Developing countries and the framework for negotiations on foreign direct investment in the World Trade Organization, American University Journal of International Law and Policy 12 (1997), 1015–1061; *Jan McDonald*, The Multilateral Agreement on Investment: heyday or mai-day for ecologically sustainable development?, Melbourne University Law Review 22 (1998), 617–656; *Francisco Sercovich*, Best practices, policy convergence and the WTO trade-related investment measures, CEPAL review 64 (1998), 93–100; *Kenneth J. Vandevelve*, Sustainable liberalism and the international investment regime, Michigan Journal of International Law 19 (1998), 373–399; *Robert Stumberg*, Sovereignty by subtraction: the Multilateral Agreement on Investment, Cornell International Law Journal 31 (1998), 491–597; *Thomas Brewer & Stephen Young*, Investment Issues at the WTO: the architecture of rules and the settlement of disputes, JIEL 1 (1998) 3, 457–470; *Riyaz Dattu*, A journey from Havana to Paris: The fifty-year quest for the elusive multilateral agreement on investment, Fordham International Law Journal 24 (2000), 275–316; *Peter T. Muchlinski*, The rise and fall of the Multilateral Agreement on Investment: where now?, International Lawyer 34 (2000), 1033–1053; *David Schneidermann*, Investment rules and the new constitutionalism, Law and Social Inquiry 25 (2000), 757–787; *Kenneth J. Vandevelve*, The economics of bilateral investment treaties, Harvard International Law Journal 41 (2000), 469–502; *Eva C. Nieuwenhuys* (ed.), Multilateral regulation of investment, 2001; *Stephen Woolcock*, Investment at the WTO, The World Trade Organization millennium round 2001, 161–179; *Bernard Hoekman & Kamal Saggi*, From TRIMS to a WTO agreement on investment?, Developing countries at the WTO 2001, 201–214; *Bhagirath Lal Das*, Dangers of negotiating investment and competition rules at the WTO, 2001; *Asoke Mukerji*, The WTO debate on trade and investment and the "development dimension", Journal of world investment 2 (2001) 4, 731–759; *Pierre Sauve*, Scalling back ambitions on investment rule making at the WTO, Journal of world investment 2 (2001) 3, 529–536; *Mark Coulen*, Foreign investment at the WTO, Mulilateral regulation on investment 2001, 181–203; *Alan M. Rugman*, New rule for international investment: the case for a multilateral agreement on investment (MAI) at the WTO, Trade liberalization, competition and the WTO 2002, 176–289; *Nagesh Kumar & Jaya P. Pradhan*, Foreign direct investment, externalties and economic growth in developing countries: some empirical explorations and implications for the WTO negotiations on investment, 2002; *Jürgen Kurtz*, A generell investment agreement in the WTO? Lessons from chapter 11 NAFTA and the OECD multilateral agreement on investment, JIEL 23 (2002) 4, 713–789; *Esther Kentin*, Prospects for rules on investment in the new WTO round, Legal issues of economic integration 29 (2002) 1, 61–71; *Cynthia D. Wallace*, The legal environment for a multilateral framework on investment and the potentieal role of the WTO, Journal of world investment 3 (2002) 2, 289–325; *Alan M. Rugman & Gavin Boyd* (eds), The World Trade Organization in the new global economy: trade and investment issues in the millenium round, 2003; *Kevin C. Kennedy*, A WTO Agreement on Investment: A solution in search of a problem?, JIEL 24 (2003) 1, 77–188; *Carlos Correa & Nagesh Kumar*, Protecting foreign investment: implications of the WTO regime and policy options, 2003; *Americo Beviglia Zampetti & Torbjörn Fredriksson*, The development dimension of investment negotiations in the WTO: challenges and opportunities, Journal of world investment 4 (2003) 3, 399–450; *Nagesh Kumar*, Investment on the WTO agenda: a developing countries perspective and the way forward for the Cancun Ministerial Conference, 2003; *Working party of the Trade Committee-prep. by Michael Gestrin*, The investment architecture of the WTO, Orginazation of economic co-operation and development: OECD-Papers 3 (2003) 4, 252, 1–21; *Victor Mosoti*, The WTO Agreement on Trade Related Investment Measures and the flow of foreign direct investment in Africa, Pace international law review 15 (2003) 1, 181–201; *David Woodward*, Financial effects of foreign direct investment in the context of a possible WTO agreement on investment, 2003; *Nagesh Kumar*, Trade and investment in the WTO, Doha development agenda 2003, 392–413; *Maurin Irish* (ed.), The auto pact: investment, labour and the WTO, 2004; *Tillmann R. Braun*, Investment protection under the WTO law: new developments in the aftermath of Cancún, 2004.

725 The problem of investment rules for the world trade order is, with respect to trade in goods, partly dealt with in the **Agreement on Trade Related Investment Measures (TRIMS)** and, for the field of trade in services, in a few provisions of the GATS (Cf. paras 565 *et seq.*). Both regulations, however, take into account only to a limited extent the general problem of regulating foreign investment in its relationship with the rules on world trade.

726 The Agreement on Trade Related Investment Measures **addresses the particular issue** of the **inconsistency** of a number of investment measures **with** the **prohibition of quantitative restrictions** and the **principle of national treatment** (Art. 2 TRIMS). It features possible examples of inconsistent measures by means of an "indicative list" in the Annex. The Agreement is clearly tailored around the GATT Panel decisions concerning the Canadian Foreign Investment Review Act.[18] However, it deals with only a particular subset of issues involved in transborder investment issues.

727 Transborder investment plays a major role in the world economy. Even if undertaken only for investment purposes, it causes an influx of capital into the host country. Where the investor thereby also pursues entrepreneurial motives by investing in an enterprise or his own business, other production factors, in particular technologies, are also regularly transferred. This results in an important impetus **for economic development** in the host country. Foreign direct investment inflows reached

[18] *Canada – Administration of the Foreign Investment Review Act*, Report of the Panel adopted on 7 February 1984 (L/5504 – BISD 30S/140).

a total volume of 1.3 trillion US$ in 2000, although since that peak, the global inflows declined for three years in a row to 560 billion US$ in 2003.[19]

728 Restrictive **regulation of foreign investment** was, and still is to a certain extent, **common** in many countries, and by no means only in developing countries. Foreign investment has played a highly controversial role in the context of the North-South conflict. Having gained political independence, the developing countries claimed their right to sovereignty also in economic terms and in particular disliked the persisting economic connections with the former colonial powers. The often threatened, and in some cases completed, expropriation of investments long dominated international economic diplomacy.[20]

729 The **investment controls** introduced at the time by many developing countries were for the most part based on approval requirements which were often tied to extensive control of **foreign exchange and capital movement**. With these came a number of conditions which were meant to serve different national objectives of economic and development policy. The utilization of local natural resources, raw materials, supply and labour was essential in the sense of **"local content"**, which was often defined as a certain share of the total added value and required of the investor. In addition, objectives were commonly set for export returns to be generated, and the duties relating to technology transfer and training. Moreover, exclusive jurisdiction was often given to the courts of the host country. Altogether, these regulations rendered business activities difficult and gave rise to considerable **legal uncertainties**.

730 The World Bank contributed to overcoming the tensions and legal uncertainties thus created by establishing the **International Centre for Settlement of Investment Disputes (ICSID)**[21] a forum for settling investment disputes by arbitration, and the **Multilateral Investment Guarantee Agency (MIGA)**[22] as a multilateral institution for the insurance of investment risks. In addition, the OECD and the International Chamber of Commerce (ICC) established non-binding

---

[19] See UNCTAD World Investment Report 2004 UNCTAD/WIR/2004 (Overview), 2 *et seq.*

[20] See the overview by *Lowenfeld*, International Economic Law, 2002, 405 *et seq.*; from the perspective of public international law in general *Shaw*, International Law, 5th ed. 2003, 737 *et seq.*, with further references.

[21] Convention on the Settlement of Investment Disputes between States and Nationals of Other States of 18 March 1965, UNTS Vol. 575, 159.

[22] Convention Establishing the Multilateral Investment Guarantee Agency, of 11 October 1985, ILM 28 (1981), 1233.

guidelines for enterprises carrying out international activities in order to accommodate the concerns and welfare interests of the host countries.[23]

731 In the 1980s, the major industrial countries also started to conclude **bilateral investment agreements** with important potential host countries. These treaties soon exceeded the mere regulation of investment protection with regard to possible expropriations and included regulations on permissible forms and subjects of investment regulation and, to an extent, principles of non-discrimination.[24] This revealed a change in the policy of industrialised countries. They now questioned individual elements and instruments of investment control that had long been accepted as an expression of sovereignty in economic terms.

732 From the viewpoint of capital exporting countries, and before bilateral investment treaties provided a positive experience, the few WTO provisions on investment in the WTO were considered insufficient. An attempt to substitute the complex tangle of more than 1,000 bilateral treaties with a homogenous multilateral regulation had been made by the OECD between 1994 and 1998 with the negotiations on a **Multilateral Agreement on Investment (MAI)**. The MAI failed for a number of reasons: apart from the lack of appropriate participation by developing countries, the very far-reaching and yet, in the eyes of the public, inadequate regulations on environmental and social issues arguably contributed to this failure in the end. It may be that many states, in return for their participation in a multilateral investment regulation, expected concessions in other fields which could not be negotiated and granted in the framework of the OECD.[25]

733 It is thus no surprise that the subject of investment was again introduced in the WTO as early as 1996 at the Ministerial Conference in Singapore. It led to the setting up of the permanent **Working Group on Trade and Investment**.[26] Ever since, the representatives of the WTO Members have been analysing and discussing the relationship between world trade and investment, including their possible effects on economic growth and development, the existing international investment

[23] The OECD Guidelines for Multinational Enterprises: Text, Commentary and Clarifications, DAFFE/IME/WPG(2000)15/FINAL, 31 October 2001, <http://www.olis.oecd.org/olis/2000doc.nsf/LinkTo/daffe-ime-wpg(2000)15-final>; see also OECD, The UN Global Compact and the OECD Guidelines for Multinational Enterprises: Complementarities and Distinctive Contributions, DAF/INV(2005)6, 26 April 2005.

[24] See in detail *Dolzer & Stevens*, Bilateral Investment Treaties, 1995 and the statistical data of ICSID, at <http://www.worldbank.org/icsid/treaties/treaties.htm>.

[25] The OECD published documentation on the negotiations, at <http://www1.oecd.org/daf/mai>.

[26] Declaration of the Ministerial Conference in Singapore, 13 December 1996, WT/MIN/(96)/Dec., para. 20.

treaties as well as the advantages and drawbacks of negotiation on an investment framework under the umbrella of the WTO.[27] Notwithstanding this existing extension of the WTO to the subject of investment, the attempt of 29 Members at the Seattle Ministerial Conference in 1999 to reach a decision on the initiation of negotiations on a multilateral investment treaty was not successful. At the Doha Ministerial Conference (paras 799 *et seq.*), the Members did agree that negotiations might begin after the 5th Ministerial Conference subject to certain conditions.[28] The Cancún Draft Declaration envisaged a further clarification and the determination of modalities for negotiations to be adopted by the General Council.[29] The Declaration, however, altogether failed to achieve consensus (para. 804) and the General Council decided to withdraw the issue from the work programme of the Doha Round in December 2004.[30]

734 A regulation would make sense, however, only if it went beyond a repetition of common provisions contained in bilateral agreements.[31] Apart from **unifying** the bilateral regulations, it would be sensible to grant **most-favoured-nation treatment** and **national treatment** before and after the investment. One could imagine providing for such exceptions following the model of the GATS (paras 561 *et seq.*) and allowing for transitional periods for developing countries.[32]

735 Still unsolved is the problem of **competition-distorting effects of state financial investment incentives**. However, there does not as yet seem to be sufficient support for abandoning such investment incentives. The United States, for example, signalled during the negotiations on the Multilateral Agreement on Investment (para. 732) that it was not willing to give up investment incentives and has also claimed constitutional concerns relating to binding effects for its states.[33]

736 To the extent that relevant consensus between the states with regard to a WTO investment agreement cannot be established, a careful extension of the existing **TRIMS** is a promising alternative. For example, it would be possible to extend the illustrative list, contained in the Annex

---

[27] See the Report on the Meeting held on 10 and 11 June 2003, WT/WTGI/M/22, 17 June 2003.

[28] WT/MIN(01)/DEC/W/1 of 14 November 2001, para. 20 *et seq.*

[29] Draft Cancún Ministerial Text, Second Revision, JOB(03)/150/Rev.2 of 13 September 2003, para. 14.

[30] Decision Adopted by the General Council on 1 August 2004, WT/L/579 of 2 August 2004, para. 1, *lit.* g.

[31] See the report of the Working Group, (see footnote 27 above), para. 27.

[32] See *Muchlinski*, The rise and fall of the Multilateral Agreement on Investment: where now?, International Lawyer 34 (2000) 3, 1033, 1051.

[33] *Graham*, A note why multilateral negotiations failed at the OECD, and how such negotiations might be crafted to succeed in the WTO, in: Private Investments abroad – problems and solutions in international business in 1999, 3.

to the TRIMS, of the investment measures which fall under the principle of non-discrimination.[34] Furthermore, one could also question the regulations on the mandatory conclusion of joint ventures with local and national partners, as well as compulsory technology transfers and export obligations in terms of the sale abroad of a certain percentage of products.

737 A further development could come from **Art. 9 TRIMS,** which provides for a **review** of the agreement by the Council for Trade in Goods. The continuing consultations, however, still show clear differences of opinion. It is disputed whether an examination of the socio-economic effects of trade-related investment measures should be undertaken on the basis of the experiences of developing countries. The investigation is to be carried out by UNCTAD – possibly with the participation of the WTO.[35]

738 However, already the Doha Ministerial Conference agreed to postpone the transitional period under Art. 5.3 TRIMS and there are discussions on including in the agreement provisions on **special and differential treatment** of developing Members.[36]

II. *The WTO and Environmental Issues*

Daniel C. Esty, Greening the GATT: Trade, Environment, and the Future, 1994; *William M. Reichert*, Resolving the trade and environment conflict: the WTO and NGO consultative relations, Minnesota journal of global trade 5 (1996), 219–246; *Daniel P. Blank*, Targeted-based environmental measures: a proposal for the new WTO Committee on Trade and Environment, Stanford environmental law journal 15 (1996), 61–129; *Duncan Brack*, International Trade and the Montreal protocol, 1996; *David E. Kaczka*, A primer on the shrimp – sea turtle controversy, Review of European Community & International Environmental Law 6 (1997), 171–180; *Jill Lynn Nissen*, Achieving a balance between trade and the environment: the need to amend the WTO/GATT to include multilateral environmental agreements, Law and policy in international business, 28 (1997), 901–928; *Richard H. Steinberg*, Trade-environment negotiations in the EU, NAFTA, and WTO: regional trajectories of rule development, AJIL 91 (1997), 231–267; *Geert van Calster*, The Shrimp/Turtle Report: marine conversation v. GATT conversation?, European environmental law review 7 (1998), 307–314; *Duncan Brack*, The Shrimp-Turtle case: implications for the multilateral environmental agreement – World Trade Organization debate, Yearbook of international environmental law 9 (1998),

[34] *Read*, International investment in the WTO: prospects and challenges in the shadow of the MAI, Bond Law Review 11 (1999) 2, 360, 383, available under <http://www.bond.edu.au/law/blr/contents.htm>.

[35] So far no consensus has been reached on the terms of reference for a joint UNCTAD/WTO study on different aspects of TRIMS and how they actually affected countries during the course of and since the entry into force of the TRIMS Agreement, for the review process see the protocols of the sessions of the Council for the Trade in Goods, most recently W/C/M/79 of 20 May 2005, 2.

[36] See Report (2004) of the Committee on Trade-Related Investment Measures, G/L/705, 3 November 2004, paras 8 *et seq.*

13–19; *Rohan Hardcastle*, Environmental trade measures under siege: the WTO US shrimp case, Asia Pacific journal of environmental law 3 (1998), 157–171; *Axel Bree*, Article XX GATT – Quo vadis?: The environmental exception after the Shrimp/Turtle Appellate Body Report, Dickinson journal of international law 17 (1998), 99–134; *Howard Mann*, Of revolution and results: trade-and-environment law in the afterglow of the Shrimp-Turtle case, Yearbook of international environmental law 9 (1998), 28–35; *Marlo Pfister Cadeddu*, Turtles in the soup?: An analysis of the GATT challenge to the United States Endangered Species Act Section 609 Shrimp Harvesting Nation Certification Program for the Conservation of Sea Turtles, Georgetown international environmental law review 11 (1998), 179–207; *Jennifer Wanken*, The Shrimp-Turtle case before the World Trade Organization, Colorado journal of international environmental law and policy (1998), 27–39; *David A. Wirth*, Some reflections on turtles, tuna, dolphin, and shrimp, Yearbook of international environmental law 9 (1998), 40–47; *Rita M. Wisthoff-Ito*, The United States and shrimp import prohibitions: refusing to surrender the American Goliath role in conversation, Maryland journal of international law and trade 23 (1999), 247–290; *Matthew Brotmann*, The clash between the WTO and the ESA: drowning a turtle to eat a shrimp, Pace environmental law review 16 (1999), 321–352; *Dukgeun Ahn*, Environmental disputes in the GATT/WTO: before and after US-Shrimp Case, Michigan journal of international law 20 (1999), 819–870; *Bruce Neuling*, The Shrimp/Turtle case: implications for Article XX of GATT and the trade and environment debate, Loyolo of Los Angeles international and comparative law journal 22 (1999), 1–50; *Gregory Shaffer*, United States – import prohibition of certain shrimp and shrimp products, AJIL 93 (1999), 507–514; *Benjamin Simmons*, In search of balance: an analysis of the WTO Shrimp/Turtle Appellate Body Report, Columbia journal of environmental law 24 (1999) 2, 413–454; *Bret Puls*, The murky waters of international environmental jurisprudence: a critique of recent WTO holdings in the Shrimp/Turtle controversy, Minnesota Journal of global trade 8 (1999), 343–379; *Suzanne Pyatt*, The WTO Sea Turtle decision, Ecology law quarterly 26 (1999) 4, 815–838; *Geert van Calster*, The WTO Appellate Body in Shrimp/Turtle: picking up the pieces, European environmental law review 8 (1999), 111–115; *Arthur E. Appleton*, Shrimp/Turtle: untangling the nets, JIEL 2 (1999), 477–496; *Gretchen L. Gaston & Randall S. Abate*, The Biosafety Protocol and the World Trade Organization: can the WTO coexist?, Pace International Law Review 12 (2000), 107–152; *Robert E. Hudec*, The relationship between international environmental law to international economic law, in: *Fred L. Morrison & Rüdiger Wolfrum* (eds), International, Regional and National Environmental Law 2000, 133–168; *John H. Jackson*, The Jurisprudence of GATT and WTO, 2000, 414–448; *Christopher C. Joyner & Tyler Zachary*, Marine conversation versus international free trade: reconciling dolphins with tuna and sea turtles with shrimp, Ocean development and international law 31 (2000), 127–150; *Petros C. Mavroidis*, Trade and environment after the Shrimps-Turtles litigation, JWT 34 (2000) 1, 73–88; *Andes Rueda*, Tuna, dolphins, shrimp & turtles: what about environmental embargoes under NAFTA?, Georgetown international environmental law review 12 (2000), 647–692; *Ryan L. Winter*, Reconciling the GATT and the WTO with multilateral environmental agreements: can we have our cake and eat it?, Colorado Journal of International Environmental Law and Policy 11 (2000), 223–255; *Frederick M. Abbott & Thomas Cottier & John H. Jackson*, The limits of international trade, Proceedings, American Society of International Law 94 (2000), 219–224; *Tania Voon*, Sizing up the WTO: trade-environment conflict and the Kyoto Protocol, Journal of transnational law & policy 10 (2000) 1, 71–108; *Nicola Notaro*,

The EC and WTO trade and environment case law, The Cambridge yearbook of European legal studies 3 (2000), 327–350; *Duncan French*, The changing nature of "environmental protection": recent developments regarding trade and the environment in the European Union and the World Trade Organization, Netherlands international law review 47 (2000) 1, 1–26; *Pinninti Krishna Rao*, The World Trade Organization and the environment, 2000; *Steve Charnovitz*, World Trade and the environment: a review of the new WTO report, Georgetown international environmental law review 12 (2000) 2, 523–541; *John A. Barrett*, The global environment and free trade, Indiana law journal, 76 (2001) 4, 829–887; *Francesco Francioni*, Recent WTO cases on trade and environment, The global community: yearbook of international law and jurisprudence 2001, 123–130; *Richard Eglin*, Keeping the T in the WTO: Where to next on environment and labour standards, North American journal of economics and finance 12 (2001) 2, 173–191; *Gary P. Sampson*, Effective multilateral environment agreements and why the WTO needs them, The world economy 24 (2001) 9, 1109–1134; *Gregory C. Shaffer*, The World Trade Organization under challenge, The Harvard environmental law review 25 (2001) 1, 1–93; *Laura Yavitz*, The WTO and the environment, Journal of natural resources & environmental law, 16 (2001/2002) 2, 203–255; *Sabrina Shaw*, Trade and environment in the WTO, JWT 36 (2002) 1, 129–154; *Sydney M. Cone*, The environment and the World Trade Organization, New York Law School journal of human rights, 19 (2003) 1, 245–257; *Archna Negi*, The WTO Asbestos case, The Indian journal of international law 43 (2003) 1, 93–107; *Trish Kelly*, The WTO, the environment and health safety standards, The world economy 26 (2003) 2, 131–151; *Klaus Liebig*, The WTO and the trade-environment conflict, Trade and environment 2 (2003), 635–654; *Peter-Tobias Stoll*, How to Overcome the Dichotomy between WTO Rules and MEAs?, ZaöRV 62 (2003), 439–458; *WTO-Trade and Environment Division*, Trade and environment at the WTO, 2004; *Nicola Notaro*, Judicial approaches to trade and environment, 2004; *Jochem Wiers*, Trade and environment in the EC and the WTO, 2004; *Mark Harris*, Beyond Doha: clarifying the role of the WTO in determining trade environment disputes, Balancing act 2004, 307–332; *Gary P. Sampson & John Whalley* (eds), The WTO, trade und environment, 2005.

739 A close **relationship full of conflicts** connects the world trade order to international environmental policy and its institutions. It originates in the fact that a great deal of environmental pollution is economically induced and often related to international trade flows. There is concern that trade liberalization, and the connected and hoped-for economic growth, may on the one hand further increase the environmental burden, and on the other hand interfere with the obligations undertaken by WTO law to carry out state measures for the protection of the environment.

740 When looking at other forms of economic integration, e.g. the European Union, it becomes clear that trade liberalization requires the **harmonization** of formerly national – in many cases – **protective policies**. This is guaranteed in the European example through the institutional framework of the EU and the broadening of its competences.

741 At international level, such institutional extension to the competences of the WTO is not anticipated. Environmental issues are better dealt with by other international agreements and institutions. The consolidation of aspects of trade and the environment, especially necessary in terms of sustainable development, thus essentially requires **coordination and cooperation** between these **different international sectoral arrangements.**

742 The WTO explicitly refers to environmental issues. The first paragraph of the **preamble to the WTO Agreement** addresses the objective of **sustainable development**, and aspires to achieve it "both to protect and preserve the environment and to enhance the means for doing". This reveals the influence of the United Nations Conference on Environment and Development (UNCED) of 1992, which had emphasized the principle of sustainable development. From an institutional perspective, it is in particular the Committee on Trade and Environment (CTE) that deals with environmental issues within the WTO.[37]

743 The relationship of the WTO to environmental matters poses several problems. In this context, the **relationship of the WTO with existing Multilateral Environmental Agreements** (MEAs) plays a momentous role. This question was dealt with primarily by the Committee on Trade and Environment, which analysed a large number of such international agreements for possible contradictions with WTO regulations. According to the findings of this research, so far the potential for conflict is limited.[38]

744 This is first and foremost due to the fact that the possible **area of contact** between environmental agreements and the rules of the WTO is **limited**. Environmental agreements provide only to a very limited extent for elements of regulation with regard to trade in goods and services.

745 In this context, **prohibitions on trade in certain products** have to be mentioned first. Such prohibitions are included in the rules of the Montreal Protocol on Substances that Deplete the Ozone Layer[39] with regard to ozone-damaging substances, in the Washington Convention on International Trade in Endangered Species,[40] and in the Basel Convention on the Control of Transboundary Movements of Hazardous Wastes.[41]

---

[37] Decision on Trade and Environment, adopted at the Ministerial Conference in Marrakesh, 14 April 1994, see at <http://www.wto.org/english/docs_e/legal_e/legal_e.htm>.

[38] The reports and working papers are referenced in the document of the WTO Secretariat WT/CTE/INF/5/Rev.5, 28 June 2005. The relationship between the MEA and the WTO law is also subject of the negotiations in the "Doha Round", see WT/MIN(01)/DEC/1, 20 November 2001, paras 31–33.

[39] See Montreal Protocol on Substances That Deplete the Ozone Layer, dated 16 September 1987, ILM 26 (1987) 1550.

[40] Convention on International Trade in Endangered Species of Wild Fauna and Flora (CITES) of 3 March 1973, ILM 12 (1973), 1085 with annex 1096.

[41] Basel Convention on the Control of Transboundary Movements of Hazardous Wastes and Their Disposal of 22 March 1989, ILM 28 (1989), 657.

746 The latter agreement leads to a second category of mechanisms, which **allows Members** to **object to the import of certain goods** subject to certain conditions and special procedures. Corresponding mechanisms are provided for, other than in the Basel Convention, in the Rotterdam Convention with regard to pesticides and hazardous chemicals[42] and in the Protocol on Biosafety to the Convention on Biological Diversity with regard to living modified organisms.[43]

747 In a similar manner, the **Agreement on Straddling and Highly Migratory Fish Stocks to the United Nations Convention on the Law of the Sea**[44] stipulates that the participating countries may, on the basis of an effective system for the conservation of highly migratory species, prohibit the catching of fish and further transport of catches which were fished in defiance of the conservation rules. A dispute on these lines between Chile and the European Union was discussed by the dispute settlement mechanism of the WTO and the International Tribunal for the Law of the Sea, but was eventually settled by agreement.[45]

748 Apart from this small number of regulations which exert influence on trade with respect to environmental effects, **supportive measures of environmental law, and technology transfer and information transmission regulations** are discussed. For example, the requirement of wider application and utilization of traditional knowledge in accordance with Art. 8 *lit.* j of the Convention on Biological Diversity (CBD) has been debated with regard to the TRIPS (see para. 664).

749 The solution of the conflicts and disputes between the rules of an environmental agreement and those of the WTO, which are possible but not very likely, has been discussed many times. In this context it must be differentiated carefully. In cases in which **all WTO Members concerned are also parties to the environmental agreement in question**, the issue appears as a case of conflicting obligations of public international law. In this respect, the general interpretation rules of international law, such as the principle of *lex posterior* or *lex specialis*, come into consideration. The view prevails, that WTO rules hardly hinder Members, which are parties to an environmental agreement to apply its provisions among themselves.

---

[42] Convention on the Prior Informed Consent Procedure for Certain Hazardous Chemicals and Pesticides in International Trade of 11 September 1998, ILM 38 (1999), 1.

[43] Cartagena Protocol on Biosafety to the Convention on Biological Diversity of 29 January 2000, ILM 39 (2000), 1027.

[44] UN Agreement on Straddling and Highly Migratory Fish Stocks of 4 December 1995, ILM 34 (1995), 1547.

[45] See the agreement between the EU and Chile, *Chile – Measures Affecting the Transit and Importation of Swordfish*, WT/DS193/3, 6 April 2001.

750 More problematic are cases concerning the application of a provision of an environmental agreement to which **one of the participating Members is not a party**. An especially incisive, even if so far only theoretical, example is the prohibition of trade in ozone-hazardous substances with countries not party to the Montreal Protocol. In such cases it must be examined whether the environmental agreement, pursuant to the different approaches discussed hitherto, may possibly claim validity beyond its membership. If this is not the case, measures of a Member may be justified in accordance with the general exceptions (paras 151 *et seq.*), or the TBT or the SPS Agreement, independently of the fact that they were adopted in execution of an environmental agreement.

751 In some of the newer environmental agreements, the question of the relationship with other international agreements and, in particular, the world trade order is mentioned explicitly. The Rotterdam Convention and the Protocol on Biosafety, for example, contain identical provisions in their preambles, the significance of which, however, is largely considered to be limited. It can hardly be expected that a solution to possible situations of conflict will emerge from these cross-references.

752 The potential for conflict between the international environmental and trade orders is, however, not only limited to cases in which a conflict between the provisions of environmental agreements and those of the WTO is revealed. Of increasing importance, particularly due to the principle of sustainable development and the demand for a mutually supportive interrelationship between environmental and economic policies, is the question of **implementing or enforcing** environmental agreements. This often concerns the **application of economic instruments** the compatibility of which with the rules of the WTO necessitates a detailed analysis.

753 Of considerable relevance for the relationship between trade and the environment are **unilateral measures** taken by individual states. In a number of disputes which have been subject to much critical public attention, the considerable leeway of and limits on individual states in undertaking such measures have become clear.

754 Examples of such disputes are two Panel Reports of the GATT (**"Tuna I"**[46] and **"Tuna II"**[47]), regarding United States' import bans on tinned tuna directed at protecting dolphins from certain dangerous modes of

[46] *United States – Restrictions on Imports of Tuna*, DS21/R, 3 September 1991 (known as Tuna/Dolphin I).

[47] *United States – Restrictions on Import of Tuna*, DS29/R, 16 June 1994 (known as Tuna/Dolphin II).

tuna fishing. After the establishment of the WTO, a Panel and the Appellate Body had to decide on regulations of US policies on air pollution control concerning the improvement of the quality of petrol and providing for certain different transitional regulations for national or foreign refineries (***United States – Gasoline***). Later, a case came up for decision that – as in the tuna cases – provided for import restrictions on shrimps with regard to fishing methods which were potentially dangerous to marine turtles (***United States – Shrimp/Turtle***).[48] With regard to both subject matter and legal reasoning there are close relations with disputes in the field of health protection, for example, the hormone and asbestos cases.

755 The legal clarification of the possibilities of unilateral environmental measures advanced by these disputes primarily concerns the interpretation of **Art. XX GATT 1994** (paras 174 *et seq.*). As an exception, first ***lit.* b** comes into consideration. According to this, Members are not prohibited from adopting or implementing measures "necessary to protect human, animal or plant life and health". Moreover, with regard to justifying GATT-inconsistent national measures, ***lit.* g**, which concerns measures "relating to the conservation of exhaustible natural resources if such measures are made effective in conjunction with restrictions on domestic production or consumption", must be considered.

756 In the cases dealt with so far, the dispute settlement bodies did not have to give their final opinion on the relationship between these two exceptions, as they avoided this by reference to judicial economy. However, there is a **clear tendency** first to examine the exception for measures relating to the conservation of exhaustible natural resources in accordance with Art. XX *lit.* g GATT 1994 is noticeable. This is essentially so because, contrary to a widely used former interpretation, the term "natural resources" by no means comprises only mineral and other non-living natural resources, but also living resources.

757 Apart from its scope of application as regards the subject matter of Art. XX *lit.* g GATT 1994, which has been widely interpreted, the geographical aspect of this exception has also been interpreted widely. With regard to the protection of maritime creatures, the **geographical scope of application,** since the Shrimp-Turtle decision, has extended to all **maritime areas** over which the Member in question can claim sovereign rights. Accordingly, it will be sufficient if stocks or single individuals of the protected species pass through these maritime areas at least temporarily in the course of migration. Moreover, the exception in Art. XX *lit.* g GATT 1994 requires that the measure must promote the **con-**

[48] *United States – Import Prohibition of Certain Shrimp and Shrimp Products*, WT/DS58/AB/R, 12 October 1998.

servation of such species. In this context, the relationship between the means applied and the objective pursued must also be considered.

758 The measures must finally be undertaken in the context of **restrictions on national production or national consumption**. This requirement brings to mind the requirement of national treatment. However, the latter is not demanded in this respect in the strict sense of the word and would also not make sense. We are concerned here with a kind of "even-handedness"[49] and, in particular, a requirement of efficiency. Accordingly, trade effective measures may be applied only if national production and consumption are restricted at the same time.

759 The protection of the environment has, however, played an important role in the interpretation not only of Art. XX *lit.* g GATT 1994, but also of the *chapeau* (paras 192 *et seq.*). Of considerable significance is in particular the approach, from the requirement to refrain from unjustified discrimination when applying measures to the imposition of an obligation of Members to negotiate. In the seminal decision in *United States – Shrimp/Turtle*, it was pointed out that the United States was obliged (1) to initiate **negotiations** (2) with all Members concerned (3) in good faith, and (4) only then to apply measures, if permitted. In the case at hand, the Panel and Appellate Body had criticized the failure to conduct negotiations with all Members concerned. The subject of the obligation is the negotiation but, *nota bene*, not reaching an agreement.

760 It has hitherto been less clearly indicated when such an obligation exists. There are indications in the two Tuna disputes (para. 754), which were based on similar facts. It was considered relevant that the objectives of the measures required the **cooperation of other states**. In the Tuna and the Shrimps/Turtle cases, the measures – import bans on tuna products and shrimps – served the goal of imposing fishing methods which do not endanger dolphins and marine turtles. The measures can thus achieve their purpose only if third states change their behaviour with regard to the import ban. In the Tuna cases it was correctly pointed out that the sovereignty of other Members is thereby put into question.

761 If one considers Art. XX GATT 1994 to be a system of exceptions for the preservation of the sovereignty of Members (para. 175), one will readily conclude that its utilization must not lead to compromising the sovereignty of other Members. Typically, environmental protection deals with products and protective measures that cannot be classified according to the criterion of sovereignty in an unambiguous and delimiting manner. With regard to the overlaps that thus arise, it is necessary to find ways of carefully balancing **competing sovereignty claims**. The obligation to negotiate accommodates these considerations.

[49] *United States – Gasoline*, WT/DS2/AB/R, 29 April 1996, 19.

762 A limit to the system of exceptions in Art. XX GATT 1994 also becomes evident. The provision is based on the assumption that certain protection interests can be associated with the Members, and can be pursued by them through the application of measures within the limits of the provision. In this respect, other and generally multilateral forms must be found in order to reconcile trade interests and protection concerns at a time where many environmental concerns are global in nature.

III. *World Trade Order, Minimum Social Standards and Human Rights*

Social Standards: *Steve Charnovitz*, The Influence of International Labour Standards on the World Trading Regime: A Historical Overview, International Labour Review 126 (1987), 565–584; *Lars P. Feld*, Sozialstandards und die Welthandelsordnung, Aussenwirtschaft 51 (1996) 1, 51–73; *Keith E. Maskus*, Should Core Labor Standards Be Imposed Through International Trade Policy?, Worldbank Policy Research Working Paper Nr. 1817 (1997); *Steve Charnovitz*, The International Labour Organization in its second century, in: *Rüdiger Wolfrum & Jochen A. Frowein* (eds), Max Planck yearbook of United Nations law, 4 (2000), 147–184; Chantell *Taylor*, NAFTA, GATT, and the current free trade system: a dangerous double standard for worker's rights, Denver Journal of International Law and Policy 28 (2000) 4, 401–435; *Christoph Scherrer & Thomas Greven*, Sozialstandards im internationalen Handel, Enquete-Kommission des Deutschen Bundestages „Globalisierung der Weltwirtschaft", AU Stud 14/11, 2001; *Yasmin Moorman*, Integration of ILO core rights labor standards into the WTO, Columbia Journal of International Law 39 (2001) 2, 555–582; *Clyde Summers*, The battle in Seattle: free trade, labor rights, and societal values, University of Pennsylvania Journal of International Economic Law 22 (2001) 1, 61–90; *James Thuo Gathi*, Re-characterizing the social in the constitutionalization of the WTO: A preliminary analysis, Widener Law Symposium Journal 7 (2001) 1, 137–173; *Jim Rollo & Alan Winters*, Subsidiarity and governance challenges for the WTO: environmental and labour standards, Developing countries and the WTO 2001, 185–200; *Richard Eglin*, Keeping the T in the WTO: Where to next on environment and labour standards, North American journal of economics and finance 12 (2001) 2, 173–191; *Hans-Michael Wolffgang*, Core labour standards in world trade law, JWT 36 (2002) 5, 883–901; *Sean Turnell*, Core Labour Standards and the WTO, ELRR 13 (2002) 1, 105–126; *Keith E. Maskus*, Regulatory standards in the WTO, World trade review 1 (2002) 2, 135–152; *Tom Nankivell*, Living, labour and environmental standards and the WTO, 2002; *Andrew J. Samet*, Doha and global labor standards, The international lawyer 37 (2003) 3, 753–759; *Robert W. Staiger*, The international organization and enforcement of labor standards: the role of the WTO, International labor standards 2003, 271–308; *Peter Muchlinski*, Human rights, social responsibility and the regulation of international business, Non-State actors and international law 3 (2003) 1, 123–152; *Catherine Button*, The power to protect, 2004; *Chantal Thomas*, Should the World Trade Organization incorporate labor and environmental standards? Washington and Lee law review 61 (2004) 1, 347–404.

Human Rights: *Erika de Wet*, Labor standards in the globalized economy: the inclusion of a social clause in the General Agreement on Tariff and Trade/World Trade Organization, Human rights quarterly 17 (1995) 3, 443–462; *Patricia Stirling*,

The use of trade sanctions as an enforcement mechanism for basic human rights: a proposal for addition to the World Trade Organization, American University international law review 11 (1996) 1, 1–46; *Asif H. Qureshi,* International trade and human rights from the perspective of the WTO, in: *Friedl Weiss* (ed.), International economic law with a human face (1998), 159–173; *Pascal Couchepin,* Soziale und umweltbezogene Fragen innerhalb des WTO-Systems: die Antwort der Schweiz, Aussenwirtschaft 53 (1998) 4, 487–494; *Adelle Blackett,* Whiter social clause? Human rights, trade theory and treaty in interpretation, Columbia human rights law review, 31 (1999) 1, 1–80; *Ernst-Ulrich Petersmann,* The WTO Constitution and human rights, JIEL, 3 (2000) 1, 19–25; *Arthur E. Appleton,* The World Trade Organisation: implications for human rights and democracy, Human rights and democracy for the 21st Century – 1998 International Law Session 2000, 415–462; *Salman Bal,* International free trade agreements and human rights: reinterpreting Article XX of the GATT, Minnesota journal of global trade 10 (2001) 1, 62–108; *Christoph Spennemann,* The WTO Agreement on Government Procurement, ZEuS 4 (2001) 1, 43–95; *Ernst-Ulrich Petersmann,* Time for Integrating Human Rights into the Law of Worldwide Organizations, JMWP 7/2001; *Caroline Dommen,* Raising Human Rights Concerns in the World Trade Organization: Actors, Processes and Possible Strategies, Human Rights Quarterly 24 (2002) 1, 1–50; *Sarah H. Cleveland,* Human Rights Sanctions and International Trade: A Theory of Compatibility, JIEL 5 (2002) 1, 133–189; *Caroline Dommen,* Trading Rights? Human rights and the WTO, 2002; *Robert Howse,* Human rights in the WTO: whose rights, what humanity?, EJIL 13 (2002) 3, 651–659; *Ernst-Ulrich Petersmann,* Constitutionalism and WTO law, The political economy of international trade law: essays in honour of Robert E. Hudec, 2002, 32–67; *Christiana Ochoa,* Advancing the language of human rights in a global economic order, Boston College Third World law journal 23 (2003) 1, 57–114; *Frank Schorkopf & Christian Walter,* Elements of Constitutionalization: Multilevel Structures of Human Rights Protection in General International and WTO-Law, German Law Journal 4 (2003) 12, 1359–1374; *Ernst-Ulrich Petersmann,* Human rights and the law of the World Trade Organization, JWT 37 (2003) 2, 241–281; *Ernst-Ulrich Petersmann,* Constitutional economics, human rights and the future of the WTO, Aussenwirtschaft 58 (2003) 1, 49–91; *Stephen J. Powell,* The place of human rights law in the World Trade Organization rules, Florida journal of international law 16 (2004) 1, 219–231; *Ernst-Ulrich Petersmann,* The "human rights approach" advocated by the UN High Commissioner for Human Rights and by the International Labour Organization, JIEL 7 (2004) 3, 605–627.

763 The relationship of the WTO with international regulations and organizations concerning minimum social standards and human rights is in dispute between the WTO Members.

1. *Minimum Social Standards*

764 The granting of minimum standards concerns the regulation and enforcement of **rights of employees**, as laid down, for example, in the different **conventions of the International Labour Organization** (ILO). The rights granted in the ILO conventions are often also referred to as **core labour norms**, while, for the rest, the terminology is inconsistent.

It is argued in part that the core labour norms are regarded as elements of social standards, which also comprise subjects such as minimum wages, social insurance obligations and labour protection.

765 The problem in terms of the relationship between trade and social standards is the **effects on competition**. Particularly in some industrialised countries **"social dumping"** is discussed in the sense that imports from countries with less far-reaching and effectively secured regulations on labour relations could endanger national economic sectors and jobs. In industrial nations, higher social standards are deeply rooted in society and the social order, and their prevalence is normatively secured. It is thus necessary for the granting of trade preferences be made dependent upon adherence to certain minimum social standards.

766 In the related discussion, a **core inventory of social guarantees** and standards of different breadth has been suggested which, with regard to uniformity of competitive conditions, is to be generally applicable. Apart from generally accepted minimum standards, such as the prohibition on child labour and some standards for dealing with dangers in the workplace, it is contentious whether the right of employees to establish organizations, collective bargaining and regulation of labour conditions, as well as certain basic elements of social security, should also belong to such a proposed core inventory of social standards.

767 The **legal nexus with such standards** of the world trade order is possible in two ways. First, one must think of exceptional powers wielded by individual states. A first rudimentary starting point is contained in Art. XX *lit.* e GATT 1994, which grants states exceptional authority with regard to products of prison labour (para. 188). An extension of this exceptional authorization would be conceivable *de lege ferenda*. In this way, Members could be granted considerable leeway to reject goods produced under circumstances not in compliance with minimum social standards. Still further, one could consider providing for state import bans on all goods originating in a Member which cannot or does not want to guarantee social standards.

768 It is, however, also conceivable – again *de lege ferenda* – that social standards, which are to be particularly specified, be enforced by means of the instruments of the WTO in the community interest of the Members. Any possible violation of such minimum standards could then be condemned in dispute settlement proceedings, and could ultimately be sanctioned by the suspension of trade preferences. A precondition for this would be that the corresponding standards were integrated into the legal order of the WTO in such a way as to create enforceable obligations of the Members.

769 A starting point for such proposals, which were already made in the early years of the GATT 1947, in particular by the United States, France, and Scandinavian countries, is the common assessment that minimum social standards are provided for in an unsatisfactory manner at the international level. It is true that the ILO, which can look back on a long history and which institutionally accommodates the interests of employees, employers and governments, can very easily show a record of success in regulating social standards. Since its establishment in 1919, the ILO has adopted about 200 conventions relating to essential issues of social organization and security, which in many fields must be considered rather progressive. However, the degree of membership of the individual conventions and standards differs as a result of the classical structure of lawmaking within the ILO, and their implementation and enforcement are often insufficient.

770 In this view, the **enforcement** of minimum social standards **via the WTO** would indeed constitute an important progress. However, the accompanying repercussions on the system of rulemaking within the ILO must also be taken into account. The organization's activities and the relatively far-reaching willingness of states to agree to certain minimum social standards are based on a specific expectation for application and enforcement. This expectation refers to the classical system of legal obligation and enforcement in the framework of the ILO, and would be significantly altered should minimum social standards now become enforceable by way of trade sanctions. It may be assumed that, due to the considerable differences in interests and opinions between states worldwide, ILO lawmaking would largely fall apart if states had to become aware of the fact that minimum social standards could, where required, be enforced by means of trade sanctions.

771 In addition, many developing countries with very low income levels are opposed to linking minimum social standards with the WTO. Higher social standards are linked to higher production costs. The developing countries, whose **decisive comparative advantage** consists in low labour costs, are understandably worried about losing their competitive advantage and investment incentive following the introduction of social standards into the WTO.[50] The effort to establish an obligation of minimum social standards is considered to be an attempt by the industrialised countries to protect their markets against competitive pressure from the

[50] *Siebert*, Die Angst vor der internationalen Arbeitsteilung – eine Auseinandersetzung mit den Globalisierungsgegnern, Aussenwirtschaft 57 (2002) 1, 7, 15 *et seq.; Summers*, The Battle in Seattle: free trade, labor rights, and social values, University of Pennsylvania Journal of International Economic Law 22 (2001) 1, 61 *et seq.*

developing countries through "new protectionism". The group of developing countries within the WTO thus regards the ILO as the competent and more appropriate forum for this subject.

772 After numerous past attempts by industrialised countries to put the topic of minimum social standards on the WTO's agenda had failed, some progress has been made in this controversy since 1998 through increased activities by the ILO.The International Labour Conference of the ILO in June 1998 adopted a **"Declaration on Fundamental Principles and Rights at Work"**, which obliges all contracting parties to comply with fundamental labour rights. These core labour norms concern freedom of association (ILO Convention No. 87 of 1948), the right to collective bargaining (ILO Convention No. 98 of 1949), the prohibitions on child labour (ILO Conventions No. 138 of 1973, No. 182 of 1999), forced labour (ILO Conventions No. 29 of 1930 and No. 105 of 1957), and [on] discrimination in employment and occupation (ILO Convention No. 111 of 1958) as well as on gender-specific wage discrimination (ILO Convention No. 100 of 1951).[51]

773 At the same time, the International Labour Conference adopted for the first time during its session in May/June 2000 measures for the enforcement of a convention on the basis of **Art. 33 ILO Charter**.[52] The provision is part of a procedure which requires a contracting party to implement its obligations under the ILO Conventions. In the case at hand, the parties were requested to take appropriate (sanctioning) measures because of continued violations by Myanmar (Burma) of the Forced Labour Convention. The European Union reacted by abandoning tariff preferences for Myanmar, adopting restrictions on entry for government members and reducing diplomatic activity.[53]

774 In the Doha Ministerial Declaration of 2001, Members were again able to agree only to a compromise wording. It confirmed the Declaration of Singapore of 1996, in which the ILO was recognized as the competent organization with reference to cooperation between the WTO and the ILO.[54] Furthermore, it referred to activities within the ILO. The ILO Working Group on "Social Dimension of Globalization" –

[51] See at <http://www.ilo.org/dyn/declaris/DECLARATIONWEB.INDEXPAGE>. See further OECD, Trade, Employment, and Labour Standards: a Study of Core Workers' Rights and International Trade, 1996 in the revised version of 2000, COM/TD/TC/DEELSA/ELSA (2000), 4.

[52] Resolution of 14 July 2000, at <http://www.ilo.org/>.

[53] See Commission Regulation (EC) No. 300/2005 of 22 February 2005 amending Council Regulation (EC) No 798/2004 renewing the restrictive measures in respect of Burma/Myanmar, EC OJ L 51/13 of 24 February 2005; Council Common Position 2005/340/CFSP of 25 April 2005 extending restrictive measures against Burma/Myanmar and amending Common Position 2004/423/CFSP, EC OJ L 108/88 of 29 April 2005.

[54] Declaration of the Ministerial Conference of Singapore of 13 December 1996, WT/MIN/(96)/Dec, para. 4.

coinciding with the Doha Ministerial Conference – on 12 November 2001 decided to set up a commission of high-ranking personalities, which was to deliver a report proposing a solution to the problem. The 26-member World Commission on the Social Dimension of Globalization published its voluminous report in February 2004.[55]

775 Before concluding this subject, two further approaches to the enforcement of minimum social standards must be noted: on the one hand, there are attempts to persuade enterprises to bind themselves to a **code of corporate conduct**,[56] on the other hand the use of **labelling** may make consumers aware of the conditions of production of goods and influence them in their purchasing decisions.

2. *Human Rights*

776 In parallel to the discussion about minimum social standards, the opinion is voiced that trade policy measures should **also** be permitted or adopted **in order to sanction the violation of human rights**. In this respect – as mentioned in the section above – unilateral measures on the basis of respective exceptions or the inclusion of human rights standards in the law of the WTO are conceivable.

777 Between minimum social standards and human rights there are several connections and overlaps. However, the emphasis is different in the case of human rights. Distortion of competition, an important aspect in the context of minimum social standards, plays only a subordinate role with respect to human rights. Central to the discussion about human rights protection in world trade is, on the contrary, the question whether the world trade order should recognise a **"civilizing minimum"** in the sense of ensuring basic human rights standards.

778 The proposals for the general orientation of the WTO on the protection of human rights are also a **reflection of the success of the organization**. The effective dispute settlement procedure with its legally binding decisions and the – even if limited – enforcement mechanism are perceived as apt instruments for strengthening international human rights protection.

779 The provisions of Art. XX *lit.* e GATT 1994 shows that human rights protection has so far played a very limited role in the law of the WTO.

---

[55] *ILO*, A fair globalization: Creating opportunities for all, Report of the World Commission on the Social Dimension of Globalization, 2004, <http://www.ilo.org/public/english/fair-globalization/report/index.htm>; compare also UN General Assembly Resolution A/RES/59/57 of 2 December 2004.

[56] *OECD*, Codes of Corporate Conduct, Working Party of the Trade Committee, 2000, TD/TC/WP(99)56/REV1 and the UN-initiative UN Global Compact, at <http://unglobal-compact.org>.

Unilateral trade policy measures explicitly aimed at the protection of human rights have been adopted in a few cases but met with harsh criticism regarding their legality and their political impact. The US American state of **Massachusetts** had wanted to make the acceptance of public bids dependant on the fact that the bidder had no business relations within or with Myanmar (Burma).[57] At the federal level in the United States, the **Helms-Burton Act**[58] and the **D'Amato Act**[59] were adopted. The Helms-Burton Act, *inter alia*, allows US American citizens to bring an action for damages against foreign enterprises investing in expropriated American property in Cuba (Title III), and obliges American authorities to prohibit entry to the United States for the management and stockholders of such enterprises (Title IV). The D'Amato Act provides for mandatory sanctions against foreign enterprises directly supporting the development of oil and gas production in Iran and Libya with investments worth more than 20 million US$.[60] The law of the WTO in this context serves to limit the national scope for action.

780 The – at first sight evident – idea of pursuing the interest in the effective enforcement of human rights via the primary use of the world trade order appears at a closer look to be extremely difficult to handle. In many cases the **facilitation and extension of trade** in and with the relevant states may very well initiate a change towards the better protection of human rights. Furthermore, it is not certain how violations of human rights will be weighted in an individual case and how the proportional application of the WTO instruments for the purposes of sanctions could be assured.[61]

IV. *Democratization of the WTO?*

Jan Tumlir, International Economic Order and Democratic Constitutionalism, ORDO 34 (1983), 71–83; *Peter-Tobias Stoll*, Freihandel und Verfassung, ZaöRV 57 (1997) 1, 83–146; *Peter Hilpold*, Das Transparenzprinzip im internationalen Wirtschaftsrecht, EuR 34 (1999) 5, 597–620; *Steve Charnovitz*, Opening the WTO to nongovernmental interests, Fordham International Law Journal 24 (2000) 1,

[57] Mass. Gen. Laws ch. 7, §§ 22G–M (1996). The law was repealed because it conflicted with federal law, see. Crosby v. National Foreign Trade Council, 120 S.Ct. 2288 (2000). See also para. 773 above.

[58] Cuban Liberty and Democratic Solidarity (LIBERTAD) Act of 1996, Pub. L. No. 104–114, 110 Stat. 785 (1996) = 22 U.S.C.A. § 6021 *et seq.*

[59] Iran-Libya Sanctions Act of 1996 (D'Amato Act), Pub. L. No. 104–172, 110 Stat. 1541 (1996) = 50 U.S.C.A. §§ 1701 as amended by the ILSA Extension Act of 2001.

[60] See in detail on this matter the report of the European Commission "Report on United States Barriers to Trade and Investment", December 2003, 7 *et seq.*, <http://trade-info.cec.eu.int/doclib/docs/2003/december/tradoc_115383.pdf>.

[61] For an overview of national experiences with such sanctions policy see *Cleveland*, Human Rights Sanctions and International Trade: A Theory of Compatibility, JIEL 5 (2002) 1, 133 *et seq.*

173–216; *Arthur E. Appleton*, The World Trade Organisation: implications for human rights and democracy, Human rights and democracy for the 21st Century – 1998 International Law Session 2000, 415–462; *Armin von Bogdandy*, Verfassungsrechtliche Dimensionen der Welthandelsordnung, Kritische Justiz 34 (2001) 3, 264–281 (part 1), 34 (2001) 4, 425–441 (part 2); *Meinhard Hilf*, New Economy – New Democracy?, in: Claus Dieter Classen (ed.), Festschrift für Thomas Oppermann, 2001, 427–438; *Markus Krajewski*, Verfassungsperspektiven und Legi-timation des Rechts der Welthandelsorganisation (WTO), 2001; *idem*, Democratic Legitimacy and Constitutional Perspectives of WTO Law, JWT 35 (2001) 1, 167–186; *Harlem Désir*, Report on Openness and democracy in international trade, European Parliament, A5-331/2001, EC OJ C 112/207 of 9 May 2002; *Eric Stein*, International Integration and Democracy: No Love at First Sight, AJIL 95 (2001) 3, 489–534; *Robert E. Howse & Kalypso Nicolaïdes*, Legitimacy and Global Governance: Why Constitutionalizing the WTO Is a Step Too Far, in: *Roger B. Porter & Pierre Sauvé & Arvind Subramanian & Americo Beviglia Zampetti* (eds), Efficiency, Equity, and Legitimacy, 2001, 227–257; *John O. McGinnis & Mark L. Movsesian*, The World Trade Constitution, Harvard Law Review 114 (2001) 2, 512–605, *Deborah Z. Cass*, The 'Constitutionalization' of International Trade Law: Judicial Norm-Generation as the Engine of Constitutional Development in International Trade, EJIL 12 (2001) 1, 39–75; *Gregory C. Shaffer*, The World Trade Organization under challenge: democracy and the law and politics of the WTO's treatment of trade and environment matters, Harvard Environmental Law Review 25 (2001) 1, 1–93; *Claude E. Barfield*, Free trade, sovereignty, democracy: the future of the World Trade Organization, Chicago journal of international law 2 (2001) 2, 403–415; *Robert E. Hudec*, Free trade, sovereignty, democracy, World trade review 1 (2002) 2, 211–222; *Americo Beviglia Zampetti*, Democratic legitimacy in the World Trade Organization, JWT 37 (2003) 1, 105–126; *William J. Antholis*, Towards a democratic world trading system: four challenges for the WTO, Doha development agenda 2003, 143–162; *Robert Howse*, How to begin to think about the "democratic deficit" at the WTO, International economic governance and non-economic concerns 2003, 79–101; *Peter M. Gerhart*, The World Trade Organization and participatory democracy, Vanderbilt journal of transnational law 37 (2004) 4, 897–934; *Ernst-Ulrich Petersmann*, Challenges to the legitimacy and efficiency of the world trading system, JIEL 7 (2004) 3, 585–603; *David E. Skaggs*, How can parliamentary participation in WTO rule-making and democratic control be made mor effective in the WTO?, JIEL 7 (2004) 3, 655–658; *James Bacchus*, A few thoughts on legitimacy, democracy, and the WTO, JIEL 7 (2004) 3, 667–673.

781 In recent years, a worldwide strong **critical current** against the institutions of the world economy has arisen among the public. While the World Bank and the International Monetary Fund have for decades been criticised by the academic community and non-governmental organizations (NGOs), such defensive position is a new phenomenon for the WTO. The considerable attention paid to the World Trade Organization, of which the public has been aware at least since the Seattle Ministerial Conference in 1999, shows that the WTO has developed beyond the position of a mere technical international organization, and has been politicised.[62]

[62] See *Stein*, International integration and democracy: no love at first sight, AJIL 95 (2001) 3, 489, 530.

782 The **reasons** for this development can first be found in the widespread conviction that the establishment of the WTO has led to a further cession of national decision-making authority at the international level. The ability of citizens to participate in the regulation of issues directly affecting them would be reduced. It was thus a typical example of the continuing loss of national power executed by direct democratically legitimized institutions. This argument results in the accusation of the existence of a "democratic deficit", familiar from the European integration process.[63]

783 This criticism is directed at the incongruity between decisions at WTO level and the will of those who are ultimately affected by them. From a normative perspective, the question of **legitimization** is raised; from a societal perspective this question concerns the **acceptance** of such decisions. Democratic legitimization in the sense of classical constitutional law, i.e. through a close and uninterrupted relationship of all exercise of sovereign power with the sovereign, cannot be achieved at international level in the same way as within a State. Furthermore, the members of the international community lack the homogeneity necessary to head for more inclusive forms at international governance.[64] The lack of a supra-regional consensus with respect to the necessary contents of the concept of democracy is evident.

784 Other approaches to the solution of the "democratic deficit" concern the **transparency** of the WTO, that is the openness of its procedures and decision-making processes. Transparency is a precondition for an open discourse and for criticism. This discussion differentiates between internal and external transparency.

785 The term **"internal transparency"** comprises measures guaranteeing the effective participation of Members in the work of the WTO. The fact that this topic is a subject of discussion at all is surprising because in the WTO, as an international organization based on public international law, the principle of the sovereign equality of states applies. Practice shows, however, that formal equality and effective participation may, and in practice often do, fall apart. Many Members maintain no or only a very small representation at the headquarters of the WTO in Geneva, so that they are cut off from consultation and the daily business of the organization. In addition, there is a practice of informal consultations between individual Members and groups of Members during the Ministerial Conferences, where the number of participants is deliberately kept small. In these "green room" negotiations

[63] See, e.g., *Hilf*, New Economy – New Democracy?, in: *Classen* (ed.), Festschrift für Thomas Oppermann, 2001, 427 *et seq.*; *Krajewski*, Democratic Legitimacy and Constitutional Perspective of WTO Law, JWT 35 (2001) 1, 167, 175 *et seq.*

[64] This argument also speaks against a further development of the WTO into a supranational organization.

important trade policy pre-decisions are in effect taken between the relevant trade blocks. In consequence, a majority of the Members – often those having the status of developing countries – are factually excluded from decision-making. They have no access to these forums and can no longer exert much influence on the substance of decisions in the official committee sessions. These practices and facts have in the past caused a radical loss of confidence among WTO Members.

786 Following the Seattle Ministerial Conference in 1999, which essentially failed as a result of the opposition of a number of developing countries, discussions were initiated within the WTO to improve internal transparency.[65] In the course of this discussion process, the Members, for example, agreed to principles for the preparation of the Doha Ministerial Conference in 2001. Furthermore, an Advisory Centre on WTO law was established in Geneva for the least developed countries (LDCs), which was to make available to them assistance and technical **resources to enable them to participate in the WTO** and in dispute settlement (para. 258). The Doha Development Agenda recognizes that technical assistance and capacity building are core elements of the development dimension of the multilateral trading system.[66] In 2004, the WTO Secretariat for the first time issued a Technical Assistance Plan that organizes the enhancement of resources in developing and least-developed countries to address trade policy issues and concerns and to facilitate an effective participation in the negotiations.[67] Moreover, the Doha Develop-ment Agenda Global Trust Fund, supported by the industrialised countries on a voluntary basis, was set up in order to finance specific projects of the WTO Secretariat for education and training over the next few years. Finally, the WTO manages several technical cooperation programmes in collaboration with other international agencies, namely the so-called Integrated Framework (IF), which is a technical cooperation programme specifically for Least-Developed Countries (LDCs) in collaboration with the International Trading Center, IMF, World Bank, UNCTAD and UNDP.[68]

---

[65] See Ministerial Declaration, adopted on 14 November 2001, WT/MIN(01)/DEC/1, 20 November 2001, para. 10. The relevance of the topic "internal transparency" is exemplified by the discussion in the General Council on Iran's request for accession, WT/GC/M/92, 7 April 2005, 1 *et seq.*

[66] Doha Work Programme, Decision Adopted by the General Council on 1 August 2004, WT/L/579, 2 August 2004, *lit.* d.; see also Ministerial Conference, Declaration adopted on 14 November 2001, WT/MIN(01)/DEC/1, 20 November 2001 paras 38 *et seq.*

[67] WTO Secretariat, Technical Assistance and Training Plan 2005, WT/COMTD/W/133/Rev. 2, 16 December 2004

[68] WTO Plan of Action for the Least-Developed Countries of 13 December 1996, WT/MIN(96)/14, 7 January 1997; Joint Communiqué by the Six Core Agencies of the Integrated Framework – IMF, ITC, UNCTAD, UNDP, World Bank and WTO, WT/IFSC/5, 15 July 2003.

787 The term **"external transparency"** embraces the participation of civil society and particularly of NGOs in the WTO internal procedures. **Art. V:2 WTO Agreement** first provides for consultations and cooperation with non-governmental organizations, for which the General Council has adopted guidelines.[69] This regulation, however, covers only a small area, and, for example, leaves open questions concerning access to documents, the participation of representatives of non-governmental organizations in sessions of WTO bodies, and, in particular, the issue of a right to representation in the context of the dispute settlement procedure. NGOs have formulated a corresponding claim for participation which has been recognized by some Members and has been the subject of discussion in WTO bodies since the establishment of the organization. In particular the Members of the QUAD Group made relevant proposals for reform.[70] Among the Members there is, however, no consensus on the opening of the WTO's internal procedures and, in particular, the direct involvement of NGOs. A large group of developing countries holds the opinion that the information of the public was a primary responsibility of the respective national governments. The WTO was an intergovernmental organization, in which the governments of states were represented.[71] Moreover, one has to bear in mind that NGOs – beside their often supportive work – represent only specific interest and cannot claim any normative legitimacy conveyed by the constitutional architecture of a democratic state to the government. The **Report by a Consultative Board**, chaired by former GATT Director-General *Peter Sutherland*, on the "Future of the WTO: Addressing Institutional Challenges in the New Millennium", which was published in January 2005, noted that the WTO had succeeded in improving transparency to a significant extent. However, the report acknowledges that additional external transparency and civil society engagement would have considerable disadvantages, such as disproportionate burdens imposed on developing countries in engaging with non-WTO Members and loss of confidentiality in trade negotiations. The Consultative Board recommended that the primary responsibility in this matter rests with Members.

788 As regards dispute settlement, the Appellate Body undertook an important step in strengthening the role of civil society in the world trade

[69] Guidelines for Arrangements on Relations with Non-governmental Organizations, WT/L/162, 23 July 1996.

[70] See e.g., the WT/GC/W/92, 14 July 1998 (EC/EU); WT/GC/W/106, 13 October 1998 (US/Canada); WT/GC/W/413, 11 October 2000 (US); WT/GC/W/415, 17 October 2000 (Canada), and WT/GC/W/419, 2 November 2000 (Norway).

[71] For a taste of the formal difficulties involved in the discussion of the subject of external transparency, see the Protocol of the Session of the General Council, WT/GC/M/57, 14 September 2000, 59 *et seq*. The Members were not even able to reach consensus on whether or not this topic could be discussed at length under "miscellaneous" on the agenda.

order. In several decisions it was made clear that the Panel, in accordance with Art. 13 DSU, and the Appellate Body, in accordance with Art. 16(1) of its working procedures, may accept petitions and statements of non-governmental organizations and individuals (**amicus curiae briefs**) (para. 259). This practice of the Appellate Body has, however, demonstrated with how much fervour such institutionalized involvement by societal groups is opposed by some Members.[72]

789 A further model for improving the democratic legitimization of the WTO is also discussed under the key term **"parlamentarization"**. This could be realized either by the increased involvement of national parliaments, both in the negotiations and in the work of the WTO, or through a separate WTO parliament. There are two role models to the creation of a **parliamentary assembly within the WTO**: the conventions[73] of national parliamentarians at the Seattle and Doha Ministerial Conferences as well as the corresponding project of a working group of representatives of the European Parliament.[74]

790 Every attempt at the parliamentarization of the WTO, be it in the form of an institution equipped with decision-making power or as a discussion forum, is confronted with the problem of the above mentioned lack of homogeneity between the WTO Members. The Members' political and economic development is highly diverse, leading to a considerable divergence of interests. The crucial argument against the institutionalization of a classic parliamentary representation within the WTO is, however, the fact that the WTO is far from being a community that is able to organize a public process of communication and to form a common will. The WTO is a functionally differentiated **international organization with a claim to universal application** in the *field of world trade.* It does not have any supranational sovereign power of its own, but acts within the international treaty framework ratified by the Members according to their respective national constitutional laws. An independent parliamentary assembly is therefore not necessary in any way.

791 The complexity of the world trade order should further not encourage anyone to hastily disregard the existing, and hitherto untapped, **potential**

[72] See the Protocol of the Special Session of the General Council of 23 January 2001, WT/GC/M/60 paras 7 *et seq.* The Council convened at the request of Egypt, after the Appellate Body in the Asbestos case had asked to submit amicus curiae briefs, WT/DS135/9, 8 December 2000.

[73] See the speech of former General Director *Moore* before the interparlamentary assembly in Seattle on 2 December 1999, at <http://www.wto.org/english/thewto_e/minist_e/min99_e/english/press_e/pres159_e.htm>.

[74] See the Resolution of the European Parliament on Openness and Democracy in International Trade of 25 October 2001, paras 28 *et seq.*, and Bulletin Quotidien Europe No. 8081 of 29/30 October 2001, 15.

for reform at the national level. The important influence of the US Senate on American trade policy is based on the constitutionally guaranteed division of foreign affairs powers between the President and the Senate.[75] The national parliaments could, on the one hand, increase their presence and influence in their governments' negotiating teams and, on the other hand, reflect on a new definition of their role in foreign relations.[76] By means of an adjustment of national constitutional law according to the US model, parliaments could in principle avoid the problem of a later "ratification situation". In order not to conflict too strongly with the foreign affairs power, being a classic prerogative of the executive branch, the constitutional separation of competences could be limited to international treaties in the context of the world trade order.

792 NGOs' criticism of the WTO and the process of internationalization should not make forgotten, that in most countries, economic interests already collide with social and environmental policy interests at the *national* level. From this perspective, objectors from society emphasise that they are a minority at the national level.[77] Otherwise, it would be possible to influence the position of the state in question in the WTO bodies via the national political process. For example, such consensus on the *imperative* enforcement of minimum social standards has been achieved neither in the United States nor in the European Union.[78]

793 In any case, the **normative and societal legitimation** of the WTO needs to be improved. A first set of measures has already been adopted to ensure more effective participation by all Members and an equal share of the benefits of the world trade order. A further necessity is the reform and enhancement of existing mechanisms. This concerns in particular the establishment of external transparency, a further differentiated and systemized legal order as well as continued efforts to agree on societal demands and convictions.

794 This process is referred to in part as the **constitutionalization of the world trade order**. The concepts behind this term are, however, not uniform. In any case, this vague term comprises the elaboration of institutions and norms for the further legimization of the world trade order.

---

[75] *Leebron*, in: *Jackson & Sykes* (eds.) Implementing the Uruguay-Round, 1994, 175, 177 *et seq.*, and above paras 681 *et seq.*

[76] See the speech by former General Director *Moore* before the Parliamentary Assembly of the Council of Europe on 23 January 2002, <http://www.wto.org/english/news_e/spmm_e/spmm75_e.htm>.

[77] See *Kelly*, The WTO and global governance: the case for contractual treaty regimes, Widener Law Symposium Journal 7 (2001) 1, 109, 131.

[78] *Gantz*, Failed efforts to initiate the "Millennium Round" in Seattle: lessons for future global trade negotiations, Arizona Journal of International and Comparative Law 17 (2000) 2, 349, 350 *et seq.*

V. *The New World Trade Round ("Doha Round")*

Jagdish Natwarlal Bhagwati, After Seattle: free trade and the WTO, International affairs 77 (2001) 1, 15–30; *The Economist*, Globalisation and its critics, A survey of globalisation, 29 September 2001; Short articles in JIEL 5 (2002) 1, 191–219; *Petros C. Mavroidis*, The Meeting in Doha, JWT 36 (2002) 2, 167–169; *WTO*, The road to Doha and beyond, 2002; *WTO*, Doha declarations, 2002; *Frederick M. Abbott*, The Doha Declaration of the TRIPS Agreement and Public Health, JIEL 5 (2002) 2, 469–505; *Steve Charnovitz*, The legal status of the Doha Declarations, JIEL 5 (2002) 1, 207–211; *Matthias Meyer*, A new trade deal for developing countries?, Aussenwirtschaft 57 (2002) 2, 151–158; *William A. Lovett*, Bargaining challenges and conflicting interests, American University international law review 17 (2002) 5, 951–1002; *Terence P. Stewart*, After Doha, 2002; *Sūryaprasāda Suvedī*, The road from Doha, The international and comparative law quarterly 52 (2003) 2, 425–446; *Larry A. DiMatteo*, The Doha declaration and beyond, Vanderbilt journal of transnational law 36 (2003) 1, 95–160; *Marc Baccetta*, Industrial tariff liberalization and the Doha Development Agenda, 2003; *Ross P. Buckley* (ed.), The WTO and the Doha Round, 2003; *Pieter Jan Kuijper*, A legal drafting group for the Doha Round, JWT 37 (2003) 6, 1031–1036; *Marcus Peter*, The Cancún experience, ZEuS 6 (2003) 4, 619–642; *Duncan Matthews*, WTO decision on implementation of Paragraph 6 of the Doha Declaration on the TRIPS Agreement and Public Health, JIEL 7 (2004) 1, 73–107; *Clete D. Johnson*, A barren harvest for the developing world?, Georgia journal of international & comparative law 32 (2004) 2, 437–472; *Basudeb Guha-Khasnobis* (ed.), The WTO, developing countries and the Doha Development Agenda, 2004; *Joseph E. Stiglitz & Andrew Charlton*, The development round of trade negotiations in the aftermath of Cancún, Commonwealth Secretariat, 2004.

795 Since 1947, altogether eight world trade rounds have taken place under the GATT, in which further tariff reductions as well as the enhancement and reform of the World Trade Organization were negotiated.[79] The Uruguay Round ended in 1994 with the establishment of the WTO. The Members intend to use the organization to develop an "integrated, more viable and durable multilateral trading system".[80] The development of such a multilateral trading system is a very long process. The dynamic element becomes apparent within the existing system in the form of the so-called "built-in agenda" – the Agreement on Agriculture and the GATS contain the obligation to initiate negotiations before the end of 1999 (paras 586, 714). However, the initiation of a new world trade round has been the subject of a long debate.

796 The attempt to initiate this new comprehensive round of negotiations ("Millennium Round") at the **third WTO Ministerial Conference in Seattle in 1999**, however, failed. The Members, influenced by considerable, partly violent public protests, were not able to agree to issue

[79] Geneva (1947); Annecy (1949), Torquay (1950), Geneva (1956), Dillon (1960–61), Kennedy (1964–67); Tokyo (1973–79), and Uruguay (1986–94).

[80] See the 4th consideration of the Preamble of the WTO Agreement.

a mandate for negotiation. The contrasts between the Members' positions, the inadequate preparation of the conference, and the surrounding circumstances even resulted in the Members not adopting the usual Ministerial Declaration.

797 The failure of the Ministerial Conference and, along with it, the planned "Millennium Round" had several causes: the central ones are a change in the self-perception of individual Members and groups of Members as well as a considerably greater awareness of the consequences of trade liberalization and its interrelations with development policy topics. A majority of the developing countries have reached the conclusion that in the Uruguay Round the industrialized countries managed to pursue their interest well while the result of negotiations was not to the advantage of developing countries. Thus, the developing countries have created a link between the initiation of further negotiations on tariff reduction and improved market access on the one hand, and the cooperation of the industrialised countries with regard to the implementation of agreements and increased awareness of the level of development on the other hand. A dispute arose in particular over whether the negotiations, as requested by most industrialised nations, should also extend to environmental and social standards.

798 Once the government delegations of the Members had recovered from the "shock of Seattle", a number of **confidence-building initiatives** were started with the goal of perhaps giving the development process of the world trade order the desired dynamic at the next Ministerial Conference in late 2001. For example, an initiative was undertaken at the political level in the EU for the better integration of the least developed countries into the global economy, under which all goods from these States except for weapons (**"Everything but Arms"** Initiative) should in principle be granted tariff- and quota-free access to the Common Market.[81]

799 The diplomatic and political efforts were successful. In the context of the **fourth Ministerial Conference at Doha**, representatives of the Members agreed on 14 November 2001 on a new round of negotiations.[82] The mandate of the "Doha Round" comprises the following

---

[81] The implementation of the EBA-Initiative was achieved by means of Council Regulation (EC) No. 416/2001 of 28 February 2001 amending Council Regulation (EC) No. 2820/98 applying a multiannual scheme of generalized tariff preferences for the period 1 July 1999 to 31 December 2001 so as to extend duty-free access without any quantitative restrictions to products originating in the least-developed countries, EC OJ L 60/43 of 1 March 2001. For extensive remarks on the EBA Initiative, see <http://europa.eu.int/comm/trade/miti/devel/eba1.htm>.

[82] In the official documents of the WTO, the term "round" is not used in consideration of the negative position of many developing countries with regard to a new world trade round.

topics, which are to be dealt with in the context of either negotiations or a working programme: the implementation of existing obligations; agriculture; services; market access; TRIPS; the Singapore issues, i.e., investment, competition policy, trade facilitation, and public procurement; WTO rules (anti-dumping, subsidies, and regional agreements); dispute settlement; environmental protection; electronic commerce; small economies; debts and finance; technology transfer; technical aid and resource allocation; Least-Developed Countries; and special and differential treatment (S&D).

800 The negotiations are supervised by a **special committee** (Trade Negotiations Committee, TNC) under the authority of the General Council. The Committee was set up on 1 February 2002 and is led by the Director-General of the WTO "ex officio". This regulation is a compromise, given the significant differences in opinion between the Members. It reflects the above mentioned principal positions of the industrialised and developing countries with regard to a "new round" (para. 797). A group of developing countries – among which were Pakistan, Tanzania, Uganda, Kenya, Zimbabwe, Jamaica, Honduras, and China – wanted the TNC to be chaired, in an annual rotation, by representatives of the Members of the rank of ambassador, in order to assure the appropriate consideration of their interests. The compromise on the issue is accompanied by principles and practices of organization and procedure meant to ensure, in particular, transparency and the representation of all WTO Members.[83] New negotiation committees have been established to discuss market access and WTO rules; the remaining topics are to be negotiated in special sessions of the competent, existing WTO bodies.

801 The trade round's agenda already shows that the **different interest groups** among the WTO Members had to lower considerably their expectations with regard to their positions and to accept compromises. It must be emphasized in this context that the negotiations on agriculture include the reduction of all forms of export subsidies, aiming at lifting them one by one. This aspect will cause considerable internal difficulties for the European Union because it will make changes to the Common Agriculture Policy (CAP) unavoidable. In June 2003, the EU Ministers of Agriculture were able to adopt the necessary reform steps. In the future, farmers in the EU will receive a single farm payment, independent from production, which is linked to the respect for environmental

[83] Statement by the Chairman of the General Council, TN/C/1, 4 February 2002. With regard to transparency and the participation of all WTO Members reference is made to the remarks of the chairman of the General Council, WT/GC/M/57, 14 September 2000, paras 132 *et seq.*

and food safety, animal and plant health and animal welfare standards as well as the requirement to keep all farmland in good agricultural and environmental condition (so-called "cross-compliance"). Furthermore, some market policies will be revised by price cuts and direct payments to larger farms will be reduced.[84] Hence, the EU moved the vast majority of its direct payments to farmers into the "Green Box" of non-trade-distorting subsidies (para. 519). The Ministerial Declaration further contains a number of development-friendly provisions, which accommodate the interests of the developing and least-developed countries.[85] On the other hand, the industrialised nations have managed to have the Singapore topics as a matter of principle be included on the agenda of the new world trade round. The initiation of concrete negotiations is, however, subject to a corresponding declaration, to be adopted by explicit consensus, at the fifth Ministerial Conference.

802 Particularly remarkable also is the agreement immediately to initiate negotiations on three topics from the fields of **trade and environment**: (i) the relationship between WTO regulations and multilateral environmental protection agreements (MEA), (ii) procedures for regular information exchange between the MEA Secretariats and the corresponding WTO bodies, and (iii) the reduction or abolition of tariffs and non-tariff trade barriers for environmentally relevant goods and services.[86] The Ministerial Declaration is accompanied by a voluminous decision on questions relating to implementation[87] and by a declaration on the **TRIPS agreement and public health**, which, amongst others, recognizes that the TRIPS Agreement does not prevent Members from adopting measures for the protection of public health (para. 672). This important regulation, which needs to be viewed against the background of the HIV, malaria, and tuberculosis epidemics in many developing countries, settled a long standing dispute with the industrialised countries

[84] The reform approach is implemented by three regulations: Commission Regulation (EC) No. 795/2004 of 21 April 2004, EC OJ L 141/1 of 30 April 2004; Commission Regulation (EC) No. 796/2004 of 21 April 2004, EC OJ L 141/81 of 30 April 2004; Commission Regulation (EC) No. 2237/2003 of 23 December 2003, EC OJ L 339/52 of 12 December 2003.

[85] In detail, this concerns the statements on technical aid and "capacity-building" (paras 38–41), the confirmation of the working programme for LDCs, Integrated Framework (paras 42–43), the obligation to the objective of tariff- and quota-free market access for goods originating in LDCs, the establishment of working groups on debt and finance, as well as technology transfer, the notice of the framework agreement on special and differentiated treatment proposed by the developing countries (WT/GC/W/442), the agreement on a procedure for the extension of the transition period according to Art. 27.4 ACSM, and the obligation of the WTO budget commission to prepare a financial plan for technical aid.

[86] Ministerial Conference, Declaration adopted on 14 November 2001, WT/MIN(01)/DEC/1, 20 November 2001, para. 31.

[87] Decision on Implementation-related Issues and Concerns, WT/MIN(01)/W/10, 14 November 2001.

over the extent of patent protection and the availability of basic medication for poorer countries.

803 The implementation, adoption and entry into force of the results of the negotiations are dealt with as part of a **"package deal"**, i.e., they can only be accepted or rejected by the Members in their entirety.[88] Exceptions exist for improvements and clarifications of the Dispute Settlement Understanding.[89] Should Members be able to reach agreement in individual topics ahead of time, the negotiated agreements can be brought into force in a preliminary manner. The negotiations were to close at the latest by **1 January 2005**.

804 The fifth **Ministerial Conference**, which was held in **Cancún** in September 2003, however, ended without a declaration, because the Members could not reach consensus on agricultural issues and on the "Singapore issues".[90] It became clear that the anticipated time frame for the negotiations was unrealistic and that the dissent among WTO Members and Member Groups reached a substantive dimension. Nevertheless, the conference saw a major success on the question of intellectual property protection and public health. The Members reached consensus and adopted a **decision** that waives a Member's obligation under Art. 31 *lit.* f TRIPS to produce pharmaceuticals under compulsory licencing predominantly for the domestic market (para. 647).[91] This and other measures, such as the withdrawal of the Singapore issues from the work programme (para. 799) and especially in connection with technical assistance (para. 786), foster confidence-building on the part of developing countries. Therefore, it is not unreasonable to assume that the Ministieral Conference in autumn 2005 in **Hong Kong** will take substantive steps towards the successful conclusion of the trade round. The termination of the negotiations is deliberately projected for 2007.

805 Whether the world trade order represented by the WTO has a viable future is also a question of how concurring trends in the multilateral trading system develop. The proliferation of **Regional Trade Agreements** (RTAs) is perceived as a danger for the most-favoured-nation principle, because regional trade agreements are discriminatory by nature (para. 114).[92]

---

[88] Ministerial Declaration WT/MIN(01)/DEC/W/1, para. 47.

[89] The deadline for these negotiations was May 2003, WT/MIN(01)/DEC/W/1, para. 30.

[90] Compare the Cancún Draft Declaration JOB(03)/150/Rev.2, 13 September 2003 and the cover letter of the draft ministerial text of 31 August 2003, <http://www.wto.org/english/thewto_e/minist_e/ min03_e/min03_e.htm>.

[91] Implementation of paragraph 6 of the Doha Declaration on the TRIPS Agreement and public health, Decision of the General Council of 30 August 2003,WT/L/540, 1 September 2003.

[92] Detailed *Crawford & Fiorentino*, The Changing Landscape of Regional Trade Agreements, WTO Discussion Paper No. 8, 2005.

OUTLINE OF STRUCTURE

INDEX